PARTIES OUT OF POWER IN JAPAN, 1931–1941

PARTIES OUT OF POWER IN JAPAN

1931-1941

Gordon Mark Berger

PRINCETON UNIVERSITY PRESS
PRINCETON, NEW JERSEY

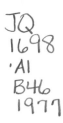
Copyright © 1977 by Princeton University Press
Published by Princeton University Press, Princeton, New Jersey
In the United Kingdom: Princeton University Press, Guildford, Surrey

Library of Congress Cataloging in Publication Data will
be found on the last printed page of this book

This book has been composed in Linotype Caledonia

Printed in the United States of America
by Princeton University Press, Princeton, New Jersey

To My Parents

Preface

AT the beginning of the Shōwa era, Japan's major political parties regarded themselves and were regarded as full-fledged members of the "political establishment." Their power extended from a firm base in the Lower House of the Imperial Diet to alliances and coalitions with the nation's other political elites: the Court, nobility, military leaders, business magnates, and career bureaucrats. Local party supporters included families who exercised a pervasive influence over the economic, social, and political life of their communities, and had in many cases enjoyed this influence for several generations. Men who belonged to or aligned themselves with one or another of the parties could be found in the House of Peers, the Privy Council, the bureaucracy, and even the Army. Above all, the parties between 1924 and 1932 monopolized the premiership, creating a series of party Cabinets in place of the older style of "transcendental government." While positions in party governments were often allocated to nonparty men, the premier's party invariably held a large majority of ministerial portfolios during these years. Despite frequent scandals and complaints about the parties' lack of morality, they seemed assured of a prominent position in Japanese politics. As a distinguished American student of Japanese politics wrote in early 1932, " 'Transcendentalism' may still be destined to enjoy brief interludes of power, but party cabinets may fairly be assumed to have become the established rule."[1]

Less than a month after these words were published, the

[1] Harold S. Quigley, *Japanese Government and Politics: An Introductory Study* (New York and London: Century Co., 1932), p. 233.

parties lost control of the premiership, and never regained it under the imperial political system. Indeed, by 1940, all political party organizations had disappeared from Japanese politics. In less than a decade, they appeared to plummet from a position of growing influence to impotence and obscurity. The polycentric "old order" was scathingly and almost universally denounced as inappropriate to Japan's ethical standards and political needs; and the parties were dissolved as the prologue to the establishment of a monolithic and highly moralistic "new political order." Ever since, it has been common to associate the political parties with the prewar democratic movement, and to see in their dissolution and displacement by new institutions the inauguration of a dismal era in which "democracy, representative government, and the party movement based upon these had been assigned to oblivion."[2]

The fact remains, however, that while the influence of party politicians waned during the 1930s, it was not obliterated. Although democracy in prewar Japan failed to mature, party politicians reached the zenith of political power, retained and fulfilled several important functions even as party power declined, and had already begun to regain positions of political prominence by the end of the Pacific War. The concept of the political party as a means of organizing participants in the political process and allocating political power among them remained viable even after 1940. Throughout the war, ex-party politicians and bureaucrats often thought about creating new parties, and after Japan surrendered in 1945, many of their plans were realized through the postwar parties.

Prewar party power at its height was not contingent upon the democratic movement; nor was the decline of party power necessarily occasioned by the weaknesses of Japanese liberalism. The continuing interest in organizing parties

[2] Robert A. Scalapino, *Democracy and the Party Movement in Prewar Japan* (Berkeley and Los Angeles: University of California Press, 1953), p. 347.

during the war likewise had little to do with liberalism or democratic thought. The large majority of politicians who associated themselves with party organizations did so not out of ideological commitment but rather as a means of pursuing power and implementing policy objectives. It is clear, then, that the history of the political parties in imperial Japan must be examined apart from the study of democracy's failures, and in the dual context of how policies were made and how men competed for political power.

The purpose of this study is thus to examine the political party as a vehicle for the acquisition, allocation, and exercise of political power in late imperial Japan.[3] It begins with a brief chapter reviewing the sources of party strength prior to the early Shōwa era. The next three chapters focus on the extent, causes, and dynamics of the parties' decline as power holders. The final three chapters deal with two questions linking the political parties to Japan's efforts at national mobilization for war. First, how well were party politicians able to weather the growing attack made on their institutional and traditional sources of power in the name of national unity and total mobilization? Second, how successful were they in turning the quest for unity and a mobilized citizenry into assets in the defense and possible enhancement of their power?

The study suggests that while the military elites may have

[3] The left-wing or proletarian parties of the early Shōwa era have been carefully studied in a variety of works, and are therefore excluded from the purview of this study except insofar as they relate to the history of the major parties established earlier (the *kisei seitō*). On the prewar history of social-democratic parties, see George O. Totten, *The Social Democratic Movement in Prewar Japan* (New Haven: Yale University Press, 1966). The prewar history of the Japan Communist Party is related in Rodger Swearingen and Paul Langer, *Red Flag in Japan: International Communism in Action* (Cambridge: Harvard University Press, 1952); Robert A. Scalapino, *The Japanese Communist Movement 1920–1966* (Berkeley and Los Angeles: University of California Press, 1967); and George M. Beckmann and Okubo Genji, *The Japanese Communist Party 1922–1945* (Stanford: Stanford University Press, 1969).

enjoyed a preponderance of influence in setting the foreign and defense policies of Japan after 1936, they were unable to monopolize political power prior to Japan's attack on Pearl Harbor at the end of 1941. The collapse of the Army's efforts in 1940 and 1941 to establish a totalitarian one-party system signified the continuing viability of coalition government rather than dictatorship, and the persistence (rather than obliteration) of party influence and traditional party support groups in the countryside. Even after the Pacific War had begun, the military was obliged to share power with the civilian bureaucracy and, indeed, with members of the defunct political parties. The resilience of party power was demonstrated by the national elections of 1942, by the reappearance of party leaders in the Cabinet after 1943, and by the successful defense by party men and their local allies of their position as an important channel linking the citizenry with the state. The preservation of a modicum of party influence nationally and locally, and its enhancement after 1942, set the stage for the parties' reemergence and rapid recovery of power following Japan's surrender.

While I am, of course, solely responsible for whatever errors of fact and argument may appear in these pages, I should and wish to indicate at the outset that I could not have written this study without the assistance and invaluable criticism of many people. In the course of my research, I was supported by National Defense Modern Foreign Language Fellowships between 1964 and 1967 and again in 1970. Yale University provided additional financial support during the writing of the Ph.D. dissertation from which this book emanates. A particular note of thanks must be extended to the staff of the United States Educational Commission in Japan, which provided me with much good advice, assistance, and three consecutive Fulbright research grants in 1967, 1968, and 1969. Later study in Japan was underwritten by the Japan Foundation in 1973, and funds from a University of Southern California Research and Publication Grant have aided in the preparation of final drafts.

Whatever merit may appear in this work is directly attributable to the stimulation and guidance of a number of Japanese historians in the United States and Japan. I owe my original interest in Japan and in history to David Abosch, whose instruction I received as an undergraduate. Now that I myself have written a doctoral thesis and assumed the responsibilities of full-time teacher and researcher, I am as much amazed as grateful that he was willing to teach me the Japanese language and the rudiments of the historian's craft without compensation while carrying a full course load and attempting to complete his own dissertation. The inspiration and direction for my study of the politics of the 1930s came from James B. Crowley. More than anyone else, he has shaped my approach to Japanese history and encouraged the development of whatever critical faculties I possess. As chairman of my doctoral committee at Yale, he has read this work in several forms, and made innumerable suggestions on how to improve it. I have also benefitted from the generosity of many others who gave of their time to read and comment critically on this study at various stages. They include John W. Hall, Jonathan Spence, Gary Allinson, John Dower, Peter Duus, F. G. Notehelfer, Richard Smethurst, George Akita, and Suzanne Berger Keniston. I am also deeply indebted to Margaret Case for her editorial assistance.

Most of the written and oral materials used in preparing this book were obtained in Japan. I owe an inexpressible debt to the many people there who provided me with interviews, access to materials, and introductions. I have listed in the bibliography the names of those who granted me some of their valuable time to discuss prewar politics; here, I wish to thank them collectively for their candor and good will in responding to my often ill-phrased and misdirected questions. For guiding me through materials at the National Diet Library, I express my appreciation to Ōkubo Toshiaki, Tsunoda Jun, and Tayama Shigeru. The late Kishi Kōichi of the Institute of Asian Economic Affairs was extremely generous in providing me with access to microfilmed Navy Ministry records on Shōwa political and military affairs. The late Nishiura Susumu, head of the Historical Section of Japan's Self-Defense Agency, was kind enough to place much of the huge documentary collection of his office at my disposal; and the late Inaba Masao and Hara Shirō of his staff provided me with direction and insights of particular value. Nagaoka Shinjirō, of the Foreign Ministry Archives Section, assisted me in the examination of records on political party activity in the Foreign Ministry archives. I wish also to thank Konoe Fumitaka and the Konoe family for permission to examine the unpublished papers of Prince Konoe Fumimaro at the family library in Kyoto. Nawa Osamu of the Konoe family library (*Yōmei bunko*) facilitated my efforts to sift through these papers and extract some meaning from them. I am also grateful to Kamei Kan'ichirō for permitting me to examine his personal papers.

I am delighted to have the opportunity to express my profound gratitude to the Japanese scholars who have shared their time and exhaustive knowledge of Shōwa history with me. Hayashi Shigeru, then Professor at the Tokyo University Institute of Social Science Research, served as my faculty advisor during my graduate study in Japan, and provided me with a wealth of materials and instruction germane to my research topic. Itō Takashi of Tokyo University has assisted me in more ways than it is possible to enumerate. The frequent references in this study to Itō's published works do not begin to indicate my indebtedness to him as a mentor and friend. He and a number of his colleagues, including Mitani Taichirō, Satō Seizaburō, Sakai Yukichi, and Banno Junji have been a constant source of stimulating ideas on Shōwa history and the Japanese political process.

Figures 1 and 3 were supplied by Mainichi shinbunsha; Figures 2, 4, 5, and 6 were supplied by Chūō kōronsha. I am grateful for the permission to use them.

Finally, I wish to acknowledge the support I received throughout the several stages of this project from my wife, Karen, who assumed many of the domestic responsibilities I should have shouldered, in order that I might devote myself more fully to the completion of this study.

Throughout this book, I have followed what has become the standard and appropriate practice of rendering Japanese names in accordance with Japanese custom, with the family name preceding the personal name. The names of Americans of Japanese ancestry have been cited in accordance with the American custom of placing the personal name before the family name.

I have followed the method of romanization of Japanese words used in the 1954 edition of Kenkyūsha's *New Japanese-English Dictionary*. Exceptions to this procedure appear only in the case of the place names Tokyo, Kyoto, and Osaka, for which long marks have been omitted.

Contents

Illustrations

Abbreviations

DR   Bōeichō bōei kenshūsho senshi-shitsu, *Daihon'ei rikugunbu*, 2 v.

IMTFE   International Military Tribunal for the Far East.

KF   Yabe Teiji, *Konoe Fumimaro*, 2 v.

NKSG   Nihon kokusai seiji gakkai, ed., *Taiheiyō sensō e no michi*, 8 v.

SKS   Harada Kumao, *Saionji-kō to seikyoku*, 9 v.

YKUS   Yokusan undō shi kankōkai, ed., *Yokusan kokumin undō shi*.

PARTIES OUT OF POWER IN JAPAN, 1931–1941

CHAPTER I

Sources of Party Power in Early Shōwa Japan

INTRODUCTION

By the end of World War I, Japan's major political parties constituted an important segment of the nation's ruling elite. Under the guidance of Hara Kei and others, they parlayed their control over the budget in the Lower House of the Diet and their role as the representatives of the people into a position of prestige and power through adroit compromises with other elite groups. As Tetsuo Najita's study of Hara's career suggests, moreover, the parties were able to win positions of influence only after shedding their intemperate and total opposition to the claims made by other elite groups to a share of political power. Party leaders recognized the need to accommodate nonparty elite groups in the political system, and sought to establish a working relationship with them. A further precondition of party growth was accepting the institutional framework for political competition and policy making provided by the Meiji Constitution. From the late 1890s, Hara remained convinced that the constitutional system could serve as a hospitable environment for his party, the Rikken seiyūkai, to grow and prosper. His eventual selection as premier in 1918 proved the wisdom of this confident assessment.[1]

Party acceptance of the Meiji political order implied a commitment to the principle of imperial rule, as well as the institutions established by the Meiji oligarchy and codified

[1] Tetsuo Najita, *Hara Kei in the Politics of Compromise 1905–1915* (Cambridge: Harvard University Press, 1967). See also Peter Duus, *Party Rivalry and Political Change in Taishō Japan* (Cambridge: Harvard University Press, 1968).

in the Constitution. Even after Hara's death in 1921, few party men ever contemplated any formal constitutional amendment or ideological challenge to the concept of imperial sovereignty. No responsible member of either major party affirmed the principle of popular sovereignty, even during the era of "Taishō Democracy" in the 1920s. However much advocacy of popular sovereignty might theoretically have bolstered the position of the two major parties vis-à-vis other elite groups, party members remained keenly cognizant of the fact that their positions of influence and prestige rested on their commitments to the Meiji Constitution and its definition of imperial sovereignty.

While at times the parties wielded the threat of institutional reform as a lever in the competition for power with other elite groups, neither party in fact ever committed itself to the sponsorship or defense of any legislation to strengthen the legal position of the Lower House of the Diet in relation to the other organs of the state. Rather than endeavoring to expand their own influence by extending the legal jurisdiction of the one state organ in which they enjoyed preeminence, they sought instead to extend party influence into other organs. Under Hara, the Seiyūkai gained access to the premiership and selection of the civilian ministers of state for the first time. By 1924, the two major parties had won Prince Saionji Kinmochi's recognition of their preeminent claim to this position. This constituted an important victory, since it was the venerated Saionji's prerogative as elder statesman (*genrō*) to designate whom the emperor would appoint as premier. Similarly, the parties continually sought throughout the 1920s to extend their influence into the *Kizokuin* (House of Peers or Upper House), *Sūmitsuin* (Privy Council), and imperial bureaucracy. Although party influence never penetrated deeply into the military services, overtures were made successfully to General Tanaka Giichi to become president of the Seiyūkai in April 1925, and a similar offer to General

4

Ugaki Kazushige was contemplated, if not made, by the Rikken minseitō.[2]

By the beginning of the Shōwa era in 1926, the parties had had considerable success in penetrating organs of state hitherto monopolized by nonparty elite groups. While the parties were not the sole arbiters of national policy and the allocation of political power, it appeared certain that party Cabinets would continue for some time. Indeed, this period of party-led governments was regarded, even by most nonparty elites, as one of "normal constitutional government," a logical development from the political settlement of the Meiji era.

The Parties as Power Brokers and Conflict Managers

The success of the parties in competing for political power and responsibility was largely attributable to the careful attention they gave to formulating a role for themselves in the political structure that would invite support and cooperation from other elites. During the period of party government, party support or membership led to appointments and enhanced influence not only in the Lower House and Cabinet, but in the House of Peers, Privy Council, and bureaucracy as well. The parties gained the support of those nobles, civil servants, and military leaders who sought personal advancement and prestige, as well as official positions. Thus, the relationship between parties and nonparty elites became mutually interdependent in the 1920s.

By strengthening ties with nonparty elites, the parties

[2] See Itō Takashi, *Shōwa shoki seiji shi kenkyū* (Tokyo: Tokyo daigaku shuppankai, 1969), p. 24. For a discussion of Tanaka's growing ties with the Seiyūkai during the Hara government's term in office, see Mitani Taichirō, *Nihon seitō seiji no keisei* (Tokyo: Tokyo daigaku shuppankai, 1967), pp. 263–68 and notes 30 and 31, p. 271.

provided networks that integrated diverse elite views and ambitions. Their ability to function as informal arenas of elite conflict proved of particular importance, since the formal structure of state had been carefully fragmented by the framers of the Constitution and Cabinet system. The Cabinet, as established in 1885 and revised in 1889, was a weak body in many respects. Its most significant weakness lay in the lack of leverage given the premier over his ministers. Although the premier nominally appointed ministers to serve in his government, he was not empowered to dismiss them. Ministers were not responsible for their actions to the premier, only to the throne. From a legal standpoint, this gave them relative independence in their dealings with the premier and with each other. Furthermore, since each minister was equal before the throne, it was necessary to have unanimous approval for any Cabinet policy submitted for imperial ratification. If a division of opinion existed within the Cabinet, the emperor technically could be drawn into the political controversy to resolve the issue at hand. Except for rare occasions, however, recourse to direct imperial intervention in decision making was eschewed because of the possible detrimental effect an active political role would have on the majesty and prestige of the throne. In order to preserve the authority of the emperor untarnished by political criticism of his actions, Meiji leaders developed the practice of resolving issues before they reached the throne for formal decision.

The resolution of controversial issues by consensus within the Cabinet was often a difficult task. Primary responsibility resided with the premier, who nevertheless had little institutional or legal leverage vis-à-vis the other ministers. Unless he proved able to unite the Cabinet in support of specific policies, the premier had little alternative to tendering his resignation. Conversely, any minister could, in theory, force the resignation of the government by obstinately refusing to sanction a policy. Much has been made of this "fatal flaw" in the Cabinet system, particularly with regard to its exploitation by Army and Navy ministers.[3] However, the Cabinet's institutional weakness was, at the same time, specifically designed to be a check on the arbitrary actions of a premier. Indeed, the Cabinet structure faithfully mirrored the concerns of the men who ruled Japan during the 1880s. These men comprised a coalition of factions (*hanbatsu*) from the former domains of the Tokugawa era, and were organized under the leadership of prominent oligarchs. In order to assure the continuity of this coalition, representatives of each major faction were selected to serve as ministers, regardless of who was appointed premier. By providing them with the power to veto or force amendment of the policy proposals of the premier's faction, the Cabinet system diminished the possibility that one faction or another would become disenchanted with the coalition and leave it. The structural weakness of the system thus perpetuated rule by consensus. When views became irreconcilable, of course, governments collapsed; but they were invariably replaced by Cabinets drawn from the same political factions, with power shifting but slightly among the leading oligarchs.

The system worked particularly well in its early years, despite the inherent diffusion of political power. One reason for this success was the relatively small number of competing groups and factions which had to be represented within the Cabinet. Another stemmed from the fact that faction leaders shared common experiences and a unity of purpose as the founders of the Meiji state. As Restoration leaders such as Itō Hirobumi, Yamagata Aritomo, and Matsukata Masayoshi retired from active positions in the government, they maintained this unity through their consultations as *genrō* and through their continuing influence over protégés who now ran the government machinery. Throughout the period of "clan governments" (*hanbatsu*

[3] See, for example, Yale Candee Maxon, *Control of Japanese Foreign Policy* (Berkeley and Los Angeles: University of California Press, 1957).

7

seiken), Cabinet unity and accord among the political elites were maintained by the extra-Cabinet activities of the *genrō* as supreme conflict managers.

As the number of elites requiring accommodation in the political system proliferated during the early years of the twentieth century, the *genrō* continued to serve as informal unifiers and ultimate arbiters of national policy. By 1924, however, only one *genrō*—Prince Saionji—was still alive. Throughout his political career, Saionji adhered firmly to one political principle: while the emperor was indeed sovereign, he must never become involved in politics, or be charged with political responsibility. It was only through a clear separation of the throne from the political arena, Saionji believed, that imperial authority and the stability of the Japanese state could be assured. Saionji himself was seventy-five in 1924, and realized that the *genrō* institution and the managerial functions it performed in politics would pass into history with his death. Unless other extra-Cabinet agencies could be developed for harmonizing elite views and ambitions, therefore, only the emperor could unify Japan's elites and complex state organization through personal imperial intervention in Cabinet politics. Such a possibility was anathema to Saionji, and from the middle of the Taishō era (1912–1926) he began an anxious quest for his own successors. On the one hand, he began turning over the functions of national unification to the growing political parties, notably the Seiyūkai. At the same time, the elderly courtier began grooming a group of young nobles, led by Prince Konoe Fumimaro, to succeed him as a mediating force at Court among the competing elites and as the trusted political advisors of the throne.[4]

By 1918, the parties had already begun to demonstrate their ability to use their ties with nonparty elites to assume the collective *genrō* function of harmonizing political,

[4] On the Court's role in the politics of the early Shōwa era, see David A. Titus, *Palace and Politics in Prewar Japan* (New York: Columbia University Press, 1974).

bureaucratic, and economic pressures. Many party leaders were themselves ex-bureaucrats, who brought with them into the parties their close connections with coteries of ministry officials. The large business combines (*zaibatsu*) dominating Japan's economy also learned to work through the parties, exchanging financial support for the satisfaction of their political demands and aspirations.[5] An important start had been made towards establishing the parties as an extra-Cabinet forum of elite conciliation, and once the Seiyūkai attained control of the Cabinet, party connections expanded into other areas as well. During the 1920s, even military leaders with political aspirations began to channel their activities through the party forum. General Tanaka's accession to the Seiyūkai presidency in 1925 en route to the premiership was the most outstanding example of the degree to which the political party had become a focal point for the clash and resolution of elite political differences and ambitions.

PARTY ROLES IN POLITICAL PARTICIPATION AND
LEGITIMIZATION

The Meiji Constitution in theory ascribed to the emperor the sole source of political legitimacy. In fact, however, the people had to give their assent to the imperial choice of governments, if only tacitly by refusing to rebel against the government and throne. Stated in the extreme, even the nineteenth-century oligarchs of early Meiji Japan governed only with the consent of the people. To stabilize their own

[5] For a discussion of the interpenetration of party and business elite groups at its height, see Arthur E. Tiedemann, "Big Business and Politics in Prewar Japan," in James W. Morley, ed., *Dilemmas of Growth in Prewar Japan* (Princeton: Princeton University Press, 1971), especially pp. 279–83. Also Ichihara Ryōhei, "Seitō rengō undō no kiban: 'zaibatsu no tenkō' o shōten to shite," *Keizai ronsō*, LXXII.2 (February 1955), 106–22 and "Seitō rengō undō no hasan: 'Teijin jiken' o shōten to shite," *Keizai ronsō*, LXXII.3 (March 1955), 161–82.

positions, the oligarchs sought to emphasize popular obedience to the monarch and his ministers by education, exhortation, and—at times—by repression of dissidence. The
latter method, for example, was employed in the 1870s and
1880s against the early parties who advocated popular participation in politics and a limited monarchy or popular
sovereignty.[6] Moreover, the Constitution was designed to
buttress the position of the oligarchy against popular challenge by its clear statement of imperial sovereignty. Nevertheless, the oligarchy recognized that the process of "catch-
ing up" with the Western powers required the citizenry to
bear a heavy burden, particularly in the form of taxation
levied on landholders to modernize and strengthen Japan's
economy and military forces. Not only the oligarchy's powers, but the doctrine of imperial sovereignty that rationalized those powers, might well be subject to challenge unless
the people recognized the legitimacy of the new political
system. Although they were skeptical of the political wisdom of the masses and jealous of their own powers, the
drafters of the Constitution deemed it wise to provide a
means for those who paid the most taxes to establish some
sort of identification with the state through participation
in national affairs. They therefore created a Lower House
in the Diet to represent "the people," and permitted the
half-million taxpayers who paid fifteen yen or more in
annual taxes to vote for Lower House members. The Election Law of 1889 promulgated in conjunction with the Constitution thus extended the franchise to roughly one percent
of the total population.

[6] For an account of the growth of political parties in the early Meiji
era, see Scalapino, *Democracy and the Party Movement*; and Nobutaka Ike, *The Beginnings of Political Democracy in Japan* (Baltimore:
Johns Hopkins University Press, 1950). For an incisive account of
the oligarchy's response to the pressures for broader participation in
government during the early Meiji era, see George Akita, *Foundations of Constitutional Government in Modern Japan, 1868–1890*
(Cambridge: Harvard University Press, 1967).

10

The popularly elected Lower House of the Diet was not a powerful institution. Its creators meant it to foster a sense of the legitimacy of the Constitution and the regime, not to exercise any meaningful check on the Cabinet and other organs of government. It was intended to be a vehicle that allowed popular political participation while confining it. The Lower House did have the power to veto the government's budget and any additional tax levies that might be proposed by the government. It was further empowered to approve or veto all laws proposed by the Cabinet, and to approve bills on its own initiative. However, these powers were largely circumscribed by the oligarchs through powers granted to the other institutions of government under their control. In cases where the Lower House vetoed the annual budget, for example, the Cabinet was empowered to operate on the basis of the previous year's budget. Legislation that did not obtain Lower House approval might be enacted, at least on a temporary basis, through direct imperial ordinance. Bills passed by the Lower House at its own initiative might be stymied by the refusal of the Upper House to approve the legislation, or by the veto of the Privy Council.[7]

The Lower House was thus born from the oligarchy's attempt to forestall a dual crisis of legitimacy and participation.[8] During the ensuing forty years, the political parties based in the Lower House played a vital role

[7] A concise summary of Diet prerogatives may be found in Misawa Shigeo and Ninomiya Saburō, "The Role of the Diet and Political Parties," in Dorothy Borg and Shumpei Okamoto, eds., *Pearl Harbor as History: Japanese-American Relations, 1931–1941* (New York and London: Columbia University Press, 1973), pp. 321–22.

[8] Joseph LaPalombara and Myron Weiner, eds., *Political Parties and Political Development* (Princeton: Princeton University Press, 1966), p. 18 elaborates on these crises in a general context. The conceptualization of the functions of the Lower House parties in terms of legitimizing elite power, as well as in terms of their roles as conflict managers and agencies for popular political integration, is suggested by the authors' chapter i and conclusion.

11

in ensuring the success of this attempt. Ironically, however, the oligarchs paid dearly for their success, since the parties cooperated only in exchange for a growing share of the oligarchs' executive power, and finally for a commanding position in the Cabinet. From the first national election in 1890, the Lower House was controlled by members of the political parties. They were elected primarily by obtaining the support of prominent rural leaders (*meibōka* or *chihō yūryokusha*) who traditionally dominated the public affairs of their communities, and controlled almost without exception the way the voters in their communities cast their ballots.[9] Popular participation in the political process thus took the form of local leaders defining and articulating community interests by throwing the unanimous support of the community's voters behind one candidate or another. Elected candidates organized themselves into political parties in the prefectural assemblies or in the Lower House, and through bloc voting they articulated the interests of their local supporters at the upper levels of national politics. The parties in the Lower House managed to use its limited institutional powers to exercise greater leverage on the oligarchs in the executive than had been thought possible. Between 1890 and 1905, financing two wars and the govern-

[9] From 1890 through the 1920s, the electorate was predominantly rural, reflecting not only the locus of Japan's population, but also the fact that the tax qualifications for suffrage excluded the urban classes who did not hold land and therefore did not pay a land tax. The *meibōka* were often local landlords, but others were bankers, businessmen, local politicians, or educators. See Peter Duus, "The Era of Party Rule: Japan, 1905–1932," in James B. Crowley, ed., *Modern East Asia: Essays in Interpretation* (New York: Harcourt, Brace & World, 1970), p. 193. Even in the cities, voters tended to have been recent emigrants from the countryside, and followed village customs of voting in accordance with the directives of "urban *meibōka*." See Masumi Junnosuke, "Josetsu," in Nihon seiji gakkai, ed., *Nenpō seijigaku 1972: "Konoe shintaisei" no kenkyū* (Tokyo: Iwanami shoten, 1973), p. 3.

ment's program of military and industrial development required unexpected increases in taxation and the annual budgets. Since Lower House vetoes would require the Cabinet to operate on insufficient funds budgeted the previous year, some form of compromise with party forces became necessary. Many oligarchs, including Yamagata Aritomo, argued that the parties only represented special interests. Yamagata and his followers in the bureaucracy, House of Peers, and armed forces saw themselves as "neutral" groups who "transcended" private interests, and consequently believed that they, and not the parties, should determine national policy. Hence, there was strong opposition to the appointment of Cabinet officers and high-ranking ministerial officials on the basis of party affiliation. However, the oligarchs were faced with the frustration of their plans for modernization and expansion without Lower House support; and ultimately, they were obliged to establish a *modus vivendi* with the parties that permitted party men to participate in the upper levels of the executive branch of government in exchange for Lower House approval of the budget and tax bills.

The parties rationalized their intrusion into other institutions of government in ways that strengthened the legitimacy of the imperial system. They insisted, for example, that under a benevolent imperial ruler, the will of the sovereign and his subjects should be as one, and that the emperor's advisors in government—his ministers—should therefore include popularly elected representatives of the people. They added that an imperial government divorced from the will of the people as articulated by the men of the Lower House would deprive the emperor of advice he needed to rule benevolently, and endanger the majesty (and political legitimacy) of the throne. Buttressed by elite fears of more radical challenges to their political control in the wake of World War I, the parties succeeded in having this concept of representative imperial government widely ac-

13

cepted at the elite and popular levels of articulate public opinion as "normal constitutional government" by the 1920s.[10]

In collaboration with the *meibōka* in the villages, the parties also provided useful channels for expanding political participation without surrendering control of politics to the masses. When greater taxation was required after the Sino-Japanese War to develop Japan's military strength against the menace of Czarist Russia, the government was obliged to lower the taxation qualification for the suffrage to ten yen, doubling the number of participants in the electoral process to almost one million voters.[11] Two special tax levies in the wake of the Russo-Japanese War, designed to finance the expenses of the conflict and refurbish the armed forces, greatly increased the number of taxpayers meeting the ten-yen qualification, while a reduction of the tax requirement for suffrage to three yen in 1919 raised the number of voters to 2,860,000.[12] The Universal Male Suffrage Act of 1925, designed to expand political participation further under controlled conditions in order to defuse social and economic unrest, eliminated all tax qualifications and quadrupled the electorate to 12,500,000.

Political participation by the expanding electorate flowed through channels established at the end of the nineteenth century, linking the citizen to the state through the *meibōka*, Diet member, and party. Newly enfranchised villagers voted as the traditional leaders of their community directed, and successful candidates sought to repay their supporters with "pork barrel" concessions gained through party pressures on the executive. Even during most of the 1920s, when a rash of tenant-landlord disputes and labor-management conflicts made it apparent that the interests of the political

[10] For specific examples of the way in which party figures rationalized party power, see Suzuki Yasuzō, *Seitō ron* (Tokyo: Nippon hyōronsha, 1943), pp. 85–86, 119–21.

[11] Quigley, *Japanese Government*, p. 252.

[12] *Loc. cit.*, and Mitani, *Nihon seitō seiji no keisei*, pp. 188 and 257.

14

bosses and the bulk of their constituents were not necessarily synonymous, the traditional authority of *meibōka* in
the villages and their counterparts in the cities usually remained strong enough to command the allegiance of their
communities in matters related to politics and business in
Tokyo. The *meibōka*-Diet member-party linkage worked to
minimize any challenges by new political participants to
the exercise of power by the elite groups—party and nonparty—who controlled national affairs.

PARTY ORGANIZATION AND THE JIBAN

By the beginning of World War I, the parties' tactics for
obtaining and maintaining a major share of political power
beyond the Lower House had been clearly defined. For
twenty-five years, party members had agreed that party
power could be enhanced within the constitutional system,
and that amending the rules of the political game would
be unnecessary to achieve control of the Cabinet. The
major tactical question dividing party leaders during this
period had been whether their objectives could best be
achieved through a coalition of all parties in the Diet
against the oligarchs and their protégés, or striking bargains
with their adversaries in order to increase party power.[13]
Hara and the Seiyūkai pursued the latter course with such
success that the tactics of compromise attracted a growing
number of adherents among party men. In 1913, Katsura
Tarō—a protégé of the *genrō* Yamagata Aritomo—and a
group of anti-Seiyūkai Diet men formed a new party called
the Dōshikai to serve as an alternative to the Seiyūkai in
striking compromises between the Lower House and the
other elite groups. The Dōshikai, in its later incarnations
as the Kenseikai and Minseitō, became the Seiyūkai's chief

[13] Duus, "The Era of Party Rule," pp. 184–85, and Tetsuo Najita,
"Inukai Tsuyoshi: Some Dilemmas in Party Development in Pre-
World War II Japan," *American Historical Review*, LXXIV.2 (Decem-
ber 1968), pp. 499–505.

15

competitor for party influence until the parties dissolved in 1940.

Although splinter groups and proletarian parties subsequently obtained a small share of seats in the Lower House, Japan's party system from 1913 to the late 1930s was basically one of two-party confrontation. The two major parties became known as *kisei seitō*, the "established" or "entrenched" parties, a term that denoted a grudging and somewhat critical recognition of their success in breaking into the national power elite. Each of the *kisei seitō* consisted of a number of active politicians, most of whom were members, ex-members, or aspiring members of the Lower House and prefectural assemblies. They were not organized around policy positions, ideologies, or class interests, but rather by personal loyalties to the men who led them. The party usually had a small directorate of perhaps ten men, clustered around a central figure who served as party president or, if the president was a figurehead, the men who actually ran party affairs. Each of the prominent members of the party had his own following of lieutenants, subordinates, and followers exhibiting varying degrees of loyalty to him. The leading positions in the party organization were given to those who could enhance party power. Prince Saionji, for example, served as Seiyūkai president for several years, and lent to the party his prestige as a Court noble and protégé of Itō Hirobumi. Others with strong connections to leading banking and commercial institutions might be given important posts in exchange for obtaining funds for the party's activities and electioneering. Men with careers in the bureaucracy had policy expertise and personal contacts in the ministries and were valuable to the parties as managers of elite conflict. Home Ministry officials had the additional advantage of enjoying close ties with the community leaders (*meibōka*) where they served, and could prove effective vote-getters when they retired and contended for seats in the Lower House. Other experienced politicians might enjoy important party positions because

16

of their favorable press (Ozaki Yukio and Inukai Tsuyoshi) or their skills in organizing election campaigns (Adachi Kenzō).

Whatever the background of the party leadership, it was absolutely essential from the viewpoint of party growth and effective political action that members be infused with a strict sense of party discipline, and vote as a bloc. Failure to do so would weaken the party's power in the Lower House, and make it an unattractive partner for alliances with nonparliamentary elite groups. Moreover, a party divided and isolated in the Lower House lacked the leverage to extract "pork barrel" commitments from the government, and suffered at the polls as a consequence. Similarly, a party fragmented by internal differences was a poor agency for the management of conflict among the other elite groups, and could not merit serious consideration by the *genrō* for Cabinet leadership. The preservation of unity in parties not bound by common policy commitments or particular ideologies was a difficult task; but when outstanding party leaders such as Hara were able to bind party members to them by personal loyalty and self-interest, they made their parties a vital force in national affairs.

The size of a party's delegation had a direct effect on the influence it could wield. Minor parties counted for little with the other elite groups or in parliamentary affairs, except in rare situations when they might cast the decisive votes in support of one or the other of two evenly balanced major parties. Small parties could hardly be regarded as embodying the popular will on any broad scale, and were thus of little value in legitimizing elite governments through their participation in the Cabinet. They also had little attraction for ambitious members of other elite groups who wished to advance their fortunes through the parties.

It is, however, difficult to define the precise point at which a party's delegation in the Lower House became large enough to warrant consideration as a senior partner in the Cabinet coalition. The path to controlling the pre-

17

miership and organizing the Cabinet did not depend on a prior Lower House majority. A government party was usually able to employ the advantages of being in office to win a majority or plurality of Lower House seats in an election held following its accession to power. No new government party ever entered office with majority control of the Lower House, and only one failed to achieve at least a plurality in the ensuing election.[14] The one exception occurred in 1924, when the "Peers Cabinet" of Kiyoura Keigo called an election while allied only to a splinter group from the Seiyūkai, the Seiyū hontō. Entering the election, the Seiyū hontō held a plurality of Lower House seats, with 149 members, but faced a three-party coalition against it. The election reduced its delegation to 111 members, and obliged the Kiyoura government to resign in favor of a Cabinet organized by the leaders of the victorious three-party coalition. The experience of the Seiyū hontō demonstrated that, while a party did not need a majority in the Lower House to attain office, it required somewhat more than 150 seats to contest successfully a national election against a larger opponent. No other party so small was ever again invited to join or organize a Cabinet coalition as the sole government party.

Each party was therefore attentive to the tasks of maintaining and, perhaps, enlarging its delegation in the Lower House. By offers of financial support or party leadership positions, a major party often succeeded in recruiting independent Diet men into its ranks or weaning away dissident cliques of men from opposing parties. The key to building a large party lay at the polls, however, and in the triangular relationship that developed among the parties, the Home Ministry, and the *meibōka*. The Home Ministry was the government agency directly charged with maintaining public order and supervising election procedures in the cities

[14] The three-party coalition that entered office in 1924 did, however, command a majority of the Lower House seats in combination.

18

and villages. In addition to election supervision, the ministry ran the police system and the system of local government; it held responsibility also for public works, the national health programs, the Shintō shrines, urban planning, and land development programs. After the Russo-Japanese War, the ministry became a natural target of the parties' effort to extend their influence through the machinery of government. As home minister in the Saionji Cabinet, Hara sought to replace the chief prefectural administrative officers—the governors (*chiji*)—with men more sympathetic to the fortunes of the Seiyūkai. The *chiji* were among the most important of the Home Ministry officials from the parties' viewpoint, for they had the authority to supervise elections and disburse funds to local communities.[15]

Hara also placed officials sympathizing with his party in charge of police work. At election time, police department leaders could perform useful services for the party with which they collaborated. They often prosecuted the opposition candidates for electoral violations real and imagined, while ignoring the conduct of government party candidates. At times, they harassed opposition party campaigners and incarcerated opposition candidates for questioning during the final days of a campaign. Frequently, they selected election supervisors whose views were favorable to the government party and whose pockets were filled with progovernment votes to be stuffed into ballot boxes where necessary.[16] These techniques had been used by the oligarchs earlier in an effort to stymie party success at the polls. Hara and subsequent home ministers of party origin were now quick to employ them to the advantage of their parties. Control over the election apparatus, along with access to mass media and the ability to deliver on "pork barrel" pledges to

[15] Najita, *Hara Kei*, pp. 38–45.

[16] For an enumeration of police tactics in election intervention, see the comments of Home Minister Wakatsuki Reijirō in 1924, cited in Quigley, *Japanese Government*, p. 266, n. 20.

19

community leaders, were the elements that guaranteed victory for the incumbent party in every national election except 1924.[17]

Control of these Home Ministry posts was thus a valuable asset to the parties, but no less valuable was the good will and support provided party candidates by the *meibōka* in the local communities. In a figurative sense, the *meibōka* stood athwart the road into the local community from Tokyo's power centers. The lowest link in the chain of regional administration descending from the Home Ministry was the administrative town (*machi, chō*) or village (*mura, son*), which represented an amalgamation of "naturally" constituted local communities or hamlets (*buraku, aza, ō-aza,* etc.). The *meibōka* not only dominated the affairs of the "natural" local communities, but were also selected locally (with Home Ministry ratification) to serve as mayors of the administrative towns and villages. Some even rose to serve as county (*gun*) officials between 1890 and 1923, when this unit of administration was abolished. They also provided the local leadership for a variety of semiofficial bodies linking the local community and administrative towns and villages to the center in Tokyo: the industrial guilds (*sangyō kumiai*), agricultural associations (*nōkai*), and, in concert with local veterans, the *Zaigō gunjinkai* (Imperial Military Reservist Associations).

Candidates for elective office from the *kisei seitō* generally acknowledged the local authority of the *meibōka*— many, indeed, were of *meibōka* origins themselves—and used it to build a firm electoral base (*jiban*). Significantly, there were no *kisei seitō* branches in the local community, and apart from appearances by well-known party figures during election campaigns and the frequent distribution of illegal funds from party coffers through the candidate and political bosses to voters, there was little systematic con-

17 Robert A. Scalapino, "Elections and Political Modernization in Prewar Japan," in Robert E. Ward, ed., *Political Development in Modern Japan* (Princeton: Princeton University Press, 1968), p. 283.

tact between the party and the electorate. The candidates were the only continuing representatives of party interests locally. These men spent a great deal of time cultivating personal relationships with *meibōka* in their districts. Family ties and the bestowal of monetary and other favors by the candidate could generate some local support, as could the intervention of police authorities at election time; but in the final analysis, the crucial factor in building a stable base of community support was whether the *meibōka* had personal confidence in him and believed he was faithfully and effectively articulating their interests at the prefectural or national level. Usually, it was the man, and not his party, that mattered most, and candidates with strong *jiban* had little difficulty being reelected to office even after changing party affiliations several times.

The parties, then, were elite organizations, small in membership and oriented towards the interests of local and national elite groups. They consisted of groups of men bound together into coalitions of mutual interest and personal loyalty, and sought to operate beyond the confines of the Lower House through similar coalitions of mutual interest and personal loyalty with nonparty elite groups. While their organizations and modes of operation were hardly characteristic of party systems in democratic societies, they served to articulate local interests at a national level and to legitimize elite government among the limited number of citizens who saw the state as being of any real consequence in their lives. In return for the effective performance of these functions, party members achieved power outside of the Lower House, and retained the local support of their *jiban*.

LIMITATIONS AND ATTACKS ON PARTY POWER

From the foregoing discussion, it is clear that the political parties were never able to control either national or local politics themselves, but worked in collaboration with na-

21

tional and local elite groups to expand party influence. Coalition, compromise, and "limited pluralism" in the distribution of power among elites remained the salient characteristics of Japanese politics.[18] The functions performed by the parties in the political system made them a valuable asset to other elite groups, but since party power was in many cases enhanced at the expense of other elites, a strong sense of competition and desire to limit party influence pervaded the ranks of groups with whom the parties worked. Deeper examination of the relationships among the parties, *meibōka*, and the Home Ministry demonstrates the nature and degree of opposition to party influence as the parties moved into the power elite.

The *meibōka* guarded their power jealously, and resisted all efforts by parties or the state to bypass them in mobilizing or controlling the citizenry. At the turn of the century, traditional local elites supported Yamagata Aritomo's several programs for frustrating the growth of party influence locally, in order to prevent the subordination of traditional patterns of power holding and community leadership to the criterion of party loyalty.[19] Subsequently, when the national parties made their peace with the *meibōka* and relied on them to mobilize the electorate in exchange for "pork barrel" concessions, it was the Home Ministry and other ministries of the central government that became *meibōka* adversaries. As the agencies of the central government conducted frequent attempts to extend official controls into the villages where political power had been monopolized previously by *meibōka* families, the traditional leadership looked

[18] That is, in contrast to the unlimited pluralism of democratic systems, not all members of the polity were regarded as legitimate participants in the political process and competition for power. See Juan J. Linz, "An Authoritarian Regime: Spain," in Erik Allardt and Yrjo Littunen, eds., *Cleavages, Ideologies and Party Systems* (Helsinki, Finland; Distributor, Academic Bookstore, 1964), pp. 298–300.

[19] For the only real party challenge to *meibōka* authority in 1906–1907, see Najita, *Hara Kei*, pp. 45–57.

to party men to help them repel the center. In time the parties came to be strong defenders of *meibōka* authority against inroads by the bureaucracy.

During the decade after the Russo-Japanese War, *meibōka* and their communities were subjected to a variety of efforts to integrate them into the life of the state. Through military service or exposure to the local chapter of the *Zaigō gunjinkai*, villagers became increasingly aware of the relevance of the state in their lives, and in that sense were integrated into the life of the state through the armed forces.[20] Efforts by the *Zaigō gunjinkai* and the Education Ministry to train good subjects of the emperor through education may also have had some effect on heightening the villager's awareness of himself as a member of the nation as well as the local community. Above all, however, it was the Home Ministry that became more deeply involved in the daily lives of the Japanese people than any other agency of the central government. The ministry conducted a variety of programs subsumed under the rubric of "local improvement" (*Chihō kairyō undō*). The ministry's goals were to strengthen the rural economic base for Japan's further industrialization as a major power, shift the primary loyalties of the agrarian communities from the village to the state, and rationalize the system of local government.[21] According to the official history of the Home Ministry,

[20] For a discussion of the origins and purposes of the *Zaigō gunjinkai*, see Richard J. Smethurst, "The Creation of the Imperial Military Reserve Association in Japan," *Journal of Asian Studies*, xxx.4 (August 1971), 815–28; for an extended discussion of this and other Army-patronized organizations, see Richard J. Smethurst, *A Social Basis for Prewar Japanese Militarism: The Army and the Rural Community* (Berkeley and Los Angeles: University of California Press, 1974).

[21] For details, see Kenneth B. Pyle, "The Technology of Japanese Nationalism: The Local Improvement Movement 1900–1918," *Journal of Asian Studies*, xxxiii.1 (November 1973), 51–65, and Kano Masanao, "Sengo keiei to nōson kyōiku: Nichi-Ro sensō-go no seinen-dan undō ni tsuite," *Shisō*, #521 (November 1967), pp. 42–59.

The movement took several specific forms: the creation
of auxiliary organizations to facilitate the penetration of
national administration, the education of villagers
through individuals or organizations, and an emphasis
on rejecting political conflict and party orientation. . . .
Huge organizations were created with the local community (buraku) as the basic unit, in order to facilitate the
penetration of national administration. Included among
them were the Zaigō gunjinkai, the Red Cross Association, the Patriotic Women's Association, the tax payment
and savings guilds, the nōkai and sangyō kumiai. All of
these bodies used the pressures to conform that were
present in the buraku and five-man groups (gonin-gumi),
creating an imposed "spontaneity" to convey national
administration into the community. They were brought
together under the supervision of the administrative chain
of command running down from the governors through
the county chiefs to the mayors.[22]

These efforts to integrate the local community into the
life of the state through semiofficial organizations and the
Home Ministry bureaucracy had profound implications for
the relationship among the meibōka, parties, and the ministry. Meibōka became more sensitive to the goals of the
nation's leadership, but also looked to the parties to defend
their traditional authority against invasion from above. The
parties' "unholy alliance" with the meibōka thus reduced
the possibility of effective bureaucratic penetration in the
countryside, and added tensions to the collaboration of the
parties and Home Ministry under Hara and subsequent
home ministers of party origin. Leading officials were torn
between their desire to expand the ministry's influence locally, and the recognition that they could be cashiered if
they displeased the home minister and his party's local

[22] Taikakai (Gotō Fumio), ed., Naimushō shi (4 vols., Tokyo:
Chihō zaimu kyōkai, 1970), ii, 435 (hereafter cited as Naimushō
shi).

supporters. Indeed, between 1905 and 1925, the parties were remarkably successful in using the home minister's office to penetrate the upper levels of the bureaucracy. In the Home Ministry the governorships and chief police positions were converted into political appointments.[23] Officials affiliated with one party were assured of posts when that party became the government party, but were also certain to be replaced when a new government party came into office. Those who resisted affiliation might serve under either major party, or might equally be bypassed altogether for top positions. The insecurity of nonaffiliation reduced the ranks of those who adhered to the "transcendental" position, opposed to permitting "private interests," as represented by the parties, to sully the conduct of national affairs. Lower-ranking officials, whose positions were not subject to the spoils system, might speak contemptuously of their superiors' fawning attitude towards the parties, but in time, they, too, had to face the alternative of affiliation with a party or the likelihood of premature retirement.

Paradoxically, however, as the notion of representative government achieved wider acceptance as a means of legitimizing elite rule and permitting controlled political participation in national affairs, the opponents of party influence in the ministry began to restore their position. Following World War I, the unsettled socio-economic conditions of the city and village, new problems of social control engendered by the advent of mass society, and the prospects of a larger electorate to supervise during elections created new responsibilities and a climate of apprehension in the ministry.[24] On the one hand, ministry officials came to agree

[23] It should be noted that these and other bureaucratic positions could be held only by qualified career civil servants. It was from among these men that the parties searched for allies, and rewarded them with appointments.

[24] Industrial departments specializing in labor relations were established in some of the municipal and prefectural Home Ministry offices. The powers and responsibilities of the police were augmented to deal

25

that universal male suffrage and representative government
would be the safest and least costly means (in terms of
maintaining elite control over the citizenry) for siphoning
off discontent against elite rule. On the other hand, they
warned that the *meibōka*-party linkage and party connections with big business (*zaibatsu*) frustrated a true articulation of mass interests, and thus invited revolt from below
against the imperial system. Impelled by a new sense of
urgency, some bureaucrats argued further that the parties
not only obstructed effective control of the countryside but
impeded the general efficiency of Home Ministry administration. They noted that with each change in government,
the highest-ranking police and local government officials
were replaced by a new set of men sympathetic to the new
government party, and complained that officials were therefore not permitted to remain at their posts long enough to
implement long-range programs of social control with any
effectiveness. The high rate of turnover in the governorships and police department leadership, they contended,
could be reduced only if party access to the powers of official appointment and, more importantly, dismissal were
restricted.[25]

The Home Ministry officials who took this position found
support among civil servants in other ministries affected by

with the labor and socialist movements. The Social Policy Bureau
was established in 1920, and in 1923, the Home Ministry absorbed
from other government agencies the responsibility for dealing with
the increasing number of labor unions. Masumi Junnosuke, *Nihon
seitō shi ron* (4 vols., Tokyo: Tokyo daigaku shuppankai, 1965–1968),
iv, 165–66. A further discussion of the proliferation of Home Ministry duties may be found in Ari Bakuji, "Chihō seido (Hōtaisei hōkai-
ki): burakukai chōnaikai seido," in Fukushima Masao, Kawashima
Takeyoshi, Tsuji Kiyoaki and Ukai Nobushige, eds., *Kōza: Nihon
kindai-hō hattatsu shi—shihon shugi to hō no hatten*, vi (Tokyo:
Keisō shobō, 1959), 171 ff.

[25] For examples of these arguments, see Gordon M. Berger, "Japan's
Young Prince: Konoe Fumimaro's Early Political Career, 1916–1931,"
Monumenta Nipponica, xxix.4 (Winter 1974), 466–69.

the party patronage system, as well as among members of the House of Peers who were seeking to resist party penetration of that body during the early 1920s. As the concept of representative government gained currency during the final years of the Taishō era, elite forces inimical to the extension of party influence began searching for a new approach to popular representation. They sought now to supplant the party-*meibōka* and party-Cabinet linkages as a means of legitimizing elite rule, controlling citizen participation in politics, and further strengthening the individual's identification with the state.[26]

Officials were not the only ones to complain about the inadequacies of a representative government in which the *kisei seitō* seemed preoccupied with articulating and defending the interests of their financial supporters in the business world and their electoral backers among the *meibōka*. Journalists, intellectuals, and representatives of the nascent labor and tenant movements decried the failure of the parties to be truly representative of the masses. Frustrated by the monopoly of national power by the parties and other elite groups, and encouraged by the victory of the democratic powers in World War I and the Bolshevik Revolution in 1917, groups of liberals and socialists called for a thoroughgoing overhaul of the political system to make representative government more representative. While the moderate reform movements concentrated on the enactment of universal male suffrage (deferred under Hara's government and not implemented until 1925), more radical groups agitated for the rejection or overthrow of the imperial system. With the passage of the suffrage act in 1925 in tandem with a new law authorizing police crackdowns on radical left-wing movements, party governments sought to mitigate this opposition with a combination of concessions and repression. The liberal and democratic-socialist movements were reoriented towards advancing within the imperial system as the *kisei seitō* had previously, while the com-

[26] *Ibid.*, pp. 467–71.

27

munist movement was repeatedly forced underground or shattered by waves of arrests. Nevertheless, a strong feeling pervaded Japan in the mid-1920s that the *kisei seitō* would have to broaden their appeal if they were to continue to play an important role in legitimizing elite rule and providing a secure channel for controlling popular political participation.

Apart from these criticisms of party power by those who had come to accept the principle of representative government, the parties were always confronted by "Japanist" forces in the elite groups and right-wing societies who denied their value on the basis of moral principle. The parties were attacked as organizations of alien origin, being mere imitations of Western institutions that had no place in imperial Japan. From this perspective, the parties were seen not as harmonizing agencies, but as embodiments of an unsightly and immoral competitive urge for personal power. Rather than unifying the people with imperial rule, they were portrayed as intruders who sundered a sacred and mystical bond between the emperor and his subjects— a bond of harmonious beauty which, when manifested in imperial benevolence and the loyal obedience of the subject, elevated Japan to a position of moral paramountcy among the other nations of the world.

The political and ideological challenges to the parties' influence by the mid-1920s denoted a persistent legacy and contemporary environment of opposition to their growth. Nevertheless, there were countervailing aspects of the domestic and international environment that contributed to the maintenance of the parties' position. To begin with, thirty-five years of government under the Constitution had established its unquestioned legitimacy as a statement of the ground rules for political competition. Even the possibility of amending the document was considered anathema at all levels of respected public opinion. Inasmuch as the Constitution guaranteed the right of popular participation in politics, the position of the Lower House was secure.

Moreover, the concept of representative government had become accepted by much of the elite establishment as a valuable way of siphoning off popular discontent while maintaining elite power. While the parties were at times accused of perverting the implementation of representative government, they were unquestionably more acceptable to the nonparty elite groups than were democrats, socialists, anarchists, and communists who rejected the validity of elite power altogether. The appearance of mass interest in the political process created alarm about the ability of the Cabinet-party linkage to channel mass political participation into the imperial system of elite rule without disturbing it, but there appeared to be no better style of political linkage available for this purpose.

The international environment of the early 1920s was also conducive to the preservation of the gains made by the parties. The Washington order established in 1922 assured Japan's security in the Western Pacific in the eyes of those who controlled the Navy, while to most observers, Japan's interests on the Asian continent seemed secure under the Washington system's provision for collaborative imperialist exploitation of China by the Great Powers. The internal upheavals taking place in the Soviet Union, while frightening to an elite establishment intent on restricting mass access to power, at least temporarily removed the "Colossus of the North" as a threat to the security of Japan's home islands and continental possessions. There were, to be sure, important figures in the Army (Araki Sadao) and Navy (Katō Kanji) who disagreed vehemently with this overall assessment, but the preponderance of opinion in the military, diplomatic, and civilian branches of government supported it until later in the decade.

This type of environment was one that mitigated anti-Western sentiment in Japan, and reduced the ideological appeal of those who condemned the parties as Western imports. Japan experienced difficulty in discerning her national identity as an Asian, Western, or purely unique society dur-

29

ing this period, but at the least, the prevailing national mood was not one of bitter hostility to things Western. Moreover, the Washington order appeared to be a prototype of the style of competition and collaboration that the parties themselves embodied in their relationship with other elites. Affirmation of Japan's foreign and military policies was thus in another sense an affirmation of the political style which fostered the growth of party power. In addition, the mood of security led to an emphasis on diplomacy and civilian control of domestic affairs as opposed to a foreign policy of brute force and military mobilization of Japan's society. Japan's security rested firmly on the policy of "cooperative diplomacy" with the Western powers, and the percentage of the annual budget siphoned off into military expenditures decreased steadily. This situation tended to enhance the power and prestige of the civilian elites, including the parties, at the expense of the Army and Navy. And finally, the parties could take much of the credit for Japan's fortuitous international position, since the Washington treaties had been negotiated by a government under Seiyūkai leadership and sustained by governments controlled by the Kenseikai.

Thus, between 1918 and 1932, the parties were able to achieve and maintain a monopoly over the premiership and a commanding influence in the Cabinet for all but two years. By the beginning of the Shōwa era, they had breached the barriers to party influence not only in the Cabinet, but in the House of Peers, Privy Council, and the bureaucracy. They had developed important working relationships in addition with the *genrō*, the Court, leaders of the armed forces, big business, and the traditional leadership in the countryside. While there were limitations on the extent of their influence and critics of their behavior, it seemed unlikely that they had already reached the apogee of their power in imperial Japan.

CHAPTER II

The Decline of Party Influence, 1930–1936

INTRODUCTION

DURING the early years of the Shōwa era, the fate of the political parties continued to be related directly to the quest for stable elite government. Political stability under the Constitution required the resolution of two perennial problems. First, because of the weak Cabinet system and the proliferation of elite groups seeking power within it, informal mediatory agencies were always a desideratum to supplement the Cabinet as arenas for the management of conflict among the elites. Second, the ruling groups faced the constant task of maintaining popular support or tolerance of their monopoly of political power. While the parties rose to power by contributing to the mitigation of these problems at the beginning of the century, they were forced by 1932 to surrender their control of the premiership. Although their loss appeared to be only temporary at the time, it proved to be permanent; party Cabinets were not resumed under the Meiji constitutional order.

One of the central questions in modern Japanese political history is why the parties suffered this loss. One opinion holds that the parties lost power to their competitors because of an unprincipled willingness to compromise with their adversaries.[1] A second attributes their collapse to the effects wrought on domestic opinion by repeated instances

---

[1] Shiraki Masayuki, *Nihon seitō shi: Shōwa hen* (Tokyo: Chūō kōronsha, 1949), p. 115; Edwin O. Reischauer, *Japan: Past and Present*, 3rd ed., rev. (New York: Alfred A. Knopf, 1964), pp. 177–78; John K. Fairbank, Edwin O. Reischauer and Albert M. Craig, *East Asia: The Modern Transformation* (Boston: Houghton Mifflin Co., 1965), pp. 587–88.

of terrorism during the early 1930s.[2] Still other historians ascribe the demise of party influence to inherent weaknesses in the parties' structure and to the limited commitment of prewar Japanese politicians to the philosophical principles of democracy.[3] While aspects of each of these explanations merit serious consideration, the central cause of the parties' sudden disadvantage in the competition for power appears to lie in a more complex nexus of changes in the domestic and international environment. Essentially, the military and bureaucratic elites were able to persuade many of their counterparts in other elites and much of the populace that Japan had entered a period of national crisis in her foreign and domestic affairs, which required an application of military and bureaucratic expertise the parties could not provide. The parties' adversaries were able to capitalize on an atmosphere of national emergency (*hijō-ji*) to replace party government with a style of Cabinet rule in which military and bureaucratic elites enjoyed preeminence. However, since the Cabinet structure remained weak, and the desire for popular acquiescence to elite rule remained strong, the cessation of party government had as a corollary the quest for new means to bind the elites together and the people to the state.

THE CHANGING CLIMATE OF PARTY RULE

The decline in party fortunes began under the Minseitō government established under Hamaguchi Yūkō (Osachi) in July 1929. The new premier quickly announced that the

[2] Shigemitsu Mamoru, *Japan and Her Destiny* (London: Hutchinson & Co., Ltd., 1958), p. 81; Nakamura Kikuo, *Shōwa seiji shi* (Tokyo: Keiō tsūshin, 1958), p. 46.

[3] Scalapino, *Democracy and the Party Movement*, p. 371 and *passim*; Imai Seiichi, "Inukai Tsuyoshi," in Tōyama Shigeki, ed., *Kindai Nihon no seijika* (Tokyo: Kōdansha, 1964), p. 327; William G. Beasley, *The Modern History of Japan* (New York: Praeger, 1963), pp. 247–48.

fundamental policies of his Cabinet would be directed towards economic retrenchment to promote recovery from the agrarian depression in Japan, and a foreign policy of close cooperation with the Western powers to protect Japan and her interests in China. Under the guidance of Finance Minister Inoue Junnosuke, the budget for 1930 was reduced to ninety percent of the previous year's figure, while preparations were made to lift the gold embargo and return to the gold standard. The government sought to curb popular consumption and stimulate personal savings, in an effort to limit purchasing power and lower prices.[4]

The fiscal and economic policies of the new government provoked strong opposition among many business and political leaders. As a gesture designed to enhance its support among bureaucrats, the government agreed to consider proposals to reform the election system and to protect officials against arbitrary dismissals. In January 1930, the Cabinet approved Home Minister Adachi Kenzō's plan to establish a Lower House Election Reform Study Commission (*Shūgiin senkyo kakusei shingikai*). The commission studied five areas of reform related to making the electoral system more representative: an extension of political education, prevention of voting abstentions, consideration of proportional representation in the Diet, public management of elections, and reform of the Lower House Election Law. It further considered ways in which the positions of officials could be protected against the parties' custom of dismissing high-ranking officials from the previous government and replacing them with other bureaucrats more sympathetic to the new government party.[5]

It was unlikely, however, that any commission headed by the leading officers of the Minseitō (Hamaguchi, Adachi, and Egi Tasuku) would make concrete proposals for eliminating the major instruments of retaining and extending

---

[4] Chō Yukio, "From the Shōwa Economic Crisis to Military Economy," *Developing Economies*, v.4 (December 1967), 574.

[5] Itō, *Shōwa shoki seiji shi kenkyū*, pp. 43–44.

party influence. The Hamaguchi government soon showed that it had no intention of yielding control over the appointment of high officials in the central and local administrative systems, or abandoning the traditional mobilization of the nation's police on its behalf during election campaigns. The Minseitō government, in fact, replaced twenty-nine of the forty-eight *chiji* with pro-Minseitō bureaucrats within a year of coming to office, and made similar personnel shifts in the police departments of the Home Ministry.[6] In the Election Reform Commission, the Seiyūkai voiced its objections to any policy that would guarantee the positions of high-ranking bureaucrats, fearing that the hegemony of the new pro-Minseitō officials would be perpetuated by any such reform.[7] In short, party men did not wish to reform a system that had sustained them for thirty years.

Despite repeated promises that the retrenchment program itself would lead to economic recovery, the Hamaguchi government was unable to check the wave of depression sweeping the country. If anything, its economic policy, based on pre-Keynesian principles of fiscal austerity, only worsened matters in the countryside.[8] Throughout 1930, criticism of the government mounted as it became clear that recovery was not taking place. When Great Britain finally abandoned the gold standard in September 1931, public support for the Minseitō's economic policies plummeted.

The government's competence in foreign affairs and national defense also came under virulent attack with Japan's signing of the London Naval Treaty in 1930.[9] Hamaguchi

[6] Arthur E. Tiedemann, "The Hamaguchi Cabinet: First Phase, July 1929–February 1930: A Study in Japanese Parliamentary Government," Ph.D. dissertation, Columbia University, 1959, p. 85. For further statistical examples of the shakeup in the bureaucracy effected by the Hamaguchi regime, see Quigley, *Japanese Government*, pp. 151–52.

[7] Tiedemann, "The Hamaguchi Cabinet," p. 87.

[8] For details, see Chō, "Shōwa Economic Crisis," pp. 575–77.

[9] For thorough discussions of the London Treaty and its ramifications in Japanese politics, see Itō, *Shōwa shoki seiji shi kenkyū*; Ito

and Foreign Minister Shidehara Kijūrō had earnestly hoped that the London Conference would produce a treaty limiting naval armaments. The possibility that the powers would agree to limit naval construction at the conference was regarded by the government as a natural and desirable extension of the system of cooperative diplomacy established at the Washington Conference in 1921–1922. Moreover, the prospect of reduced outlays for naval construction dovetailed nicely with the government's program of economic retrenchment. Prior to the opening of the London meeting, the premier outlined to the nation the government's plans for reconciling the demands of national defense with the necessity of economic retrenchment. He announced that Japan's defense would be assured by combining the Navy's demands for a Japanese cruiser force seventy percent as strong as that of the United States or Great Britain with the policy of peaceful international cooperation embodied in "Shidehara Diplomacy." As an American chargé d'affaires wrote to the United States Department of State in October 1929: "not only [has the Japanese government] so definitely committed itself to this position [the 10:10:7 ratio in cruiser strength among the United States, Great Britain, and Japan], but it has inculcated so firmly in the minds of the people the idea that anything less would imperil Japan's safety . . . it is difficult to see how it could accept anything less at the Conference and avoid serious reverberation at home."[10]

The United States and Great Britain, however, were de-

Takashi, "Conflicts and Coalitions in Japan, 1930: Political Groups [and] the London Naval Disarmament Conference," in Sven Groennings, W. W. Kelley, and Michael Leiserson, eds., *The Study of Coalition Behavior* (New York: Holt, Rinehart and Winston, 1970), pp. 160–76; and James B. Crowley, *Japan's Quest for Autonomy: National Security and Foreign Policy, 1930–1938* (Princeton: Princeton University Press, 1966), pp. 35–81.

[10] Cited in Gerald Wheeler, *Prelude to Pearl Harbor* (Columbia: University of Missouri Press, 1963), p. 168.

termined that Japan accept a 10:10:6 ratio, and threatened a bilateral alliance against Japan unless the Japanese delegation complied with this formula. Wishing to preserve friendly relations with these two powers and to continue its policy of economic retrenchment, the Hamaguchi government finally instructed its representatives in London to accept a modified version of the Anglo-American proposal. The "serious reverberation at home," however, was not long in coming. Admiral Katō Kanji, chief of the Naval General Staff, immediately accused the government of endangering national security, and questioned the competence and constitutional authority of the Cabinet to overrule the Navy in matters affecting the defense of the nation. The Seiyūkai, eager to embarrass the government party, joined Katō and the vice chief of the Naval General Staff, Vice Admiral Suetsugu Nobumasa, in condemning the government's concessions in London and its usurpation of the Navy's right of supreme command. The Seiyūkai, the Katō group, conservative members of the House of Peers, and pro-Seiyūkai members of the Privy Council soon coalesced with the intention of blocking ratification of the London Treaty.[11] Hamaguchi, however, marshaled a coalition of his own supporters in the Navy, Privy Council, and Minseitō, and was able to win approval for the terms of the treaty without resolving the constitutional question raised by Admiral Katō and the Seiyūkai. On October 2, 1930, the emperor's seal was affixed to the treaty, and the issue apparently was settled with a victory for the Cabinet policies of "cooperative diplomacy" ("Shidehara Diplomacy") and economic retrenchment.

[11] Takeuchi Tatsuji, *War and Diplomacy in the Japanese Empire* (Chicago: University of Chicago Press, 1935), p. 806. The Seiyūkai role in this coalition demonstrates the fashion in which the parties sought to coordinate nonparty elite views with their own, in order to enhance their political influence. The Seiyūkai motivation in this movement was twofold: to overturn what it regarded as a dangerous foreign policy, and to replace the Minseitō as governing party.

Just as the depression undermined national confidence in the Minseitō's expertise in the realm of fiscal policy, the treaty controversy raised and left unanswered serious questions about the competence of party-led Cabinets in formulating national defense policies. First, the Minseitō government had approved a cruiser ratio that it had claimed a year earlier would not be adequate to provide for the security of the nation. Second, the constitutional question of the right of supreme command—the prerogative to have the final say on defense matters—had not been resolved to the satisfaction of large segments of the military elite, the House of Peers, the Privy Council, or the Seiyūkai. These groups demanded that the General Staffs be given a larger role in determining the defense requirements of the nation, limiting the authority of the Cabinet in this area. They clearly doubted the competence and authority of the government to make final decisions on certain vital national policies. They judged that the threat of an Anglo-American naval alliance against Japan demonstrated the bankruptcy of the spirit and rules of post-Washington Conference diplomacy and Foreign Minister Shidehara's foreign policy.

While the Minseitō was strong enough to survive the opposition's attacks, the party's ability to provide adequate defense policies had been called into question. Both the Seiyūkai and certain Navy leaders were able to capitalize on the widespread doubts about the adequacy of the Minseitō as a governing force to extract new policy positions from the government. Hamaguchi agreed to give the military voice a wider hearing in decision-making circles, as the Seiyūkai demanded, and to consult more closely with the military in formulating future defense policies.[12] Furthermore, while Shidehara's views continued to underlie the foreign policy of the Minseitō government, the Seiyūkai had made it clear that when it came to power, it would reject Washington order diplomacy in favor of new approaches

[12] Crowley, *Japan's Quest*, p. 79.

to the defense of Japan's continental interests and the regulation of Japan's relations with the powers.[13]

Inspired by the growing disillusionment with the Cabinet's policies, a small number of impetuous young Army officers and civilian revolutionaries began plans to end party government by carrying out a coup d'état. Their initial plot culminated in the abortive March Incident of 1931. This was followed by another unsuccessful plot in October 1931, which aimed not only at overthrowing party government but also at assassinating senior Court officials who supported Shidehara's foreign policy of conciliation. In addition, Hamaguchi was shot by a civilian fanatic in late 1930, and was forced to yield control of his Cabinet and party to Wakatsuki Reijirō. He died from his wounds in August 1931.

One month later, the government was staggered by two blows that radically altered Japan's international environment and shook the foundations of Minseitō control. One of the two September shocks was Great Britain's decision to abandon the gold standard. The new British monetary policy undermined the economic policies of Finance Minister Inoue, and strengthened the hand of those who had opposed the Cabinet's decision to return to the gold standard. The other shock was, of course, the Manchurian Incident. Alarmed by signs that the movement for national reunification in China had begun to penetrate the heartland of Japanese economic and strategic interests in Manchuria, the Imperial Army had for several years been anxious to move beyond the constraints of "cooperative diplomacy" to a forceful exclusion of Chinese nationalism from the area. By 1931, the Army was agreed that a resolution of the "Manchurian problem" could not be deferred much longer. This perspective was apparently shared by the president of the South Manchurian Railway, Ōkura Kinmochi, who declared that Sino-Japanese relations had reached the

[13] *Ibid.*, p. 80.

"snapping point." The British military attaché in Peking added in a report of July 13 that "unless the protagonists speedily altered their viewpoints, something in the nature of a serious explosion will surely occur."[14] On September 18, this prophecy was fulfilled when forces of the Japanese Kwantung Army under the direction of Colonel Itagaki Seishirō and Lieutenant Colonel Ishiwara Kanji engineered the Manchurian Incident. The Kwantung Army's actions were widely applauded in Japan, though they breached the constraints of "Shidehara Diplomacy" and propelled the Cabinet's foreign policy into the same limbo as its economic program. Wakatsuki's government was now clearly in danger.

SCHISMS IN PARTY UNITY

If the Minseitō had enjoyed the support of nonparty elites during these crises, it might well have weathered again the storm of Seiyūkai opposition to its policies. As Wakatsuki himself quickly discerned, however, the London Treaty and the growing challenge to Japan's Asian interests posed by a resurgent Chinese nationalism made it unlikely that his government would receive that support. The Minseitō found both military services resolutely committed to seeking a greater voice in the formulation of defense policy. The Seiyūkai, moreover, was now publicly committed to making foreign policy independent of the attitudes of the Western powers in order to assure the security of Japan's continental interests.

Thus, despite the continued support of the *genrō* and a core of Minseitō supporters in the civilian nonparty elites, the government party's ability to formulate an acceptable

[14] *Ibid.*, pp. 104 and 82–121; also see Sadako N. Ogata, *Defiance in Manchuria: The Making of Japanese Foreign Policy 1931–1932* (Berkeley and Los Angeles: University of California Press, 1964), and Takehiko Yoshihashi, *Conspiracy at Mukden: The Rise of the Japanese Military* (New Haven: Yale University Press, 1963).

39

synthesis of national policies to deal with the Manchurian and economic problems had now been called into question. Similar doubts existed within the Minseitō as well, and were coupled to a deep dissatisfaction with the party's efficacy as power broker. The role of Home Minister Adachi Kenzō in forcing the Wakatsuki government to resign gave ample proof of the unhappiness felt even in the Minseitō with the party's policies and distribution of power. Wakatsuki believed his Cabinet and its policies could survive the Manchurian Incident only if the Seiyūkai's support could be won. To prompt the Seiyūkai's defection from the opposition, he was willing, as president of the Minseitō, to surrender a share of his party's power and authority to the opposition party.[15] In late October, Wakatsuki broached the possibility of a Minseitō-Seiyūkai coalition Cabinet to Adachi. The Home Minister, who was vice president of the Minseitō and aspired to the presidency, enthusiastically endorsed the proposal and began to work assiduously for it.

Adachi realized that a two-party coalition would make it possible to abandon the gold standard and reimpose the gold embargo, overthrowing Finance Minister Inoue's policy of retrenchment. Coalition with the Seiyūkai would also imply a rejection of Shidehara's "weak-kneed" policy of defending Japan and her interests through peaceful cooperation with the Western powers. Adachi had not originally favored the policies of Inoue and Shidehara, and he welcomed the formulation of a coalition as an opportunity to reverse them. Furthermore, he knew that a coalition with the Seiyūkai would lead to a reallocation of power within the Minseitō and the Cabinet. Adachi had been denied the presidency of the Minseitō after Hamaguchi's death because Shidehara and Inoue had opposed him. The overthrow of their policies in a new Cabinet would reduce their stature

[15] Wakatsuki Reijirō, *Kofūan kaikoroku* (Tokyo: Yomiuri shinbunsha, 1950), p. 384. For a detailed analysis of the foreign policy problems underlying and contributing to the Minseitō's difficulties, see Crowley, *Japan's Quest*, pp. 133–49.

within the party, and would of course mean their resignations from the government. Adachi foresaw the possibility of becoming premier himself, or the *éminence grise* in a coalition government, and believed his position in the Minseitō would be greatly enhanced as well.[16]

As Adachi undertook to win approval from the Seiyūkai leadership for Wakatsuki's plan, Shidehara and Inoue began to voice strong opposition to any inclusion of the Seiyūkai in the government.[17] With obvious justification, they suspected their foreign and economic policies would be sacrificed in the interests of such a coalition. Wakatsuki could not easily ignore the views of these ministers: they represented important Minseitō links with business and the bureaucracy. The premier promptly decided to abandon the coalition Cabinet plan, and announced on November 14 that he would continue to serve as chief officer in a purely Minseitō Cabinet. However, Adachi and an important group of Minseitō members refused to surrender the coalition plan. Though the Minseitō's elective strength had never been greater, the Home Minister went on record publicly as willing to support a change in the composition of the government.[18] Party advisor Tomita Kōjirō, executive secretary Yamaji Jōichi, and other leading or promising party figures such as Nagai Ryūtarō, Nakano Seigō, and Kazami Akira all actively joined Adachi in promoting a coalition Cabinet to replace the government dominated by their own party. Their rupture with Wakatsuki and the government finally came to a climax on December 11, when the home

[16] It has been suggested that Adachi sought the premiership for himself. See Maejima Shōzō, *Nihon fuashizumu to gikai* (Kyoto: Hōritsu bunkasha, 1956), p. 271. It has also been argued that he wished to be the power behind an Inukai regime (*ibid.*, p. 275) or an Ugaki government. See Suda Teiichi, *Kazami Akira to sono jidai* (Tokyo: Misuzu shobō, 1965), p. 83.

[17] "Nagai Ryūtarō" hensankai (Matsumura Kenzō), ed., *Nagai Ryūtarō* (Tokyo: Seikōsha, 1959), p. 296.

[18] Adachi Kenzō, *Adachi Kenzō jijōden* (Tokyo: Shinjusha, 1960), p. 263.

41

minister refused to attend an emergency Cabinet session or to resign from his post. Unable to unify the Cabinet, Wakatsuki had to submit his government's resignation the following day.

The Seiyūkai was also divided internally at this juncture, although not yet as seriously as the Minseitō. Committed to overthrowing the government party and its policies, the mainstream of the Seiyūkai, under Inukai Tsuyoshi and Suzuki Kisaburō, preferred a new Cabinet they would dominate to a coalition in which they would share power with the Minseitō. However, Kuhara Fusanosuke—the executive secretary of the Seiyūkai—enthusiastically joined Adachi in promoting the creation of a coalition Cabinet. Kuhara was eager to overturn Inoue's financial policies,[19] and might ordinarily have confined his efforts against the Cabinet to supporting the Seiyūkai mainstream's demand for a Seiyūkai government. But while Kuhara's influence within the party was growing, it was not yet equal to that of Suzuki Kisaburō. Kuhara was convinced that Suzuki would be the chief beneficiary in the allocation of positions and influence in the party and government, if a Seiyūkai Cabinet were established. Rather than have his own political ambitions thwarted by a government of his party, Kuhara preferred to work for a coalition Cabinet led by General Ugaki Kazushige.[20]

Despite the efforts of Adachi and Kuhara, a coalition government was never formed. Prince Saionji named Inukai

[19] Much of Kuhara's personal fortune had apparently been invested on the speculation that the gold embargo would be reimposed in Japan. Maejima, *Nihon fuashizumu to gikai*, pp. 271–72, 275.

[20] *Ibid.*, p. 275. Others in the Seiyūkai who supported the coalition Cabinet proposal included Okazaki Kunisuke, Mizuno Rentarō, Tokonami Takejirō, Mochizuki Keisuke, Yamamoto Jōtarō, Mitsuchi Chūzō, Maeda Yonezō, Akita Kiyoshi, and Uchida Shinya. These men were the leaders of the anti-Suzuki forces in the party. By 1935, five of them—Mizuno, Tokonami, Mochizuki, Akita, and Uchida—had either resigned or been expelled from the Seiyūkai. See Nashimoto Sukeyoshi, *Suzuki Kisaburō* (Tokyo: Jidaisha, 1932), p. 82.

to succeed Wakatsuki as premier, and Inukai excluded the Minseitō from his Cabinet. Shortly thereafter, Adachi defected from the party in which he had been vice president, and in 1932 he formed the small Kokumin dōmei party with other defectors from the Minseitō cause. Kuhara remained in the Seiyūkai, but continued seeking to enhance his own prestige and the influence of his party by promoting close ties with the Army.[21]

The first important political development under Inukai's government was the general election of February 20, 1932. As was frequently the case during the period of party government in prewar Japan, the incoming government sought to confirm its authority and establish control of the Lower House by calling and winning a general election. When Inukai became premier, the Seiyūkai's strength in the Lower House was 174 seats, compared to 273 for the Minseitō. In the 1932 elections held under the Seiyūkai administration, the ruling party garnered 301 seats in the Lower House, and the Minseitō dropped to 146 seats.[22] Although it was not impossible for Saionji to turn to the Minseitō in the future to form a Cabinet, the fact that the Minseitō held less than half the Seiyūkai total of Diet seats made such a possibility unlikely. The Minseitō would need another general election, one not held under Seiyūkai auspices, to demonstrate its popular strength and regain the *genrō's* confidence. The precipitous decline of Minseitō strength in the 1932 election thus resulted in a four-year party strategy of opposing party (Seiyūkai) government and supporting two "national unity" Cabinets led by retired admirals. The party's commitment to "parliament-centered government" was tempered finely by a pragmatic assessment of its own re-

[21] He had, of course, previously indicated such tendencies in successfully recruiting General Tanaka Giichi into the party in 1925.

[22] The figures for the respective party strengths prior to the 1932 election are based on the 1930 election results. See Kōmei senkyo renmei, ed., *Shūgiin giin senkyo no jisseki* (Tokyo: Toppan insatsu kabushiki kaisha, 1967), p. 137.

quirements as a minority group holding fewer than one-third of the seats in the Lower House.

The second important incident of the Inukai reign was the appointment of Suzuki Kisaburō as home minister a month after the elections. Suzuki's appointment suggested that he had sufficient power within his party to be selected as the next president of the Seiyūkai.[23] The significance of Suzuki's ascent to the position of Inukai's heir apparent became clear within two months, when Inukai's assassination forced Saionji to consider whether or not to make Suzuki premier.

The activities of Mori Kaku, the fiery chief Cabinet secretary of the Inukai government and influential Seiyūkai leader, were also of great importance in the eventual termination of party government. According to his biographer, Mori's political philosophy shifted in early 1931 to "dictatorial tendencies that would deal with the period of emergency."[24] Mori broke with Inukai's continental policy early in 1932, and like Kuhara and Adachi, he looked outside his party for channels through which his ambitions and policy views could be promoted. Despite the overwhelming victory of the Seiyūkai at the polls in February, Mori began to campaign actively for the establishment of a new Cabinet, led by Baron Hiranuma Kiichirō, the vice president of the Privy Council. In Mori's view, a Hiranuma government in which both parties were represented would prove the best instrument for consolidating Japan's position in Manchuria and China. Before Mori's efforts could bear fruit, Inukai was assassinated on May 15 by a group of young radical Navy cadets. He was the third prominent Japanese to die violently in 1932, for Inoue Junnosuke (the former finance minister) and industrialist Dan Takuma had been struck down earlier in the year.

[23] Nashimoto, *Suzuki*, pp. 14–15, and Itō, *Shōwa shoki seiji shi kenkyū*, pp. 217–18, 220.

[24] Yamaura Kan'ichi, *Mori Kaku* (Tokyo: Mori Kaku denki hensan-kai, 1940), p. 788.

SUSPENSION OF PARTY CABINETS

The "May 15th Incident" has been accorded an important place in early Shōwa history, for Inukai's death marked the end of party government. The termination of party rule has been equated with the final defeat of liberalism and democracy at the hands of a burgeoning radical fascism and militarism.[25] Historians have contended that the "liberal" Saionji was reluctant to put an end to party rule even temporarily, but was obliged to do so in order to cool the passionate opposition and terrorism of Army and ultranationalist groups directed against the political parties. In this view, the parties sought to preserve party government, but were overwhelmed by the Army and right-wing civilian groups. A closer examination of political conditions in May 1932 suggests that the issue was somewhat more complex.

In late 1931 and early 1932, Adachi, Kuhara, Mori, and their followers endeavored to change the relationship of the parties to the Cabinet. They set aside the notion that one or the other of the major parties should control the Cabinet, and advocated that governments be led by a two-party coalition and a nonparty figure such as Baron Hiranuma or General Ugaki. None of their efforts received the blessing of the mainstream elements in either party, nor did they win the approval of Saionji. Even the nonparty civilian and military elites agreed to the elder statesman's designation of Inukai as premier of a government dominated by one party.

By May 1932, however, the political situation had changed considerably. The Minseitō, drastically weakened by Adachi's defection and the crushing defeat at the polls in February, was eager to regain a share of Cabinet posts in the government that would succeed the fallen Inukai. Izawa Takio, an influential Minseitō supporter in the House

[25] G. Richard Storry, *The Double Patriots: A Study of Japanese Nationalism* (Boston: Houghton Mifflin Co., 1957), p. 124; Scalapino, *Democracy and the Party Movement*, p. 243.

of Peers, now lobbied for a coalition Cabinet that would give Wakatsuki's party a seat in government councils.[26] Within the Seiyūkai as well, there was growing support for a government led by someone other than the party's new president, Suzuki Kisaburō. Inukai's selection as party president in 1929 had been a maneuver designed to postpone the day of reckoning in the competition for party hegemony between the supporters of Suzuki and Tokonami Takejirō.[27] With Inukai's death, this rivalry again surfaced in a competition for the highly coveted presidency and access to the premiership. The situation was further exacerbated by Kuhara's rising strength in party councils, and by his determination to frustrate Suzuki's quest for control over the party.[28] Mori, furthermore, had not abandoned his plans to make Hiranuma the next premier. The anti-Suzuki forces were numerous but divided. They were unable to prevent Suzuki's selection as the new president of the Seiyūkai, but they were determined to deny him the prestige and additional political leverage attendant to the premiership.

Suzuki's rise to political prominence was not the result of the crisis of the moment. He had had a long, illustrious, and stormy career in the Ministry of Justice, and together with Hiranuma had guided the fortunes of the ministry during the late Meiji and Taishō eras. Suzuki followed Hiranuma into politics in 1924, serving as the justice minister in the short-lived Kiyoura Cabinet. In 1927, he became home minister in the Tanaka Seiyūkai government, and simultaneously joined the Seiyūkai. Despite his oft-expressed antipathy for party politics,[29] he soon proved adept at the political

[26] Yamaura, *Mori Kaku*, pp. 796, 812. Izawa was also a patron of Gotō Fumio, and was largely responsible for Gotō's appointment as minister of agriculture and forestry in the new government.

[27] Itō, *Shōwa shoki seiji shi kenkyū*, pp. 219–20.

[28] Nashimoto, *Suzuki*, pp. 6–9, 76 and *passim* for Suzuki-Kuhara-Tokonami factional relations.

[29] See the remarks of Suzuki's close associate, Oka Kishichirō, in Suzuki Kisaburō sensei denki hensankai (Yamaoka Mannosuke), ed.,

infighting characteristic of Japanese party factionalism. His appointment as home minister in March 1932 marked him clearly as Inukai's successor (see Figure 1).

Suzuki's emergence as a major force in Seiyūkai politics illustrates as well as do the activities of Adachi, Kuhara, and Mori the danger of equating party politics in the 1920s and 1930s with a commitment to political liberalism or party government on the English pattern of alloting control of the Cabinet to the party holding a parliamentary majority. Along with his close association with Hiranuma, a consistent and vigorous critic of liberalism and the parties, Suzuki himself was quite explicit in outlining his own views on the role of the parties and Diet in the Japanese polity (*kokutai*). On the eve of the first general election held under universal male suffrage in 1928, Home Minister Suzuki issued a stinging attack on the Minseitō's advocacy of "parliament-centered government."

> According to our Constitution, the Cabinet is organized principally upon the august invocation of imperial sovereignty. It is inexcusable that our country be compared to others where Cabinets are directly formed by the majority party. From its inception, the Seiyūkai has been obedient to the principle of government centered on the emperor. . . . By contrast, the present platform of the Minseitō cites "a need to carry through politics centered on the parliament." This is a most disquieting concept, which I must say violates the great spirit of our nation's sacred Constitution. The governance of imperial Japan is completely subject to the control of the emperor; it is very clearly politics centered on the emperor.
>
> Concepts like parliament-centered politics are Anglo-American notions flowing from the current of democracy, and are inconsistent with our nation's *kokutai*. They obscure the great principle that sovereignty lies entirely

Suzuki Kisaburō (Tokyo: Suzuki Kisaburō sensei denki hensankai, 1945 and 1955), p. 217.

FIGURE 1. Inukai Tsuyoshi (left center) was Imperial Japan's final party prime minister. Assassinated on May 15, 1932, he was succeeded at the helm of the Seiyūkai by Suzuki Kisaburō (center right).

with the emperor. They violate the great spirit of the imperial Constitution. They are absolutely intolerable. I call upon the people to assess the situation coolly, and to permit the fullest operation of the Constitution, faithfully giving body to its great spirit.[30]

Invocations of loyalty to the throne could hardly be faulted, but Suzuki's remarks on the emperor as the only source of control in the governing of Japan, particularly when made in the context of a partisan political election campaign, were anathema to Saionji. The elder statesman's entire career had been devoted to isolating and protecting the throne from politics. It was precisely because of his desire to find an alternative to direct imperial involvement in politics that Saionji had originally promoted the parties as responsible agents of national government. Because of his antipathy for the "direct imperial rule" (*shinsei*) ideology, Saionji not only regarded Suzuki with hostility, but was a vigorous and consistent opponent of the political ambitions of Suzuki's comrade, Baron Hiranuma (see Figure 2).

Faced with the task of recommending a new premier to the throne in May 1932, Saionji had to choose between Suzuki or a figure outside the political parties. Selecting Suzuki would enable him to avoid, as he had in 1921, setting the "dangerous precedent" of turning a party out of power because of the assassination of its president,[31] and would also permit the continuation of party government. On the other hand, it would install as premier a man who derided the significance of the Diet, who was "like a younger brother" to Hiranuma, and who pointedly contended that the throne, rather than the Lower House parties, was the only force capable of unifying Japanese politics under the Meiji Constitution. Suzuki was further regarded by Saionji as a principal architect of the Seiyū-

[30] *Ibid.*, p. 236.

[31] Harada Kumao, *Saionji-kō to seikyoku* (9 vols., Tokyo: Iwanami shoten, 1950–1956), I, 220 (hereafter cited as SKS).

49

FIGURE 2. The venerated Prince Saionji Kinmochi was the sole surviving *genrō* in the 1930s, and his trips to the Imperial Palace were invariably a sign of political crisis.

kai's attack on the London Naval Treaty and the Washington order Saionji had helped to construct.[32] He was, moreover, unpopular at Court, in the House of Peers, and among some bureaucratic groups for his blatant manipulation of the police in the 1928 election.

Saionji found the political situation further complicated by the Army's well-known opposition to another party Cabinet, by the Minseitō's desire to recoup some of its recently lost influence, and by a determined movement in the Seiyūkai to deny Suzuki the premiership. The *genrō* found little support from party forces for an adherence to the principle of having the majority party control the Cabinet. Wakatsuki, as president of the Minseitō, advocated a Cabinet led by Admiral Yamamoto Gonnohyōe; Izawa actively supported the appointment of Admiral Saitō Makoto.[33] Acting Premier Takahashi Korekiyo—former president of the Seiyūkai and beneficiary of Saionji's resolve against "setting a dangerous precedent" eleven years earlier—advised Saionji against the formation of another Seiyūkai government.[34] Within the Seiyūkai, only Suzuki's faction and Hatoyama Ichirō, Suzuki's brother-in-law, remained firm advocates of a new Seiyūkai government under Suzuki.

In short, most party politicians, whom historians regard as the strongest advocates of party government, refused to support it in May 1932. Among those who surrounded the emperor at Court, the factional struggle in the Seiyūkai was seen as a serious obstacle to the perpetuation of Seiyūkai rule. Even before Inukai's death, Kido Kōichi (then secretary to the lord keeper of the privy seal) indicated the anxieties of the Court politicians when he noted on April 3, 1932:

> In the current situation, it will not be possible to count on even the Seiyūkai, with its more than 300 members in

[32] *Ibid.*, p. 177.

[33] "Nagai Ryūtarō" hensankai, ed., *Nagai Ryūtarō*, p. 310. Izawa's personal animosity towards Suzuki dated back to their days as bureaucrats together. See Nashimoto, *Suzuki*, pp. 84–85.

[34] Yamaura, *Mori Kaku*, p. 816.

the Diet. If the recent atmosphere of uncertainty should grow worse, it will be necessary to make preparations to deal with a possible replacement of the current government. The biggest problem to be faced in that regard is deciding on a premier. Admiral Saitō would seem the most appropriate choice, but should the plans of Hiranuma's supporters prove too strong, one possibility might be to form a Cabinet under both of them. I rather think it would be difficult to create such a coalition, but were it possible, it would be good.[35]

Thus, as the *genrō* went about finding a consensus on the selection of a new Cabinet, it became very clear that the overwhelming opinion at Court and in the Diet, to say nothing of the Army and the ultranationalist right wing, was opposed to a Seiyūkai government under Suzuki. Even Hiranuma, eyeing the premiership himself, opposed the appointment of his old colleague as premier. Finally, on May 22, Saionji invited Admiral Saitō to succeed Inukai as the premier of a "national unity" Cabinet.

In retrospect, Saionji's decision to suspend party government was not simply the result of a struggle between the forces of "liberalism" in the Diet and at Court and the forces of militarism and fascism in the Army and right wing. To be certain, the terrorist attacks on Inoue, Dan, and Inukai cast a dark shadow over the selection of a new premier; and the *genrō* certainly wished to alleviate the danger to national stability posed by military and right-wing assassination plots. But the political dilemma of the shattered Minseitō, the factionalism of the Seiyūkai, and Saionji's own antipathy for Suzuki's political record were equally important factors in the decision to select a premier from outside the parties. The elder statesman, whose responsibility it was to recommend to the throne a man who could harmonize the competing elites into a stable governing coalition, found

[35] Kido Kōichi, *Kido Kōichi nikki* (2 vols., Tokyo: Tokyo daigaku shuppankai, 1966), I, 153.

little elite support for Suzuki. Ironically, the only objections to the suspension of majority party rule in May 1932 came from Suzuki, a man who had eloquently expressed his own disdain for parliament-centered politics on election eve, 1928.

The appointment of Admiral Saitō was as much a specific rejection of Suzuki and the disunited Seiyūkai as it was an abandonment of party government. The *genrō*, the Court, and the parties regarded the new government as an "interim" regime, which would serve only briefly until the parties could again assume a central role in coordinating elite views into national policies and allocating political power among the elites. Saionji evidently hoped that, given time, the parties could close ranks internally and again fulfill the task of "assisting the imperial rule." Once their internal strength was restored, the parties might be able to check the political ambitions of the Army, and prevent Japan from following a foreign policy that Saionji felt certain would provoke the Western powers and endanger the nation.

PARTY TIES TO "NATIONAL UNITY" CABINETS

Suzuki also believed that Saitō's appointment was only a temporary setback. Hence, the Seiyūkai as well as the Minseitō provided party leaders as ministers of state in the new government. Five Cabinet posts in the Saitō government were held by representatives of the *kisei seitō*. But the parties quickly disappointed Saionji. Anxious to demonstrate their willingness to support and lead the national consensus on important policies, they joined together within a month of Inukai's death to express the Diet's unanimous support for recognizing the newly created state of Manchukuo. Wakatsuki's party would continue in the months ahead to support the Saitō government fully, believing that the Minseitō's only chance for a complete return to power would come after a general election held under the neutral auspices of an "interim" government (see Figure 3).

Figure 3. Following the death of Inukai Tsuyoshi, party government gave way to "national unity" cabinets. The first such cabinet governed from May 1932 to July 1934, and included (rear row, from left), Hatoyama Ichirō (education), Araki Sadao (army), Nagai Ryūtarō (development), Nakajima Kumakichi (commerce), Koyama Matsukichi (justice), and Gotō Fumio (agriculture and forestry). The front row (from left) includes Mitsuchi Chūzō (railways), Uchida Yasuya (foreign affairs), Saitō Makoto (prime minister), Yamamoto Tatsuo (home affairs), and Minami Hiroshi (communications).

By April 1933 the Seiyūkai attitude towards the continuation of the Saitō regime had become ambivalent. Suzuki had supported the Cabinet, expecting that it would rule only briefly before he became premier. He now became restless over the delay in Saitō's resignation. His opponents within the Seiyūkai, on the other hand, were gratified that the Saitō government obstructed their president's ambition to control the Cabinet.[36] When Admiral Saitō finally did step down in July 1934, Saionji was confronted with a situation analogous to 1932. The Army again opposed party control of the Cabinet. The Minseitō was happy with its share of power and willing to support another "interim" Cabinet until elections could be called. The balance of elite opinion opposed returning control of the Cabinet to the majority party. Further, it became clear to Saionji between 1932 and 1934 that both parties were willing to support the creation of Manchukuo and a foreign policy rooted in Japan's military strength. The *genrō* could no longer hope that a revival of party government would result in any dramatic reversal in foreign policy. He therefore recommended to the throne that a "national unity" Cabinet be retained, with Admiral Okada Keisuke as the new premier.

Rebuffed a second time, Suzuki and the Seiyūkai mainstream flatly refused to cooperate with the new government. While the Minseitō readily agreed to have two of its leaders serve as ministers in Okada's Cabinet, Suzuki refused to permit Seiyūkai participation in the government. When Yamazaki Tatsunosuke, Tokonami Takejirō, and Uchida Nobuya of the anti-mainstream factions accepted portfolios in the new Cabinet, they were immediately read out of the party.[37] The Seiyūkai further opposed the establishment of a Cabinet Policy Council (*Naikaku shingikai*), although the original proposal for such an organ had been made by

[36] Maeda Yonezō denki kankōkai (Aritake Shūji), ed., *Maeda Yonezō den* (Tokyo: Itō-setsu shobō, 1961), pp. 282–85. See also Nakamura, *Shōwa seiji shi*, pp. 117–18.

[37] Nakamura, *Shōwa seiji shi*, p. 120.

Yamamoto Jōtarō, a Seiyūkai leader. When Mochizuki Keisuke and Mizuno Rentarō chose to become members of the Council, they, too, were forced to leave the party.[38]

If the parties were to maintain their roles as coordinators of elite opinion and channels through which power was allocated, Suzuki's strategy of refusing to cooperate with the Okada government proved a serious error. Despite the approval expressed by most elites for the "national unity" Cabinet proposed by Saionji in 1934, Suzuki refused to recognize the legitimacy of this style of government. However laudable the party's consistency in advocating party government may have been in theory, it was hardly conducive to instilling confidence in the Seiyūkai's sense of responsibility for maintaining domestic harmony and stability. Already, radical opponents of the parties were demanding that any Diet politician selected as Cabinet minister be required to resign from his party before assuming office. In the final analysis, however, it was the attitude of the mainstream of the majority party that forced Yamazaki, Tokonami, and Uchida to leave their party in order to assume ministerial positions. In short, the Seiyūkai voluntarily excluded itself from the responsibility of formulating policies for the nation. Suzuki's strategy could hardly have been better calculated to lend credence to the old antiparty argument that the *kisei seitō* cared more for their own private interests than for the welfare of the nation.

Suzuki and his party soon paid the price for their ill-conceived strategy. In December 1935, those who had been dropped from the Seiyūkai roster formed the Shōwakai party. Three months later, as a result of the general election on February 20, 1936, the Seiyūkai bloc in the Lower House was reduced by almost 130 seats to 174, while the Minseitō

[38] Okada Keisuke taishō kiroku hensankai, ed., *Okada Keisuke* (Tokyo: Okada Keisuke taishō kiroku hensankai, 1956), pp. 303–304. The original proposal for the *Naikaku shingikai* had been made by Yamamoto Jōtarō during Inukai's tenure as premier. See Maeda Yonezō denki kankōkai, ed., *Maeda Yonezō den*, pp. 256–64.

won 205 seats. Suzuki himself was defeated in his campaign to retain a seat in the Diet. It was now only a matter of time before the party would have to find a successor to Suzuki as president. Within a year, the party was deeply split between the Maeda Yonezō-Nakajima Chikuhei group and the Hatoyama faction, both of which sought to gain control of the Seiyūkai by seizing the party presidency. Never again was the party really able to act effectively as a unified force in Cabinet politics.

The Minseitō fared only slightly better. After Adachi's futile attempt to create a coalition Cabinet in 1931, the Minseitō leadership firmly opposed his reinstatement in the party.[39] Late in 1932, Adachi and the small group following him out of the Minseitō completed the break by forming the Kokumin dōmei. Although the party's electoral strength suffered from Adachi's defection, party unity was retained. Wakatsuki continued as president until his resignation in late 1934, and Machida Chūji was formally designated his successor in January of the following year. During the Saitō and Okada Cabinets, the Minseitō continued to support the "national unity" governments, in the belief that its strength would increase in any election held under neutral auspices. Unofficial efforts were also made by party leaders such as Kawasaki Takukichi and Nagai Ryūtarō to enhance the party's position by seeking a coalition with dissident Seiyūkai elements, and by forming a new party centered on the Minseitō and led by a distinguished national figure like General Ugaki or Prince Konoe Fumimaro.

The official party strategy was finally rewarded with the announcement by Premier Okada that a general election would be held on February 20, 1936. On February 25, it was announced that the Minseitō had won 205 seats in the new Diet. Combined with the twenty seats won by the

[39] Kawasaki Takukichi denki hensankai, ed., *Kawasaki Takukichi* (Tokyo: Ishizaki shoten, 1961), pp. 436–44, documents the Minseitō mainstream's success in frustrating a movement in the party to reinstate Adachi.

Shōwakai and with several other independent supporters, the Minseitō might have been able to form a coalition of sufficient strength to merit Saionji's consideration in the formation of a new Cabinet. Unfortunately for the party, the nonparty elites were less inclined to tolerate party government now than they had been at the beginning of the decade. It is important to review some of the reasons for this change in attitude, since they help to explain the decline in party influence.

A New Climate Strengthens the Case Against the Parties

By February 1936, both major political parties had been subjected to intensive attacks from "reform" and "Japanist" right-wing groups and from an increasing number of important leaders in the Army, Navy, and bureaucracy. At the same time, well-publicized party scandals further damaged the image of the parties as legitimate organs of political leadership.[40] Right-wing ideologues for many years had regarded the very existence of the parties and party government as the manifestation of evil doctrines of Western liberalism that were "inconsistent with the nation's political essence." After 1930, when the depression wreaked havoc on the societies and economies of the Western democracies, these polemicists naturally cited the socio-economic distress of those nations as additional and convincing evidence of the ineffectiveness of parliamentary government.[41] Moreover, Japan's gradual diplomatic estrangement from

[40] Perhaps the most damaging scandal was the "Teijin Incident." See Tiedemann, "Big Business and Politics in Prewar Japan," pp. 294–96. All of those indicted by the prosecutors were found to be not guilty in 1937, but not until considerable damage had been done to their reputations and the reputations of the parties.

[41] Naimushō keiho-kyoku chōsa-shitsu (Hirotsu Kyōsuke), *Saikin wagakuni ni okeru gikai seido kaikaku ron* (Secret), March 1936, pp. 30–31.

the Western powers bred a growing reaction against Western styles and institutions within the country, and strengthened the position of those who criticized the competitive party system as incompatible with Japan's national essence. These attacks on the parties and political liberalism were certainly obstacles to the maintenance or extension of party influence during the 1930s. In themselves, however, they were not sufficient causes for the decline of party power and prestige. Parties had often been attacked for their corruption even during the period of their remarkable growth from 1905 to 1930. Moreover, elite acceptance of the parties during this earlier period hinged not on a commitment to political liberalism but on a pragmatic assessment of the parties' value in harmonizing elite views and serving as intermediary agencies between the Japanese people and their government. A simple critique of liberalism and Western influence was not sufficient cause for the elites suddenly to reject party government.

Between 1932 and 1934, Japan embarked on a series of new economic policies to fight the depression and develop the military strength of the nation. These policies required a larger state role in economic affairs, and even "moderate" political writers questioned the ability of party politicians to deal with sophisticated policies related to the proliferation of state functions in the national economy.[42] An even more significant departure from the policies of the 1920s took place in the realm of foreign affairs and national defense. The anti-Japanese militancy of Chinese nationalism and the threat of an Anglo-American naval alliance directed against Japan persuaded many Japanese leaders that "cooperative diplomacy" could no longer preserve the nation's security or her interests on the mainland. Reflecting this disillusionment, the Inukai government quickly recognized the legitimacy of the Kwantung Army's actions in Man-

[42] For an overall review of these policies, see Takahashi Makoto, "The Development of War-Time Economic Controls," *Developing Economies*, v.4 (December 1967), 653–56.

59

churia and extended formal recognition to the newly created puppet state of Manchukuo. In the fall of 1933, Saitō's Cabinet "proposed to neutralize the influence of the Soviet Union, the Nationalist government of China, and the Anglo-American nations by a diplomacy rooted in the efficacy of Japan's military forces."[43] Building a military force capable of dealing successfully with all of Japan's hypothetical adversaries was, as it turned out, quite beyond the military and economic capabilities of the nation. Nevertheless, the responsibilities for executing these plans were accepted by all of the nation's political elites, including the *kisei seitō.*

These new national policies were in one sense indicative of a shift taking place in the balance of power among the elites, and in another sense productive of further changes in the locus of power. They required careful attention to the views of those with technical expertise germane to their implementation. Hence, the years after 1932 were marked by increased recognition for the bureaucratic and military elites, who claimed to have specialized knowledge required for the successful execution of Japan's national policies. The weight of bureaucratic and military influence among the elites began to increase with the depression, the London Treaty controversy, and the military's response to Chinese nationalism; it was augmented thereafter by the policies of the Saitō and Okada governments. While civilian and military bureaucrats capitalized on the events of the early 1930s to enhance their relative position among the elites, the parties suffered from growing skepticism about their ability to make meaningful contributions to the integration and implementation of national policy.

Minobe Tatsukichi, for example, typified the disillusionment with party politicians as national leaders. The best known interpreter of Japan's Constitution, Minobe was a distinguished professor of law at Tokyo Imperial Univer-

[43] Particulars of this policy were subsequently made explicit in Cabinet decisions of July and December 1934 and October 1935. See Crowley, *Japan's Quest*, pp. 195–99, 231.

sity, a member of the House of Peers, and during the 1920s, an important advocate of party government.[44] His constitutional views supported the growth of party influence among the elites, and the eventual success of the parties in gaining control of the Cabinet in the late 1920s and early 1930s. By 1934, however, he questioned publicly the wisdom of allowing Diet politicians to decide the nation's policies. He wrote that the Diet had previously considered only political issues, such as the freedom of assembly and speech, or the extension of the franchise. Customarily, economic planning had been left to the discretion of those engaged in economic activities, and there had been relatively little demand for legislation in the area of economic policy.[45] All a man had needed earlier to be a satisfactory arbiter of national policy in the Diet was a modicum of common sense. However, with the desire for economic recovery from the depression, Minobe pointed out that a member of the Diet now had to be well versed in economic affairs as well as political issues. There was a growing demand for laws to control finance, production, and labor, and to reform the capitalist structure of the economy. The state's role in the economic life of the people was growing at a rapid pace; and politics had become integrally related to economic questions, especially to questions of state economic controls. Policy judgments had to be based on specialized knowledge, rather than simply on common sense. These judgments could not be left to the idle consideration of amateurs; the role of the specialist was becoming increasingly important. Minobe explained that the Diet's initiative in drafting legislation was very slight; with the exception of bills unrelated to

[44] See Frank O. Miller, *Minobe Tatsukichi: Interpreter of Constitutionalism in Japan* (Berkeley and Los Angeles: University of California Press, 1965), especially pp. 130–38.

[45] This was true only in a relative sense. The government's role in modern Japan's economic development was always an important one. In relative terms, however, the volume of state tasks in the 1930s was far greater than previously.

economic matters (such as revisions of the Diet law and the election laws), the Diet now functioned only to ratify the proposals of specialists in the executive branch of government. Its members were no longer qualified to do otherwise.[46]

Minobe was, of course, quite correct in noting that the Diet had rarely functioned as a policy-making body even during the 1920s. Most legislative proposals historically emanated from the various ministries, not from the floor of the Diet. Moreover, the parties did not give a great deal of weight to serious policy study within their own organizations. While both major parties had Political Affairs Research Councils (*Seimu chōsakai*), the importance of these councils in determining party positions was far less than in today's Liberal-Democratic party.[47] Party positions were decided instead by top party leaders, who sought the support of other elites for the party by working for compromises among elite positions and adjusting party views to the consensus they might reach. However, Minobe's critique was not limited to party performance in the Lower House. What he now maintained was that Diet members (i.e., party politicians) were no longer qualified to deal with legislative proposals. Whereas they had formerly coordinated competing policy viewpoints into national policy through party channels outside of the Diet, Minobe now asserted that they did not possess the specialized expertise to deal intelligently with sophisticated problems of economic and social policy planning and integration. Therefore, it was no longer desirable to allocate to the parties a central role in governing the nation or determining Cabinet policies. Minobe now doubted that the Diet had any future as a legislative branch

[46] Minobe Tatsukichi, "Waga gikai seido no zento," *Chūō kōron,* #553 (January 1934), pp. 9 ff.

[47] *Asahi shinbun,* August 28, 1962, p. 2. Quigley, writing prior to the demise of party government, noted that "the principal deficiency, surely a notable one for 'research' committees, is the absence of scientific members." Quigley, *Japanese Government,* p. 248.

of government, or that subsequent Cabinets should be formed on the basis of Lower House majorities.[48]

Minobe was not the only highly respected intellectual who had earlier advocated parliamentary government but now questioned the ability of the parties to formulate sophisticated policies related to national defense and economic recovery. In an atmosphere of domestic and international crisis, Japan's political and intellectual leaders saw the need for technical expertise and comprehensive national planning in terms of drafting and implementing policies of national survival. The low level of specialized knowledge among party politicians—decried even in the past—now became a serious deterrent to the resuscitation of party influence. Rōyama Masamichi reflected the disappointment and anxieties of the supporters of representative government when he wrote in 1935:

Presently, the Diet's achievements have been limited to criticizing the government's policies and administration on one ground or another. No concrete policy proposals, however, have been submitted by Dietmen. During the days of party government, it was perhaps possible for an opposition party to fulfill its function as the opposition without making constructive criticism or definite proposals. Today, on the other hand, when we consider if the parties can again take hold of the reins of power, it must be said that their failure to evince a positive attitude in this area is a demonstration of their inadequacy.[49]

As civilian and military technocrats amassed prestige and influence during the "period of national emergency," the position of the parties among the elites began to decline, and their sophistication in policy matters tended to diminish even further. Once they had lost their prestigious position in the government, it became difficult for them to

[48] Minobe, "Waga gikai seido no zento," p. 11.
[49] Rōyama Masamichi, *Gikai, seitō, senkyo* (Tokyo: Nippon hyōronsha, 1935), p. 69.

recruit men who could provide them with the technical expertise needed to regain the confidence of the other elites. The Seiyūkai found no new recruits like Tanaka Giichi or Takahashi Korekiyo, who had brought expertise to their party in their fields of specialization. Difficulties in recruitment for the majority party may have been due in large part to its strategy of purging members who accepted posts in the Okada government. Meanwhile, the extreme weakness of the Minseitō between 1932 and 1936 limited its attractiveness as an avenue to power and prestige. The assassinations of Inoue Junnosuke and Hamaguchi, and the death of Egi Tasuku by natural causes, robbed the party of several knowledgeable and respected leaders. A member of the Minseitō later recalled that after 1932 it became increasingly difficult for his party to recruit bureaucrats and financiers to the party's standard, as they preferred to deal directly with nonparty elites themselves.[50]

THE IMPAIRMENT OF PARTY FUNCTIONS

The parties' ability to provide rewards for party membership naturally declined as they became less influential in government. Moreover, once they had lost control of the Cabinet, the bureaucracy was able to procure stiffer guarantees of officials' positions in government. In the context of a disastrous agrarian and business depression, even party leaders were obliged to join the nonparty elites in conceding the need for a stabilization of administrative leadership. In late 1932, the Saitō government established a Commission on the Guarantee of Officials' Status (*Kanri mibun hoshō iinkai*) with the power to review the retirement of officials. With the creation of this commission, it became impossible for new governments to fire officials simply on the basis of their political affiliations. In February 1933, an Imperial Ordinance (*Junsa mibun hoshō-rei*) was issued

[50] Matsumura Kenzō, in "Nagai Ryūtarō" hensankai, ed., *Nagai Ryūtarō*, p. 310.

guaranteeing the status of police officials. This edict prevented new governments from arbitrarily replacing police officials with men sympathetic to the new regime. In addition to stabilizing the police administration of the nation, it reduced the leverage governments could exert on the police force, thereby making it difficult for them to force the police to intervene in elections on behalf of one party or another.[51]

These two measures were of enormous significance. They made government officials far less dependent for their occupational security on the regime in power, and prompted a reinforced sense of bureaucratic independence. By and large, they also eliminated the parties' ability to penetrate the bureaucracy, thereby reducing the parties' capacity to serve as foci of competing elite viewpoints and harmonizers among the elites. They represented a successful culmination of the bureaucratic effort to limit party influence in the ministries, particularly in the Home Ministry.

With the decline of party influence and prestige, party recruiting efforts suffered, and other elites increasingly bypassed party channels in promoting their views and interests. Between the elections of 1928 and 1937, the number of Dietmen recruited from the bureaucratic, military, and business elites declined steadily, as seen in Table 1.[52] Even

Table 1

Election	Diet Seats	Ex-officials	Ex-military	Ex-bankers	Businessmen
1928	466	41	4	5	92
1930	466	36	3	2	82
1932	466	39	1	1	79
1936	466	27	0	0	72
1937	466	9	3	1	72

[51] Shiraki, *Nihon seitō shi*, p. 154, and *Naimushō shi*, i, 404–405.

[52] Figures from *Dai Nippon teikoku tōkei nenkan* (1939), p. 365. It should be noted that compilations on the backgrounds of Diet members were based simply on the member's own judgment of his

within the Diet, there were signs that the *kisei seitō* had declined as avenues of political advancement. After 1932, the number of Diet members who chose to remain aloof from either of the two major parties increased (Table 2).[53]

Table 2

Election	Seiyūkai	Minseitō	Others	Percentage of Others in Total
1928	217	216	33	7 percent
1930	174	273	19	4 percent
1932	301	146	19	4 percent
1936	174	205	87	19 percent
1937	175	179	112	24 percent

The trends revealed in these tables suggest the decline of *kisei seitō* and even Lower House membership as a method of obtaining power and prestige. There were, then, two mutually reinforcing trends that undermined the party position among the elites. As the civilian and military bureaucracies capitalized on the atmosphere of crisis and the strongly felt need for administrative expertise in policy making, they nudged the parties from control of the Cabinet. Similarly, as the parties surrendered some of their power and prestige they found it increasingly difficult to recruit members from the other elites who would strengthen party ties with these other elites and raise the level of party sophistication in national policy questions. The interplay of these two tendencies resulted in a downward spiral of party power among the elites.

---

background, and that definitions of the appropriate category may have varied from member to member. The table should be read with the further caveat that it refers only to successful recruits, i.e., those who managed to obtain seats in the Diet.

[53] Figures taken from Kōmei senkyo renmei, ed., *Shūgiin giin senkyo no jisseki*, pp. 138–42.

Changing Requirements of Mass Control

The position of the parties as intermediaries between the government and people—as organs that might channel popular political participation without disrupting the political system—came under severe attack during the early 1930s. The parties had long contended that they were the only organizations at the national level that represented the "voice of the people" in government. While they were subject to constant criticism for their imperfections in the performance of linking popular representation with elite government, most of their critics in the past had at least grudgingly recognized them as useful intermediary agencies for maintaining mass tolerance of elite rule. Indeed, their operation in this capacity had been an important reason for the earlier acceptance by the other elites of party power within and beyond the Lower House. In the period from 1932 to 1936, however, the parties' claim to this intermediary position was fiercely disputed by challengers to party power, and the nonparty elite groups approached a consensus on the view that the parties as then constituted had little to contribute towards resolving new problems of mass control.

Those elements of the attack on the parties in this regard that were a carry-over from the previous decade require little further elaboration. Again in the 1930s, parties were accused of corrupting the channel between the people and the government through their close association with the special interests of big business and traditional local elite groups, and of ignoring national interests in the pursuit of party power and private interests. As in the case of the attack on the parties as impediments to stable and rational bureaucratic administration, however, it was not the inherent persuasiveness of the parties' opponents that carried the day in the 1930s, but the new domestic and international environment and the demands it raised that lent support to the case against party power. The economic and foreign

67

policy crises Japan's leaders perceived in the early 1930s shifted their concern from perfecting a system of absorbing popular political energies into the imperial system to developing channels between the people and the state through which the nation's spirit, energies, and resources could be mobilized for national survival. While the importance of popular representation in government was never explicitly denied, and radical proposals for perfecting popular representation were considered, the ruling elites' priorities gradually focused on centralizing local administration and strengthening the citizenry's identification with the state through ideological mobilization.

The need to resuscitate the depression-shattered agrarian economy and to provide larger tax revenues for underwriting Japan's national defense program made the economic relationship between the local community and the state more important than at any time since the early Meiji era. Hitherto, many of the key responsibilities of local administration had been reserved for the villages, local semiofficial bodies, and the traditional rural elite to carry out. Indeed, the trend of the 1920s seems to have been towards real "local autonomy" (*jichi-ken*).[54] Local village groups were responsible for fire prevention, health and welfare, aid to the destitute, and tax collection during this period. In the wake of the depression, however, the burden of these and other essential tasks increased beyond the financial capacities of these semiofficial local groups, and the central government began to play a larger role in supporting them financially and assuming some of their burdens. As in other nations during this period, the sheer volume of state intervention in local affairs began to increase rapidly, and the fate of the local economy became contingent on new relationships being established between the central government and the community.

[54] *Naimushō shi*, II, 177–93; Ari, "Chihō seido," pp. 183–84. For a dissenting view, see Akagi Suruki, "Kokumin sai-soshiki," in Nihon seiji gakkai, ed., *"Konoe shintaisei" no kenkyū*, pp. 28–29.

68

Hence, the demand for state intervention in local economic affairs arose not only from the requirements of the nation's foreign and defense policy goals, but from overburdened local communities and their leaders. The response of the government to this demand between 1932 and 1935 was twofold. On the one hand, the Saitō government undertook, with Diet approval, an extensive program of public works construction to absorb the growing class of unemployed laborers and to provide off-season work for the impoverished peasant. The power to approve and fund these vital projects was vested in the prefectural governors.[55] The second aspect of the Saitō government's program was a "Plan for the Economic Resuscitation of Agrarian and Fishing Villages" (*Nōsan gyoson keizai kōsei keikaku*).[56] The principal agencies involved in funding and implementing these programs were the Home Ministry and the Ministry of Agriculture and Forestry. The former sought to stimulate a spirit of "self-assistance in resuscitation" (*jiriki kōsei*) among the peasantry, and to inject elements of a well-planned and organized local economy into the village. Traditional leaders of the *buraku*—the mayor, presidents of the local *nōkai* and *sangyō kumiai*, and school principals—were to direct a new community organization, the Economic Resuscitation Committee, and lay plans for the economic development of their village. They were also to engage in a spiritual movement extolling the virtues of neighborly cooperation (*rinpo kyōjo*) and to work in collaboration with government programs of agrarian recovery to restore the economic health of the community.

The Ministry of Agriculture and Forestry, for its part, initiated a five-year plan for expanding the *sangyō kumiai*, which aimed at placing one such *kumiai* in every village of the nation. All peasants were to join the *kumiai*, and it was

[55] *Naimushō shi*, i, 410; ii, 506–509.
[56] *Ibid.*, i, 410–11; ii, 509–516; Ari, "Chihō seido," pp. 168–73, 185. See also Ishii Kin'ichirō, "Nihon fuashizumu to chihō seido," *Rekishigaku kenkyū*, #305 (1965), p. 2.

to become the center of agrarian life by integrating the economic functions of buying, selling, and credit dispensation for the peasant. In contrast to the Home Ministry's emphasis on the *buraku*, traditional leadership, and the new Economic Resuscitation Committee, the Ministry of Agriculture and Forestry envisioned the *sangyō kumiai* as the basic village organization for implementing the economic resuscitation of the countryside and integrating the agrarian economy into the national economy.[57] Inasmuch as the *sangyō kumiai* was being reoriented from an organ dominated by the village elite towards becoming a nationwide guild of peasants, wealthy and poor alike, it posed an even greater threat to the structure of local power relations than the Home Ministry program. Combined with the fact that a nationwide organization of peasants buying jointly would exert great pressures on the small and medium-sized enterprises that sold fertilizer and other goods to farmers, this threat stimulated a vigorous anti-*kumiai* campaign among business circles and local elite groups represented in the *nōkai*.

Apart from highlighting local and bureaucratic rivalries, however, the program of economic resuscitation was significant in the new relationship between the state and local community it portended. While it took into account local requirements for recovery, the program's main features were: a rationalization and unification of organizations concerned with local government; an emphasis on overall economic planning on a village-by-village basis; and an integration of local economic administration into the controlling network of the central government. In comparison to the official efforts at national integration following the Russo-Japanese War, the economic programs of the early 1930s

[57] See Ishida Takeshi, "Movements to Protect Constitutional Government—A Structural Functional Analysis," in George O. Totten, ed., *Democracy in Prewar Japan: Groundwork or Façade?* (Lexington, Mass.: D. C. Heath and Co., 1965), p. 89.

represented far more intense intervention, organization, planning, and control by the central government in the life of the local community.

The direct effects of these programs on the position of the *kisei seitō* were quite serious. To begin with, the parties had been at least partially bypassed as agencies for the articulation and satisfaction of local economic demands by the governors, whose security of position was now guaranteed against the spoils system, and whose powers over the disbursal of funds and approval of local public works projects made them a focal point of attention among local community leaders. Second, the plight of local communities imposed heavy popular pressures on the local elites to permit state intervention in the community. In many areas, village leaders continued to resist the reorganization of local economic life and the centralization of local administration. Despite the ominous backdrop of growing agrarian unrest, which "appeared on the verge of going beyond the realm of simple tenancy disputes,"[58] the parties continued to support the local elites by criticizing the extension of state influence in the village as "bureaucratic despotism." The net effect of the parties' fidelity to their local supporters, however, was to discredit them further in the eyes of the nonparty elites. During these crisis years of the early 1930s, they were branded as the enemies of village harmony, and the charge that they represented only narrow class interests took on additional bite. A citizenry more concerned with where its next meal was coming from than with elections looked increasingly to the bureaucracy for the satisfaction of its demands, and put the parties on the defensive in the struggle for national and local influence. The Army, capitalizing on its new-found public support following the Manchurian Incident, fanned antiparliamentary sentiments further by chastising the parties for trying to "separate the military and the people" whenever there were Diet criti-

[58] *Naimushō shi*, II, 503.

cisms of the military budget or the growing military voice in political affairs.[59]

As bureaucratic organizations moved to the offensive in the competition for power with the parties, and took a commanding position as the agencies of national integration, they found themselves limited in one important respect. There were no available means of replacing the system whereby party members were elected to the Lower House as the major political linkage between the citizenry and the state. While the importance of this linkage receded in comparison to the economic linkage during the depression and recovery, it remained significant to a ruling elite anxious to control mass political energies.

There were essentially three avenues of action open to the bureaucracy as it dealt with the question of mass political participation in the 1932–1936 period. The first was control by repression. This approach was manifested in the constant pressure placed on the Communist movement by the Home Ministry police, culminating in the mass arrests and "conversion" (*tenkō*) of the last remaining Communist Party leaders in 1932–1933. This final crackdown destroyed the only direct challenge to the imperial system. Repression was accompanied by efforts to "purify" the existing electoral process so that it more accurately resembled a manifestation of the popular will and operated independently of the *meibōka*-party alliance. A series of officially sponsored "election purification movements" was carried out under the guidance of Gotō Fumio (minister of agriculture and forestry from 1932 to 1934, and then home minister to 1936), Maruyama Tsurukichi, Horikiri Zenjirō, and Tazawa Yoshiharu—all former Home Ministry bureaucrats who had sought to "purify" the electoral process in the 1920s in order to reify their concept of a representative government free

[59] See Watanabe Tōru, "Gunmin rikan mondai," in Kyoto daigaku bungaku-bu kokushi kenkyū-shitsu, ed., *Nihon kindai shi jiten* (Tokyo: Tōyō keizai shinpōsha, 1958 and 1966), p. 146.

of party and *meibōka* influence.[60] They began with a law in 1934 that struck at the heart of local party influence, providing punishments for the "buying" of votes, limitations on the amounts of funds to be used in campaigns, and a broadened definition of culpability in matters concerning these and other election law violations. Citizen committees were organized to campaign for clean local elections in 1935, and again for the 1936 general election. Through the publication of pamphlets, radio addresses, lectures, and movies, the campaign against the practices traditionally employed by the parties and *meibōka* at election time were attacked vigorously and brought to public attention. Similar campaigns were waged annually to 1942, although they gradually reflected the official shift from electoral politics to spiritual mobilization as a means of political integration, and became movements for the local promotion of state ideologies.[61]

The final bureaucratic approach to dealing with the question of popular discontent and political participation took the form of channeling dissent into the "purified" electoral process. Surprisingly, the principal vehicle for this endeavor was the Shakai taishūtō (Shadaitō, or Social Masses Party), a fusion of several proletarian parties oriented toward parliamentary government. Created in 1932, the Shadaitō was small and anticapitalistic in orientation, but it had the advantages (from the bureaucratic standpoint) of opposing the *kisei seitō* and *meibōka*, supporting the imperial system and economic controls, and serving as a potential magnet for political dissidents who might otherwise seek means of political expression outside that system. According to Kōno Mitsu, a contemporary Shadaitō leader, the Home Ministry's Police Bureau Chief, Karazawa Toshiki, believed that the Shadaitō should receive covert official support in order to serve in this capacity, and he used the "election purifica-

[60] See Berger, "Japan's Young Prince," pp. 467–71.
[61] *Naimushō shi*, I, 419–20; II, 359–61.

tion movement" to foster a moderate growth of the party. Kōno's recollection seems confirmed by that of an ex-bureaucrat from the Finance Ministry, Sakomizu Hisatsune, a close associate of Karazawa's who served as Premier Okada's secretary. Sakomizu recalls that he acted as the conduit for one million yen from the Sumitomo *zaibatsu* to the Minseitō for use in the 1936 general election. Before passing the money along to its proper recipients, Sakomizu took the liberty of giving "20,000 or 30,000 yen" to the Sha-daitō, in order to limit the success of the Seiyūkai in the election and strengthen the position of the small proletarian party.[62]

THE PROBLEMS OF PARTY DECLINE

By the early 1930s, many of the early supporters of representative government had become strongly skeptical of the efficacy of the parties' role in the Diet and Cabinet. When fused with the doubts of military and civilian non-party elites regarding the parties' ability to formulate "emergency" economic and defense policies, this skepticism posed a formidable obstacle to the resuscitation of party influence. Within the parties as well, dissatisfaction with the allocation of influential party posts led to internal party

[62] Hara Akira, Itō Takashi, and Nakamura Takafusa, eds., *Gendai-shi o tsukuru hitobito* (4 vols., Tokyo: Mainichi shinbunsha, 1971–1972), i, 84–85; iii, 61–62. See also, Sugihara Masami, *Atarashii Shōwa shi* (Tokyo: Shin-kigensha, 1958), p. 87; and Kamei Kan'ichirō, *Gojū-nen "gomu fūsen" o otte*, ed. Sangyō keizai kenkyū kyōkai jimu-kyoku (Tokyo: n.p., 1968), p. 21. Both Tiedemann and Ichihara have suggested, on the basis of Ikeda Seihin's memoirs, that the *zaibatsu* ceased supporting the political parties before the 1936 election. While it is true that big business began to seek alternative, and more direct, ways of defending its position and interests, Sumitomo's support of the Minseitō in the 1936 election would seem to cast doubt on the thesis of the complete abandonment of the parties by the *zaibatsu* at this juncture. See Ikeda Seihin, *Kao: zaikai kaiko* (Tokyo: Sekai no Nihonsha, 1949), pp. 183–84; Tiedemann, "Big Business and Politics," pp. 295–96; Ichihara, "Seitō rengō undō no kiban."

74

bickering and disunity. The enforcement of party discipline—a vital adjunct of the parties' ability to translate elite views into national policies—became increasingly difficult. During the Saitō and Okada governments, the parties' competitors for political power in the military and civilian bureaucracies were able to roll back party influence in the Cabinet and replace it with their own.

As the parties lost political power and prestige, the two perpetual problems of the Meiji constitutional order re-emerged. To preserve political stability, some "extra-Cabinet" agency was still required to harmonize and reconcile competing elite views and ambitions; and the elites continued to worry about maintaining popular tolerance or support for their policies and political control. The mainstream leadership of the *kisei seitō* continued to reaffirm their faith that "the crux of the imperial will as manifested in constitutional politics is popular participation in politics, or, in other words, parliamentary politics. It is becoming ever more true that the fate of the state must be determined by the strength of the party politicians."[63] Few outside the parties, however, were prepared to agree, and many alternatives to party government were proposed. Specialists in the military and civilian bureaucracies contended that only by entrusting the management of the nation to them could the technological expertise and skills in mass social, economic, political and military organization be applied successfully to the crises Japan faced. Reformists on both the left and right argued that consensus among the elites and popular support for state policies could be obtained only with the formation of a single, totalitarian mass-based political party, closely linked to the government as in the Soviet Union, Germany, and Italy. A third group—the "Japanist" right wing—was imbued with an appreciation of and confidence in the historical ability of the nation to rally behind the

[63] From a speech by Minseitō leader Sakurauchi Yukio, in Ikeda Chōya, ed., *Rikken Minseitō seisaku kōenshū* (Tokyo: Meiseisha, 1935), pp. 379–82.

75

emperor in times of danger. "Japanists" maintained, ardently if vaguely, that Japan could surmount the current crisis and achieve its national goals only if the government strengthened the inherent ties existing between the throne and people (*kunmin itchi*) and established some form of direct imperial rule (*shinsei*).

These proposals were deeply troubling to Prince Saionji, who had earlier hoped that representative government might regulate elite competition and preserve popular tolerance for imperial governments. Although it was evident that the *kisei seitō* no longer commanded sufficient support among the other elites to permit the immediate reversion to party government, he was unwilling to countenance the totalitarian alternatives of the right wing or the technocratic formulas advanced by military and civilian bureaucrats. The *genrō* saw little alternative to "national unity" Cabinets; despite the comeback of the Minseitō in the election of February 1936, Saionji and Admiral Okada were apparently prepared to maintain the present Cabinet in power, and shore up the prestige and functions of palace officials to enhance their mediatory role among the elites.

The day after the election results had been announced, however, the Okada government's term in office was bloodily and abruptly ended. On the morning of February 26, 1936, some 1400 troops of the First Division of the Imperial Japanese Army occupied the Diet, Army Ministry, and Headquarters of the Tokyo Metropolitan Police. By the time Tokyoites had begun commuting to their offices and shops, the privy seal (ex-Premier Admiral Saitō), finance minister (Takahashi Korekiyo), and inspector-general of Army education (General Watanabe Jōtarō) had been slain, while Saionji and the retired Makino Nobuaki, Saitō's predecessor as privy seal, barely escaped the clutches of their would-be assassins. Admiral Suzuki Kantarō (the grand chamberlain) was severely wounded and left for dead by the rebellious troops, and Premier Okada's life was spared only by a case of mistaken identity that cost the life of his brother-in-law.[64]

By the afternoon of the 29th the rebellion had been put down, but the feeling of crisis persisted. Okada reappeared after a period during which he had been presumed dead, and submitted his resignation to the throne. Saionji was now charged with the responsibility of recommending to the throne a premier who could restore calm to the nation, work with Army leaders to restore discipline in the officer corps, and bring all the elites together in an effort to solve the pressing national problems that had provoked the rebellion. Saionji had been very much disturbed by the shifts in political power and policy orientation occurring under the Saitō and Okada regimes. Continuing to believe that Japan's interests would be best served by a resumption of "cooperative diplomacy" with the Anglo-American powers, he had turned to Saitō and Okada as alternatives to Suzuki Kisaburō and Hiranuma Kiichirō—bitter critics of "cooperative diplomacy"—or a Cabinet led by Army officers. Nevertheless, the Army's influence in policy making had grown rapidly and manifested itself in foreign policy decisions that explicitly rejected the diplomacy of the Washington order. Domestically, Hiranuma's supporters remained a formidable political force, spreading from the bureaucracy into the parties, military, and Privy Council. The genrō regarded Hiranuma as a right-wing "fanatic," however, and refused to appoint him to the premiership.[65] On the other hand, strong opposition to the foreign policy views of Saionji and what remained of his Court circle precluded the appointment of a more "liberal" politician to head the Cabinet.

The genrō realized that the February 26th Incident had been suppressed because of the swift and resolute opposi-

[64] The most comprehensive treatment of the events of the 26th is Ben-Ami Shillony, *Revolt in Japan* (Princeton: Princeton University Press, 1973).

[65] SKS, IV, 85.

tion to the rebels shown by the emperor. He wished to assure, however, that no situation would again arise in which the throne would become involved in political decision making, or charged with responsibility for political decisions. The new premier would somehow have to bring the elites together into a Cabinet that insulated the throne from politics, as Okada had failed to do. This Cabinet would have to evoke popular support as well, to preclude the possibility of further rebellions against the imperial government. "At this juncture," the aging *genrō* concluded, "there is no one other than Konoe."[66]

Saionji's nomination of Konoe Fumimaro as the nation's leader was a significant reflection of the dilemmas created by the recession of party influence. Prince Konoe's interest in reform, his youthful good looks, his social heritage as a scion of the ancient Fujiwara noble family, and his apparent ability to retain the support of a broad spectrum of political groups had made him a likely candidate for future national leadership since the mid-1920s. He had begun his career as Saionji's protégé, and was obviously being groomed to succeed the *genrō* in the delicate task of mediating elite conflict and insulating the throne from political responsibility. Serving as president of the House of Peers during the early 1930s, however, Konoe's political sympathies and foreign policy views developed well to the right of Saionji's, and the elder statesman began lamenting his protégé's parochialism and evident willingness to be a "tool" of right-wing causes.[67] Nevertheless, thanks to his noble birth—he was the only active politician in the 1930s who had blood ties to the imperial house—Konoe maintained a position of importance at Court, while also enjoying the respect of radical right-wing and young officer groups who vilified and now murdered Court politicians as "evil advisors" of the throne. In recommending him as premier, Saionji hoped desperately

[66] Yabe Teiji, *Konoe Fumimaro* (2 vols., Tokyo: Kōbundō, 1952), I, 326 (hereafter cited as KF).
[67] SKS, IV, 215.

that Konoe would be able to absorb and control the radical calls for "direct imperial rule" in the imperial system without shattering it. At the same time, he counted on Konoe's Court heritage to incline the young prince towards fulfilling in the premiership the mediatory and insulating roles Saionji had earlier envisioned for the parties in the Cabinet.

Konoe's policy differences with Saionji, and his refusal to preside over liquidating the influence of the Imperial Way faction of officers in the Army following the February 26th insurrection, led him to reject Saionji's entreaties that he accept the premiership. Nevertheless, Konoe's nomination marked his emergence as the dominant political personality of the late 1930s, and signaled the beginning of the "Konoe era."[68] From the contemporary perspective of the political parties and the larger perspective of Japan's political history, Konoe's importance was derived from the ways in which he sought to fashion a new unity among the nation's competing political elites, and how he dealt with the problem of mobilizing the masses into the life of the state. His approach to these problems placed him at the center of a number of movements to restore party influence through the creation of a new political party. However, he also played a vital role in the parties' decline, seeking the erosion of their legislative prerogatives in the Diet, their disintegration as disciplined groups, and their dissolution in 1940. From the middle of the 1930s, as the quest began for satisfactory alternatives to party Cabinets and party representation, Prince Konoe assumed a central role in national politics.

[68] For one user of this term, see Yamaura Kan'ichi, *Konoe jidai to jinbutsu* (Tokyo: Takayama shoin, 1940).

CHAPTER III

The Rise of the Military in Domestic Politics, 1932–1937

INTRODUCTION

BETWEEN 1932 and 1936, nonparty elites became strong enough to prevent the revival of government by the discredited parties. During this period, the parties ceased to function as agencies for the reconciliation of conflicting elite viewpoints and ambitions, and power shifted quickly towards the civilian and military bureaucracies. However, since divisions and disunity among the governing elites were no longer regulated by party mediation, or structured by two-party competition for the premiership, they quickly became a serious obstacle to the formulation and execution of coherent Cabinet policies. Factionalism in the Army and "sectionalism" in the civilian bureaucracy became the bugaboos of stable elite rule. Within the Army, conflicting concepts of national defense crystallized around competing personalities and groups of officers. Moreover, the two services were unable to agree on priorities in their national defense proposals. Military and civilian bureaucrats were frequently at loggerheads over the primacy of military or socio-economic planning, particularly when limited funds had to be allocated either to the defense budget or agrarian recovery. Ministries fought each other jealously to retain or extend their range of administrative authority and responsibility. Within the bureaucracy, conservative officials were increasingly challenged by reform-minded officials in their own bureaus. Bureaucratic specialists challenged the supremacy of their generalist counterparts in both civilian and military ministries.

"National unity" governments lacked the leverage to mitigate this ever-present competition among and within elites.
Essentially, they represented a throwback to the days of
"transcendental" (nonparty) government. Without the
genrō-led *hanbatsu* of the Meiji and early Taishō periods or
the parties of the 1920s to manage conflict, however, the
function of integrating policies and ambitions devolved
upon the fragile Cabinet system and the Court. The governments of Admirals Saitō and Okada consisted of representatives from several important elites, but without the extra-
Cabinet role of a controlling *han* faction or political party,
it was difficult to maintain all ministers' support for government proposals. Cabinet-level compromises enabled Saitō
and Okada to govern, but these compromises often led to
makeshift and inconsistent national policies. The most damaging of these arrangements was, of course, the defense
policy, which incorporated Army and Navy strategic concerns and demands without adequately assigning priorities
to them.

As the parties attempted to recoup their lost fortunes
under "national unity" governments, they were confronted
by a challenge of major proportions, the rapid growth of
military—particularly Army—influence in foreign and domestic affairs. The enhanced status of the military derived
from a variety of factors. First, a growing segment of party
and nonparty elite groups subscribed to the military definition of the problems Japan confronted abroad, and to military prescriptions for the resolution of those problems.
Second, the military proved to be as ambitious politically
as the civilian elites. Many military leaders considered, and
some sanctioned, a wide variety of unorthodox techniques
to compete for power: coups d'état, terrorism, and the creation of faits accomplis in China to generate national support
for their policy positions. The ultimate goal of these approaches was a military monopoly of political power. At the
same time, however, certain military figures sought to use
strategies of elite competition which, in light of the parties'

81

earlier successes, might now be regarded as orthodox: penetrating other institutions of government from a secure institutional base, and serving other elites as an agency for the mediation of competing viewpoints and ambitions. Moreover, by the end of 1936, some Army officers had also begun to formulate a new and radical approach to the problems of linking the masses to the state, through a new type of political party.

The years from 1932 to 1937 composed a transitional era for both the military and civilian competitors for power. For less patient Army leaders, these years provided opportunities to explore the limits of effectiveness for their unorthodox approach to the acquisition of political influence. Assassinations, threats, and pressures from autonomous military action in the field were combined with an assault on the constitutional prerogatives of civilian institutions and elite groups. However, following the abortion of the February 26th Incident, advocates of these unorthodox tactics in the struggle for power found themselves either ousted from the roster of active-duty officers, or largely excluded from the mainstream of Army thinking. While a few influential Army planners such as Ishiwara Kanji could still dream of an Army dictatorship at the beginning of 1937, most Army leaders were coming to recognize that the collaboration of civilian elite groups was essential to the achievement of the Army's policy objectives. From 1937 onward, therefore, the politics of compromise clearly supplanted the plans of coup d'état and brute force as the prevailing political tactics of the Army.

Against the onslaught of attacks from the Army and civilian bureaucracy, the parties found themselves in grave difficulties during much of the period from 1932 to 1937. *Genrō* patronage, which had from the beginning of the century been a vital element in their ascent to power, was now withdrawn, and focused instead on nobles and Court advisors surrounding the throne as the principal vehicles for harmonizing elite competition within the confines of the constitutional system. The Army, as indicated, sought its own style of conflict management among the elites. Prince Konoe gradually emerged as a mediator of elite viewpoints, functioning with an eye towards satisfying the civilian and military components of the ruling elite. For the parties to regain, or even maintain, what influence they enjoyed under "national unity" governments, it seemed necessary to review carefully the possible alternatives for sharing power in an elite system.

In the process of this review, the parties found themselves divided on how best to restore their power. On the one hand, the mainstream leadership of both parties assumed the wisdom of continuing the two-party system in the Lower House, and believed that majority control of the Lower House by a popularly elected party was sufficient to regain control of the premiership. Mainstream leaders in both parties were uninterested in revising long-approved strategies in competing for power with other elite groups. They adhered closely to the old patterns of alliance, with the *zaibatsu* (for funds), the *meibōka* (for votes), and the military and bureaucracy (for individual leaders and links with nonparty elite groups). Both mainstreams also continued to articulate their belief that competitive parties and the existing election system were central to the fusion of and identification by the people with the government. The Minseitō's patient tactics of cooperation with Saitō and Okada in anticipation of the 1936 election, and parallel efforts to wean away discontented Seiyūkai members into a new Minseitō-centered majority party, were predicated on building a new majority through conventional means. The Suzuki-Hatoyama tactic of withholding the support of the Seiyūkai majority from the government was likewise based on confidence that majority control of the Lower House could be parlayed into control over the premiership. Hatoyama Ichirō of the Seiyūkai nicely summarized the mainstream position in January 1936:

So long as the legitimacy of the parties' existence is undeniable, it is obvious that those who, through elections,

83

represent the popular will—that is, Diet members—should be the central focus of politics. Bureaucrats and soldiers who have the slightest desire to become involved in politics should undergo the baptism of elections and taste their bitterness before they are deemed spiritually qualified to be fused with the masses. . . . Politics should be left to the politicians, administrative matters to the bureaucrats, and national defense to the soldiers. We must once again establish our original system of divided responsibilities.[1]

Despite the essential continuity in the thought and behavior of the mainstream leadership, the period from 1932 to 1937 was transitional for the parties in several ways. Two styles of "anti-mainstream" response to the loss of party power emerged, and gradually began to undermine the control of the mainstream and the preeminence of its philosophy in party circles. Both styles focused on the creation of a new party. The more radical of the two styles favored the creation of a one-party system (*ikkoku ittō*). Such a system was predicated on the implicit assumption that the election system must be transformed from a vehicle for political competition into a tool for the ritual expression of public support for the government party. Under a one-party system, *meibōka* would still serve as the principal agents for mobilizing political participation by voters, but they would have no choice as to which candidate or party should be supported. Locally, therefore, the party and elections would continue to represent the popular will formally, and fuse a "united" citizenry with the state. Nationally, the party would enjoy a total monopoly of power in the Lower House, and oblige the Cabinet to conform to its will. The new system was thus designed to reassert control over the Cabinet by party forces, and to bring about "harmony" in

[1] Hatoyama Ichirō, "Jiyū shugisha no techō," *Chūō kōron*, January 1936, cited in Kawasaki Hideji, *Yūki aru seijika-tachi* (Tokyo: Sengoku shuppansha, 1971), pp. 267–68.

the people's relationship to the state and among the institutions of the imperial government through the new party's dominance.

The second type of anti-mainstream thinking tended towards the establishment of a new majority party comprised of anti-mainstream forces from the two major parties. There was little fundamental difference between the attitude of politicians in this group and the position of the mainstream leadership regarding party functions and the political system. They took issue with the mainstream, however, on the question of how to restore power in an era of rising military and bureaucratic influence in government. Even at the expense of traditional party ties with allies in the bureaucratic and business elites, they were willing to form new alliances with the military and "revisionist" bureaucrats over the programs of enlarged defense budgets and greater economic controls. In exchange, they sought a share of power in the Cabinet for anti-mainstream forces, and respect for the constitutional position of the Lower House, parties, and election system as a vital intermediary and harmonizing linkage between the people and the state. As the mainstream leaders looked to the *zaibatsu* for financial support, these anti-mainstream groups tended to rely on funds from so-called "new *zaibatsu*," businesses that flourished in an atmosphere of military spending and inflationary budgets. Moreover, many anti-mainstream groups obtained secret funds from the Army or Cabinet in exchange for backing specific programs in the Lower House.[2]

The debate over how to restore party power during the mid-1930s highlighted not only the gradual disintegration of party discipline but the types of alternatives considered by party men to promote their ambitions and the policies they supported. Moreover, it mirrored the larger debate among the elites over the desirability and nature of proposed policies and reforms in the political and economic

[2] Kawasaki, *Yūki aru seijika-tachi*, p. 93.

systems. The diversity of proposals for the preservation of party influence in the face of the changing political environment and the challenge of the Army thus marks the mid-1930s as an extraordinarily interesting and complex period in the history of Japan's political parties. It also suggests that, while the parties were losing power in the Cabinet, they remained a potent force in national politics. Finally, a discussion of their role during these years also serves as an introduction to the issues and responses that resulted in the parties' ultimate dissolution in 1940.

The Army's Intrusion into Domestic Politics

The Army took a greater interest in politics and the political process during the 1930s for a variety of reasons.[3] Young officers and many of their superiors were dissatisfied with the Cabinet's approach to the defense and expansion of Japan's continental interests, and felt a strong sense of mission to rectify the errors of "Shidehara Diplomacy." Many also sympathized with the plight of the agrarian villages, being themselves of agrarian origin or feeling a paternalistic concern for men under their command who suffered as their families starved or sold off daughters to teahouses in the red-light districts of Japan's cities. For many young officers radicalized by these crises, there seemed no remedy other than to overthrow constitutional government and replace it with direct imperial rule (*shinsei*) under military stewardship. Several coups d'état were therefore planned by young officers between 1931 and 1936, the most dramatic being, of course, the February 26th Incident.

For other officers, however, domestic politics and the

[3] For detailed treatments of military thinking in the 1930s, see Crowley, *Japan's Quest*; Maxon, *Japanese Foreign Policy*; Shillony, *Revolt in Japan*; Robert J. C. Butow, *Tojo and the Coming of the War* (Princeton: Princeton University Press, 1961); and Mark R. Peattie, *Ishiwara Kanji and Japan's Confrontation with the West* (Princeton: Princeton University Press, 1975).

economy became germane to their concerns mainly because of new ways of thinking about national defense. Drawing on lessons learned from the European experience in World War I, many Army planners addressed themselves to the proposition that in any future war, Japan would be obliged to mobilize all of the material, human, and spiritual resources of the state in the prosecution of "total war." As Colonel Nagata Tetsuzan remarked to a businessmen's group in 1927, "National mobilization (*kokka sōdōin*) is the task of marshaling the entire society of the state in times of need, moving from a peacetime footing to a wartime footing. The state must then organize, unify and utilize all available resources, material and human, producing a maximum national strength as war power."[4] From this perspective, the strength of the economy, the physical health of the citizenry, and the spiritual cohesiveness of the nation became vital weapons in the arsenal of national defense, and legitimate subjects of concern to the military. When the nation found itself "in times of need" during the 1930s, the "total war" planners in the Army pushed through the traditional barriers to military participation in the political and administrative processes of the state.

The Army and Navy Ministers had, of course, always participated in politics through their roles in the Cabinet, but during the 1930s other officers also obtained important positions in new Cabinet agencies. For example, in 1934 the Army won the battle to create a Manchurian Affairs Bureau (*Tai-Man jimu-kyoku*) to administer Japan's relationship with the newly created state of Manchukuo. Through this office, the power of the Foreign and Overseas Development Ministries to exercise any voice over Manchurian affairs was eliminated, and complete control was placed under Army officers.[5] In 1935, the Okada Cabinet created two new

---

[4] Nagata Tetsuzan, *Kokka sōdōin* (Osaka: Osaka mainichi shinbunsha, 1928), p. 14.

[5] For a full discussion of this issue, see Robert M. Spaulding, Jr., "The Bureaucracy as a Political Force, 1920–1945," in Morley, *Dilemmas of Growth*, pp. 67–76.

Cabinet agencies, the Cabinet Policy Council (*Naikaku shingikai*) and, under it, a Cabinet Research Bureau (*Naikaku chōsa-kyoku*). The former body consisted of a "supplementary Cabinet": prominent party politicians, businessmen, and members of the House of Peers were invited to provide integrated policy recommendations for the Cabinet's consideration. The Research Bureau was established to facilitate its work. Drawing on skilled technocrats from the important ministries, including the Army and Navy, the Research Bureau permitted a new channel for the participation of military personnel in civil administration. Within two years, the bureau was expanded into the Cabinet Planning Board, becoming the focal point for integrating the important policies of the bureaucracy and the hub of mobilization planning for the Cabinet. Its parent body, the Policy Council, had been formed primarily to strengthen the integrating power of the weak "national unity" government, and was dissolved when the Okada Cabinet left office.

Nagata Tetsuzan was not only the guiding force behind the plans for converting Japan into a fully mobilized state, but he seemed to be as astute a student of the politics of compromise and coalition as Hara Kei had been in his time. First, he lobbied assiduously for the creation of these new governmental agencies, which allowed subordinates like the young Colonel Suzuki Teiichi to serve in key policy-making positions in the bureaucracy. Rejecting the viability of military rule by coup d'état, Nagata spent the years from 1931 to 1935 cultivating a wide range of supporters and sympathizers among the other elite groups in other institutions of government. He formed an extremely close working relationship with "new" or "revisionist" bureaucrats throughout the civil service, who were ardent nationalists eager to reform the Cabinet system and create a planned or controlled economy in ways that paralleled Nagata's thinking.[6] He became cordial with Harada Kumao (Saionji's

[6] The "revisionist" bureaucrats have been carefully analyzed by Spaulding, *ibid.*, pp. 60–80, and in "Japan's 'New Bureaucrats,' 1932–

secretary), Kido Kōichi, and Prince Konoe, the young nobles who were key links between the Court and the day-to-day world of politics. And finally, he sought to reach some form of accommodation with the Lower House that would allow the passage of legislation required to create the economic and military foundations for national mobilization. Much of his work with the Diet appears to have taken the form of laying the groundwork for parliamentary support from the Shadaitō for Army programs.[7] When the Army published its "manifesto" on the desirability of national mobilization in 1934, Shadaitō leaders Asō Hisashi and Kamei Kan'ichirō quickly endorsed it. They particularly agreed with the Army's call for economic controls, and believed that cooperating with Nagata would move Japan a step closer towards socialism as well as expanding popular support for their party.[8]

Nagata appears to have had less success with the politicians of the *kisei seitō*. He worked closely with Akita Kiyoshi, an ex-Seiyūkai member and speaker of the Lower House, to strengthen the Diet machinery for policy study through the creation of standing committees on policy research.[9] There is little evidence, however, that he was able to make any headway in forming a coalition of parliamen-

---

45," George M. Wilson, ed., *Crisis Politics in Prewar Japan: Institutional and Ideological Problems of the 1930s* (Tokyo: Sophia University Press, 1970), pp. 51–70.

[7] Sugihara, *Atarashii Shōwa shi*, p. 74; and author's interview with Kamei Kan'ichirō, Tokyo, October 14–15, 1969. Nagata's chief liaison man with the Shadaitō was Major Shinjō Kenkichi.

[8] Totten, *Social Democratic Movement*, pp. 92–93. The Army's "manifesto" was the famous "Army Pamphlet of 1934." See Rikugunshō shinbun-han, *Kokubō no hongi to sono kyōka no teishō* (Tokyo: Rikugunshō shinbun-han, October 10, 1934). For a brief discussion of its contents in English, see Crowley, *Japan's Quest*, pp. 208–10. Kamei claimed to have influenced the drafting of the pamphlet in an interview with the author, October 14–15, 1969.

[9] Sugihara, *Atarashii Shōwa shi*, p. 74, and Kamei interview with the author, October 14–15, 1969.

tary forces that would support Army legislative proposals in the area of economic reform. It is difficult to know how he would subsequently have adjusted his approach to the Diet, for on August 12, 1935, Nagata was slashed to death by an officer of the rival Imperial Way faction of the Army. His assassin, Colonel Aizawa Saburō, condemned Nagata for having forced the removal of an Imperial Way general from a key Army post, and for having consorted with socialists, business magnates, and scheming bureaucrats.

It was during Aizawa's well-publicized trial for murdering Nagata that the February 26th Incident occurred. After the insurrection had been put down, Aizawa and several rebellious young officers were sentenced to death or imprisonment, and the Imperial Way faction of senior officers who had given them moral support was purged from the Army. Despite the eclipse of the insurgents and their backers, however, the Army did not revert completely to the political approach of the late Nagata. On the one hand, the new Army leadership insisted, as Nagata had, on maintaining firm control over subordinate officers, to prevent further acts of rebellion in the name of national reformation. The new leaders were also willing to work, as Nagata had, through the existing structure of elite politics in order to accomplish the reforms they deemed essential to the nation's defense and welfare. On the other hand, having perceived the lukewarm response by many bureaucratic and parliamentary figures to Nagata's program, the new leadership was more strident and somewhat more heavy-handed than Nagata had been in demanding that the legitimate policy-making organs of state—notably the Cabinet and Diet—adopt as national policy the Army's views on restructuring the administration, reforming the economy, and strengthening the military. Accompanying this tough-minded negotiating position were intimidating warnings from officers such as Ishiwara that the failure of the Cabinet and Diet to sanction the Army's proposals might lead to even stiffer demands and the possibility of still another coup d'état.

Before the Army's reform demands were drafted and made public, however, the Cabinet made an administrative decision that has since provoked considerable historical controversy. In 1899, Yamagata Aritomo had arranged the issue of an imperial decree to the effect that only generals and admirals on active duty could be appointed to hold the Army and Navy ministerial portfolios. The decree was another in Yamagata's attempts to forestall the expansion of party influence beyond the Lower House, and under strong pressure from the Seiyūkai in 1913, the decree was amended to permit the appointment of generals and admirals on the inactive list as well. This amendment presumably opened the way for the appointment of retired officers with party ties (active-duty officers were enjoined from aligning with the parties), but its ultimate effect was primarily symbolic.[10] No retired officer was ever called upon to hold a service ministry portfolio.

Following the February 26th Incident, the leadership in the Army insisted that the decree be restored to its original form, to prevent the reintroduction of Imperial Way faction influence into the Army through the appointment of one of the just-retired Imperial Way generals as a future Army minister. In view of the nation's recent brush with Imperial Way-styled revolution, both major political parties and all of the civilian ministers in the new Cabinet organized by career diplomat Hirota Kōki accepted the Army's demands without strong complaint.[11] The Army and Navy ministers were thus subject to control only by their own services, and the refusal of one service to provide an active-duty officer of general or admiral rank for a Cabinet it disliked could prevent the formation of a Cabinet or terminate its existence. Historians have therefore made much of this decision by the Cabinet. One insists that the revised decree allowed

[10] Najita, *Hara Kei*, pp. 178–82.

[11] Shiraki, *Nihon seitō shi*, p. 217; Hirota Kōki denki kankōkai, ed., *Hirota Kōki* (Tokyo: Chūō kōron jigyō shuppan, 1966), pp. 178, 196, 198.

"the Army to control the life and death of Cabinets." Another calls the decision "the most important single step that put the military on the road to supremacy."[12]

In fact, however, the effect of the new regulation on elite competition for power was minimal. Even between 1913 and 1936, the services had been too important a component of the political elite to ignore in the formation of Cabinets and national policy. During that period, no service minister was ever appointed without the explicit consent of the service he led. Consequently, every service minister appointed during these twenty-three years was an officer on active duty. The simple fact remained that the weak Cabinet system required the maintenance of consensus among important elite groups, and the rupture of that consensus—by a service minister or an important civilian, such as Adachi in 1931—would spell the demise of that particular government. Indeed, the newly designated Army minister following the February 26th Incident used the threat of non-participation in the Hirota Cabinet to influence the selection of civilian ministers even before the regulations regarding service ministers' appointments had been changed. The net effect of the new regulations was simply to prevent the formation of governments which, under strong Army or Navy opposition, would have proven short-lived under the old system. As Privy Seal Yuasa Kurahei correctly observed in January 1937, "the regulations regarding the appointment of Army ministers are not any problem. The central issue is the strong opposition of the Army [in this case to a proposed government led by Ugaki Kazushige]. Even if a Cabinet were formed [by circumventing the new rules] . . . it would immediately collapse."[13]

The Army's institutional prerogatives worked to its advantage after 1936 in assuring control over its own officers and affairs, but a constitutional and Cabinet system that per-

[12] Iwabuchi Tatsuo, *Yabururu hi made* (Tokyo: Nihon shūhōsha, 1946), p. 76; Chitoshi Yanaga, *Japan since Perry* (Hamden, Conn.: Archon Books, 1966), p. 525.

[13] Hirota Kōki denki kankōkai, ed., *Hirota Kōki*, pp. 197–98.

mitted elite groups to barricade themselves against intrusion from outside challenges became a disadvantage when the Army sought to become the predominant force in politics. Short of another coup d'état—which the emperor, Navy, and civilian elites would certainly oppose—the further enhancement of Army influence would depend on its ability to find levers of control over the elite groups in the Lower House and civil service. The threat of another coup might serve from time to time as one lever; compromise and the satisfaction of nonmilitary elites' policy goals and ambitions might be another. Ultimately, however, the Army sought to control the civilian elites through officially sanctioned institutional reforms. Between the creation of the Hirota government in March 1936 and the collapse of the Hayashi Cabinet in May 1937, the difficulties of attaining this goal were brought home poignantly for the first—but certainly not the last—time.

MILITARY PROPOSALS FOR INSTITUTIONAL REFORM

After the Hirota Cabinet was formed, the services took the formal initiative for the first time in attempting to draft Cabinet policies of economic and administrative reform. The economic interests of party supporters and political prerogatives of the Diet were often the immediate targets of these reform proposals, and party politicians were not slow to recognize the challenge of the military's initiative. Even as preparations were made for the December opening of the Diet session, the parties had begun sniping at the services' reform programs, while rumors flew of secret Army plans to push for a political party law to limit party activity in the Diet, exclude party members from the Cabinet, and restrict the franchise.[14] The parties found themselves joined in the struggle against the Army by the bureaucracy, which

[14] Hata Ikuhiko, *Gun fuashizumu undō shi* (Tokyo: Kawade shobō shinsha, 1962), pp. 177–78, n. 5; Shiraki, *Nihon seitō shi*, pp. 221–22; SKS, v, 129 (entry of August 2, 1936); Misawa and Nimomiya, "The Role of the Diet and Political Parties," p. 330.

strongly resented military efforts to intrude on its prerogatives through institutional reform.[15]

The approach to administrative reform sanctioned by the two service ministers was extremely provocative. The first section of their plan called for (1) establishing an organ under the prime minister's office to deal with the budget and policy research; (2) strengthening the Cabinet's Propaganda Agency; (3) creating a Personnel Agency under the premier's office to control and reform personnel administration; (4) merging the Development Ministry with the Foreign Ministry, and the Ministry of Agriculture and Forestry with the Ministry of Commerce and Industry; (5) expanding agencies concerned with the control of trade, fuel, electricity, and so on, and with rationalizing the administration of industrial development; (6) reorganizing and strengthening the offices that administered air and rail transport, communications, shipping and port maintenance, and placing a special emphasis on the rapid development of the civilian air industry; (7) transferring the Bureau of Shrines from the Home Ministry to the Education Ministry, and promoting popular morale and physical training. The second section of the services' official administrative reform proposal called for reforms in local administration consistent with the reforms urged for the central administrative offices.[16] This plan represented the first step taken by the services, and the Army in particular, toward reorganizing the economic, political, and administrative structure of the nation as a "national defense state" (*kokubō kokka*) with a capability of full mobilization (*sōdōin*) for total war (*sōryokusen*).

The implications of these sweeping proposals were deeply resented by most bureaucrats. Although they were in no way contrary to the Constitution, they implied the elimination of a large number of official posts, and the removal of

[15] Spaulding, "The Bureaucracy as a Political Force, 1920–1945," pp. 72–74.

[16] Hirota Kōki denki kankōkai, ed., *Hirota Kōki*, pp. 241–42.

administrative jurisdiction over several areas from one ministry to another. They also contained a recommendation for the creation of a new and powerful budget and policy research organ, which would supersede the individual ministries in power and prestige. The military did obtain support from "revisionist" officials in the Cabinet Research Bureau who were generally sympathetic with the services' reform plans. Their own positions would be strongly enhanced if budgetary affairs were added to their jurisdiction, and if their agency were placed directly under the premier's supervision. Indeed, in April 1936 they had already drafted an administrative reform proposal that went well beyond the proposals forwarded by the Army and Navy in the fall of 1936.[17] On the other hand, officials whose influence and jobs were endangered by these reforms were quick to voice their opposition to the services' arguments. Even within the military bureaucracy, there was strong opposition to the establishment of a budget and research organ or a personnel agency that would be responsible to the premier and not the individual ministries.[18]

Faced with a sharp division of bureaucratic opinion, Premier Hirota judiciously submitted the proposals from both the Research Bureau and the military to the ministries for review. He appointed a Four-Ministers Conference (consisting of the ministers of railways, finance, communications, and education) to consider aspects of the reforms related to the central administrative system, and a Five-Ministers Conference (consisting of the ministers of commerce and industry, home affairs, justice, development, and agriculture and forestry) to study the proposals for the reform of the local administration and Diet systems. In effect,

[17] Ko-Baba Eiichi-shi kinenkai, *Baba Eiichi den* (Tokyo: Ko-Baba Eiichi-shi kinenkai, 1945), pp. 262–63.

[18] Nihon hyōron shinsha, ed., *Yōyōko: Minobe Yōji tsuitōroku* (Tokyo: Nihon hyōron shinsha, 1954), p. 112. *Nishiura Susumu-shi danwa sokkiroku,* I (Nihon kindai shiryō sōsho B–1) (Tokyo: Nihon kindai shiryō kenkyūkai and Kido nikki kenkyūkai, 1968), 201.

Hirota was consigning these programs to certain amendment or evisceration by submitting them to the ministries.
In view of the challenges they posed to the vested interests
of numerous officials, the programs were unlikely to receive
a favorable reception, especially at the senior levels of
officialdom. As one observer pointed out, Hirota had little
alternative to following this procedure, in view of the strong
opposition to reform. "A plan of this kind," wrote Baba
Tsunego of the Research Bureau's proposal, "is bound to
meet with the opposition of the majority of the Cabinet
members and can only be carried out at the risk of bringing
the whole government down."[19]

The Army's program of economic and administrative reform was designed to rationalize economic and administrative institutions and facilitate the implementation of military plans for the conversion of Japan into a national
defense state. The program was part of an even bolder plan
being formulated under the direction of Colonel Ishiwara
Kanji, head of the War Leadership Section of the Army
General Staff and Nagata's principal heir as the architect
of mobilization planning. Under the direction of Ishiwara
and his advisors—the "Manchurian Group"—two consecutive Five-Year Plans were drafted in 1936, which aimed at
assuring Japan's security in face of the Anglo-American
naval forces and the Russian Army.[20] These plans would
oblige Japan to move towards a state-controlled economy,

[19] Baba Tsunego, "Hirota's 'Renovation' Plans," *Contemporary Japan*, v.2 (September 1936), 175.

[20] See Tsunoda Jun, ed., *Ishiwara Kanji shiryō: Kokubō ronsaku* (Tokyo: Hara shobō, 1967), pp. 139–47. The "Manchurian Group" included the chief of the Kwantung Army General Staff (Lieutenant General Itagaki Seishirō), chief of the Army Ministry Bureau of Mili-
tary Affairs (Major General Isogai Rensuke), chief of the Manchurian Department of the Bureau of Military Affairs (Major Katakura Tada-shi), and, among civilians, Miyazaki Masayoshi, Asahara Kenzō and Sogō Shinji. For biographical data on Asahara and Sogō, see Nakajima Kōsaburō, *Fūunji: Sogō Shinji den* (Tokyo: Kōtsū kyōdō shuppansha, 1955), especially pp. 257–60.

and would further necessitate a cautious foreign policy vis-à-vis the Anglo-American powers and China to avoid premature military commitments while Japan's military and economic strength was being developed. Emphasis was therefore placed on developing the Manchurian and Japanese economies under careful state direction, and stabilizing the delicate situation in China by diplomatic means. The first Five-Year Plan would focus on building up the Army to deal with the Soviet Union; the second Five-Year Plan would stress the Navy's development to assure Japan's Pacific security.

Implementation of these plans naturally required the assent of three major elite groups: officials in the civilian bureaucracy, the parties in the Lower House, and businessmen whose interests would be vitally affected by the imposition of a controlled economy. By late 1936, bureaucratic opposition to the Army's program of administrative reform had become manifestly apparent, and the forthcoming Diet session promised the spectacle of stiff party resistance to the proposed limitations on the powers of the Lower House, the prerogatives of the parties, and the economic autonomy of big business. While Army Minister Terauchi Hisaichi prepared to face the Diet with threats of possible military insurrection if the civilian elites did not accept the official service proposals, Ishiwara concluded that the Cabinet and Lower House would be unwilling to sanction either the official proposals or his own, more ambitious program.[21] He

21 Ishiwara's program of domestic reform focused on four points: 1) establishing a Manchukuo-style National Affairs Board (*kokumuin*) to replace the Cabinet system; 2) establishing state ownership and management of key industrial enterprises; 3) creating a new mass political party; and 4) military dictatorship within five years. It was, therefore, even more extreme than the proposals forwarded by the Army minister, though the two programs had much in common. Terauchi's warnings of another insurrection probably referred to his estimate of what Ishiwara might do in the face of civilian rejection of the official military reform proposals. For details, see Hata Ikuhiko, "Sanbō: Ishiwara Kanji" (Part III), *Jiyū* (November 1963), pp. 146–

97

RISE OF THE MILITARY, 1932-1937

therefore asked his political advisor, Asahara Kenzō, to devise an appropriate method for dealing with the political opposition. Asahara had been a labor leader at the Yawata Steel Works during the Taishō era, and was elected as a proletarian party representative to the Diet from Fukuoka in 1928. He was well acquainted with Mori Kaku, and after the Manchurian Incident, Mori introduced him to several Army officers, including Suzuki Teiichi. He later gained the confidence of General Hayashi Senjūrō, Major Katakura Tadashi, and Ishiwara, and was also involved in planning a reform of the Manchurian Kyōwakai.[22]

Drawing on his experiences with the Kyōwakai and with mass organization, Asahara reported to Ishiwara that the best approach to the Diet would be the establishment of a new mass political party, which might gain control of both the Cabinet and the Lower House. He anticipated that the party he envisioned could gain a Lower House majority within five years. In the interim, he envisioned the possibility of a new Cabinet each year, with each Cabinet implementing one major reform of the Ishiwara program before being driven from power. For the moment, the political goal of the Ishiwara group would be to replace the Hirota government with one led by General Hayashi or Prince Konoe. Lieutenant General Itagaki Seishirō, a close associate of Ishiwara's since the late 1920s and currently serving

47; Miyazaki Masayoshi, *Tōa renmei ron* (Tokyo: Kaizōsha, 1938), p. 79; Asahara Kenzō, "Seiken dasshu go-ka-nen keikaku," in Ōtani Keijirō, *Shōwa kenpei shi* (Tokyo: Misuzu shobō, 1966), p. 326; and Peattie, *Ishiwara Kanji*, pp. 185–222. Many of Ishiwara's proposed administrative reforms closely paralleled the reforms enacted in the Manchurian administrative system in July 1937. See Tōgo Shiba, ed., *Japan-Manchoukuo Year Book, 1941* (Tokyo: Jyapan-Manchukō nenkansha, 1941), p. 619.

[22] For the Kyōwakai, or Hsieh Ho Hui, see Hirano Ken'ichirō, "Manshūkoku Kyōwakai no seijiteki tenkai," in Nihon seiji gakkai, ed., *"Konoe shintaisei" no kenkyū*, pp. 231–83; Ozaki Hotsumi, "Manshūkoku to Kyōwakai," *Chūō kōron*, #640 (December 1940), pp. 90–98; and Peattie, *Ishiwara Kanji*, pp. 168–74 and 311–16.

as the chief of the Kwantung Army General Staff, would be installed as Army minister, and within five years would become the premier with dictatorial powers.[23]

Asahara's new party proposal was reflected in Ishiwara's plan to create a new "National Socialist Party" (Kokken shakaitō) with one million members. The premier would serve as president of the party. Ishiwara intended that the party gain an absolute majority of Diet seats, and that it wield actual control of state-run enterprises.[24] This plan was coupled with the "Manchurian Group's" effort to convert the Kyōwakai in Manchukuo into a dictatorial party that would control Manchurian politics and administration, and develop the economic resources of Manchukuo. Indeed, the Kyōwakai was to serve as a model for and collaborator with the new party in Japan, in order to foster effective liaison in the creation of a Japanese-Manchurian sphere of economic and military self-sufficiency.

PARTY RESPONSES TO THE MILITARY CHALLENGE

While the parties agreed to the formation of Admiral Saitō's "national unity" government in May 1932, they were deeply troubled by the erosion of party power during the next few years. Late in 1933, *kisei seitō* politicians sought to arrange a two-party coalition that might check the decline of their prestige, and reestablish party control over the premiership. However, this "movement for a two-party coalition" (*seitō rengō undō*) encountered severe obstacles both within and without.[25] Party politicians found themselves aligned in the movement along two axes defined by the allocation of power within their respective parties. Control of the Seiyūkai rested largely in the hands of Suzuki

[23] See Asahara, "Seiken dasshu go-ka-nen keikaku," in Ōtani, *Shōwa kenpei shi*, p. 326.
[24] Hata, "Sanbō: Ishiwara Kanji" (Part III), p. 147.
[25] For a general treatment of the coalition movement, see Ichihara, "Seitō rengō undō no kiban," "Seitō rengō undō no hasan."

99

Kisaburō and Hatoyama Ichirō, while Wakatsuki Reijirō presided over a Minseitō in which the leading force was the colorless but indefatigable Machida Chūji. Hatoyama and Machida represented the "mainstream" axis of alignment within the coalition movement, and found themselves confronted by an "anti-mainstream" axis composed of Kuhara Fusanosuke's collaboration with Minseitō politician Tomita Kōjirō. The Hatoyama-Machida group worked toward countering growing military influence through a simple coalition within the context of a two-party system; it was supported by the Mitsui *zaibatsu* and the Banchōkai, another business group. Kuhara and Tomita were seeking to expand the coalition Cabinet campaigns promoted by Kuhara and Adachi Kenzō during 1931 and 1932 into the development of a new political party, which would be the only party in existence.[26] This new party would collaborate more closely with the military and bureaucratic advocates of continental expansion, larger military budgets, and greater economic controls, than with the *zaibatsu* forces who backed the "mainstream" leadership. Funds would be provided by Kuhara, who presided over a giant "new-*zaibatsu*" industrial complex.[27]

Early in 1934, the coalition movement finally disintegrated under the pressure of the tensions between these two competing alignments and the attacks on the mainstream leadership (and its financial backers) from the right wing and the Army.[28] By midsummer, however, the parties were again seeking a new approach to the competition for power with the other elites. The Okada Cabinet was organized in July, and the parties were obliged to yield control of the key Finance and Home Ministry portfolios to non-

[26] See Kuhara Fusanosuke-ō denki hensankai (Mima Yasuichi), ed., *Kuhara Fusanosuke* (Tokyo: Kuhara Fusanosuke-ō denki hensankai, 1970), pp. 413, 431, 434.

[27] See, for example, Kuhara Fusanosuke, *Kōdō keizai ron* (Tokyo: Chikura shobō, 1933), p. 74 and *passim*.

[28] For details, see Ichihara, "Seitō rengō undō no hasan."

party figures from the bureaucracy. The composition of Admiral Okada's government thus caused a great deal of anxiety in both major parties. Suzuki and Hatoyama believed Suzuki was entitled to the premiership and withheld the support of the majority party as a weapon to persuade the other elites to accept their viewpoint. Kuhara offered tactical backing for Suzuki's stance, hoping to replace Okada with a more militant government. Between these two Seiyūkai positions lay two groups of old adversaries who now favored working with the government in formulating national policies: Tokonami's faction, and the "old Seiyūkai group," which had remained in the Seiyūkai when Tokonami and Hatoyama bolted to form the Seiyū hontō in the early 1920s. At Okada's request, Tokonami, Yamazaki Tatsunosuke, and Uchida Nobuya broke with their party's official position in July and accepted positions in the new Cabinet. They were immediately read out of the party, and in December, Akita Kiyoshi resigned from both the Seiyūkai and his position as Speaker of the Lower House to protest against the party's policy of noncooperation. "Old Seiyūkai group" leader Maeda Yonezō remained in the Seiyūkai, but found himself pressed by Suzuki and Kuhara to refuse all contact with the Okada government.[29]

As the splits within the Seiyūkai over party strategy began to widen, Maeda recruited the remarkable and talented Nakajima Chikuhei to his camp. Nakajima was an ex-naval aviation officer who had abandoned his military career to become the founder and president of Japan's first civilian-organized aircraft manufacturing company. By 1931, his planes had been adopted by the Army as standard equipment, and his company flourished with the growth of subsequent military budgets. He was also a successful candidate for the Diet in 1930, and joined the Seiyūkai shortly thereafter. He quickly came to public attention with a stinging attack on Shidehara's defense of the London Naval

[29] SKS, IV, 135–36, 143.

Treaty, and moved rapidly towards the upper echelons of party leadership. While still a freshman member of the Diet, he was appointed by Maeda (the minister of commerce and industry in the Inukai government) to be parliamentary vice minister (*seimu-jikan*) of the Ministry of Commerce and Industry. Such appointments were rare for men who had been elected less than two or three times, but Nakajima was clearly an exceptional man. He owed much of his strength within the Seiyūkai to his considerable fortune, which he used freely to promote his own career and the success of his party. He urged an increase in state controls over the economy, in the interests of a strong national defense. He was an ardent advocate of strengthening the defensive capabilities of both services, a position not inconsistent with his entrepreneurial interests in the defense industry. Although he was originally a follower of the Suzuki-Hatoyama leadership in the Seiyūkai, by 1935 he and Maeda had become the focal point of the Seiyūkai forces opposed to the Suzuki-Hatoyama policy of confrontation with the Okada government. While the two men were bitter enemies of Kuhara, they also began considering seriously the possibility of creating a new political party.

Similar thinking was also evident in Minseitō circles, where Kawasaki Takukichi, the party's secretary general, held a pivotal position between the "mainstream" leadership under Machida and the "anti-mainstream" forces sympathetic to Tomita and the recently departed Adachi Kenzō. In the wake of the bitter Army and right-wing attacks on the "mainstream" leadership in the parties and the loss of party power in Okada's government, Kawasaki concluded that the Minseitō might require more than simply a successful election to regain control over the premiership. In order to strengthen the party's position immediately, he and other Minseitō leaders agreed that the formation of a new party would be desirable. As Kawasaki outlined the alternatives to retiring party president Wakatsuki in late 1934, the most congenial possibility would be a fusion of the Minseitō, the "old Seiyūkai group," Tokonami's ex-Seiyūkai group, and a part of Adachi's Kokumin dōmei. The Tokonami and "old Seiyūkai" factions could bolster the new party, but would be too small to prevent the Minseitō from dominating it. Kawasaki hoped that the new party could persuade General Ugaki to serve as president, since Ugaki had excellent connections at Court through Saionji, and was believed to be acceptable as premier to the nonparty elites.[30] Kawasaki and Machida invited Ugaki to become the leader of a Minseitō-dominated party in January 1935. While the retired general showed some interest in the offer, he insisted on January 17 that the new party be a complete fusion of Seiyūkai and Minseitō forces, as Kuhara and Tomita advocated.[31] The Minseitō leaders were unable to accept this condition, and on January 18, Machida himself became president, filling the vacancy left by the retiring Wakatsuki two months earlier.

There were several points of interest in these factional maneuvers of 1934 and early 1935. First, the "mainstream" leaders of both *kisei seitō* had not only confirmed their commitment to a competitive party system, but had abandoned even the "coalition" plan of working in concert with their competition to reassert party control over the premiership. Second, the Suzuki-Hatoyama group was slowly becoming isolated in the Seiyūkai: Tokonami's faction was defecting, and both the Kuhara and "old Seiyūkai" groups were considering the formation of new parties. Third, neither mainstream leadership was willing to endorse a complete merger of the two *kisei seitō*, as proposed by Kuhara, Tomita, Adachi, and Ugaki. And finally, both mainstream and antimainstream leaders seemed uninterested in changing the fundamental relationship of their small elite organizations

[30] Itō Takashi, " 'Kyokoku itchi' naikaku-ki no seikai saihensei mondai: Shōwa jūsan-nen Konoe shintō mondai kenkyū no tame ni," *Shakai kagaku kenkyū*, xxiv.1 (1972), 60–61.

[31] *Ibid.*, pp. 63–64; Ugaki Kuzushige, *Ugaki Kazushige nikki* (3 vols., Tokyo: Misuzu shobō, 1968–1971), ii, 991–92.

to the masses. They simply did not regard the masses as a source of political energy and power that might project them again into a position of prominence among the other elite groups.

The question of converting the parties to mass organizations first became important to "anti-mainstream" leaders between 1935 and early 1937. Spurned by General Ugaki, Kawasaki concentrated his efforts to procure a prestigious leader for his proposed new party on Prince Konoe, the president of the House of Peers. Kawasaki saw in Konoe a man who could attract Seiyūkai members—particularly the "old Seiyūkai" group led by Maeda and Nakajima—into the new party and refurbish the lackluster image of the Minseitō. Working through Kiya Ikusaburō, a journalist on cordial terms with Konoe and many "old Seiyūkai" adherents, Kawasaki was able to arrange a series of monthly talks with Maeda, Nakajima, and Konoe in late 1935.[32] Konoe agreed that Army dominance of domestic politics would be unhealthy, and joined these talks to explore the possibility of a new party to counterbalance the rising influence of the military. His principal innovation, however, was to suggest that a simple coalition of several Seiyūkai and Minseitō factions would not have sufficient popular appeal to compete with the Army. While the proposed coalition of parliamentary groups might serve as the basis for a new party, political forces outside the two major parties engaged in mass organization would be necessary in the coalition for an effective recovery of party power.[33]

By the end of 1935, Kawasaki, Maeda, and Nakajima had offered Konoe the presidency of their proposed new party.[34] The prince refused to commit himself, but two months later, when he served as the "midwife" in the birth of the Hirota

[32] Although the dating is at times inaccurate, the standard source on these talks remains Kiya Ikusaburō, *Konoe-kō hibun* (Wakayama: Takanoyama shuppansha, 1950), p. 9, and *passim*.

[33] *Ibid.*, pp. 8–9.

[34] SKS, IV, 389, 392–93. Also, Iwabuchi, *Yabururu hi made*, p. 74.

government, Kawasaki and Maeda were given Cabinet port-folios. Less than three weeks later, Kawasaki suddenly be-came ill and died, and the initiative in his new party move-ment shifted to the Maeda-Nakajima group in the Seiyūkai. They moved slowly, for Konoe's advice regarding the in-fusion of nonparty and mass-based forces into the new party was not especially palatable. Most *kisei seitō* politicians continued to think in terms of their alliances with tradi-tional local leadership for political mobilization, and not in terms of mass organizations locally. Only Nagai Ryūtarō, an anti-mainstream leader in the Minseitō, urged the forma-tion of a new, mass-based political party.[35]

Meanwhile, Kuhara—the chief proponent of a one-party system—changed his political tactics during 1935. Seeking to replace Okada's government, he temporarily abandoned his quest for a new party, and concentrated on working against the Cabinet and its backers.

The creation of a new party [he now revealed] is nothing but an idiot's dream. It's the Cabinet itself which needs improvement more than the parties. It's easy enough to talk about creating and destroying parties, but it's not so easy to destroy overnight the different bases (*jiban*) each party has built up over the years. . . . Now is the time to cleanse ourselves of the spirit of leadership pro-vided by the bloc of senior Court statesmen (*jūshin*), and purge ourselves of the policy of following in the wake of the West. Now is the time to demand a demonstration of the Japanese spirit![36]

Kuhara's crusade against the shortcomings of the *jūshin* and their "puppet," the Okada government, was paralleled by the Seiyūkai's continuing criticism of the government and the party's refusal to collaborate in the formulation of na-tional policies in the Cabinet or Cabinet Policy Council.

[35] See "Nagai Ryūtarō" hensankai, ed., *Nagai Ryūtarō*, pp. 304 ff.
[36] From a speech by Kuhara on June 4, 1935, in Kuhara Fusano-suke-ō denki hensankai, ed., *Kuhara Fusanosuke*, pp. 448–49.

Kuhara, however, did not limit his activities to those of the party's mainstream leadership. Instead, he found common cause with civilian right-wing groups and radical young Army officers who opposed the parties as vigorously as they detested Saionji, the *jūshin*, and Okada. Late in 1935, Kuhara made several donations of funds to these groups, and some of the funds were used by the young officers in the February 26th Rebellion.[37] While Kuhara was later exonerated from implication in the rebellion for lack of evidence, he and the concept of a one-party system (a complete fusion of the Seiyūkai and Minseitō) disappeared from the field of party activity and party thinking until 1937.

Two significant and interrelated events in late 1936 and 1937 again brought the *kisei seitō* leadership face to face with the possibility of renewed power through a mass-based political party. The first event was a frontal collision between the "mainstream" leadership of the two parties and the Army during the 70th Diet session. The second event was the appearance of a new coalition of forces involving Colonel Ishiwara, Prince Konoe, and the nation's leading financiers and *zaibatsu* representatives. The first event demonstrated to nonparty elites the residual strength of the Diet and political parties as a political force; the second made party collaboration with these elites in the ratification and implementation of new national policies a potential means for the restoration of party power.

The Ogikubo Talks and the Five-Year Plans

From the opening of the 70th session of the Diet on December 26, 1936, both major parties indicated they were firmly opposed to the domestic program of the military. Their attack reached a crescendo on January 21, with sustained criticisms of the reform program and the increasing invasion of the military into the processes of domestic policy

[37] See *ibid.*, pp. 455–78, and Shillony, *Revolt in Japan*, pp. 87–95.

making. Hamada Kunimatsu of the Seiyūkai rose in the Diet to reiterate the official party viewpoint, and prompted Army Minister Terauchi to retort in an irritated fashion that Hamada's criticism of military influence in politics seemed to impugn the name of the emperor's loyal soldiers. The feisty Hamada demanded that Terauchi quote the section of his speech which had demeaned the honor of the imperial Army, and promised to commit *harakiri* if Terauchi could substantiate his charge. He added the wry suggestion that Terauchi could atone for his unwarranted riposte on him by similar methods if the Army minister proved unable to locate evidence of Hamada's low regard for the Army.[38]

Hamada's speech confirmed a growing conviction in the Army that the political parties under their present leadership would never sanction the domestic reform policies of the Hirota government. The Military Affairs Section of the Army Ministry concluded:

The government's policy speeches and questioning of them took place today, in the Upper House during the morning, and the Lower House in the afternoon. The questions of Hamada Kunimatsu in the Lower House displayed a complete contempt for the armed forces. In both word and gesture Hamada evidenced his disdain for Army Minister Terauchi. His final grandstanding at the podium, and the warm applause he received from both the Minseitō and Seiyūkai indicates that the problem does not lie with Hamada alone. It was a display of the anti-military feelings of the parties in general. We must conclude that it is impossible to discuss the various policies of overall reform (*shosei isshin*) with them.[39]

[38] For the text of Hamada's speech and the exchange that followed, see the records of the minutes of the Lower House session: *Kanpō gogai—Shōwa 12–nen 1–gatsu 22–nichi, Shūgiin giji sokkiroku dai–3–shū*, pp. 35–45.

[39] "Gunmuka seihen nisshi," entry for January 21, 1937, cited in Hata, *Gun fuashizumu undō shi*, p. 301. "*Shosei isshin*" was the reform slogan of the Hirota government.

Terauchi drew the same conclusion. Immediately following
Hamada's display of parliamentary pyrotechnics, the exas-
perated Army minister retired to the Cabinet's anteroom
and demanded that Hirota dissolve the Lower House and
call new elections. In view of the opposition to this proposal
by the four ministers from the parties, the Cabinet now
found itself badly split.[40]

Colonel Ishiwara had anticipated the political problems
Terauchi now encountered. His own approach to implementing economic and administrative reforms focused on
creating a new mass political party and a Cabinet under
General Hayashi or Prince Konoe. In December, as the Diet
was about to convene, a journalist acting on Ishiwara's behalf visited the home of Konoe's associate, Count Arima
Yoriyasu, to inquire about rumors of a new party involving
part of the Seiyūkai. He urged Arima, a former Seiyūkai
member, to serve as mediator among the quarreling Seiyūkai factions. Although this summons was phrased obliquely,
Arima quickly agreed to comply, and on December 26, he
convened a secret meeting of several influential political
leaders at his private residence in the Ogikubo section of
Tokyo. It quickly became evident, however, that the larger
purpose of the meeting was to discuss the formation of a
new Konoe-led party and a new government led by General
Hayashi, rather than to mediate the factional dispute within
the Seiyūkai.[41]

[40] Ibid.

[41] SKS, v, 210; Arima Yoriyasu, Seikai dōchūki (Tokyo: Nihon
shuppan kyōdō kabushiki kaisha, 1951), pp. 118–19. Arima believed
that Sogō Shinji, acting as Ishiwara's agent, organized the Ogikubo
meetings, and decided who would participate in them. See Arima
Yoriyasu, Hitorigoto (Tokyo: Koizumi insatsu kabushiki kaisha,
1957), pp. 79–80. Others believed that Nakajima was involved in
setting up the talks. According to Ishiwara's diary, he visited the
Nakajima factory on January 16, 1937. Tsunoda, Ishiwara Kanji
shiryō, p. 130. However, his visit there on the day before the final
Ogikubo meeting may not have been connected with the talks, since
a professional interest in the aircraft industry may well have prompted
the colonel to visit the factory.

The participants in the Ogikubo conversations included General Hayashi, Admiral Abo Kiyokazu, Yūki Toyotarō, Obara Naoshi, Nagai Ryūtarō, Maeda Yonezō, Nakajima Chikuhei, Yamazaki Tatsunosuke, Gotō Fumio, and Arima. These men were hardly in a position to mediate an internal dispute in the Seiyūkai. Hayashi and Abo had almost no direct connections with the politicians of the Diet. Yūki was one of the nation's most influential bankers. Obara had been the minister of justice in the Okada Cabinet and was contemplating an offer to join the Minseitō. Nagai Ryūtarō was the one *kisei seitō* leader known to favor the formation of a new mass-oriented political party. Maeda and Nakajima represented the faction in the Seiyūkai intent on forming a new party. Yamazaki had already been expelled from the Seiyūkai in 1934 for cooperating with the Okada government and belonged to the small Shōwakai party. Gotō was a retired bureaucrat who had served as minister of agriculture and forestry and home minister between 1932 and 1936. His chief involvement in national affairs thereafter was through his intimate connections with three semiofficial mass organizations in the countryside, the *sangyō kumiai*, election purification movement, and youth associations (*seinendan*). Arima was a close political associate of Prince Konoe, and was also a strong proponent of converting the *sangyō kumiai* into a nation-wide political organization.

The first Ogikubo discussion ended with a simple exchange of political views.[42] Nakajima noted that he expected the Hirota government to collapse in the near future, and he recommended that the group meet again soon. Following this advice, the participants convened again in Ogikubo on January 5 and January 17, 1937. During these two sessions, a consensus was reached on the advisability of establishing a new political party led by Konoe, and

[42] The best account of these meetings appears in Arima's diary entry for February 4, 1937, cited in Itō Takashi, "Shōwa jūsan-nen Konoe shintō mondai kenkyū oboegaki," Nihon seiji gakkai, ed., *"Konoe shintaisei" no kenkyū*, p. 138, n. 3.

supported strongly by both military services.[43] According to one published report, the party was to include only eighty or ninety men from the Seiyūkai, fifty or sixty from the Minseitō, and a dozen or so Shōwakai adherents.[44] Nevertheless, the presence of the new party advocates from the *kisei seitō* anti-mainstream groups, and the evident interest of Gotō and Arima, suggested that the new party might well be a combination of parliamentary and mass forces, as Konoe himself had earlier recommended.

While the prince's attitude towards the new party remained opaque, his actions in late 1936 spurred the hopes of both Ishiwara and the Ogikubo discussants that he would look favorably on the party. Significantly, Konoe shifted in November from a long-standing public position of criticism vis-à-vis the parties to a surprisingly strong defense of the Diet and affirmation of the potential value of a "good party." Opposing the rumored Army plan to limit party activities in the Diet and Cabinet, he observed that

> in actual practice, we have seen that when non-party men form transcendental Cabinets, they frequently clash with the Diet. . . . Yamagata suffered from this in particular, and it was the reason why Prince Saionji finally joined a party. So I have serious doubts that a clear separation of the Diet from the government will facilitate relations between the two.
>
> . . . In the final analysis, there is no acceptable alternative to forming a good political party, and operating in a framework where the Diet supervises the executive branch of the government.[45]

Provided that the participants at the Ogikubo talks were willing to bring parliamentary and mass organizations to-

[43] *Ibid.*, pp. 138–39.

[44] Nagata Tetsuji, "New Political Party Still Object of Many Leaders," excerpt from *Bungei shunjū*, March 1937, translated in *Contemporary Opinions*, #165, February 25, 1937, p. 19.

[45] Remarks made by Konoe on November 11, 1936. See KF, I, 351–52.

gether in the new party's structure, there appeared to be a reasonable chance Konoe would agree to leading this "good political party."

However, Konoe's decision on joining the new party at this juncture hinged on other factors as well. The prince regarded party membership—even party leadership—as inconsistent with his noble heritage. Nobles had been strictly enjoined from participating in party affairs during the period in which his political attitudes were formulated, and the strongest advocate of noble "transcendence" of party involvement had been his father, Prince Konoe Atsumaro. The younger Konoe defined his own political role in the Shōwa era as being that of a mediator, who might foster consensus and compromise where the parties would not or could not act effectively as conflict managers.[46] Konoe's attitude towards Ishiwara's party would therefore be determined by the degree to which he felt Ishiwara's plans could obtain consensual support among other elites represented in the government, and whether the parties under their current leadership would block the implementation of these plans once consensus had been reached among the other elite groups. Konoe would wish to examine the movements of the party and nonparty elites closely before deciding whether or not to violate his own code of noble political ethics and participate in a new party.

He consequently took a close interest in the intraelite negotiations and conflict over Ishiwara's plans for administrative reform and economic development. There was clearly strong bureaucratic opposition to the elimination of several ministries and creation of supraministerial Cabinet agencies to control personnel and the budget. Only the "revisionist" bureaucrats centered in the Cabinet Research Bureau seemed anxious to see this aspect of the military's program implemented. There was also a great deal of controversy raised by Ishiwara's economic program, which had been drafted by Manchurian Railways employee Miyazaki

[46] See Berger, "Japan's Young Prince," for the formation of Konoe's early political attitudes.

Masayoshi. Miyazaki's "Five-Year Plan for the Empire's Income and Expenditures from 1937" consisted of a five-year schedule for the broad development of Japanese and Manchurian industry, embodying a special emphasis on defense-related industries, such as aircraft and munitions production. It called for greater state controls and planning throughout the economies of both nations, and a massive increase in government spending. To finance the increased government outlays in developing defense industries, it proposed a greatly expanded national budget, flotations of national bonds, and substantial tax increases.[47] The plan found support among the "revisionist" bureaucrats, and indeed, the huge 1937 budget submitted by Finance Minister Baba Eiichi in late 1936 resembled the figures in this plan closely enough to suggest that Baba, too, embraced Ishiwara's economic plans.[48] The reaction of prominent *zaibatsu* figures, however, was far less enthusiastic. As Ikeda Seihin of Mitsui commented to Baron Harada in late November, "The present financial plans [of Finance Minister Baba] are simply the fruits of the program of the middle-echelon Army officers and the Kwantung Army. We should be aware of the extremely bad influence this will have in financial circles."[49] Businessmen objected not only to the size of

[47] Tsunoda, *Ishiwara Kanji shiryō*, p. 141, and Miyazaki, *Tōa renmei ron*, p. 79. Miyazaki's program was predicated on an informal assurance given the Army Ministry from the Finance Ministry that the Army's budget would total roughly three billion yen between 1937 and 1942. See Tsunoda, *Ishiwara Kanji shiryō*, p. 143; Yatsugi Kazuo, *Shōwa dōran shishi* (3 vols., Tokyo: Keizai ōraisha, 1971–1973), I, 352; International Military Tribunal for the Far East, *Proceedings* (Tokyo, mimeographed, 1945–1948), p. 18286 (hereafter cited as IMTFE, *Proceedings*). The Army's budget for 1936 was 515 million yen. IMTFE, *Proceedings*, p. 8540.

[48] Nakamura Takafusa, "Nihon sensō keizai no jōken: Nit-Chū sensō zengo" (Tokyo daigaku kyōyō gakubu), *Shakai kagaku kiyō*, xv (March 20, 1966), 73.

[49] SKS, v, 198.

Baba's budget and the proposed imposition of state controls on their enterprises, but also to the tax reform proposals of the Hirota government, which had stipulated that taxes would be levied on property and combined income, rather than income at the source.

It was in anticipation of this dissent among the civilian elites and in the Diet that Ishiwara had proposed to ram his program through a Cabinet led by General Hayashi or Konoe, and a Diet controlled by a Konoe-led new political party. Konoe sympathized with several facets of Ishiwara's program—particularly administrative reform and a proposed foreign policy of detente with the Anglo-American powers and China while Japan concentrated on building up her defenses against the Soviet Union.[50] Nevertheless, he recognized the strength of business and bureaucratic opposition to Ishiwara's plans. He no doubt knew also that Ishiwara's program exceeded the desires of even the leadership of the Army, and that the Colonel's intrigues and plans for intervention in politics had aroused the animosity of a number of senior officers.[51] Konoe concluded that a great deal of compromising would be necessary before a consensus among nonparty elites could be attained, and reform legislation enjoying Cabinet support presented to the Lower House. The formation of a new political party to push Ishiwara's plans through the Diet thus seemed premature. Moreover, Gotō Fumio indicated that the *kisei seitō* representatives at the Ogikubo talks were not genuinely interested in creating a party based on mass organizations.[52] For Konoe, this meant that the *kisei seitō* politicians were still unwilling to create the "good political party" he had recommended to Kawasaki in 1935 and publicly endorsed in

[50] KF, I, 351; SKS, v, 195; Iwabuchi, *Yabururu hi made*, p. 63.

[51] IMTFE, *Proceedings*, p. 18312; *Nishiura Susumu-shi danwa sokkiroku*, I, 159.

[52] See Kiya Ikusaburō, *Seikai gojū-nen no butai-ura* (Tokyo: Seikai ōraisha, 1965), pp. 160–61.

November 1936. Thus, in late January 1937, Konoe informed Arima that he was unwilling to assume the leadership of the new party proposed at the Ogikubo talks.[53]

Following Army Minister Terauchi's demand for a dissolution of the Diet in late January, political conflict among the elites intensified and peaked. Maeda Yonezō, serving as railways minister in Hirota's government, suggested that the impasse reached between the Army and the Diet as manifested in Terauchi's *"harakiri"* exchange with Hamada Kunimatsu might be resolved by the formation of a new political party.[54] Presumably, this was a reference to the plan being discussed in the Ogikubo talks, but since Arima had informed Terauchi that the immediate prospects of a new party were dim, the Army minister brushed Maeda's suggestion aside.[55] The Cabinet was then divided between the party representatives, who opposed a dissolution of the Diet, and Terauchi, who insisted on new elections. Despite efforts by Navy Minister Admiral Nagano Osami to mediate the dispute, Premier Hirota was unable to obtain a consensus among his ministers, and submitted his government's resignation. Terauchi then met the press and stated that his actions had not been motivated simply by Hamada's insulting remarks, but by the realization that the Army's views of Japan's situation were considerably different from the views consistently expressed by the leaders of both parties in the Diet session.[56]

As party men looked back on the events of the Hirota government, they could take satisfaction in having demonstrated to the Army and other elite forces that the Diet was still a force to be reckoned with in national affairs. Together with powerful forces in the bureaucracy, they had beaten

[53] Itō, "Shōwa jūsan-nen," p. 138, n. 3.

[54] "Gunmuka seihen nisshi," entry for January 22, 1937, cited in Hata, *Gun fuashizumu undō shi*, p. 301.

[55] Itō, "Shōwa jūsan-nen," p. 138, n. 3.

[56] "Gunmuka seihen nisshi," entry for January 23, 1937, cited in Hata, *Gun fuashizumu undō shi*, p. 302.

back the radical reform proposals directed by the Army against the Diet and the bureaucracy, and had launched a withering barrage of criticism against military pressures in the domestic political arena. In league with the civil service and the *zaibatsu*, they had issued a sharp reminder to the Army that power could not be monopolized by any single elite group under the Meiji political system, and that the same system that provided the military with a secure institutional base could also be used to defend the institutional prerogatives of the bureaucracy and the parties themselves. For its part, the Army was coming to the same conclusions. While Ishiwara pressed insistently for his administrative and economic reform proposals and the creation of a dictatorial party, his position was soon to be repudiated and only those sections of his scheme for a national defense state that could obtain the sanction of major civilian elite groups would henceforth be endorsed by Army ministers. While General Hayashi assumed the premiership between January and June 1937, the Army's leadership worked to tone down the most radical aspects of Ishiwara's program, and to obtain the support of prominent businessmen, such as Ikeda and Yūki, for the five-year plan. Ishiwara had anticipated that a Hayashi Cabinet could be the first step towards Army dictatorship and a useful tool in implementing reform. In the course of organizing his government, however, Hayashi was obliged to move closer to the official Army viewpoint. Initially, he seemed determined to carry out Ishiwara's program, and invited the services to name Lieutenant General Itagaki and Admiral Suetsugu to the Army and Navy portfolios. Both services declined this offer, and nominated other men instead. The businessmen tapped by Hayashi, Ikeda and Tsuda Shingo, also declined offers of Cabinet seats. It was only when Hayashi threw Ishiwara's representative out of "Cabinet Formation Headquarters" and indicated he would moderate the policies of his government in order to survive as premier that he began receiving support. As most of the radical administrative and eco-

115

nomic proposals of the "Manchurian Group" were scrapped, Ikeda proposed that Yūki be named finance minister, and in early February, he himself became governor of the Bank of Japan.

Under the auspices of the new government, the business, bureaucratic, and military elites began working out compromises based on Ishiwara's program that would be acceptable to all of them. As Ikeda phrased it to Harada, the fundamental problem was harmonizing the requirements of national defense with the existing economic structure:

> The Ishiwara plans present some difficult problems; the Army's demand for a replenishment of national defense must obviously be dealt with in accord with the dictates of international conditions. The basis of the present economic structure must remain intact. . . . If we do exactly as the most powerful of the middle-echelon elements in the Army [Ishiwara and his supporters] wish, that structure will collapse and lead to chaos. On the other hand, however, we cannot disregard national defense.[57]

In other words, the Ikeda-Yūki approach to national economic policy was conceived against a desire to curb the radical aspects of the proposals made by Miyazaki and Baba, while seeking a defense policy that would be acceptable to both the Army and the business world. This new approach was seen by the press as a more conciliatory policy by business towards the Army than had been evidenced hitherto, and it was promptly labeled "tie-up finance": an effort to join the viewpoints of business and the military.

Under Yūki's direction, a number of key Finance Ministry personnel were reinstated from the purge conducted by Baba during his tenure in office. The new officials—Kaya Okinori, Ishiwata Sōtarō, and Aoki Kazuo—were either skilled liaison men between the ministry and the Army, or

[57] SKS, v, 254–55 (entry of February 10, 1937).

experts whose special talents were particularly needed in the formulation of an ambitious national defense and economic development program.[58] To win the support of the Lower House and the business world, the Cabinet agreed to shelve the offensive tax reform proposals of the Hirota government and the total budget was pruned by Yūki from the original 3.13 billion yen proposed by Baba to a still heady but palatable 2.77 billion yen. Furthermore, the plans to introduce legislation nationalizing control of the nation's electric power industry were deferred and reworked to appease business and parliamentary opposition.[59] Of the wide variety of administrative reforms proposed in 1936, the sole reform enacted by the Hayashi regime was the enlargement of the Cabinet Research Bureau into a Planning Office (*Kikakuchō*) in May 1937.[60] To reciprocate, Ikeda agreed to send Izumiyama Sanroku of the Mitsui Bank to represent him in negotiations with the Army and Ishiwara's staff over revisions in the five-year plan for military supply industries. Izumiyama began his work on April 1, assured that Ikeda, Ishiwara, and Konoe were determined to have these plans formulated and executed.[61] By May 15, the negotiators had developed an overall plan for the development of Japanese and Manchurian military supply industries, and on May 29, the final Army Ministry plan was offi-

[58] Kaya had been the leading budgetary expert of the ministry before his demotion under Baba, and for years had been charged with harmonizing the budgetary demands of the military with overall economic and financial policy. See Aritake Shūji, *Shōwa keizai sokumen shi* (Tokyo: Kawade shobō, 1952), p. 355. Ishiwata now became the chief of the Tax Bureau, while Aoki was given the important task of serving as a liaison man between Yūki-Ikeda and the Army. SKS, v, 282.

[59] Aritake, *Shōwa keizai sokumen shi*, pp. 342–51.

[60] Yamazaki Tanshō, *Naikaku seido no kenkyū* (Tokyo: Takayama shoin, 1942), pp. 142–43.

[61] Izumiyama Sanroku, *Tora daijin ni naru made* (Tokyo: Tōhō shoin, 1953), pp. 106–107. Izumiyama's papers related to the negotiations of 1937 have been published. See *Nichi-Man zaisei keizai kenkyūkai shiryō* (3 vols., Tokyo: Nihon kindai shiryō kenkyūkai, 1970).

cially drawn up as "The Essentials of a Five-Year Plan for Key Industries."[62]

The Army Ministry now sought to facilitate acceptance of its plan by emphasizing that while "a considerable degree of controls" would be needed to procure funds, "it is considered advisable to avoid causing an abrupt change in the empire's current capitalistic economic structure in executing this program."[63] The ministry went one step further and deleted all references to the institutional and administrative reforms originally advocated by Ishiwara, in an effort to mitigate the hostility of the bureaucracy. Confident that this plan represented a sound compromise among the business world, the Army General Staff planners led by Ishiwara, and the ministry's own views, Army Minister Sugiyama Hajime gave his approval to the plan and submitted it to the Cabinet. As if to confirm the wisdom of Sugiyama's judgment, Minister of Commerce and Industry Godō Takuo responded to the presentation of the program by calling for swift government action to meet the pressing need for expanding productive power.[64]

Before the Hayashi government could take any further action on the policies presented by the Army minister, however, it was obliged to resign under Diet pressure on May 31. The general's downfall derived from the fact that his overall policy of compromise and accommodation with men like Ikeda and Yūki did not extend to the Lower House.

[62] The plan is detailed as it stood on May 1, 1937, in a chart in Nakamura Takafusa, *Senzen-ki Nihon keizai seichō no bunseki* (Tokyo: Iwanami shoten, 1971), pp. 246–47. See also Tsunoda, *Ishiwara Kanji shiryō*, pp. 148–50, and IMTFE, *Proceedings*, pp. 8260 ff. A supplementary proposal was also drafted for the development of the aircraft and weapons industries. See "Gunjūhin seizō kōgyō go-ka-nen keikaku yōkō" in Inaba Masao, Shimada Toshihiko, Tsunoda Jun, and Usui Katsumi, eds., *Nit-Chū sensō (1)* (Gendai shi shiryō VIII) (Tokyo: Misuzu shobō, 1964), pp. 752–70.

[63] Tsunoda, *Ishiwara Kanji shiryō*, pp. 148–52.

[64] Nakamura, "Nihon sensō keizai no jōken," p. 75.

Three "anti-mainstream" Diet politicians—Nakajima, Nagai, and Yamazaki—had been offered Cabinet portfolios, but only on the condition that they first resign from their parties.[65] Presumably, this condition was designed to set the stage for the formation of a new political party to lead and unify public opinion and provide Diet cooperation for the government's policies of reform in the Lower House. Uncertain about the future of the proposed new party, Nakajima and Nagai refused Hayashi's offer, and only Yamazaki agreed to resign from the small Shōwakai to become minister of agriculture and forestry.

Moreover, once the government's moderate program and reduced budget proposals had cleared the Diet, Hayashi suddenly, and without provocation, prorogued the Lower House on March 31, and announced that new elections would be held to "purify the Diet." Army Minister Sugiyama and Justice Minister Shiono Suehiko (an associate of Baron Hiranuma) both questioned the wisdom of Hayashi's decision, but neither was willing to oppose it to the extent that Cabinet unity would be ruptured.[66] In all likelihood, Hayashi's real objective in calling new elections was to provide the opportunity for a new reform-oriented political party such as had been discussed at the Ogikubo talks to emerge under Konoe's leadership. Particularly in light of the successful compromises being reached among the military, business, and bureaucratic elite groups, Hayashi may have felt Konoe was ready to assume control of the Diet forces through the new party. Indeed, on April 8, the premier called on Konoe and urged him specifically to assume the leadership of a new party.[67] Hayashi's stratagem backfired, however, and cost him the premiership. Konoe refused to organize any party in the midst of an election

[65] "Asahara Kenzō nikki," cited in Hata, *Gun fuashizumu undō shi,* pp. 314–17; and Konoe's remarks to Harada in KF, i, 367.

[66] KF, i, 374.

[67] *Ibid.,* p. 375.

campaign, and both of the major parties did well in the elections against reformist opponents. The parties accused Hayashi of irresponsible conduct in launching a personal vendetta against them, and pressures mounted on the premier to resign. Politically embarrassed, Hayashi sought to use the threat of still another dissolution of the Lower House to quiet his opponents, but when the Army refused to endorse this approach to control over the Diet, Hayashi tendered his resignation.

Army Minister Sugiyama immediately indicated that the Army did not wish to see a military man succeed Hayashi. He was clearly anxious about the conflict between the Army leadership's desire for compromise with other elites and Ishiwara's insistence that his reform program be carried out, whatever the cost. Although Sugiyama had feared in January that Konoe might become a "robot" of the Ishiwara group, the prince's commitment to reaching a compromise among Army, business, and bureaucratic elites now convinced him that Konoe's appointment would be "most convenient" for defusing a potentially explosive situation. Ex-Army Minister Terauchi also warned of Ishiwara's plans, and urged that Konoe be made the new premier.[68] General Hayashi, on the other hand, wished Konoe to succeed him in order to carry out many of Ishiwara's designs. He repeatedly sought to have Konoe form the new party Ishiwara had planned, and to assume the premiership in order to execute the reform program that Hayashi had been unable to carry out. Baron Hiranuma, Privy Seal Yuasa, and the leaders of both major political parties also regarded Konoe favorably, and it appeared that a consensus on the prince had been reached.[69] Saionji was now the sole obstacle to Konoe's appointment as premier. While the *genrō* considered the situation "unfortunate,"[70] Army opposition to a military man had narrowed the choice to his former protégé or Baron

[68] SKS, v, 310–14.
[69] Kido, *Kido Kōichi nikki*, i, 562 and 567.
[70] SKS, v, 323.

Hiranuma. Since the latter was still anathema to Saionji, Konoe was summoned into the imperial presence on June 1, and given the mandate to form a new government.

THE FIRST MONTH OF THE KONOE GOVERNMENT

Prince Konoe had been closely apprised of the agreements reached among the Army Ministry, the General Staff, Ikeda, and the Finance Ministry during the spring. He was clearly eager to end the debilitating disputes over domestic policy that had paralyzed and destroyed the last two governments. A new government firmly committed to the execution of the Army Ministry proposal for industrial development would at least focus the energies of the empire on the Soviet threat for the ensuing five years, while ameliorating relations with the Anglo-American powers. At the same time, he hoped that the creation of a sphere of self-sufficiency in Japan, Manchuria, and North China would free Japan from her dependence on the Western powers for raw materials. Perhaps on the basis of this new policy an international "New Deal" could be promulgated, in which Japan, as a "have-not" country, would take her rightful place among the great powers of the world.[71] In affirming the desirability of the new policy, Konoe "recognized the basic path of destiny which our people must follow, although I wished to move as firmly and gradually down it as possible. To that end, I would check as much as possible the group in the military which easily became reckless and impatient, while also accepting those of their demands which were rational."[72] Konoe believed this approach of-

[71] For Konoe's thoughts on an international "New Deal," a concept discussed by Colonel Edward House, see Konoe Fumimaro, "Hausu taisa ni kotau," in Konoe Fumimaro, *Seidanroku*, ed. Itō Takeshi (Tokyo: Chikura shobō, 1936), pp. 225–30.

[72] KF, I, 225. Konoe's adoption of the Army Ministry's plan at the outset of his premiership is somewhat ironic in view of his later claims that he and "the military" were constantly at odds during the first Konoe government.

121

fered the best available prospect for achieving the "domestic harmony" he so cherished. Conjuring up a picture of a Cabinet and country united in pursuit of this goal, the prince agreed to form a new government.

It became clear immediately that Konoe's "guiding principle" of national unification would be the Army Ministry's May 29 compromise plan for industrial development. For example, the three prime contenders for the important post of finance minister were Kodama Kenji (former governor of the Yokohama Specie Bank), ex-Finance Minister Baba Eiichi, and the incumbent Yūki. Kodama, however, refused to accept the budgetary plans formulated in the five-year plan, and was immediately dropped from consideration. Baba had strong support in the Army, but Konoe did not wish to upset the fragile relationship that had been established with the "tie-up finance" approach of Ikeda and Yūki. To conciliate Baba's backers, however, Konoe appointed him to serve as home minister, with the intention of asking Yūki to retain the finance minister's portfolio. Yūki, however, was unwilling to serve in the same Cabinet with Baba, and thus his vice minister, Kaya Okinori, was promoted to the finance minister's post in order to maintain the "tie-up" between the Finance and Army Ministries.[73]

Konoe followed a similar formula in the selection of his other ministers. Earlier in the year, he had shown his sympathies for Ishiwara's group by hinting that he would not serve as premier unless Lieutenant General Itagaki and Admiral Suetsugu were appointed to the Army and Navy Ministry portfolios. In June, however, such appointments might well have upset the compromise approved by Army Minister Sugiyama. Konoe thus agreed readily to the retention of Sugiyama and Navy Minister Yonai Mitsumasa in their current posts.[74] For his commerce and industry minister, Konoe selected Yoshino Shinji, a brilliant career official who held that "it was a matter of common sense in

[73] KF, I, 381; SKS, VI, 4.
[74] Arima, *Seikai dōchūki*, p. 128; KF, I, 381; SKS, VI, 4.

formulating economic policies of a country to strive at all costs for the building up of necessary industries in order to guarantee its independence and security."[75] Konoe sought to strengthen the Cabinet's position vis-à-vis the Diet by appointing Nagai Ryūtarō of the Minseitō and Nakajima Chikuhei of the Seiyūkai to ministerial posts. It was not by chance that they, rather than other party leaders, were selected to represent the Diet in Konoe's "national unity" government. Nagai belonged to a faction that had advocated the nationalization of the electric power industry for several years; and inasmuch as this policy was an integral aspect of the five-year plan, it was expected that he would prove an effective and outspoken supporter of the new government's policies. Nakajima, on the other hand, was a vigorous advocate of air power, and could be expected to promote the plans for developing Japan's aircraft industry. Not only was he an inveterate supporter of plans to bolster Japan's defenses against the Soviet threat, but as an entrepreneur, he had much to gain from increased government purchases of aircraft. He, too, therefore, was expected to support the Army's five-year plan. The remaining Cabinet appointments were also settled quickly. Hirota Kōki was appointed foreign minister, a decision that gratified Prince Saionji. Hiranuma's forces were represented in the government by Justice Minister Shiono, a hold-over from the Hayashi regime. Yasui Eiji became the education minister, Arima Yoriyasu the minister of agriculture and forestry, and Ōtani Son'yū the minister of overseas development. All owed their appointments to personal ties with Konoe.

Despite the skill with which Konoe had assembled his Cabinet, adroit political leadership would be required to consolidate or even maintain accord among the various forces represented in the government. Following the first Cabinet meeting, Kaya and Yoshino issued a joint statement of the government's "three fundamental principles" of eco-

[75] IMTFE, *Proceedings*, p. 18207. The new minister of commerce and industry was the younger brother of Yoshino Sakuzō.

nomic policy: a commitment to the expansion of productive power, a maintenance of the balance of international payments, and a harmonization of the demand for materials with available supplies. Their statement was taken as serving notice on the Army that the laudable goal of expanding productive power would not be pursued to the detriment of a sound economy. Demand would be stimulated by new funds only to the degree that materials were actually available for purchase and exports covered imports, rather than automatically in accord with the blueprint of the Army's five-year plan.[76] Ishiwara and Miyazaki countered with a position paper reiterating the need for some of the tax and administrative reforms and economic controls that had originally been pared out of the plan by the Army Ministry.[77] Sugiyama and Vice Minister Umezu Yoshijirō found themselves caught between the General Staff planners and the economic bureaucrats, and the potential for conflict in the Cabinet cast a pall over its early meetings.

Konoe dealt gingerly with both groups when he convened a meeting on June 15 to discuss the Army Ministry's five-year plan for the first time at the Cabinet level.[78] Rather than attempt to deal with the thorny issues of state economic controls, regulation of supply and demand of capital and material, and administrative reforms, the discussion was structured towards an evaluation of the overall desirability of the goals of the plan and methods by which the citizenry could be brought to cooperate in attaining them.

Given the context in which the premier had placed the question, it was not difficult for the ministers to concur on three major points:

[76] KF, i, 386; Takahashi Makoto, "The Development of War-time Economic Controls," p. 658; Tsunoda, *Ishiwara Kanji shiryō*, p. 151; Yoshino Shinji, *Shōkō gyōsei no omoide: Nihon shihon shugi no ayumi* (Tokyo: Shōkō seisaku shi kankōkai, 1962), p. 356.

[77] Miyazaki's paper was titled "An Outline of the Policies Related to the Execution of the 'Essentials of the Five-Year Plan for Key Industries,'" drafted June 7, 1937. See Tsunoda, *Ishiwara Kanji shiryō*, p. 142.

[78] For an account of this meeting, see KF, i, 392.

1. It was desirable to expand the economic strength of the empire, as the Army Ministry proposed.
2. The particular problems emanating from the Army's plan should be submitted to the Planning Office for further study before legislation was formally drafted for the consideration of the Cabinet as a whole and the Diet.
3. The role of the citizenry in providing increasing amounts of funds for capital investments and the purchase of imported raw materials was acknowledged to be of crucial importance.

The first and second points of the Cabinet's agreement were at the same time an endorsement of the Army Ministry plan and an evasion of most of the central problems its implementation would provoke. The third point revealed that there was Cabinet accord on certain critical questions. The Army plan for industrial development had originally incorporated an important compromise between the Ishiwara-Miyazaki proposals and the viewpoints of Ikeda, Yūki, and the Finance Ministry. While recognizing the necessity of promoting citizens' savings and restrictions on the consumption of nonessential goods and raw materials, the Army Ministry had rejected Ishiwara's plan for a mass political party as the agent of popular control in favor of the Finance Ministry's insistence that the encouragement of popular savings and reduced consumption be done on a voluntary basis. In outlining the approach to be used in fostering citizen cooperation with the five-year plan, the Army Ministry simply advocated "a great popular movement to check consumption and encourage thrift and saving." Konoe himself gave support to this approach by publicly disavowing interest in forming any new parties.[79] There was thus a strong

[79] *Contemporary Japan*, vi.2, 331. For the Finance Ministry's position on the campaign to promote citizens' savings and limit consumption voluntarily, see the recollections of Kaya Okinori in Andō Yoshio, ed., *Shōwa keizai shi e no shōgen*, ii (Tokyo: Mainichi shinbunsha, 1966), p. 190. For the Army Ministry's position, see Tsunoda, *Ishiwara Kanji shiryō*, p. 151.

125

consensus on the limits of mass mobilization for the plan, which only Agriculture and Forestry Minister Arima failed (or chose not) to notice at the June 15 Cabinet meeting. Arima noted cogently that the adoption of the Army Ministry's plan would inevitably increase the financial burdens of the rural population, while enhancing the wealth and productive capacities of urban industrialized areas. Speaking to Yoshino's proposal for a "spiritual" mobilization campaign to facilitate realization of the plan's objectives, Arima implied that something more substantial—a political movement or new party embracing the rural population and representing its interests—might be more suitable to win public cooperation. However valid Arima's observations might have been about the reluctance of the agrarian population to underwrite a program of dramatic industrial growth, the rest of the Cabinet refused to consider the utility of a new political party to galvanize rural support for the five-year plan. When Home Minister Baba and Education Minister Yasui quickly endorsed Yoshino's suggestion, the Cabinet agreed on a nonpartisan campaign to mobilize national support and encourage savings and reduced consumption. The home and education ministers were then charged with the responsibility of drafting plans for initiating the campaign.

The initial foreign policies of the Konoe government indicated a desire to avoid confrontations with the Anglo-American powers and China, as required by the five-year plan. Foreign Minister Hirota, working through his ambassador in London, embarked immediately on a series of discussions with Great Britain touching on all issues pending between the two nations.[80] For its part, the General Staff sought to assure that the Japanese armies in North China would not provoke any untoward incident that might interfere with the proposed industrialization plan.[81] On July 6,

[80] Hirota Kōki denki kankōkai, ed., *Hirota Kōki*, pp. 256–57; Tōgō Shigenori, *Jidai no ichimen: Tōgō Shigenori gaikō shuki* (Tokyo: Hara shobō, 1967), p. 114.
[81] Crowley, *Japan's Quest*, p. 320.

Hirota indicated that Japan would make no further effort to win China's favor or incur her ire, however unhappy Japan might be.[82] The way seemed clear for the government to harvest the fruits of the joint efforts of the Army, businessmen, and economic bureaucrats during the first half of 1937. The "tie-up" might now be extended into a firm working alliance.

As the parties moved into the "Konoe era," it was possible to assess their power position with a fair degree of clarity. During the 70th Diet session, they had confronted the Army successfully, and in combination with the business and bureaucratic elites, had forced the military at least temporarily to reduce those policy demands they found most offensive. Within the Diet, they remained the paramount force, and retained control over the institutional powers of the Lower House to block legislation and budgetary proposals. Moreover, as they demonstrated during the general elections in 1936, and again most emphatically in 1937, the strength of their members' *jiban* was relatively stable. While almost a quarter of the members elected to Diet seats in 1937 remained aloof from the *kisei seitō*, signifying a definite decline in the parties' prestige, their position within the Lower House was still secure against challenge from non-*kisei seitō* forces.

Viewed from other perspectives, however, the years from 1932 to 1937 took a heavy toll in terms of party power. In the Cabinet, their position was reduced from controlling the premiership to holding only one or two significant ministerial portfolios. They still retained networks of communication with nonparty elites—business, the civil service, the military—but were placed in the position of seeking support from these elites for the advancement of their fortunes and policy goals without providing the reciprocal service of integrating the demands and ambitions of nonparty groups. While the *zaibatsu* welcomed their support in the Lower

[82] Bōeichō bōei kenshūsho senshi-shitsu, *Daihonei rikugunbu*, I (Tokyo: Asagumo shinbunsha, 1967), 429 (hereafter cited as DR, I).

House, businessmen such as Ikeda moved directly into the political negotiating process with other elite groups rather than confine their political activities and pressures to channels provided by the parties. Important groups of bureaucrats with the technical expertise highly desired during this period of national crisis looked towards the Army rather than the parties for the implementation of their policy goals and the fulfillment of their personal ambitions. These developments had an important bearing on the allocation of power within the parties, as well. Frustrated by the inability of their leaders to confer power and prestige on them, junior party members became susceptible to supporting opponents of the mainstream leadership, whether the opposition came from anti-mainstream figures within their party or nonparty elites, such as the Army. Anti-mainstream leaders were similarly vulnerable to the blandishments of nonparty elites, and welcomed the opportunity to use new alliances with nonparty elite groups to enhance their positions within their parties (see Figure 4).

Of the two major parties, the Minseitō appeared to survive the erosion of party power somewhat better than the Seiyūkai. The Minseitō's victory in the 1936 elections bolstered the prestige of Machida and his mainstream colleagues, and sparked the party's hope of gaining a central position in future Cabinets. While one faction, led by Nagai, agitated for the creation of a new party, most Minseitō supporters preferred to follow where Machida would lead them. The Seiyūkai, on the other hand, was badly shaken by its defeat at the polls in 1936. Its president, Suzuki Kisaburō, was defeated in his bid for reelection, and shortly thereafter, became seriously ill. In early 1937, Suzuki indicated his desire to resign as party president. On February 18, four "proxies" were appointed to execute the duties of the presidency, while Suzuki's retirement was deferred pending the decision of the party on a successor.[83] A minor-

[83] Watanabe Kazuhide, *Kyojin Nakajima Chikuhei* (Tokyo: Hōbun shorin, 1955), pp. 320–22.

FIGURE 4. Despite the completion of the imposing new Diet building in 1936, the growing power of the Home Ministry and its police force, along with other nonparty elite groups, seemed to push parliamentary politics into the background.

ity of members, led by Maeda and Nakajima, actively supported the government's domestic reform proposals and were ready to organize a new political party under Konoe. This effort coincided with Ishiwara's plans to form a new party in early 1937. However, a majority of the Seiyūkai, under the control of Suzuki and his brother-in-law Hatoyama, opposed the reform proposals and proclaimed their unwillingness to support the concept of a national defense state.

The election of April 1937 increased the Seiyūkai's strength by one seat to 175 (the Minseitō lost twenty-six seats to 179), but did not fundamentally affect the distribution of power within the party. By June, however, Nakajima's position had been strengthened by his appointment to a Cabinet position by Konoe. Later that year, Konoe

129

established a committee of Cabinet counselors (*naikaku sangi*) to advise him on policies related to the China Incident, and anti-mainstream leaders Maeda and Akita Kiyoshi were favored with appointment. In addition to the patronage of nonparty elites, the Seiyūkai anti-mainstream under Maeda and Nakajima enjoyed growing strength by virtue of Nakajima's enormous expenditure of personal funds on party activities. With the party's ties to the *zaibatsu* weakening, and Kuhara and his funds temporarily divorced from the party, Nakajima's power in the party continued to increase.

As the "Konoe era" dawned, the nonparty elites in "national unity" Cabinets continued to face the problem of harmonizing Cabinet positions with the views of the Lower House, and began considering again the problem of strengthening citizen identification with the policies of the state. In dealing with the former issue, Konoe showed an interest in capitalizing on the breakdown of party discipline to facilitate the Cabinet's dealings with the Lower House. He patronized men like Maeda, Nakajima, Yamazaki, and Nagai, for example, enhancing their prestige within the parties and weakening mainstream control and influence over the party membership. It seemed increasingly likely that if he ever formed a new government party, it would be dominated by the anti-mainstream figures of the parties rather than the established leadership.

Nevertheless, as the Ogikubo talks had demonstrated, even the anti-mainstream elements of the *kisei seitō* were by and large unprepared to restructure their parties to conform to the political and economic mobilization requirements of nonparty elites. While they were sympathetic to the idea of providing Lower House support for many Cabinet proposals of economic controls and military development in exchange for a share of Cabinet power, the anti-mainstream politicians were as yet uninterested in developing party organizations based on mass participation and control. This weakened their appeal somewhat to men such as Ishiwara and Asahara, and damned them as popular mobilization became a central aspect of the policies formulated by the coalition of forces under Prince Konoe. While Konoe himself seemed anxious to develop new institutions for the mobilization of the citizenry and the promotion of mass identification with the policies of his government, his sense of identity as a noble made him reluctant to become directly involved in any party organization. Moreover, he was deterred from involvement with the *kisei seitō* politicians by virtue of their insistence on maintaining their local alliances with the *meibōka* to insulate the public from all but the most perfunctory participation in the political process. Thus, despite his strategy of patronizing the anti-mainstream party leaders to facilitate the Cabinet's relations with the Lower House, there was little inducement for him to accede to their requests that he lead them in a new party organization. By simultaneously patronizing the anti-mainstream factions to this limited degree, and publicly abjuring any intention to form a new party against the mainstream leadership, Konoe hoped to retain what he regarded as an appropriate "noble" distance from the parties, while preserving a working relationship as premier with the Lower House.

Consequently, when the question of intensifying the degree of citizen participation in national affairs was raised in the early weeks of the Konoe government, the premier supported bureaucratic proposals for a "spiritual mobilization" drive conducted by official and semiofficial organizations rather than seeking the creation of a new party centered on incumbent Diet politicians. Konoe had long believed that the party-*meibōka* alliance was obsolete and detrimental to mass participation and control. As premier, his convictions in this regard were strengthened, and so long as the parties showed no interest in restructuring themselves, he seemed inclined to bypass them as agencies of popular mobilization whenever possible. Ultimately, therefore, the

131

fate of the parties in the "Konoe era" would hinge on whether they drastically revised their relationship to the local community as popular mobilization agencies, and, if they did not, whether Konoe could overcome their residual national and local influence through the creation of new organs of mass mobilization.

CHAPTER IV

Parties and the Politics of Mobilization: The Challenge of the Reform Movement, 1937–1938

INTRODUCTION

THE context of elite competition for power under the Konoe government was defined by two issues: the debate over plans to transform Japan's economy and polity into systems consonant with the concept of a national defense state, and the problems of fighting and ending the war in China. Both issues commanded attention throughout the government's existence. However, the first remained the focal point of political conflict from June 1937 to April 1938; the second became dominant thereafter, and emerged as the key problem of the Cabinet until Konoe's resignation in January 1939.

During the first half of the Konoe government's rule, the compromises reached among various nonparty elite groups over the five-year plan were translated into a series of official policy proposals. Planners in the Army and the Cabinet Planning Board formulated specific programs for pervasive state ownership, management, and development of essential enterprises. They indicated that a powerful organ of mass mobilization would be necessary to channel the economic and spiritual energies of the citizenry towards the implementation of a new system of state to fulfill Japan's international objectives. However, the Army Ministry's leadership refused throughout this period to endorse Ishiwara's plans for a new dictatorial political party to overcome opposition to the national defense state concept and administer economic policies of control locally. Indeed, the

133

divorce between Ishiwara and the senior leaders of the Army grew as their disagreement over how to handle the hostilities in China became superimposed on their differing approaches to domestic political and economic reform. As Ishiwara was gradually eased out of a position of influence, the official Army political strategy continued to focus on preserving the coalition embodied in the Cabinet, and eschewed direct involvement in organizing political movements for domestic reform.

Nevertheless, beneath the top leaders of the ministry (i.e., the Army minister, vice minister, and chief of the Military Affairs Bureau), Ishiwara's supporters and other officers less sensitive to the niceties of compromise were anxious to patronize, if not organize, political supporters of their military and economic policies. They found a wide variety of groups who were also committed to political struggle against the forces that sought to obstruct the complete implementation of the Army's national defense state concept. Right-wing politicians competing for Diet seats sought to shatter the power of the parties' allies—*meibōka* in the villages and businessmen who funded party activities—by attacking the social and economic bases of their influence. Bureaucrats wishing to extend the hand of national authority into the village sought to undermine local and Diet resistance through attacks on the customary and legal prerogatives of their opponents. Representatives of urban labor and tenant farmers hoping to revise ownership-labor and landlord-tenant relationships advocated fundamental reforms of capitalism and the political system in the name of national defense. Indeed, all of these political forces sought to use the national policy of achieving Japanese preeminence in East Asia and liberation from dependence on the Western powers as a rallying point for the political mobilization of mass groups against established systems and holders of political and economic control.

These challenges had been faced squarely by the parties and their allies during the Hirota and Hayashi governments;

and they had been repelled with considerable success by relying on the institutional powers of the Lower House, the economic clout of big business, and the pervasiveness of traditional authority in the local community. At the national level, however, the parties' leadership and the representatives of big business came to accept the inevitability of some modifications in the political, economic, and social systems to mobilize the limited resources of the nation on behalf of the established foreign policy goals of autonomy and preeminence in East Asia. As demonstrated by Ikeda Seihin's participation in the compromises of early 1937, and the swelling strength of anti-mainstream party forces in the Lower House, there was a growing inclination by the opponents of radical institutional reform to seek accommodation with the Army and other "reformists," while limiting the extent of the reforms. The coalition assembled under Konoe in June 1937 represented an uneasy agreement between those who wished to reform Japan's institutions to strengthen her international autonomy, and those who wished to preserve and expand Japan's national strength by maintaining, so far as possible, her existing institutions and ties with the West.

While the potential for severe conflict in the Cabinet was considerable, the government's proposal for a citizens' savings campaign and reduced consumption showed the emergence of a consensus on the need for some form of popular mobilization to underwrite the nation's foreign policy and its ambitious plans for economic and military development. However, the careful structuring of the June 15 Cabinet meeting had demonstrated the limits of that consensus. The government thus had before it three difficult tasks to accomplish in order to preserve the coalition on which it stood. First, it must make a final decision on the specific contents of the five-year plan and attendant reform program. Second, in view of the unhappy experiences of the two preceding Cabinets, it must develop a strategy for gaining the consent of the Lower House parties and their backers for imple-

135

menting the five-year plan. Finally, it must decide if mass political mobilization against the opponents of the government would be necessary, or whether a nonpartisan mobilization campaign directed towards obtaining citizen cooperation with national policies would suffice for the achievement of the Cabinet's objectives. The government had decided on June 15 to deal cautiously with the Diet, and to eschew any political mobilization. The question remained, however, whether Konoe and the Army would retain this strategy in face of the anticipated bitter opposition to the five-year plan and related reform proposals when they were ultimately presented for the Diet's consideration.

The parties thus occupied a pivotal position in the political planning of the new Cabinet. Party members were themselves divided along the same lines of thinking about Japan's foreign policy and domestic mobilization as the rest of the political elite groups. Many found themselves torn between their roles as representatives of particular interest groups—local community leaders, local entrepreneurs, big business—and their own perception of the desirability of political and economic reform. Moreover, they had their own particular political problems: the weakening of party discipline, their loss of power in the Cabinet and prestige at the national and local levels, the decline of their importance as arenas of mediating elite conflict, the challenges to their function as links between the citizenry and the state. As the parties sought to regain their former positions of prominence, their behavior was vitally affected by these national issues and political problems.

Contrary to the expectations of most political leaders, however, the outbreak of small-scale hostilities in Peking on July 7, 1937, escalated into a major war. Until April or May 1938, the government leadership remained convinced that the hostilities would quickly be terminated through the efficacy of Japan's armed forces; thereafter, optimism · faded and the war superimposed a new set of factors on the framework of political competition and debate over domestic reform. During the first half of the Konoe Cabinet's tenure in office, the war had the primary effect of intensifying the desire of proponents of the national defense state to execute their reform plans. It provoked new and sweeping "reformist" attacks on *kisei seitō* influence in the Lower House, private enterprise and profits in the economic system, and "irrational" patterns of local mobilization under traditional community leaders. By the same token, it stirred the desire of many Diet members, businessmen, and local leaders to cooperate more closely with the government while the nation was at war.

Throughout this period, the political parties found themselves excluded from significant positions of power in the Cabinet, but still very much in control of the Lower House. Their chauvinism and patriotic response to the outbreak of hostilities in China, and their internal weaknesses, made them highly susceptible to pressures from the government to accept hitherto distasteful legislative proposals. They offered no opposition whatsoever to the huge supplementary military budgets requested in two special Diet sessions during the latter half of 1937, and enacted major pieces of "reformist" legislation during the 73rd regular Diet session in early 1938. Some historians have therefore concluded that their actions in this period "served to accelerate the deterioration of the Diet into a body that merely formalized government decisions."[1] The fact remains, however, that the parties waged a staunch defense of their prerogatives and the authority of the Diet. As the legislative battles of the 73rd Diet session demonstrated, their internal weaknesses made them vulnerable to Cabinet pressure, but not to the point of surrendering abjectly to the whims of the government. They extracted significant concessions from the government during these debates, and remained ardent and successful defenders of their allies in the village and business world. Their continuing vigor was indirectly but viv-

[1] Misawa and Ninomiya, "The Role of the Diet and Political Parties," p. 334.

137

idly attested to by the renewed determination of many "reformist" groups following the 73rd Diet session to undermine and supplant the power of the existing parties with a new organ of political mobilization.

The period from June 1937 to April 1938 was one in which the parties remained on the defensive in political competition with other elite groups, but fought rather effectively to prevent a further diminution of their influence. It was also a time in which Japan's attention abroad shifted slowly, but clearly, from a primary concern with building up the nation's military capabilities against the Soviet Union to meeting the demands of long-term, full-scale fighting in China. As the months from April 1938 to January 1939 would demonstrate, the shift in these concerns had a direct bearing on the persistence of party influence. The Konoe Cabinet's responses to the war in China, the demands of the "reformists," and the government's encounters with the Diet thus form a crucial episode in the account of the parties' role in early Shōwa politics.

The Konoe government came to power wanting to implement the delicate compromises on industrial development that had been worked out over the past year. The Cabinet was resolved to end the "Incident" in North China as quickly as possible, and return to the business of expanding Japan's industrial production and military strength. Although initially disposed to settle the Incident locally, the Cabinet soon shifted to the view that the complete defeat of Chiang Kai-shek would be a more efficacious means for the rapid solution of the troubles in China. Konoe explained that "after consultations with the Army minister, we came to believe that if we dispatched troops quickly in a demonstration of Japan's firm intention to fight, Chinese resistance would undoubtedly crumble."[2] Thereafter, the government

[2] Nashimoto Sukehira, *Chūgoku no naka no Nihonjin* (Tokyo: Dōseisha, 1969), p. 174.

repeatedly affirmed a policy of attack in China, with the confidence that Japan's troops could readily defeat the armies of the Kuomintang and Chinese Communist Party. The Cabinet's policy resulted in a gratifying string of victories when executed in the field, culminating in the fall of Nanking on December 13, 1937. It did not, however, lead to Chiang's capitulation.

Thus, between mid-December and early January 1938, the government was obliged to reexamine its China policy. Polling the views of his ministers and other responsible officials, Konoe learned that, with the exception of the Army General Staff, most leaders believed a continued war of annihilation might yet result in the early victory anticipated by the government. With the encouragement of the Diet parties and a vocal right-wing movement, the Konoe government resolved to press on with the attack. On the other hand, General Staff planners sharing the concerns of Ishiwara Kanji argued that war would become protracted if a truce were not declared. They feared that a long war against China would disrupt the five-year plan for industrial development and expansion of military supply industries, leaving Japan's northern flank vulnerable to Soviet attack. In the weeks following the fall of Nanking, therefore, Konoe embarked on a series of maneuvers designed to overcome the reluctance of the General Staff to continue the war.

Dealing with the General Staff was only one of Konoe's important political tasks at the end of 1937. A second problem was overcoming the long-standing Diet opposition to legislation that would be essential for the execution of the five-year industrial development plans. The Cabinet decided in early June to convene a special session of the Diet on July 23 to act on proposals related to these plans, and Konoe recalled the turmoil that had accompanied the previous Diet session. In light of this unsettling recollection, the premier gave every indication of approaching the forthcoming confrontation with the Diet extremely cautiously.

139

Konoe also publicly disassociated himself from any challenge to the existing parties by a new party; and on June 22, he announced that the parliamentary vice minister and councillor system would be reinstated.[3] These announcements were calculated to win the support of the majority of Dietmen who jealously defended their parties and their privileges as legislators.

Once the special Diet session convened in late July, Konoe emphasized that the unstable situation in China required unified national support for the industrial development program within the parameters of Finance Minister Kaya's "three economic principles." He indicated that controversial measures relating to reform of the administrative machinery and parliamentary system would not be submitted during this session of the Diet. In turn, he urged the Diet to provide support for the limited number of proposals on which "deliberations were not completed in the past session and those on which immediate action is required." Among the thirty-five bills submitted to the Diet were proposals to establish a Ministry of Health and Social Welfare, a special tax to finance military activities in North China, and a number of economic and financial measures required as the prologue to the five-year industrial development program. The Diet's patriotic response to Konoe's appeal was total. Following the unanimous approval of a resolution condemning "anti-Japanese forces in China who ignore the principles of international faith," the Diet quickly approved thirty-four of the thirty-five bills, including a controversial "Iron and Steel Manufacturing Law" that had been rejected during the previous session. On September 9, the 72nd Special Diet session was convened, and it, too, responded with strong support for the government's policies by voting a 2.2-billion-yen extraordinary grant for the military effort in China. This was a generous allocation, considering that the

[3] On the parliamentary vice minister and councillor system, see Misawa and Ninomiya, "Role of the Diet," pp. 323–24.

140

total national budget for 1937–1938 had previously been set at 2.77 billion yen.[4]

Konoe's success in avoiding confrontations with the special Diet sessions was a result of his prudence in submitting mild legislation for debate, his conciliatory attitude on the "new party" question, and the Diet's willingness to provide financial support for Japan's fighting men in times of war. Konoe appreciated the Diet's cooperation, but knew it would not extend to sanctioning the broad administrative reform programs embodied in the five-year industrial development program his government intended to introduce soon. He therefore sought new sources of leverage to coax the Diet in the forthcoming 73rd regular session (December 25, 1937–March 30, 1938), and to check the obstreperous opposition of the General Staff to the government's China policies. With these objectives in mind, Konoe appointed Admiral Suetsugu Nobumasa on December 14 to replace the dying Baba Eiichi as home minister. Suetsugu was an ardent supporter of the war in China, and greatly admired by many of the vociferous anti-liberal and anti-British elements who had terrorized Court officials, business leaders, and conservative politicians throughout the 1930s. His appointment was aimed at providing additional Cabinet leverage against the General Staff and the Lower House, and in this regard he proved to be an ideal selection. Since the admiral was a bitter critic of the parties, his appointment had direct bearing on the forthcoming Diet session. In view of the home minister's ability to intervene in elections, party men would be likely to avoid a showdown with the government in order to avoid a dissolution of the Diet and another general election under hostile Home Ministry supervision. Suetsugu thus strengthened Konoe's hand in dealing with opponents of reform in the Diet. The new home minister also lent weight to the Cabinet's battle against the Army

[4] Shiraki, *Nihon seitō shi*, pp. 250–51; and Tōgo Shiba, ed., *Japan-Manchoukuo Year Book, 1938* (Tokyo: Jyapan-Manchukō nenkansha, 1938), pp. 89–92.

General Staff. In a barely disguised threat to bring the right wing into the streets, Suetsugu warned the General Staff that the Japanese people would not accept a generous peace in the wake of the sacrifices paid by their sons on the battlefields of China. He was sharply critical of the General Staff's failure to press the attack in China with greater vigor to bring Chiang to his knees in surrender.[5]

Predictably, however, Suetsugu was not content to confine his activities to the Cabinet level. At precisely the moment when Konoe brought him into the government, he was engaged in a series of discussions with a number of prominent right-wing leaders to coordinate the diverse efforts of right-wing groups into a concerted attack against the *kisei seitō* grip on the Diet. Working through Akiyama Teisuke, Miyazaki Ryūsuke, and Akita Kiyoshi, the doyens of the right wing aroused demands that "the root of evil—opposition within the country—be eradicated, and political parties opposing each other be eliminated, to unite Japan on the principle of emperor-centered politics." On December 16, the right-wing leaders issued a public statement, formally calling for "the amalgamation of all political parties into one, and the formation of a powerful new political organization."[6]

[5] Kazami Akira, *Konoe naikaku* (Tokyo: Nihon shuppan kyōdō kabushiki kaisha, 1951), pp. 77–78 and 95–96; Hata Ikuhiko, "Nit-Chū sensō no gunjiteki tenkai," in Nippon kokusai seiji gakkai, Taiheiyō sensō genin kenkyūbu, ed., *Taiheiyō sensō e no michi*, IV (Tokyo: Asahi shinbunsha, 1963), 36 (hereafter cited as NKSG, IV).

[6] The term "right wing" has been used here to allude to those groups referred to as "*uyoku dantai*" by the Justice and Home Ministries. See, for example, Hōmushō kōan chōsachō, *Senzen ni okeru uyoku dantai no jōkyō* (4 vols., Tokyo: Naikaku insatsu-kyoku, 1964–1967), which is based on Justice Ministry reports, or the annual volumes of Home Ministry police reports, such as *Shōwa 12–nen–chū ni okeru shakai undō no jōkyō*. On certain occasions, the term also refers to men prominently associated with these groups, or with efforts to consolidate and unify right-wing groups. See Imai Seiichi and Itō Takashi, eds., *Kokka sōdōin (2)* (Gendai shi shiryō XLIV) (Tokyo: Misuzu shobō, 1974), 3–4 for the December 16 statement. For an

The motivations behind this summons were as variegated as the political philosophies of the men who issued it. One element of the right-wing movement, the "Japanists" or "idealist right wing" (*kannen uyoku*), rejected the competitive party system and the electoral process as nothing more than institutions and practices imported from the West. "Japanist" groups during the 1937 election refused to compete for seats in the Diet, or even to vote, for fear of falling into the "vortex of democracy." A system in which the Diet was perpetually cast in an adversary's role vis-à-vis the emperor's ministers was, to them, incompatible with the natural harmony presumed to exist between the throne and its subjects. In lieu of competing with the parties for control of the Diet, they sought an imperial prohibition of political parties, and a "drastic amendment of the election law" that would "return" the right to choose Diet members to the emperor.[7] Consequently, they wished to abolish all competitive parties, and establish a new monolithic force in the Lower House under their own leadership, dedicated to manifesting a harmonious relationship with the government. As in the 1920s, the chief spokesman for this viewpoint was Baron Hiranuma, currently president of the Privy Council.

A second cluster of right-wing activists, the "reform right wing" (*kakushin uyoku*), was also bitterly opposed to the influence of the parties, but deemed it proper to compete with them for seats in the Lower House during the 1937 election. In fact, this group hoped to achieve a monopoly of power in the Lower House in order to execute a series of radical political and administrative reforms, bringing Japan closer to the Nazi and fascist models of the totalitar-

analysis of right-wing schisms between 1936 and 1938, see Kinoshita Hanji, "Kokumin shugi undō no gen-dankai," *Chūō kōron*, #615 (December 1938), pp. 213–23. See also Itō Takashi, "The Role of Right-Wing Organizations in Japan," in Borg and Okamoto, eds., *Pearl Harbor as History*, pp. 487–509.

[7] Naimushō keiho-kyoku, *Shōwa 12–nen–chū ni okeru shakai undō no jōkyō* (Secret), December 20, 1938, pp. 258–59.

ian state. Men such as Nakano Seigō, whose million-member Tōhōkai affected black shirts in imitation of European fascists, Colonel Hashimoto Kingorō, who had planned several coups d'état at the beginning of the 1930s, and Admiral Suetsugu himself were among the most prominent members of this segment of the right wing.[8]

Although these two forces in the right-wing movement sought throughout the 1930s to unite, and their ideology and policy goals at times overlapped, their common ground was by and large limited to an antipathy for the parties. The China Incident, however, provided a new seductive banner under which to march in quest of right-wing unity and the abolition of the *kisei seitō*; and it was in pursuit of these two objectives that right-wing leaders agreed in December to launch the drive for a new, monolithic political force. They were joined in this undertaking by dissident elements from the *kisei seitō* who opposed the mainstream control of their parties. A group of fifty-one Seiyūkai members urged the Seiyūkai to dissolve itself and call upon other party men to join it in the creation of a new party. This group and representatives of the Minseitō faction led by Tomita Kōjirō (who had earlier worked for the creation of a single-party system with Kuhara Fusanosuke), were in close liaison with the right-wing forces.[9]

Konoe's appointment of Suetsugu indicated his willingness to patronize the right-wing and anti-mainstream new party movements for the twofold purpose of strengthening the Cabinet's hand in negotiations with the General Staff and reducing Diet opposition to legislation associated with the five-year industrial development plan. With Suetsugu's

[8] *Ibid.* Najita's study of Nakano rightly suggests that there were vast differences even among the figures of the "reformist" right wing. See Najita Tetsuo, "Nakano Seigō and the Spirit of the Meiji Restoration in Twentieth-Century Japan," in Morley, *Dilemmas of Growth*, pp. 375–421.

[9] Kuhara Fusanosuke-ō denki hensankai, ed., *Kuhara Fusanosuke*, p. 492.

active support, the Cabinet was able to override the views of the General Staff on January 14, and two days later, Konoe announced publicly that "the Japanese government will no longer deal with that government [Chiang's Nationalist regime] and it looks forward to the establishment and growth of a new Chinese regime."[10]

Once the General Staff had been stifled, Konoe turned to the problem of dealing with the Diet. The government planned to push through the industrial development plan by manipulating legislators' patriotism, their anxieties about the threat of dissolution, and their fears (or hopes) for the creation of a new political party dominated by the right wing. Prior to the opening of the Diet, Commerce and Industry Minister Yoshino indicated the outline of the government's strategy: "The Government takes the view that we should utilize the China Incident as an opportunity to make another decisive stride in Japan's industry and economy, and is desirous of obtaining some benefit for the future industrial and economic development of the country out of the emergency foreign trade control measure adopted in connection with the Incident."[11] The China Incident would be used domestically as justification for the establishment of policies related to the Cabinet's primary commitment— the execution of the policies discussed at the June 15 Cabinet meeting. Moreover, by encouraging the right wing's attack on the political parties and manipulating divisions within the parties, and by placing Admiral Suetsugu in command of the police and election apparatus, the government hoped the Lower House would be sufficiently intimidated to pass key reform measures related to the five-year plans.

The staggering weight of the Diet's agenda demonstrated the Cabinet's eagerness to use the China Incident and right-

[10] For an elaboration of events leading to this statement, see Crowley, *Japan's Quest*, pp. 365–75.

[11] Yoshino Shinji, "Our Planned Economy," *Contemporary Japan*, vi.3 (December 1937), 371.

145

wing agitation against the parties to push through as much legislation as possible related to the five-year plans. By the time the 73rd Diet convened on December 26, the government had decided on eighty-six major bills to be submitted for approval. Among them were two highly controversial measures, a previously rejected bill to establish state control over the electric power industry, and the national general mobilization bill.[12]

Once the Diet session opened, Konoe sought to win approval of the Cabinet's legislative package by appealing to parliamentarians' patriotism and sustaining rumors that he might form a new political party to shepherd the legislation through the Diet. In advancing this political strategy, Konoe found fertile soil in the chaotic internal conditions of the two major parties. The Minseitō remained under Machida's control, but Nagai's influence had been enhanced by his appointment as a Cabinet minister, and the Tomita group was still working actively against Machida on behalf of the one-party system proposed in December by the right-wing leaders. The war in China had the effect of encouraging Diet men of all parties to cooperate with the government; and this trend was particularly pronounced in the Seiyūkai, where the traditional Suzuki-Hatoyama policy of opposition to "national unity" governments was steadily undermined by defections among the anti-mainstream and junior members' ranks. The combination of Konoe's patronage of anti-mainstream Seiyūkai leaders and the war led to a dramatic growth in the prestige and influence of the Nakajima-Maeda group by December. Nakajima himself urged Konoe to form a new party, despite the assertion of Konoe's confidant, Kido Kōichi, that the premier was not interested in such a venture. Nakajima added that Japan should withdraw her troops from China immediately, in

[12] KF, I, 473; Shiraki, *Nihon seitō shi*, p. 256; Yoshida Kei, *Denryoku kanri-an no sokumen shi* (Tokyo: Kōtsū keizaisha shuppanbu, 1938), p. 29.

order to launch a preemptory attack on the Soviet Union.[13]
While Konoe was not inclined to accept Nakajima's foreign policies, he showed greater interest in the new party movement within the two major parties. As the Diet considered the controversial bills presented by the Cabinet, Kido advised the premier to generate support by appearing interested in the new party plans of the Nakajima-Maeda group in the Seiyūkai and the anti-Machida forces in the Minseitō.[14] Konoe concurred, and gradually evinced a sympathetic attitude toward the new party advocates both in and out of the *kisei seitō*. He also continued to use the right-wing new party movement as an essential part of his strategy to undermine the position of the mainstream leadership in both major parties.

By February, Konoe's strategy had produced a dramatic incident. Throughout the early part of the month, Nakamizo Tamakichi, a former Seiyūkai bodyguard (*sōshi*), organized a group of several hundred toughs called the Bōkyō gokokudan with covert support from Konoe and Akiyama Teisuke of the right-wing new party movement.[15] Nakamizo was also supported in this effort by Asō Hisashi, secretary general of the Shadaitō. Once Japan's leading left-wing party, the Shadaitō by late 1937 could be described more accurately as composing one element of the "reformist right wing," and it was in close liaison with Akiyama, Konoe, and the right-wing party movement. Nakamizo and his cohorts were guided by plainclothesmen from the Home Ministry police to the homes of Seiyūkai and Minseitō mem-

---

[13] Kido, *Kido Kōichi nikki*, I, 607 and 610 (diary entries of December 1 and December 16, 1937). See also Watanabe, *Kyojin Nakajima Chikuhei*, p. 334.

[14] SKS, VI, 229–31.

[15] For a full account of Nakamizo's activities, see Aoki Yasuzō, *Nanajū-nen o kaerimite*, ed. Asakura Yūji (Hachioji-shi: Aoki Hiroyuki, 1970), *passim*, especially pp. 122–80; and Itō Takashi, "Shōwa jūsan-nen," pp. 149–55.

bers, where they intimidated the parliamentarians to sign petitions favoring the formation of a new party. Konoe noted to Baron Harada that ninety Seiyūkai members had signed the petitions by February 16, and indicated that they were all supporters of the Cabinet's legislative package.[16] Since this showing was deemed inadequate, Nakamizo led his group into the party headquarters of the *kisei seitō* on February 17, and announced that his men would not withdraw until the parties had taken further positive action on the campaign to dissolve their parties. While Nakamizo's gang was prevented from remaining in the Minseitō quarters, they remained in the Seiyūkai offices well into the night before the police arrested them.

Unlike many of the frequent attacks on the parties during the 1930s, the Nakamizo Incident could not be written off simply as another quixotic explosion of right-wing hostility towards party influence. The behavior of the police indicated some collusion between Nakamizo and Suetsugu, despite the wholesale arrests and the home minister's denial of ever having known Nakamizo.[17] The Seiyūkai immediately recognized Nakamizo's relationship to the one-party system movement, and expelled two party members from Kuhara's old faction for collaborating with him. There was abundant evidence of Nakamizo's links to Akiyama and the movement to fuse the nonparliamentary right-wing groups together with the Shadaitō, Kokumin dōmei, Tōhōkai, and the one-party system advocates of the *kisei seitō* into a new party led by Konoe. Funds for the incident were evidently obtained through the premier himself, for when Harada asked Konoe on February 22 about assisting Nakamizo, Konoe could only reply lamely, "We certainly did not think he would use the funds for that purpose, but it is true that Kazami [Chief Cabinet Secretary Kazami Akira, a former

[16] SKS, VI, 229–31.

[17] *Ibid.*, p. 240. Aoki Yasuzō claims Suetsugu later apologized for the denial in a face-to-face confrontation with Nakamizo. See Aoki, *Nanajū-nen o kaerimite*, p. 154.

member of the Kokumin dōmei] and I gave him a bit of money."[18] To Konoe's chagrin, however, the Nakamizo affair only hardened opposition to the Cabinet's bills among conservative Diet members. Ostensibly suffering from a sudden and convenient cold, Konoe took to his sickbed to avoid the parliamentary fight looming ahead, while Saitō Takao of the Minseitō and Makino Ryōzō of the Seiyūkai led the Lower House attack on the national general mobilization bill.[19]

REFORM LEGISLATION OF THE 73RD DIET

The general mobilization bill was the central plank in the national defense state platform. It represented the culmination of military and "revisionist" bureaucratic thinking about how to maximize the mobilization of the nation's resources for total war. In November 1937, when hopes for an early victory in China still ran high, the Cabinet reorganized the Planning Office into the Planning Board (*Kikakuin*), and directed that the new organ "become the axial point of national general mobilization, to deal not only with the current Incident but also with providing a rapid advance in national power after the Incident has been concluded."[20] Virtually the first official duty of the Planning Board was the formulation of the general mobilization bill.

This piece of legislation was designed to permit widespread government controls over men and materiel to assure the preparedness of the nation's defenses in "times of wars and incidents." The provisions of the bill fell into two categories: measures to be taken in times of war (and, accord-

[18] SKS, vi, 243; Aoki, *Nanajū-nen o kaerimite*, p. 157; Shiraki, *Nihon seitō shi*, p. 259; Kiya, *Seikai gojū-nen no butai-ura*, p. 205; Kamei, *Gojū-nen "gomu fūsen" o otte*, p. 27; Totten, *Social Democratic Movement*, p. 103.

[19] A *shikishi* signed and dated by Konoe at the Kuwana Restaurant suggests that the prince was only "politically" confined to his own residence. See Yoshino, *Shōkō gyōsei no omoide*, p. 370.

[20] KF, i, 473.

ing to the original bill, incidents), and those that might be taken in peacetime as preparatory steps for dealing with wartime conditions.[21] In the first category fell authorizations for government steps to adjust the supply, demand, and allocation of labor to maximize wartime production. The state was empowered to draft labor into war-related industries, control wages, and extend working hours where wartime conditions warranted such measures. It was also given the authority to control production, transportation, and the export and import of materials to balance international payments, to assure an adequate supply of war materials when the requirements of wartime production increased demand. The government could also control, use, or expropriate important buildings and land deemed necessary for wartime mobilization, and order private manufacturers to install new equipment or improve existing facilities to increase production. It could also restrict or prohibit installation of new facilities where such installation would draw goods, labor, or capital away from essential war-related productive activities. To establish control over the operation of vital industries and businesses in wartime, the government was empowered to force entrepreneurs into control associations and cartels, in which the state might have a voice in the control of overall productive policies. Strict controls over financial institutions, including the power to force banks to make loans for the creation or expansion of vital facilities, were also authorized under wartime conditions by the bill. Similarly, the government could restrict profiteering or provide profit incentives in commodity prices and freight charges and take other price control measures. Finally, the government was authorized to ban the holding of meetings and the publication of newspapers when deemed necessary in wartime.

The bill also enabled the government to take several steps in peacetime to bolster the strength of the nation. The state

[21] *Ibid.*, pp. 473–74; Board of Planning, "On the National Mobilization Law," *Tokyo Gazette*, May 1938, pp. 1–9.

could register the professions and technical abilities of citizens, order schools and institutions to train additional technicians to meet anticipated wartime requirements, and direct employers to retrain their skilled workers. The government could also order manufacturers and businessmen to create peacetime reserve stocks of supplies that were essential in times of war, along lines that had already been established for the petroleum, iron, and steel industries by previous legislation. The government was also permitted under the bill to direct private businesses and research institutions to conduct experiments and research deemed vital to national defense. It could provide subsidies and profit incentives to producers of important materiel to stimulate production and expansion of facilities. Losses incurred by the enforcement of all of these measures were to be compensated by the government, in amounts to be determined by a mixed indemnity commission of officials and private representatives.

In view of the sweeping powers bestowed upon the government by this bill, many historians have regarded it as an essential instrument in converting the Japanese government into a dictatorship.[22] However, while it certainly strengthened governmental controls over citizens' lives, the struggle over its enactment revealed the continuing viability of the "limited pluralism" characterizing Japanese elite politics. And even before the bill reached the floor of the Lower House, it was obvious that the parties would have a considerable voice in determining how and when general mobilization would take place.

When discussed in Lower House committee on the first two days of February, the wartime provisions of the bill were bitterly attacked by party representatives. One parliamentary criticism was that if the proposed law were not to be invoked during the current Incident, it was unnecessary.

[22] See, for example, Asada Mitsuteru, "Kokka sōdōin-hō," in Kyoto daigaku bungaku-bu kokushi kenkyū-shitsu, ed., *Nihon kindai shi jiten*, pp. 202–203.

(This remark suggests that as early as the beginning of February, the government had intimated its willingness to postpone the implementation of the wartime sections until a resolution of the China Incident had cleared the way for refocusing the nation's energies on the five-year plans. This, in turn, suggests that the government's primary objective in submitting the bill was to deal with the five-year plans, rather than the China Incident.) Others complained that under the bill too many measures were left to governmental discretion, particularly the authority to ban meetings and the publication of newspapers. A further argument against the bill was raised by those who cited the danger of leaving the decision of when and how to invoke the law in the hands of bureaucrats alone. In response to these Lower House criticisms, the government withdrew the bill for emendation. When the Cabinet approved it for resubmission on February 19, the articles related to banning meetings and newspapers' publication had been struck from the text, and consideration was given to creating a nonbureaucratic commission to be consulted whenever the law was to be invoked.[23]

By the time the bill was submitted to the full session of the Diet, its opponents were most concerned by the fact that the bill would allow the government to institute sweeping wartime controls by imperial ordinance (*chokurei*), rather than by obtaining prior Diet approval for each measure it wished to institute. In an attempt to protect the legislative authority of the Diet, the opposition advanced the unique argument that the Diet lacked the authority to consider the bill. Saitō rose first to question the constitutionality of the mobilization proposal. He pointed out that the second chapter of the Constitution carefully defined the rights and duties of subjects; Article xxxi provided that these rights and duties were subject to change only by the invocation

[23] KF, i, 474–75.

of imperial authority during times of national crisis or war.[24] In other words, Saitō continued, the only way a subject's rights and duties could be limited as the mobilization bill sought to limit them was through imperial command (*tennō no meirei*) in times of war. The Diet, therefore, had no constitutional authority to limit these rights and duties through the passage of laws such as the mobilization bill. If the Lower House attempted to claim competence to consider the bill, Saitō concluded, it would violate the sacred imperial prerogative.

Makino Ryōzō took Saitō's argument one step further. He noted that the mobilization bill proposed would be limited to times of war or national emergency. However, he cautioned, only the emperor had the authority to ascertain when such conditions existed, and if the Diet were to decide by legal action to invoke a national mobilization law, this would imply the Diet's right to usurp the emperor's prerogative in deciding war or peace. Ikeda Hideo of the Minseitō added his view that in war or peace, decisions about national mobilization must be made by the emperor rather than the Diet. In short, opponents of the mobilization bill attempted to block its passage through the Diet by denying the legal competence of the Diet to deal with the bill. Saitō, Makino, and Ikeda all argued explicitly that the questions of war and national mobilization and the limitation of citizens' rights or duties could be dealt with only by the throne.

The government's adversaries in the Lower House had now raised the shield of the Constitution and imperial sovereignty against the Cabinet's challenge to the Diet's prerogatives. This was a highly effective technique for the

[24] Article xxxi read: "The provisions contained in the present chapter [on the rights and duties of subjects] shall not affect the exercise of the powers appertaining to the emperor in times of war or in cases of national emergency." For a summary of the arguments put forth against the mobilization bill, see Hasegawa Masayasu, *Shōwa kenpō shi* (Tokyo: Iwanami shoten, 1962), pp. 120–21.

153

opposition, and it was underscored by the counterthreat of a new party and government led by the mainstream leaders of both parties, with General Ugaki Kazushige and Ikeda Seihin.[25] These two men had been among the ten national leaders appointed by Konoe as Cabinet counselors in October 1937, and were increasingly apprehensive about the effects of the China Incident on Anglo-Japanese relations and the domestic economy. The possibility of an Ugaki-Ikeda Cabinet and a new party posed a serious threat to the government, and Konoe was obliged to come out from under his quilts to parry it. On March 2, the premier undermined his opponents' position by a combination of threats and compromises. Since much of Ugaki's strength rested on Saionji's personal confidence in him as a national leader, Konoe pointedly reminded Harada that the Army still nursed an intense dislike for Ugaki. He added that the young officers regarded opponents of the mobilization bill as Ugaki sympathizers. Konoe made it clear to the *genrō's* secretary that Saionji and the Court would have to support him and his government's program, or risk the possibility of Army-inspired terrorism against an Ugaki regime and a new party led by Ugaki or Machida Chūji.[26]

Turning to the Lower House, Konoe reassured the parliamentarians that the mobilization law would not infringe on the imperial prerogative to declare a national emergency. He agreed that the legislation contained in the bill under

[25] Plans for an Ugaki-Ikeda Cabinet appear in the diary of a close Ugaki confidant, Ōkura Kinmochi, under the entry for February 25, 1937. See *Ōkura Kinmochi nikki* (3 vols., Tokyo: Naiseishi kenkyūkai and Nihon kindai shiryō kenkyūkai, 1973–1974), III, 17. The alignment of political forces behind Ugaki mentioned here is also noted by Nomura Shigetarō as having developed by May or June 1938, but Ōkura's diary indicates earlier planning for the coalition. See Nomura Shigetarō, "Shintō undō o hadaka ni suru," *Chūō kōron*, #615 (December 1938), p. 239. For later manifestations of the same alignment, see Ōoka Jirō, "Kokumin saihensei ni odoru hitobito," *Nippon hyōron*, XIV.1 (January 1939), 173.

[26] SKS, VI, 252–53.

discussion could indeed be implemented by imperial decree in wartime, but stated that the government believed having the enabling legislation passed by the Diet as well would prove more faithful to the principles of constitutional government. He also attempted to differentiate between the Authorization Law that had just been passed in Germany, and the Japanese mobilization bill, pointing out that the latter could be invoked fully only under wartime conditions. The thrust of Konoe's remarks was that Japan was not now in a condition of "national emergency" or wartime, and that the mobilization legislation would only be invoked "in future wars, to be fought in ways difficult to predict and against enemies still unknown." The premier seemed to be saying, in other words, that the government would not invoke the mobilization law under present conditions. As a further concession to the fears over the Diet's surrender of its legislative prerogatives, Konoe indicated that members of both Houses would be represented on a National General Mobilization Council, to be consulted whenever the mobilization law was invoked.[27]

To further induce the mainstream leaders to accept his compromise offer, Konoe now renewed his professed interest in forming a new party of anti-mainstream elements or dissolving the Diet and conducting elections, as Suetsugu, Kazami, and Legislative Bureau Chief Taki Masao had advocated. On March 5, Konoe convened a "secret" meeting of the Cabinet. To heighten apprehensions that the meeting might have as its purpose the discussion of a new party under Konoe that would oppose the mainstream leadership, Konoe ordered Kazami to exclude the two party representatives in the Cabinet—Nakajima and Nagai—from the meeting. According to Arima Yoriyasu, Konoe argued at this meeting that unless the mobilization bill were quickly approved by the Diet, it could be passed only by dissolving the Diet and forming a new party, which Konoe would lead

[27] KF, I, 476–78.

to victory in the elections, and use to gain Diet approval for the bill.[28]

Details of the Cabinet meeting were soon leaked to the press and the recalcitrant parties, and Konoe's stratagem produced swift results. Within a week the Lower House agreed to approve the bill provided it could be assured of ample representation on the council. On March 16, Saitō Takao queried the government on this point, and Konoe replied on cue that nongovernment officials would compose more than a majority of the new organ's membership. With these assurances, and the threat of dissolution and a hostile Konoe-led party before them, the members of the two major parties gave their unanimous approval to the revised mobilization bill. The only objecting voice came from the disappointed Shadaitō "reformist" Nishio Suehiro, who insisted that Konoe should "more boldly point the way Japan must go, like Mussolini, like Hitler, and like Stalin!" Shocked at the suggestion that Japan might seek inspiration from Stalin, the Lower House immediately voted to expel Nishio from its membership.[29]

The mobilization bill then went to the Upper House, where the government finally and explicitly stated that the new legislation would not be invoked during the current China Incident. The Peers then approved the measure, and by March 24, it had surmounted its final parliamentary obstacles. On April 1, the National General Mobilization Law was formally decreed, and on May 3, the General Mobilization Council of fifty men, including thirty from the two Diet Houses, was established.

The Mobilization Law was unquestionably a major piece of enabling legislation, which transformed the relationship of the Cabinet to the Diet during the next eight years. It has been argued that the passage of this law "signaled the end of Diet authority in legislative matters: the role of the

[28] *Ibid.*, pp. 478–79; Arima, *Seikai dōchūki*, p. 141; SKS, vi, 245 and 253.

[29] KF, i, 478–79.

parties and the Diet in Japanese policy making had reached its lowest ebb."[30] While it did not specifically repudiate the constitutional authority of the Diet to authorize budgets and other legislative proposals, it would reduce the institutional role of the parliament in sanctioning wartime-related measures in a wide variety of areas. By the same token, however, the government was constitutionally entitled to declare a state of "national emergency" to enact mobilization by decree. In seeking the Diet's mandate instead, the government had made what appeared to be two important concessions in return for carte blanche in wartime. The first concession was an agreement to create a National General Mobilization Council in which sixty percent of the members would be from the Diet. This assured the parliament of a continuing voice in mobilization policy, though the council's advisory powers limited its leverage vis-à-vis the Cabinet. The second, and more important, concession stemmed from the government's assurance that the Mobilization Law was only to be invoked under wartime conditions, and not to deal with the China Incident. This concession had the effect of deferring invocation of the law, and of charging each decision to invoke it with a debate over whether conditions at the time constituted "wartime conditions." As the China Incident became a growing drain on the nation's resources during 1938, and the military became increasingly impatient to get on with the tasks of creating a national defense state, this concession became an important political issue. Had the China Incident not continued to escalate in 1938, it is difficult to estimate when or whether the "wartime" section of the National Mobilization Law could have been actually invoked to implement the five-year plans.

The other major item of the Cabinet's immense legislative package was the bill to establish state management over facilities for the generation and transmission of electric

[30] Misawa and Ninomiya, "The Role of the Diet and Political Parties," p. 339.

power.[31] All parties to the debate over its enactment agreed that its significance lay in the presumption that it would set the pattern for future settlements between the conservative advocates of preserving the capitalist system of enterprise to maximize Japan's national strength, and the reformist view that greater state control of the economy—approximating national socialism—was required to mobilize the energies and resources of the empire in times of national crisis. While debate over the bill was thus of particular concern to the power companies and the technocrats devising a new approach to enhancing productive power, it reflected a broader conflict of interests and opinions throughout the political and economic world.

At one extreme, military advocates of state control over essential enterprises insisted that the state must assume the ownership and management rights over the electric power industry. At the other end of the argument, the electric power companies' cartel organization, the *Denryoku renmei* (Power Company Federation), sought to preserve private ownership and management rights within the limits of public policy under which the cartel had been chartered. Okumura Kiwao, the "revisionist" bureaucrat from the Communications Ministry most directly concerned with the issue, was willing to give conditional recognition to the principle of private ownership, but complained that the freedom to pursue profits had led to monopoly capitalism.[32] Rejecting the classical liberal belief in laissez faire and the inviolability of private ownership, Okumura and other "revisionists" wished to place primacy on the interests of the state, rather than the individual entrepreneur, and to circumscribe the prerogatives of ownership by the superior

[31] The following discussion of this bill is based on Yoshida, *Denryoku kanri-an no sokumen shi*, "Nagai Ryūtarō" hensankai, ed., *Nagai Ryūtarō*, pp. 362–425, and Hashikawa Bunzō, "Kakushin kanryō," in Kamishima Jirō, ed., *Gendai Nihon shisō taikei, X: Kenryoku no shisō* (Tokyo: Chikuma shobō, 1965 and 1967), pp. 251–73.

[32] Hashikawa, "Kakushin kanryō," in Kamishima, *Kenryoku no shisō*, p. 265.

right of the state to control national resources for mobilization. His formula for this approach was to permit the continuation of private ownership of the power companies, but to place their management under state control. However, other officials, notably Communications Vice Minister Hirazawa Kaname, opposed the imposition of more than perfunctory state powers of supervision over the electric power industry, and placed greater emphasis on stimulating power production through incentives to private industry.

Diet members not only had to consider these issues, but specific political questions as well. For example, rural representatives leaned towards supporting the bill because it promised to consolidate urban and rural power districts, thereby reducing the costs of electricity in the countryside. By contrast, many Lower House representatives had close ties with the power companies, and had received strong financial backing in exchange for parliamentary support of the companies' water rights. Other members had been bureaucrats, and regarded the issue from the viewpoint of administrative efficiency. While the *kisei seitō* found themselves divided internally over the bill, the Shadaitō gave it strong support as a step towards socialism.

The form of the legislation finally presented to the Diet in early 1938 had gone through several commissions within and outside of the government, and though it was still staunchly opposed by the companies, it had been tailored to minimize their opposition and the opposition of their Diet supporters. The legislation provided for the establishment of a state-run Electric Power Generation Company (*Nippon hassōden kabushiki kaisha*) and an autonomous Electric Power Commission, comprised of private industry executives, to check "monopolistic excesses" by the company. The state company was to engage in the expansion of power production, and private companies were to transfer to it a variety of facilities in exchange for compensation at a rate to be determined by the government and the private owners jointly or, in the absence of agreement, by the state itself. A special law was to be enacted to protect

159

the rights and interest of debenture holders who secured the electric power facilities destined for transfer to the state-run company.

In the Lower House committee considering the legislation, further revisions were made to minimize the challenge to private ownership. Existing companies were to be permitted to manage their own affairs, under state direction (*kanri*), while the public company would be managed by the state and the commission. Despite opposition from the Shadaitō and Communications Minister Nagai, who criticized this step away from state controls, the revised bill then passed the Lower House by a vote of 236 to 81. The House of Peers took up the bill amidst charges that the legislation challenged constitutional guarantees of the inviolability of property rights and had a socialistic flavor. An Upper House committee further amended the procedures by which companies would be compensated for facilities transferred to the new state company. Private firms could be compensated now by simple reparations, rather than through the transfer of stock in the new company to their names. Moreover, the Upper House took issue with the method of determining the value of the facilities transferred. In the version of the bill approved by the Lower House, facilities would be evaluated on the basis of plant expenditures over the three years previous to transfer; the Upper House increased the compensation by basing it on the previous five years' expenditures. (Subsequently, a joint Upper House and Lower House committee set the figure on the basis of ten years' previous expenditures.) Finally, the Upper House struck from the bill the clause that would permit the government to have the ultimate authority to determine the value of the facilities transferred to the state company.

The same new party rumors and appeals to patriotism used by Konoe to gain party assent for the Mobilization Law were operative in propelling the Lower House towards a favorable decision on the electric power legislation. Meanwhile, Upper House opposition to passing the revised bill was checked by threats that Konoe would resign over the issue. Konoe retained considerable influence and a wide range of friendships in the Upper House from his twenty-year career in that body, and the possibility that the Peers might otherwise destroy his government contributed to their decision to approve the legislation. As predicted, the electric power legislation had major implications for subsequent attempts to transform the economic system from a capitalist orientation to one resembling national socialism. Despite the ultimate defeat of the private companies, they had won significant concessions. They were compensated handsomely for the facilities they surrendered to the new company. They retained a major voice in the affairs of the industry, both in the Power Commission and in the direction of the state company itself. Businessmen could now make a legitimate claim to direct access to new institutions of government, the state companies and commissions created to regulate industry and formulate industrial policy. The presidents of the Electric Power Generation Company were invariably drawn from the ranks of top company officials in the private sector of the industry. State controls had been approved, but in retrospect, the arrangements reached during the Diet debate over this particular legislation set a trend for making business cooperation and partnership an essential element in the operation of the wartime economy. Official controls on the business community remained lighter than over any other aspect of the economy during the war years. The political power of the business community and the parties had been somewhat, but not fatally, impaired by the reformist challenge during the 73rd Diet session.[33]

THE DRIVE FOR A NEW MASS PARTY

Assessments of the Diet session varied according to the political viewpoint of the observer. Education Minister Kido Kōichi wrote exultantly in his diary that the Diet had set a

[33] Tiedemann, "Big Business and Politics in Prewar Japan," p. 311.

new record for success by passing the eighty-six measures proposed by the government, as well as more than 110 items relating to the 1938–1939 budget.[34] However, the ability of the Diet to extract compromises from the government on key reform legislation invited the anger of powerful reformist groups in the Army, bureaucracy, and right wing. To them, the Diet's performance was ample demonstration of the need to create a powerful political mobilization organization against conservative party members and their allies locally and in the business world.

For example, immediately following the close of the Diet session, Agriculture and Forestry Minister Arima spoke as president of the National Federation of Industrial Guilds to the thirty-third general meeting of the organization about the need to become more involved in politics. Urging the guilds to abandon their traditional aloofness from political activity in order to support Konoe and his program, Arima lamented that

> I have just witnessed the debates of the Upper and Lower House, and while the Diet undoubtedly gave its careful consideration to the bills presented, and put on a show of affirming national unity and complete confidence in the government, its actual conduct represented a shocking departure from its words. Was that any way to support Konoe? In today's troubled times, the only way to help Konoe stay in office and stand his ground in implementing his plans is for those who truly wish to assist him to mobilize the power of the ordinary citizen. Just talking about national unity, or how great Konoe is, or how adroit his Cabinet is impedes, rather than assists, him when it comes to actual politics. . . . I urge you all as citizens to utilize the power of this great organization to ensure that the brilliance of Japan's national history is not stained at this moment.[35]

[34] Kido, *Kido Kōichi nikki*, ii, 632.

[35] Cited in Adachi Gan, *Kokumin undō no sai-shuppatsu* (Tokyo: Kasumigaseki shobō, 1940), pp. 14–16.

Arima went further privately; he and Chief Cabinet Secretary Kazami gave strong support to efforts by radical young members of the guilds' youth auxiliary (*Sangyō kumiai seinen renmei*, or *Sanseiren*) to create a new party and popular movement in support of reformist programs. Ultimately, Arima and Kazami hoped Konoe would assume the presidency of the new agrarian party.[36]

Some idea of the linkage made between the national defense concept and local reform issues may be gained by examining the platform of the party that emerged from Arima's April summons. The radical elements of *Sanseiren* established the *Nippon kakushin nōson kyōgikai* (Japan Reformist Agrarian Council, or *Kakunōkyō*) as a political party in October 1938. The new party's platform listed several concrete reforms it would support to enhance Japan's strength as a national defense state. Along with parroting the military demands for administrative reform and the "Japanist" plea for a "clarification of the national essence," the party's founders enumerated a number of changes in the economic system that should be effected by their party of "national unity." They included: 1) an overthrow of capitalism, and the creation of a new economic system based on the primacy of the public interest and cooperativism (*kyōdō shugi*);[37] 2) the liberation of workers from individual exploitation, and the establishment of a truly cooperative relationship between ownership and labor in enterprises; 3) solution of the land problem and increases in production

[36] It was, perhaps, such a new party that Arima had alluded to at the Cabinet meeting of June 15, 1937. See *supra*, p. 126. Arima's proposed party was to have as its chief administrative officers Adachi Gan and Toyofuku Yasuji (Arima's personal secretary). "Konoe Fumimaro-ate Kamei Kan'ichirō shokan sōkō," in Imai and Itō, eds., *Kokka sōdōin*, p. 575.

[37] The anticapitalism of the platform was aimed not only at urban capitalists, but no doubt as well at the economic foundations of the landlord-tenant relationship. For the preeminence of the economic aspects of that relationship over social aspects, see R. P. Dore and Tsutomu Ōuchi, "Rural Origins of Japanese Fascism," in Morley, *Dilemmas of Growth*, p. 185.

through the establishment of cooperatives as the basic organization of agrarian production; 4) a reduction in land taxes to enable the countryside to respond to the demands of long-term warfare; 5) state controls over financing, and an end to the monopoly of finance capital; and 6) strong controls over war profiteering and income derived from rents.[38]

Konoe never indicated any commitment to the agrarian party, but following the 73rd Diet session he did seem interested in promoting the formation of a new, mass-oriented reform party. While the Diet was in session, he had used the movement for a unified right-wing party to check Diet opposition to his government's proposals. Now, however, he extended special patronage to the new party plans developing under the auspices of one faction of the right wing, a group led by Akiyama Teisuke and Asō Hisashi. In April, he summoned Kamei Kan'ichirō (of Asō's faction in the Shadaitō) back from a European tour to join Akiyama and Asō in planning a new mass political party, and instructed Kamei to harmonize the Akiyama-Asō group's work with Arima's plans.[39] At least judging from his involvement with this group in April, it appeared evident that the premier shared the desire of other reformists for a new political support group to deal with the conservative opposition in the future. Konoe's interest in Akiyama's plans coincided with his exploration of a more conciliatory policy towards Chiang Kai-shek. Early in April, Konoe received the depressing news that the Nationalists had badly mauled Japanese forces in a battle at Taierhchuang. In the wake of this evidence of China's continuing resistance, Konoe became un-

[38] Adachi, *Kokumin undō no sai-shuppatsu*, pp. 92–93. For Arima's comment on *Kakunōkyō*, see Arima, *Seikai dōchūki*, pp. 186–88. Within months of its formation, the new party was rent by internal bickering, and was on the verge of collapse. See Naimushō keiho-kyoku, *Shōwa 14-nen–chū ni okeru shakai undō no jōkyō* (Secret), December 20, 1940, pp. 790–91.

[39] Imai and Itō, eds., *Kokka sōdōin*, pp. 573–75 and personal interview with Kamei Kan'ichirō, October 14–15, 1969, Tokyo.

certain about the possibility of a swift military victory. "Until recently," he confessed, "while I don't say I didn't appreciate the need for peace, I wasn't too wise, was I. . . . In fact Hirota and I were much too emphatic in calling for the downfall of the Chiang regime."[40] He thus began considering ways of revising the policy laid down in January under his guidance, and began to see merit in the General Staff's original argument that a full-scale war in China would interrupt defense preparations against the Soviet Union. Unless the war was quickly won, the nation's energies could not be focused on the five-year plans. The coalition and compromises of mid-1937 would collapse, bringing the government down with them. Throughout April, therefore, Konoe considered resigning or reshuffling his ministers to strengthen the Cabinet coalition, end the war, and get on with the industrial development program. Akiyama was Konoe's chief personal liaison with the Nationalist regime, as well as an advocate of forming a new "reformist" party. The premier's patronage of the Akiyama group thus indicated his growing desire to end the war quickly (even by negotiations with Chiang) and then use a new political party to overcome opposition to whatever future reforms would be required to implement the five-year plans.

Akiyama was a veteran politician and journalist, well known for his long-standing interest in China and for his behind-the-scenes political maneuvering (which earned him the sobriquet "the old man of Kōjimachi"). Early in his career, he had played a major role in gaining Japanese support for the revolutionary efforts of Sun Yat-sen, and had become associated with Konoe Atsumaro's movement for a pan-Asian federation linking Japan and China in a joint effort to end European influence in East Asia. Akiyama was not any stranger to new party movements, having taken part in the creation of the Dōshikai under Katsura Tarō.

[40] SKS, vii, 5–6 (entries of May 30 and June 3, 1938); John Hunter Boyle, *China and Japan at War 1937–1945: The Politics of Collaboration* (Stanford: Stanford University Press, 1972), pp. 137–43.

165

During the 1920s and 1930s, he retained his close connections with the Konoe family and the Chinese Nationalist movement. Indeed, shortly after the outbreak of the China Incident, Konoe and Akiyama had agreed to send Miyazaki Ryūsuke to Nanking as a personal emissary to facilitate the negotiation of a localized settlement of hostilities and lay the basis for a Sino-Japanese alliance. This effort failed when Miyazaki was seized and turned back by the *kenpeitai* (military police) in Kobe. Akiyama was simultaneously seized in Tokyo. After his release, he participated in the movement to unite the right wing and to form a new party, but by mid-1938 his close ties with the Chinese government prompted rumors among some of his erstwhile right-wing collaborators that he was actually a paid agent of Chiang Kai-shek. By August 1938, Akiyama's activities were so suspect that Home Minister Suetsugu—a former associate—ordered him placed under police surveillance.[41]

Akiyama's chief collaborators in mid-1938 included Asō and Kamei, who were prominent members of the Shadaitō. By 1937, Shadaitō representation in the Diet had grown to thirty-seven members, twice that of its 1936 strength. The increase in Shadaitō strength is often regarded as evidence of popular dissatisfaction with the growth of military influence during the mid-1930s;[42] but since it occurred precisely as the party was moving towards strong support of Army plans for a national defense state, this conclusion hardly seems warranted. The party continued moving to the right,

[41] SKS, vii, 157–59; KF, i, 405–406; Konoe Fumimaro, *Konoe Fumimaro-kō no shuki: ushinawareshi seiji* (Tokyo: Asahi shinbunsha, 1946), p. 13; letter of September 29, 1938 from Kamei to Konoe, in Imai and Itō, eds., *Kokka sōdōin*, pp. 14–21; Konoe Fumimaro, *Konoe Fumimaro shuki: heiwa e no dōryoku* (Tokyo: Nippon denpō tsūshinsha, 1946), p. 5. For additional biographical information on Akiyama, see Marius B. Jansen, *The Japanese and Sun Yat-sen* (Cambridge: Harvard University Press, 1954); Nomura Shigetarō, "Shintō undō o hadaka ni suru," p. 237; and Itō, "Shōwa jūsan-nen," pp. 14–41.

[42] For example, see Scalapino, *Democracy and the Party Movement*, pp. 383, 386–87.

and in October 1937, Kamei announced publicly that his party should no longer be regarded either as socialist or democratic.

Despite the party's electoral successes, Asō and Kamei agreed that the Shadaitō could not in the foreseeable future overtake either of the two major parties at the polls. Hence, they became interested in forming a new party, based firmly on the agrarian as well as the proletarian masses. If somehow the stranglehold of rural political control exercised by *kisei seitō*-oriented *meibōka* could be broken, they believed that the agrarian guild movement and radical elements of its youth auxiliary, the *Sanseiren*, could be forged into a powerful political force.[43] They optimistically believed that if the new party were led by Konoe, it would stand an excellent chance of becoming the preeminent force in the Diet.

What distinguished these new party plans from previous ones, however, was the fact that Akiyama, Asō, and Kamei aimed not at Diet supremacy alone but, in fact, at supplanting the Diet and much of the bureaucracy with a new organ that would become a vital part of the process of formulating and implementing national policies. The new party would consist not only of the usual group of Diet members, but a vanguard cell oriented towards ideology and political action, and a huge mass organization (*kokumin soshiki*) consisting of all existing major mass organizations: labor unions, agrarian guilds, *seinendan*, *Zaigō gunjinkai*, chambers of commerce, and so on. This mass base would provide political support for the party and government, and serve as the institutional network for the implementation of national policy locally. Kamei and Asō wished to take charge of the vanguard organ, which would lay down party ideology and programs for organizing the masses; the re-

[43] For one expression of these views, see Kamei's remarks in Kido nikki kenkyūkai (Oka Yoshitake), ed., *Kido Kōichi kankei monjo* (Tokyo: Tokyo daigaku shuppankai, 1966), p. 206 (hereafter cited as *Kido monjo*).

maining party posts and tasks, in their view, could be left for Akiyama and other politicians joining the new party. While Akiyama and Asō began to recruit *kisei seitō* and right-wing politicians, Kamei established a research team to devise party programs and organizational plans.[44]

Akiyama was assisted in his work by Akita Kiyoshi, the former speaker of the Lower House. Together, they worked through the summer trying to convince members of the Seiyūkai, Minseitō, and smaller parties and factions in the Diet to join the new party. They found an audience that was very much interested in the formation of a new Konoe-led party. Within both major parties, anti-mainstream groups were eager to form a new political force under Konoe, although they thought in terms of an elite, rather than mass, party. Strong interest was also evinced by smaller factions and parties in the Diet, who had little to lose by aggressively endorsing the party and the chance of gaining influence in the new organization. Indeed, these groups joined each other on May 16, 1938, to form the *Tōa kokusaku kenkyūkai*, an informal organization created to discuss and prepare for the creation of a new party led by Konoe. The Nakajima-Maeda faction of the Seiyūkai was the dominant force in the organization, but there were Minseitō representatives and members from the Shadaitō, Kokumin dōmei, Tōhōkai, and the old Shōwakai. Despite their common agreement on the desirability of a new party to oppose the mainstream leadership of the *kisei seitō*, these groups had great difficulty finding common ground on the issue of domestic and political reform. For instance, Ōishi Dai, a Tōhōkai member from Kōchi, reported that the *kenkyūkai* was split between those who favored an old-style political party, and those who favored a "reformist" party to spearhead major changes in the Diet and political system. Ōishi classified himself in the latter category, but complained that supporters of his view numbered only fifty com-

---

[44] Interview with Kamei, October 14–15, 1969; Itō, "Shōwa jūsan-nen," p. 157; Imai and Itō, eds., *Kokka sōdōin*, pp. 11–14.

pared to the Seiyūkai and Shōwakai advocates of the "status quo," who numbered around a hundred. He added that those of his persuasion looked to Home Minister Suetsugu as their leader, and the press reported that the admiral was indeed attempting to form a new party to carry out far-reaching political reforms.[45]

Suetsugu, of course, was one of the chief leaders of the movement to create a new party that would embrace the entire right wing and dominate, if not absorb, the other forces in the Diet. By late summer, however, he and Akiyama found themselves opponents, rather than allies as in late 1937 and early 1938. It is difficult to know precisely why the two men parted ways, but perhaps Suetsugu's adamant insistence on annihilating Chiang Kai-shek, and Akiyama's reputed sympathies with the Chinese Nationalists, had some bearing on their relationship. Moreover, Suetsugu was not convinced of the recent right-wing "conversion" of the Shadaitō, and therefore regarded Akiyama's alliance with Asō and Kamei as part of a "red" plot. At any rate, when Suetsugu sketched out his own thoughts on a new party in September, he noted that it should not include "unsavory political figures," an apparent reference to the Akiyama-Asō group. Their participation, in his view, would provoke the rest of the right wing to violent action, because of the socialistic background of Asō and Kamei. He added that the new party's rules and regulations should be care-

[45] Hōmushō kōan chōsachō, *Senzen ni okeru uyoku dantai no jōkyō*, p. 510; Nomura, "Shintō undō o hadaka ni suru," p. 237; Report from Kobayashi Mitsumasa (governor of Kōchi) to Home Minister Suetsugu, Army Minister Sugiyama, Navy Minister Yonai, and the Cabinet Information Commission Chief, May 17, 1938, *Kōjōhatsu*, #168 (Report of the Special High Police #168), entitled "Shintō mondai ni kansuru daigishi no ikō ni kansuru ken." This document is located in the Foreign Ministry Archives, Section 3 of *Honpō naisei kankei zassan*, which is listed in Cecil H. Uyehara, comp., *Checklist of Archives in the Japanese Ministry of Foreign Affairs, Tokyo, Japan, 1868–1945* (Washington, D.C.: Photoduplication Service, Library of Congress, 1954), p. 46, Classification number S1.5.0.0–1, continued.

fully defined to preclude anyone from mobilizing the party in support of any peace settlement with Chiang.[46]

The Akiyama group responded by planning to exclude Suetsugu from their new party. By early September, Akiyama and his associates seemed confident that out of the fluid situation obtaining among the parties and right wing, most of the Seiyūkai (excepting the Hatoyama mainstream faction) and a chunk of the anti-mainstream Minseitō would readily join *any* new party—mass-based or traditional-style—so long as Konoe agreed to lead it. In an effort to attract hesitant members of both major parties to his cause, Akiyama launched a massive propaganda campaign in early September, announcing through the Tokyo newspapers that the formation of the party was imminent. Posters were printed with Konoe's picture to announce the establishment of the party, and an inaugural speech drafted that would have the prince invite the leaders of all parties and factions to dissolve their organizations and join him in the establishment of the new, mass-based political party. September 16 was tentatively fixed for the public announcement of the new party's creation, and Asō prepared a list of party leaders for Konoe that designated the premier as party president and Akiyama as chief of the party's administrative section (*bakuryō-chō*). Representatives of all parliamentary groups were included in Asō's proposed roster of leaders, although in order to lure more *kisei seitō* men into the fold, the names of Asō, Kamei, and Akita did not appear. Asō was nevertheless slated to head the political section of the party, Kamei the propaganda section, and Akita the secretariat. Nakamizo Tamakichi was designated as the leader of an armed youth section.[47]

[46] KF, i, 568–69.

[47] "Arima Yoriyasu nikki," unpublished, entry for September 13, 1938. Access was gained to this important document through the good offices of Itō Takashi and Arima Yorichika. See also Nomura, "Shintō undō o hadaka ni suru," p. 238. A text of Konoe's proposed speech may be found in Kamei's unpublished papers, and a later allusion to

The ultimate political objective of the party was suggested by its formal name, *Dai-Nippontō-bu*. As one of its planners, Sugihara Masami, suggested, the word *bu* (or section) was appended to the name *Dai-Nippontō* (Great Japan Party) to parallel the word *gunbu* (military section of the government). The new party planners aimed at making the new party and the military the two basic components of a dictatorial government. Asō pressed Konoe to use the power of the state as premier to create a "national unity" party under the *Dai-Nippontō* banner, while Akita Kiyoshi recommended that Konoe and the Home Ministry apply pressures on the parties to dissolve as the prelude to the creation of a one-party system. Kamei likewise conceived of the *Dai-Nippontō* as the functional equivalent of dictatorial organizations like the Kyōwakai in Manchuria, and the proposed Shinminkai and Zenmintō in occupied China.[48]

The broad party policy proposals prepared by Kamei and his research group were heavily anti-capitalistic in orientation. As Kamei outlined his thinking to Konoe, the soundest way to resolve the ongoing China Incident was to create a system of cooperation between the peoples of the two nations. When Manchuria and her people were added to this system it would become an Oriental cooperative unit (*Tōyō kyōdōtai*)—the manifestation of a new East Asian Order. Cooperation could be achieved only when Japanese and

the printing of posters at this time is found in SKS, viii, 7. Further indication of the plans for the new party may be found in an undated letter from Asō to Konoe, reproduced from Kamei's papers in Imai and Itō, eds., *Kokka sōdōin*, pp. 82–84. The allocation of posts in the new party is also discussed in Kamei, *Gojū-nen "gomu fūsen" o otte*, p. 21, and KF, i, 566. See also Itō, "Shōwa jūsan-nen," p. 156.

[48] Interview with Sugihara Masami, February 10, 1969, Tokyo; Sugihara, *Atarashii Shōwa shi*, pp. 144–45; Itō, "Shōwa jūsan-nen," pp. 141 and 164; Imai and Itō, eds., *Kokka sōdōin*, pp. 14–21; and *Katō Yūsaburō-shi danwa sokkiroku* (Naiseishi kenkyū shiryō dai–76, 77, 78–shū) (Tokyo: Naiseishi kenkyūkai, 1969), p. 98.

171

Chinese nationalism were harmonized. Mōri Hideoto, a central figure on Kamei's research team, amplified this thesis by characterizing Japan's struggle in China as directed against "the control of China by international capitalism and communism and the submission of the Chiang regime to these forces." He added, however, that the invasion of China and the exploitation of newly occupied Chinese territory by Japanese capitalists was little different from the conduct of European and American capitalists. He stressed the importance of reaching a political accord among the peoples of Japan, China, and Manchuria through the *Tōyō kyōdōtai*, and warned that Japanese capitalists and bureaucrats who put economic concerns before these political problems would frustrate the efforts of Japan and China to create this accord. Sugihara, another of Kamei's associates, added that the principal obstacle in China to resolving the China Incident was the rush of Japanese private interest groups and individuals into newly occupied areas in quest of economic gain.[49]

The Kamei group thus held that Sino-Japanese cooperation could be achieved (and the China Incident resolved) only if Japanese capitalists were prevented from exploiting their continental neighbor. As Mōri pointed out, however, that exploitation was firmly rooted in the fact that Japan's domestic system was also based on capitalism.[50] There was no way to prevent Japanese capitalists from doing as they

[49] Imai and Itō, eds., *Kokka sōdōin*, pp. 14–21; Kamakura Ichirō (pseudonym for Mōri Hideoto), "Tōa kyōseitai kensetsu no sho-jōken," in Sugihara Masami, ed., *Nis-Shi jiken kara Tōa kyōdōtai kensetsu e* (Tokyo: Kaibō jidaisha, 1938), pp. 19–28. This book is an offprint of a collection of articles in the October 1938 issue of *Kaibō jidai*, a magazine edited by Sugihara. Inasmuch as Mōri was an official of the Finance Ministry and Planning Board, it is understandable that he used a pseudonym in publishing these views. See also Sugihara Masami, *Kokumin soshiki no seiji-ryoku* (Tokyo: Modan Nippon-sha, 1940), p. 11.

[50] Kamakura Ichirō (Mōri Hideoto), "Tōa kyōseitai kensetsu no sho-jōken," p. 22.

172

wished in China unless some political control over them was established at home. It was thus necessary to muster a powerful political force, based on popular support, to overcome the dominant political position of Japanese capitalists. Such an organization could be formed by mobilizing the entire nation through the various interest groups and organizations that enjoyed mass membership. In embracing all of the people, the new organization would admittedly include the capitalists and their supporters in the political parties, but the political power of the people when organized under strong anti-capitalist leadership would put an end to politics based exclusively on the economic interests of those who sought to exploit both Japan and China.

The party organization and program presented to Konoe by the Akiyama-Asō-Kamei group in late summer 1938 represented a bold response to the premier's appeal for support of his plans to reform the nation. The new party offered him a framework in which to resolve permanently the vexing problem of Cabinet-Diet relations by interposing a mass organization of political participation and mobilization that would control the Diet as well as the Cabinet under his leadership. However, the *Dai-Nippontō* presented some serious political and constitutional problems, as well. Party membership and position would now become new requisites for access to many civilian institutions of national and local government. Strong opposition could be anticipated to the party's assumption of responsibilities hitherto claimed by the national bureaucracy or traditional local leadership in communicating and implementing national policies in the local community. Businessmen would object strenuously to proposed party controls over their professional organizations and official bodies such as the Electric Power Control Commission, to say nothing of their general contempt for the anti-capitalistic policy proposals of the party leadership. "Japanists" would certainly attack the organization as an emulation of Nazi, Fascist, and even Communist party models, and would complain bitterly about the casual approach

173

to respecting the imperial Constitution exhibited by the new party's proponents. Finally, while some *kisei seitō* politicians might join the new party from the anti-mainstream factions, there would be strong mainstream opposition to the dissolution of all other parties and the consequent loss of mainstream influence. While the *Dai-Nippontō* offered some chance of building a new *jiban* locally, many party men would be reluctant to risk the destruction of their old power bases and the privileged position of their *meibōka* allies. Thus, as Konoe pondered the offer of the party presidency proffered by the Akiyama-Asō-Kamei group, he had to consider carefully whether he was willing to divide the country in a bitter political struggle over the nature of the new organization. Indeed, given the pluralistic nature of national politics, he had to decide whether it would even be possible to fit the party into the legal framework of the nation.

CHAPTER V

Parties and the Politics of Mobilization: The Suspension of the Reform Movement, 1938–1939

INTRODUCTION

WHATEVER the depth of Prince Konoe's interest may have been in a new political party during April 1938, the events of the late spring and summer dissuaded him from accepting the leadership of the party when it was offered to him. Konoe and his government now became fully aware of the widespread disruptive effects of the war in China on the five-year plan proposed in 1937. The five-year plan had been predicated on peace, and the government was now obliged to abandon or curtail many key aspects of the industrial development program. It was also forced, in fact, to renege on its commitment to defer invocation of the Mobilization Law until genuine "wartime" conditions existed. By the middle of 1938, it had become apparent that the "Incident" in China was indeed a "war," and that Chinese resistance would most likely make it a long-term war.

Konoe's response to these developments was to encourage the political elites to restrict the scope of their competition for power and to compromise with their adversaries for the sake of "national unity." To be certain, Konoe and other leaders had individual policy preferences and ambitions that they sought to advance over opposition during this period. Political competition and conflict did not cease. Many reformists sought to capitalize on the growing demands for national sacrifice to press the attack on their opponents, while the defenders of Japan's established forms of political, economic, and social organization sought like-

175

wise to use the mood of crisis for their own ends. However, the war also persuaded Konoe and others who were previously inclined to launch a political campaign against the "advocates of the status quo" to temper their demands, and seek a framework of collaboration in which all forces could work for the sake of meeting the nation's overseas military and economic commitments. Since Konoe was the key figure in the plans by reformists to destroy their opponents' institutional prerogatives, his refusal to lead any political movement directed specifically against the "advocates of the status quo" spelled the failure of the reformists' movement.

The parties in the Lower House were, therefore, able to preserve much of the institutionally derived power they enjoyed as popularly elected officials and "assistors of the imperial rule" in the Diet. They made many concessions to their adversaries, and became more seriously divided internally than ever before over party strategies for recovering power in the Cabinet. But since the traditional and institutional bases of their power—the *jiban*, election system, and the Lower House—remained undamaged by the reformist movement, they retained the ability to extract compromises from the government on important legislation, and defend their allies in the business and local communities against the attacks of reformist forces. By late 1938 they were reasserting their claims as a vital linkage between the people and the state, serving as organs to mobilize popular support and sacrifice on behalf of government policies.

Throughout 1939, mainstream leaders of the *kisei seitō* pursued a strategy of collaboration with the government. The Minseitō remained fairly stable internally, divided between Machida's mainstream leadership and a smaller group clustered around the "reformist" Nagai Ryūtarō. However, the Seiyūkai suffered a major upheaval within the party. Suzuki and Hatoyama were at last overwhelmed by Nakajima and the return of Kuhara Fusanosuke to the party's ranks, and the party split in two between those who supported Nakajima and those who supported Kuhara.

While Hatoyama sank into temporary obscurity, the new mainstream Seiyūkai leaders continued to reassert the function of the parties as vital agencies of popular mobilization. Like Machida and Hatoyama, Nakajima and Kuhara stressed the role of the parties as mobilizers of popular support for government policies. Unlike those two leaders, however, they all but neglected to mention the parties' second function between the state and people, that of articulating popular demands to the government. Both Seiyūkai leaders sought to regain power through the establishment of a new party in permanent control of the Diet. They talked of doing more work organizing mass groups than previously, but in fact continued to look to the *meibōka* and existing *jiban* as the basic style of local political organization and mobilization of popular support for the state and its international mission.

Most party leaders cooperated with the Hiranuma government (January-August 1939) as a manifestation of satisfaction with the cessation of attacks on their institutional prerogatives and as a strategy for the enhancement of party power. Even when Hiranuma gave way to a new Cabinet organized by General Abe Nobuyuki, party leaders assumed a position of outright support or, at the least, neutrality towards the government. Within the parties, however, a profound dissatisfaction with this approach grew among junior members, who doubted its efficacy as a strategy for the recovery of party control over the Cabinet. Abandoning hope of ever achieving power under the mainstream leadership, the younger members of the parties joined with members of the smaller Diet parties and factions to overthrow the Abe government at the beginning of 1940. The movement against Abe, however, turned out to be less an indication of anti-military sentiment than the beginning of a campaign to create a new party committed to and allied with the advocates of sweeping political reform and mass organization in the name of the national defense concept. At roughly the same time, the Army leadership also shed its reluc-

177

tance to engage overtly in political movements specifically oriented towards the implementation of its programs of reform; and the anti-leadership movement in the parties moved towards a political alliance with the Army. The anti-leadership forces in the Diet now joined the Army in rejecting the notion that a party's primary function was simply to mobilize public support for government. Together, they embraced the concept of a highly partisan "reformist" party ready to do battle against the defenders of the political and economic "status quo," and integrate the masses into the state through the new party organization.

Thus, at the very moment when another Cabinet was overthrown by parliamentary pressures, the erosion of party discipline threw party strategies and policies into turmoil. Realizing that a party without discipline was of little value in the competition for power, party leaders looked anxiously for some way to regain control over their own forces. When Prince Konoe revealed that he was once again interested in the formation of a new party, they turned to him with alacrity, and set in motion the events that resulted in the dissolution of the parties before the summer of 1940 was over.

MOBILIZATION: DEFINITIONS AND OPTIONS

The growing need for popular mobilization that impelled Konoe's interest in the original new party plan of 1938 was prompted by the requirements of the government's five-year plans for military and industrial development, the strength shown by the opponents of reform during the 73rd Diet session, and the continuing war in China. Whatever their differences in approach, many national leaders had begun to regard the mobilization of mass groups as essential to reforming Japan for the fulfillment of her policy goals in East Asia. Before considering the implications and outcome of this new interest in mass mobilization, however, it is necessary to review the general perspective and legal

178

context in which Konoe and other Japanese were likely to regard mass political organizations.

The Japanese concept of "political-ness" (having or being of a political nature) was legally codified in a series of laws regulating political activity at the end of the nineteenth century. Under the stipulations of the Regulations for Meetings and Associations (*Shūkai jōrei*, 1880), the Meetings and Political Associations Law (*Shūkai oyobi seisha hō*, 1900), and the Public Security Police Law (*Chian keisatsu hō*, 1900), any public or private gathering convened for political purposes required prior notification of the police. The Home Ministry was empowered to prohibit any activity, meeting, or organization that, in its estimation, threatened the public peace. Moreover, no military man, minor, woman, or religious leader was permitted to join a political organization (*seiji kessha*), and women and minors were not even permitted to attend political meetings.[1] It was important, then, to establish criteria for determining whether or not an organization or movement was political, in order to determine its legal status and its field of mobilizing supporters. Gotō Fumio, a career Home Ministry bureaucrat and one-time home minister, attempted to describe the criteria in the following ways:

According to the public security police law, the laws of our country—the regulations of this law define two different types of organizations; namely, the political organization, and the public organization.

First, political associations: organizations which center around activity in the Diet which will have a direct influence on the policies of the government, which try to gain public opinion and to make the people at large agree with their political views. In short, organizations with a political purpose. These organizations are called organi-

[1] Ōkubo Toshiaki, *Taikei Nihon shi sōsho 3: seiji shi III* (Tokyo: Yamakawa shuppansha, 1967), p. 319; *Naimushō shi*, II, 676 ff.

179

zations concerning politics, and generally speaking, are referred to as political organizations. All other organizations are, in this law, referred to generally as public organizations, ideological organizations, social welfare organizations, educational organizations, and organizations comprising all other kinds of social activity in their widest sense. These are grouped together as public organizations; organizations which lay particular stress on ideological problems fall under the category of public organizations.[2]

This definition of political activity and political organizations bore the imprint of the mid-Meiji political milieu in which it was first formulated. It was originally codified by a government that regarded itself as "transcending" private political and economic interests, and directed against political organizations "centering around activity in the Diet," that is, the political parties. In other words, the efforts by the parties to win popular support for their claim to "greater influence on the policies of the government" were "political," while even highly political activities by nonparty elites—affecting the nation's attitude towards the state and the population's vital interests—could be considered apolitical or "public." While the injustice of this differentiation is clear, the Meiji oligarchs were neither the first nor the last national leadership in the world to declare themselves "neutral" and "above politics." Nevertheless, as a consequence of this definition, the legal context and general perceptions of political mobilization were characterized by a differentation between one cluster of images ("partisan," "private interests," "political") and another ("transcendental," "national interests," "public").

The oligarchs who formulated these regulations and definitions did so for two reasons, both of which were related to the preservation of their power. First, they wished to contain attacks on the doctrine of unlimited imperial sov-

[2] IMTFE, *Proceedings*, pp. 1664–66.

ereignty, which legitimized the political power they enjoyed. The parties finally managed to circumvent this barrier to power by dropping their challenge to the legitimacy of the institutions of imperial government, and instead seeking to recruit the nonparty elites who held power in the various organs of state. As part of the strategy and faith of Hara Kei and other early twentieth-century party leaders, the Diet parties became staunch defenders of the legitimacy of the imperial system. Indeed, by 1925, when they were safely entrenched in the Lower House and expanding their influence into other political institutions through the nonparty elites, the parties led the defense of institutional legitimacy through new regulations on "political" organizations. The Peace Preservation Law (*Chian iji hō*) of 1925, approved by a Cabinet and Diet led by Katō Kōmei of the Kenseikai, was specifically enacted to deflect and repress challenges from the Left to the legitimacy of the institutions of imperial government.

The second reason for the regulations of the late nineteenth century was to resist challenges to oligarchic power even within the framework of the Meiji Constitution and the doctrine of imperial sovereignty. The extension of party influence beyond the Lower House into other institutions of government in the early twentieth century continued to depend on reforming the legal foundations of nonparty elite strength (such as the guarantees afforded civil servants against being hired or fired in accordance with party affiliation, the prerogative of the armed services to restrict candidates for the service portfolios to active or retired generals and admirals, the hereditary rights of the nobility to serve in the House of Peers, and so on). Since the parties remained in the position of directly challenging these established legal ground rules for allocating political power among elite groups, they were still regarded as highly "political" in their Diet strategies and mobilization efforts.

In time, perhaps, the Diet parties might have consolidated their positions of control in the other institutions of

181

government, and transformed their public identity from being challengers of established elite positions to defenders of the allocation of elite power within the legitimized imperial system. During the 1930s, for example, when party influence beyond the Lower House had already crested and was under attack from military elites who sought to expand their position in civilian institutions of government through legal reform and popular mobilization, the parties charged that the military was engaged in "politics" and was violating the traditional separation of military and civilian affairs. Military and right-wing activists who sought to strike down the *jūshin* institution, eliminate the Diet's powers, reduce the authority of the bureaucracy, and abolish the election system, were also subject to criticism for their "political" activities. In a generalized sense, "political" movements were those directed against specific elite groups claiming a monopoly over access to specific institutions legitimized by tradition, law, or the Constitution, and channels of political participation. They originated among elite and nonelite groups who often sought to redefine the canons of legitimacy in order to displace those who monopolized political power in one or more institutions of government. Alternatively, "political" movements might not challenge the legitimacy of the institutions themselves, but seek merely to undermine the legal foundations of the specific elite group's monopoly of control over an institution.

"Public" organizations and movements took several forms: spiritual, economic, ideological, and educational. "Public" mobilization often touched on the political interests and aspirations of groups whose power was legitimized by imperial rule. It was, however, inspired by a defense of the institutionally derived prerogatives of established elite groups and not by direct challenges to the legal or constitutional position of any specific elite. Thus, "Japanist," military, and bureaucratic organizations could inveigh against the parties' orientation towards private or class interests, and campaign to "purify" citizens' minds, the electoral pro-

182

cess, and the Diet of their preoccupation with "private" rather than "public" or "national" interests. These organizations were clearly acting in a political fashion, but so long as they did not challenge the canons of legitimacy sanctioning the election process or the prerogatives of Lower House members, their actions were not regarded legally as "political" movements. Similarly, when Cabinets acted to restrict the access of new groups to elite status and positions in the institutions of the imperial government, or to repress competing definitions of political legitimacy, they acted in a "public" rather than "political" capacity. Thus, party activity in the late nineteenth century was restricted by the oligarchs in the Cabinet in the "public" interest, and was limited in accordance with oligarchic definitions of "public" order. The same set of terms applied when the party-dominated Cabinet under Katō endeavored to suppress the Left through new regulations on "political" activity.

The mobilization of popular support for "national unity" and Japan's mission in East Asia was likewise "public," so long as it did not challenge the legitimacy of the imperial system or the allocation of power among elite groups in control of the various institutions of government. Such campaigns consisted, in fact, of efforts by the elites who occupied legitimized governmental institutions to mobilize the citizenry to a higher level of identification with the doctrines of legitimacy, and the policies and institutions of the imperial government. They sought to generate a stronger popular consciousness of the government's legitimacy and purposes, and an intensified degree of citizen participation in the implementation of national policies, without surrendering control over the citizenry or sacrificing elite claims to monopolize governmental institutions. "Public" mobilization of popular support and participation in this fashion often touched directly on the interest of specific elite groups, to say nothing of the interests of the citizenry as a whole. Nevertheless, it was not regarded as "political," and

183

was usually directed by a coalition of all elite groups as a means of defending their respective political and institutional prerogatives when greater demands were being imposed by the state on the citizenry.

The reformist supporters of the Konoe government were thus presented with two possible types of mass mobilization in 1938: "political" mobilization directly challenging the legitimacy of institutions or the legal premises of certain conservative elite groups' power, and "public" mobilization to insure popular support for the Cabinet's foreign and domestic reform programs. Some, like the Akiyama-Asō-Kamei group, advocated a mass-oriented campaign to abridge the powers of those institutions controlled by conservatives and to introduce new organs to determine legitimate access to political participation. Others, including most bureaucrats and a growing number of "Japanists," emphasized the desirability of "public" mobilization to minimize citizen resistance or challenges to the prerogatives and policies of the governing elites. The types of mobilization selected by the political leadership would have a profound impact on the parties' power position; and they, along with other elite groups, became vitally involved in deciding how the citizenry would be controlled and manipulated in national politics henceforth.

KONOE'S REJECTION OF "POLITICAL" MOBILIZATION

While Prince Konoe maintained his interest and connections in the movement for a new party following the close of the 73rd Diet session in March, 1938, he was also active in attempting to coopt the support of his principal rivals for power, General Ugaki and Ikeda Seihin. In May, the premier succeeded in persuading both men to join his Cabinet. Ugaki was induced to become foreign minister, with a tacit mandate to end the China Incident through diplomatic negotiations that might even involve Chiang Kai-shek, in disregard of Konoe's January 16 statement severing all ties with the Nationalist regime. Ikeda became finance minister and minister of commerce and industry concurrently, to supervise the government's economic programs as mobilization for the China Incident and the five-year plans proceeded. Both men evidently read the results of the 73rd Diet as an indication that the government would be unable to force conservatives to accept a radical reform program. They now joined the government in an effort to confine the mobilization and foreign policy policies of the regime to limits that would minimize their effect on Japan's economic and political systems, and her ties with the Anglo-American powers.

Throughout the spring of 1938, the government was forced to abridge its original programs of reform and industrial development. The war in China simply absorbed too large a share of the nation's energies to enable the Cabinet to proceed on the basis of figures for expenditure of resources and funds that had been calculated prior to the war. While hoping that the delay imposed by the war on the military and economic development plans would be minimal, the government's optimism was dashed by the sturdy Nationalist resistance to Japanese forces, particularly at Taierhchuang. Moreover, an economic report covering the first quarter of 1938 revealed that even the revised goals of the government for stimulating exports to finance required imports were not being met. The economic crisis grew worse on June 11, when the United States announced an embargo on the shipment to Japan of aircraft, armaments, engine parts, aerial bombs, and torpedoes.[3]

[3] As an example of how the war in China affected proposed expenditures under the Army's 1937 five-year plan, see the Cabinet decision of January 18, 1938, whereby the government decided to limit exports to the three-billion-yen level for 1938, and use the exchange obtained for three-billion-yen worth of imports. These figures represented a substantial reduction from the figures projected for 1938 (4.4 billion yen in exports and 5.3 billion yen in imports) in the Army's plan of May 1937. See IMTFE, *Proceedings*, p. 8498; Tsunoda, *Ishiwara Kanji shiryō*, p. 151. For the first quarter report in 1938, see IMTFE, *Proceedings*, p. 8498; and for the American embargo, see IMTFE, *Judgment*, p. 261.

These problems made it increasingly difficult to provide the imperial forces in China with munitions and tools of war over a prolonged period, while simultaneously adhering to the five-year plan proposals on which the Cabinet coalition stood. On June 23, the Cabinet was obliged to recognize that "the plan for the mobilization of commodities for 1938 decided earlier has become difficult to realize because of the extremely unfavorable foreign trade balance, owing to the decrease in exports and other reasons." It was agreed that a new set of policies must be adopted to assure that the demands for military supplies were met and domestic production increased. The government sought to curb the rising inflation created by military demand through a combination of wage limitations, price controls, transformation of the labor force to wartime production, and a campaign to encourage popular thrift and savings instead of consumption. To execute these proposals, the Cabinet was forced to conclude that certain articles in the National Mobilization Law would have to be invoked in spite of the commitments made during the 73rd Diet session.[4]

The economic impact of the China war on the five-year plans occasioned interest in more intensive forms of "public" mobilization. At the outset of the China Incident in 1937, the Cabinet had converted its plans for a voluntary citizens' drive for savings into a Movement for Mobilizing Popular Morale (*Kokumin seishin sōdōin undō*) to generate public support for the government's China policy. A loosely knit Central Federation of seventy-four (and later ninety-four) organizations, including representatives from all parliamentary groups, was created to direct the movement under the joint supervision of the Cabinet Information Commission, Home Ministry, and Education Ministry.[5] Heavy emphasis

[4] IMTFE, *Proceedings*, p. 8492. The government statement of June 23 may be found in Horiba Kazuo, *Shina jihen sensō shidō shi* (Tokyo: Jiji tsūshinsha, 1962), pp. 170–72.

[5] For a list of participating organizations, see Yokusan undō shi kankōkai (Shimonaka Yasaburō), ed., *Yokusan kokumin undō shi*

was placed on ideological propaganda to strengthen popular identification with the state and foster a sense of nationalism. Other campaigns were launched to encourage production, citizen savings, the purchase of war bonds, and thrift. However, the popular response was at best lukewarm, and a number of officials began urging that the movement be placed under the direction of one single government office with the power to coordinate more closely the activities of the various groups represented in the federation. By mid-1938, as the government prepared to limit wages and consumption, create unemployment while transforming the labor force to a wartime footing, and demand a greater degree of "spontaneous" citizen cooperation with the war effort, it was obliged to give careful consideration to strengthening its campaign for "public" mobilization.

A memorandum submitted to Konoe on July 20, 1938, summarizes the proposals made by various bureaucratic agencies to strengthen the functions and organization of the Central Federation of the Movement for Mobilizing Popular Morale.[6] First, the leadership of the mobilization movement had been ineffective and required reorganization. The piecemeal leadership of the three government offices in charge hitherto had proved ineffectual. It was thus necessary to streamline the government's supervision through one agency and provide stronger official leadership over the activities of the participating groups in the federation.

A variety of offices might assume the burden of directing the federation. The Cabinet Information Commission might be expanded into a Propaganda Ministry if spiritual mobilization were to remain the goal. On the other hand, a number of other ministries objected to being excluded from the direction of the movement. The Education Ministry held

---

(Tokyo: Yokusan undō shi kankōkai, 1954), pp. 28–30 (hereafter cited as YKUS).

[6] See "Kokumin seishin sōdōin sai-soshiki no ken," July 20, 1938, in Imai and Itō, eds., *Kokka sōdōin*, pp. 4–7.

that the main emphasis of the movement should be directed at educating and cultivating the minds of future citizens through the schools and *seinendan*, and that direction of spiritual mobilization should be under the aegis of the Education Ministry. Under newly installed Education Minister General Araki Sadao, chief ideological exponent of the Imperial Way, the ministry demonstrated its concern for "spiritual mobilization" through a relentless purge of "liberal" and "socialist" instructors in the nation's universities and secondary schools. The Home Ministry, however, also claimed a long tradition of jurisdiction over the spiritual mobilization of Japanese citizens.

Meanwhile, officials in other ministries argued that the mobilization movement should go beyond stirring up patriotism to marshal support for economic reform. The Ministry of Agriculture and Forestry and the Ministry of Commerce and Industry both contended that the movement should provide leadership in drives to increase national production and establish long-term economic foundations for a prolonged military and economic commitment to the construction of a new East Asia. The movement should thus become a "political" one, directed against the opponents of economic reform, and should be placed under the guidance of one of these two ministries.

The bureaucratic controversy over popular mobilization continued through the summer and fall, overlapping and at times becoming entangled with the plans of party politicians and right-wing leaders to form political mobilization organs themselves. From Konoe's perspective, however, the state could now ill afford the risks of sharp political conflict throughout society engendered by the creation of an intensely "political" mobilization campaign or new party, such as Akiyama's group was proposing. As attractive as a new mass party might appear in principle, the possibilities of quickly overthrowing the position of the existing parties and their local allies were slim. Given the need to mobilize

188

the nation to meet wartime economic demands, compromise replaced challenge as the most pragmatic and effective approach to reform for Konoe. The government had already obtained the enabling legislation it needed from the Lower House in the previous Diet session, and the premier could work with Ikeda on invoking the Mobilization Law without challenging or involving the Lower House parties. Indeed, Article vi of the law was invoked in July, establishing government controls over hiring and firing, wages, and length of the work day.[7] The economic problems incurred by the development plans and the continuing battle in China thus inclined the premier to opt for an emphasis on "national unity" and "public" mobilization, and abandon his earlier thoughts of "political" mobilization against those who might oppose the implementation of the five-year plan. In political terms, this thinking also suggested that Konoe would rather compromise with Ikeda under current conditions than risk another battle against business groups and their political supporters over the issue of state economic controls.

Konoe also structured his approach to foreign policy with an eye to averting widespread political divisions among the citizenry. In this case, however, compromise seemed a liability to effective "public" mobilization. While he had initially left Foreign Minister Ugaki the option of negotiating with Chiang if necessary to obtain a truce and settlement of the war, the right wing and military had organized widespread demonstrations against "Ugaki Diplomacy."[8] Setting aside the question of whether the demonstrators were truly representative of public opinion, it was clear that any compromise resolution of the "holy war" that allowed Chiang to remain in power was not politically feasible in light of

[7] Fujiwara Akira, Imai Seiichi, and Tōyama Shigeki, Shōwa shi, rev. ed. (Tokyo: Iwanami shoten, 1959), p. 160.

[8] SKS, vii, entries during August 1938 for evidence of the growing right-wing offensive.

the current distribution of power among the elites, and was potentially damaging to the "national unity" Konoe now sought.

When Ugaki proposed in early September that the government negotiate directly with Chiang, Konoe found the suggestion too radical to accept, and underscored his objections by citing the threat to public order talks with Chiang would pose.[9] Given the control over the nation's peace-keeping machinery exercised by the chauvinistic Suetsugu, any disturbances provoked by a "dramatic shift in diplomacy" were unlikely to be restrained by the police.[10] Konoe was thus unwilling to modify Japan's peace terms, and China remained unwilling to accept them. The premier offered no real support to Ugaki, and, indeed, undercut the foreign minister by backing the Army's scheme to carve control of China diplomacy out from Foreign Ministry jurisdiction and place it under a new organ, the Asian Development Board (*Kōain*). Enraged at what he believed to be Konoe's betrayal and lack of interest in negotiations, Ugaki resigned at the end of September. As Konoe abandoned his short-lived interest in negotiations, he began seeking a new rationale for the fighting on the continent, some compelling concept that the government might use to improve the effectiveness of its "public" mobilization of citizen support and sacrifice. In November, the premier announced Japan's noble purpose in China was henceforth to be the construction of a "New Order in East Asia."

THE MINISTERIAL CONFERENCES ON POPULAR MOBILIZATION

As the premier moved towards the rejection of any widespread "political" mobilization campaigns, he came under renewed pressure from the right wing to assume the leadership of the new political party. During August and early

[9] Kido, *Kido Kōichi nikki*, II, 670.
[10] SKS, VII, 90; also Kido, *Kido Kōichi nikki*, II, 667.

September, Suetsugu, Akiyama, Baron Hiranuma, and other right-wing leaders repeatedly urged the prince to form a new political organization unifying the right wing. Konoe and Kido discussed the possibilities of forming a party on September 7, 8, and 24, but the premier showed little desire to create a new organization. However, he was again subjected to pressures from the right in October, when the Akiyama-Asō-Kamei group urged him to make a final decision on its party while Suetsugu and Justice Minister Shiono again broached the issue of a different new party.[11] Konoe was aware of the fact that these men represented groups with sharply conflicting views concerning political parties and the political process. Akiyama's group wished not merely to dominate the Diet and elections but supplant them with a new organ of popular participation, the *Dai-Nippontō*. Suetsugu was willing to confine the activities of the party he proposed to the Diet, but wished to outlaw all other parties and ostracize Akiyama. Hiranuma and Shiono represented the "Japanist" viewpoint, which had emphasized "spiritual" rather than "political" mobilization, and held that popular participation through elections and a Lower House reflective of diverse popular viewpoints were inconsistent with the national essence. Despite widespread right-wing sentiments favoring unification under a new party, Konoe obviously doubted that the competing and diverse right-wing forces could reach accord. Hence, he finally sought to mitigate the new party pressures on him by suggesting that Suetsugu, Shiono, Agriculture and Forestry Minister Arima (an advocate of Konoe's leadership of a new party based on the guilds), and Welfare Minister Kido discuss the new party question among themselves and report their findings to him. Each of the ministers held different views on the personnel and functions to be embraced

---

[11] Kido, *Kido Kōichi nikki*, ii, 670–71, 673; Kazami, *Konoe naikaku*, p. 148; Shiono Suehiko kaikoroku kankōkai (Matsuzaka Hiromasa), ed., *Shiono Suehiko kaikoroku* (Tokyo: Shiono Suehiko kaikoroku kankōkai, 1958), p. 288.

by the proposed party, and Konoe's decision to pit them against each other was clearly designed to end the new party campaign.[12]

Because of illness, Arima did not attend the ministerial discussions on the new party issue until November. The remaining three ministers met in secrecy for the first time on September 27. Almost from the outset, it appeared that Konoe had seriously misjudged the distance separating the positions of Suetsugu and Shiono, for within a week, the two had taken the initiative in drafting detailed plans for the creation of a new "Imperial Japan Party" (*Kōkoku Nip-pontō*). On October 15, they presented Konoe with drafts of the platform and an announcement proclaiming the creation of the party.[13] There is no record of Konoe's reaction to the drafts, but Suetsugu and Shiono were soon complaining bitterly about the premier's "indecisive" attitude.

The new party plans underwent several revisions in October, during which the proposed name of the party was tentatively changed to the "Greater Imperial Japan Popular Party" (*Dai-Nippon kōminkai*).[14] At first glance, these new party plans were strikingly similar to those drawn up by the Akiyama-Asō-Kamei group for the *Dai-Nippontō*. The similarities were no doubt due to the fact that Suetsugu had asked the Police Bureau to draw up working drafts for consideration, and the job of drafting had fallen to Katō Yūsaburō, a member of Kamei Kan'ichirō's research team![15] In

[12] Kazami, *Konoe naikaku*, pp. 147–48. Itō has reached a similar conclusion. See Itō, "Shōwa jūsan-nen," p. 165.

[13] Kido, *Kido Kōichi nikki*, II, 677.

[14] Plans for the *Kōkoku Nippontō* are listed in Kido nikki kenkyūkai, ed., *Kido Kōichi kankei monjo sō-mokuroku*, unpublished, 1967, pp. 37–38. A draft version of the *Dai-Nippon kōminkai*, on which the following discussion is based, may be found in *Kido monjo*, pp. 361–66. See also Itō, "Shōwa jūsan-nen," pp. 166 ff, and Gordon M. Berger, "The Search for a New Political Order: Konoe Fumimaro, the Political Parties, and Japanese Politics during the Early Shōwa Era," Ph.D. dissertation, Yale University, 1972, pp. 265–74.

[15] For details on Katō's role, see *Katō Yūsaburō-shi danwa sokki-roku*, pp. 64 ff.

its revised form, however, the new party proposal differed from the *Dai-Nippontō* plan in several important ways. First, it greatly reduced the emphasis on the policy-making organs of the party. Second, while early *kōminkai* drafts did call for the gradual incorporation of mass organizations such as the *seinendan, sangyō kumiai,* and other functionally organized local bodies, the final form of the party proposal emphasized instead an identification with the Diet and local assemblies down to the village and town levels. The party was thus to be primarily a parliamentary one, designed to monopolize parliamentary and assembly affairs, but posing no apparent challenge to the administrative network of the central bureaucracy, as the Akiyama-Asō-Kamei party plans did. Third, heavy emphasis was placed on providing posts in the party for *kisei seitō* members, and apart from the organizational unity binding members at the Diet level with those down to the village assembly, the organization was strongly reminiscent of the existing parties.[16] Finally, and perhaps most important of all, the personnel running the party would differ from the *Dai-Nippontō*. Suetsugu originally planned to become the vice president and actual leader of the party under Konoe's mantle; Akiyama and the "false converts from the left" in the Shadaitō were to be denied the leadership positions they sought through the *Dai-Nippontō*.[17]

Aware of previous attempts by Suetsugu and Hiranuma (Shiono's political patron) to limit or eliminate *kisei seitō* influence, members of both major parties were profoundly suspicious of the new party when rumors of it reached them. Most feared that it represented a shift from a competitive party system to a one-party system, in which they would lose control of the Diet to new forces brought in from the right wing and bureaucracy to run the party. The only evidence of positive parliamentary interest in the party came from an unexpected source, the Suzuki-Hatoyama faction

[16] Itō, "Shōwa jūsan-nen," p. 167.
[17] *Ibid.*, p. 173, n. 2, and *Katō Yūsaburō-shi danwa sokkiroku*, p. 83.

193

of the Seiyūkai. During the fall of 1938, this faction was finally overwhelmed as the controlling force within the party, and it became clear that when a new president was elected, Nakajima would have the votes to establish a new mainstream leadership. Hence, when Miki Bukichi approached the Seiyūkai leaders on Shiono's behalf, he learned that "Hatoyama is surprisingly well informed about the situation, and would joyfully participate in a new 'national unity' party if the opportunity arose. He is not committed to the present status quo." However, Hatoyama's "joy" was not shared by the preponderance of forces in the major parties, who flatly refused to participate in the new organization.[18]

Suetsugu nevertheless appeared prepared to call all party leaders in and order them to form the new party.[19] He was dissuaded from doing so, but obviously hoped to use a new party to win parliamentary support for further reform legislation related to mobilization, and to undermine the political support business enjoyed in the Lower House. The

[18] Hatoyama's views are reported in Keishichō jōhō-ka, "Shintō juritsu undō gaikyō," November 1, 1938 (Top Secret). This official document is in the possession of Itō Takashi, who graciously permitted me to copy it. Also see Nomura, "Shintō undō o hadaka ni suru," p. 242. For a broader review of party politicians' reactions to the kōminkai plan, see the various reports of prefectural governors at the time. For example, Report of Tsuchiya Shōzō (governor of Gunma) to Premier Konoe, Home Minister Suetsugu, Foreign Minister Konoe, and Chief of the Tokyo Metropolitan Police Abe Genki, October 28, 1938 (Secret report #21,962), entitled "Daigishi no shintō mondai ni taisuru gendō no ken"; Tsuchiya to same, October 28, 1938 (Secret report #21,967), entitled "Daigishi no jikyoku gendō ni kansuru ken"; Yano Kenzō (governor of Tōyama) to Home Minister Suetsugu, Foreign Minister Arita, etc., November 2, 1938 (Secret report #385), entitled "Shintō soshiki mondai nado ni taisuru daigishi no ikō ni kansuru ken"; and Yano to same, November 14, 1938 (Secret report #394), entitled "Daigishi no jikyoku dan ni kansuru ken." These documents are located in the Foreign Ministry Archives of Japan, Section 3 of Honpō naisei kankei zassan. For further bibliographical information, see Chapter IV, n. 45 supra.

[19] Kazami, Konoe naikaku, p. 149.

home minister was an ardent advocate of measures such as the invocation of Article XI of the Mobilization Law, that empowered the government to limit company dividends and force banks to make loans for defense production. Finance Minister Ikeda adamantly refused to support Suetsugu's position, and in response was publicly attacked by Army spokesmen for his defense of the capitalist spirit.[20] The controversy highlighted the continuing tensions between reformist proponents of the national defense state concept and those who insisted drastic reforms would only weaken Japan. It demonstrated that there remained strong incentives for the reformist supporters of Suetsugu and the Army to curtail the political influence of conservative forces in both the business world and the Diet. And considering the nature of the reformist demands enumerated by Suetsugu and local groups such as Kakunōkyō, there appeared to be equally good reasons why the major parties and their *meibōka* allies would be extremely wary of any self-proclaimed new "national unity" party committed to reforming Japan.[21]

In view of the bold political objectives of the new party planners, Suetsugu and Shiono must have been infuriated by Konoe's bland dismissal of their proposal as "something which hardly differs from the existing political parties." Shiono later recalled that he was on the verge of resigning from the Cabinet in protest against Konoe's

[20] The Article XI controversy ended as had the debate over the Electric Power Bill, with a compromise that allowed the government to limit dividends to ten percent annually, but in reality gave business and the banks substantial concessions. See Tiedemann, "Big Business in Prewar Japan," pp. 310–11.

[21] Indeed, one party member noted specifically that local community leaders would oppose the *kōminkai* plan as strongly as the parties themselves did. See remarks of Matsumura Kenzō as reported by Yano Kenzō (governor of Tōyama) to Home Minister Suetsugu, Foreign Minister Arita, Cabinet Information Commission chief, and governors of Ishikawa, Niigata, Fukui, and Nagano, November 14, 1938 (Secret report #394), entitled "Daigishi no jikyoku dan ni kansuru ken," in Foreign Ministry Archives of Japan, Section 3 of *Honpō naisei kankei zassan.*

position.[22] Kido, on the other hand, was anxious to avoid provoking the major parties on the eve of a new Diet session. He urged Konoe to forsake the proposed new party, and by October 28, Konoe had shelved the plan indefinitely. Once Konoe had vetoed the formation of a new party, the Cabinet's attention shifted to bureaucratic proposals for expanding "public" mobilization. Suetsugu, Shiono, Kido, and Arima continued to meet and debate these issues, and on November 25, Education Minister Araki Sadao and Chief Cabinet Secretary Kazami Akira were invited to join the discussions. Despite repeated efforts by Arima and Kazami to direct the talks towards the formation of a new political party based on the agrarian guilds and more radical agrarian youth movements, attention remained fixed on bureaucratic proposals. On November 26, the Cabinet Information Commission submitted a plan to strengthen the spiritual mobilization movement in order to deal with the long-term task of constructing a new East Asian Order. The ministers decided to examine this plan, and Nagai, Nakajima, and the new overseas development minister, Hatta Yoshiaki, were invited to join the discussants from November 28. Henceforth, the meetings were called Eight-Minister Conferences, with Kazami the only participant of nonministerial rank.[23]

The commission plan called for a new system to mobilize political support for the government. It sought to establish new channels of mobilization running from the premier's office through the commission to the strongest nationwide organizations in the Popular Morale Central Federation— groups such as the youth associations, reservist associations, women's groups, and agrarian guilds. In other words, the government would be "united" with the people through the commission and its local network, in contrast to the era of

[22] Shiono Suchiko kaikoroku kankōkai, ed., *Shiono Suehiko kaikoroku*, p. 288.

[23] "Arima Yoriyasu nikki" (unpublished), entry for November 25, 1938 and entry for November 28, 1938. See also, Itō, "Shōwa jūsannen," p. 178.

party government, when mobilization channels ran from the government through the government party and its supporters among the *meibōka* to the people. Although there was no explicit rejection of the Diet and local assemblies as the organs through which executive policies were harmonized with popular views, the commission rejected the party-*meibōka*-local community ties as an effective channel through which to mobilize government support. In fact, the political parties were specifically excluded from participation in the mobilization drive proposed by the commission.[24]

The commission's plan to exclude the parties from an ostensibly "public" mobilization was not only a bureaucratic effort to limit party power further, but a response to a new challenge from the parties for preeminence in the spiritual mobilization movement. In mid-October, both parties took the initiative in creating a bipartisan "public" mobilization effort called the *Tōa saiken kokumin renmei* (Popular Federation for the Reconstruction of East Asia). The purpose of this movement was to reassert the parties' role as vital mobilizing intermediaries between the government and the people. All members of the Diet were to make at least three speeches in their election districts, and organize their electoral backers with a view towards gaining public cooperation with the government's policies. They were to urge popular forbearance during the period of long-term conflict on the continent, raise morale by emphasizing the benefits to be gained from Japanese exploitation of continental resources, encourage popular savings and thrift, and explain the reasons why a certain amount of economic control had become necessary. If the movement evoked any popular response, the parties planned to merge it with the Central Federation of the Movement for Mobilizing Popular Morale. Indeed, the first meeting held in the parties' mobilization drive on November 15 attracted 7,000 people, and prompted

[24] The commission plan was entitled "Chōki kensetsu taishō no tame no Kokumin seishin sōdōin kyōka hōsaku-an," and appears in *Kido monjo*, pp. 371–76.

197

a number of requests from the countryside for similar meetings. The effort to revitalize the parties' position as a crucial linkage between the people and the state had begun.[25]

Although there is no record of how the Eight-Minister Conference reacted to the commission's plan at the meeting of November 28, Communications Minister Nagai of the Minseitō is known to have suggested that his colleagues give more of their attention to the problem of creating a new political party. While Railways Minister Nakajima of the Seiyūkai replied that such a proposition no longer seemed feasible, neither of the two party men in the Cabinet supported the commission's proposal to undermine the position of the parties as intermediaries between the people and the government.[26] Similarly, the home and education ministers were unlikely to support any whittling away of their ministries' prerogatives with respect to the spiritual mobilization movement. Whatever the individual motives of the conference participants may have been, by December 1 they had shunted the commission plan aside and taken up consideration of a pair of plans drafted in the Home Ministry.

The existence of two essentially different Home Ministry proposals reflected a divergence of views within the ministry between reformist young officials of the Police Bureau and the Local Administration Bureau. Just as the Akiyama-Asō-Kamei plans for a *Dai-Nippontō* had served as the basis of Katō Yūsaburō's draft proposal for the new party deliberations of the Three-Ministers Conference in October, Katō introduced them again in modified form as the foundation for the Home Ministry's plan for "public" mobilization in November. In its new form, the plan was a proposal to convert the Central Federation of the Movement for Mobilizing Popular Morale into a "Popular Alliance for the Con-

[25] See Keishichō jōhō-ka, "Shintō juritsu undō gaikyō." Also, Jikyoku kaibō chōsajo (Tokuda Kenji), *Seikai rimen shi nenkan* (gekan) (Tokyo: Nihon bunka shuppankai, 1939), November 1938 section, p. 38.

[26] "Arima Yoriyasu nikki," entry for November 28, 1938.

struction of a New East Asia" (PACNEA).[27] As outlined by Katō and his colleagues in the Police Bureau, the goals and structure of PACNEA stood midway between Aki-yama's plan for a *Dai-Nippontō* and the concept of extend-ing bureaucratic control in the countryside. The major dif-ference between the proposal of October and the PACNEA plan was that while the former emphasized parliamentary consolidation, the latter sought to provide the framework for a fusion of civilian and official elements in formulating the administrative policies and managing the institutional apparatus for mobilizing the population. The premier was to serve as the overall chairman of PACNEA, while the home minister, education minister, and "a civilian who has a clear grasp of the significance and objectives of the China Incident" would serve jointly as vice chairmen.

The heart of the entire PACNEA organization was to be the administrative office (*jimu-kyoku*), with responsibility for planning and executing the activities of mobilized mass organizations (the *kokumin soshiki*). The permanent direc-tor of the national administrative office was to be a civilian rather than an official, and the pattern of joint civilian-official control was to be extended to the branches of the administrative office in the prefectures, cities, towns, and villages. At the upper level of the PACNEA regional hier-archy, the governors were to serve as branch chiefs, and at the lower levels, the mayors would hold the top position in the branch office. However, civilians were to serve as second in command in all regional offices. Civilian leaders were to be selected in accordance with the recommenda-tions of the civilian chief of the national administrative office, and the official leaders of the branch office. PACNEA was to become the focal point of organized activity by local citizens, absorbing and consolidating existing mass organi-zations under its aegis. As a result, *meibōka* leaders of the

[27] *Kido monjo*, pp. 358–60. The PACNEA plan was entitled "Shin Tōa kensetsu kokumin dōmei no shushi oyobi yōkō" (Home Ministry plan), Top Secret.

"local autonomy" system (*jichi seido*) would become more responsive to commands from above when integrated into the organizational framework of PACNEA, and their traditional status of leadership in nonofficial and semiofficial local organizations would be redefined in terms of official positions in the new institution.

The Police Bureau proposal obviously provoked a strong reaction among other Home Ministry officials, for an additional section of the plan, entitled "Organizational Policy," was swiftly appended before the PACNEA plan was circulated.[28] The new section was less a description of the policies to be followed by PACNEA than a proposal for an entirely different organization, called the "National Service Federation" (NSF). More than the name was different. The NSF plan was clearly the product of ministry officials who were fearful that the PACNEA organization—which conceded a large leadership role to nonofficials at both national and local levels—would intrude on their broad prerogatives in the area of local administration. In the NSF proposal, the premier was to serve formally as the president of the organization, but actual leadership was to be provided by the home minister as the sole vice president (the PACNEA plan, it will be recalled, provided for three vice chairmen, including one civilian). The vice president's staff would be organized within the Home Ministry, with branch offices in local Home Ministry offices throughout the country. There was no mention of a new administrative office, or of civilian leadership. Other ministries would be confined to a subordinate advisory role in NSF, while leaders of the groups participating in the federation would be selected as federation directors under the supervision of the home minister (vice president) and his staff.

An effort was also made to reinforce the Home Ministry's position locally. While the local structure of the NSF plan

[28] *Kido monjo*, pp. 361–62. The NSF plan was entitled simply "Soshiki hōshin" (Home Ministry plan), Top Secret.

bore some resemblance to the PACNEA plan, the overall intent was to strengthen the Home Ministry role in local affairs, and to exclude nonofficials from a voice in formulating and implementing local policies. Local units would be organized in the cities, towns, and villages, under the supervision of Home Ministry officials and mayors. These local units would consist of hamlet associations (*burakukai*) and town or ward associations (*chōnaikai*), government or public agencies, local companies, schools, factories, and all other vocational organizations. The proposed structure of the lower level of the NSF implied some major revisions in the system of local administration. Through the federation, mayors would gain added legal power to supervise and control the activities of local vocational and other nonofficial organizations. As in the PACNEA plan, the mayor's relative prestige and influence vis-à-vis town associations, assemblies, and local organizations would be enhanced through his new role in the federation. Likewise, the mayors would be brought into a legal and subordinate relationship to NSF officials at the prefectural and national levels. However, since the NSF plan excluded civilian personnel from federation leadership, all NSF officers with jurisdiction over the mayors would be Home Ministry officials. In other words, the network of Home Ministry administrative controls over the mayors and villages would be tightened through the institution of the National Service Federation. Furthermore, the federation would give legal recognition to the *burakukai* and *chōnaikai*, and integrate them for the first time into the local administration system of the Home Ministry.

Thus, under the NSF proposal, all Japanese citizens would be directly subjected to Home Ministry orders, should the government require a greater mobilization of materiel, manpower, or morale in the execution of its national policies. The goals of the NSF plan were virtually identical to other administrative proposals made by the Local Affairs Bureau of the Home Ministry in June 1938

201

(*Nōson jichi seido kaisei yōkō*).[29] At the time, the bureau's chief concern was to preserve its preeminent position in local affairs against challenges from the Ministry of Agriculture and Forestry and the Ministry of Commerce and Industry. It was also seeking to expand Home Ministry influence locally to deal with wartime mobilization problems. In this latter endeavor, it encountered the strong opposition of traditional holders of local political power (the *meibōka*), the local assemblies they still dominated, and their allies in national politics, the political parties. By injecting the local administrative reform proposals in the draft for a nation-wide NSF, the Local Affairs Bureau was apparently seeking to enact its program through the new organization.

The Home Ministry plan(s) for the creation of PACNEA or NSF were the subject of the Eight-Minister Conference on December 1. On December 3, Chief Cabinet Secretary Kazami sent Kido a new Home Ministry proposal, based on the PACNEA and NSF plans.[30] The new plan called for the creation of a National Service Association (NSA). It was based on the ministers' discussions and also on the two original Home Ministry plans.

The NSA plan revealed that the Eight-Minister Conference had been unable to agree on the fundamental issues raised by the Cabinet Information Commission plan of November 26, or the two Home Ministry plans discussed on December 1. In an effort to reach accord, the ministers had set the commission plan aside and deleted controversial sections from the Home Ministry plans. What was left as the NSA proposal was a watered-down and vaguely phrased draft that did little more than affirm the wisdom of Japan's mission in Asia and the desirability of national unity. Perhaps the ministers realized that, as Arima noted,

[29] For a discussion of these proposals, see Ari, "Chihō seido," pp. 176, 186–87; Ishii, "Nihon fuashizumu no chihō seido," p. 1.

[30] See *Kido monjo*, p. 370, for this letter. Also, for the NSA plan, entitled "Hōkokukai ni kansuru ken," Top Secret, see *Kido monjo*, pp. 366–70.

no plan could be implemented that ran contrary to Konoe's wishes.[31] And the premier showed little interest in approving any proposal that went beyond intensifying "public" mobilization through the already existing Movement for Mobilizing Popular Morale.

The NSA draft was merely a shadow of the original PACNEA plan. All mention of coordinating and fusing local groups was either deleted or referred to only vaguely. Clearly, the Eight-Minister Conference had been unable to agree on absorbing the nation's political and economic groups into the framework of a new organization or movement. Similarly, the structural aspects of the NSA plan were little more than an evisceration of the original Home Ministry plans. The premier was to serve as president, while the Home Minister and a civilian would serve as co-vice presidents. Hence, a compromise was reached between the PACNEA proposal for three vice presidents and the NSF proposal that the home minister alone should run the organization in the president's name. This compromise suggested that the long-standing official desire to unify the government's direction of the mobilization movement would be resolved by selecting the Home Ministry as the principal government agency supervising the movement. However, nonofficial figures and bureaucrats from other offices were to be appointed as NSA directors and advisors. Thus, as in the case for the Movement to Mobilize Popular Morale, the NSA could not become an instrument for displacing any of the political elite groups from the positions they currently held. Indeed, even agreement on placing the Home Ministry in charge of "public" mobilization proved illusory. Agriculture and Forestry Minister Arima indicated a growing dissatisfaction among reformists with the prospects of an officially dominated organization, particularly one dominated by the Home Ministry. Furthermore, Overseas Development Minister Hatta and Communications Minister Nagai

[31] "Arima Yoriyasu nikki," entry for November 28, 1938.

showed an inclination to abandon the attempt to create any new organization. Education Minister Araki, as well, must have been displeased by the threat to his ministry's claims of primary importance in leading the mobilization movement. Amidst the growing disenchantment of the ministers, the Cabinet assigned Home Minister Suetsugu and Araki the task of ironing out the proposal for reforming the Movement to Mobilize Popular Morale.[32] In other words, the two ministers most severely at odds in determining who should control the movement were left the job of coming to agreement. The result of this strategy was quite predictable: nothing more was heard of the project before the Konoe government's resignation a month later.

The Hiranuma Government and Popular Mobilization

The lessons of the ministerial conferences of late 1938 were not lost on Baron Hiranuma Kiichirō, who succeeded Konoe as premier on January 4, 1939. Having witnessed the failure of the new party and "political reorganization" movements at the end of his predecessor's reign, the new premier quickly let it be known that he would not challenge the parties and their local support groups, but instead hoped to win their support by conceding their importance. Immediately after receiving the imperial mandate to form a Cabinet, Hiranuma moved swiftly to assuage any misgivings party members might have about his appointment. While the makeup of his government indicated a strong sense of continuity with the past regime, Hiranuma conspicuously omitted the strongest advocates of institutional reform—Suetsugu, Arima, and Kazami—from his list of appointees. Moreover, Sakurauchi Yukio of the Minseitō and Maeda Yonezō of the Seiyūkai were given ministerial portfolios, indicating Hiranuma's willingness to work

[32] *Ibid.*, entry for December 9, 1938; and Itō, "Shōwa jūsan-nen," p. 178.

with the parties. The premier was soon even more explicit in affirming the desirability of maintaining the political status quo; shortly after taking office, he issued the following statement through his chief cabinet secretary:

Since we have constitutional politics in Japan, and since the Constitution provides for a Diet, we must give the Diet our respect. Moreover, as parliamentary politics have developed, political parties have naturally evolved in the context of running the Diet. Since they must inevitably exist, we can accomplish nothing by ignoring them. I earnestly hope that the parties will have a healthy development. I have no thoughts of a "restructuring of popular organizations" (*kokumin soshiki saihensei*) or a new political party movement.[33]

Hiranuma further conceded that

to realize parliamentary politics, parties—healthy parties—must of course be rooted in the spirit of assisting (*hoyoku*) the throne. Whatever the national policy may be, the parties must obviously decide their own approaches, in order to carry out the overall policy of the state and move towards the successful implementation of this policy. In the process, each party will obviously decide how best to serve the state. The platforms of the various parties will of course differ, but the basic point will remain *hoyoku*.[34]

In essence, the venerated dean of the "Japanist" right wing declared there was a proper and morally justifiable place in Japanese politics for parties with different platforms and viewpoints. This argument contrasted sharply with Hiranuma's earlier views and with the anti-party positions taken by many right-wing groups. It therefore pro-

[33] Cited in the interpellation of Ogawa Gōtarō in the Lower House, January 22, 1939. See *Kanpō gogai—Shōwa 14–nen 1–gatsu 22–nichi, Shūgiin giji sokkiroku dai–3–go*, p. 32.

[34] Hiranuma's response to Ogawa, *ibid.*, p. 33.

voked a great deal of controversy in right-wing circles over whether Hiranuma was still worthy of support. One group of right-wing leaders (including Iwata Ainosuke [*Aikokusha*], Kuzuu Yoshihisa [*Kokuryūkai*], Irie Taneomi and Ikeda Hiroshi [*Kokutai yōgo rengōkai*], and Honma Ken'ichirō [*Shizankai*]) issued a public statement supporting Hiranuma on February 11, 1939. They maintained that the proposals for political reform and mobilization of the preceding months were socialistic in intent, and they supported Hiranuma's decision to divorce himself from the plans.[35] On the other hand, "reformist" right-wing groups like the *Seisen kantetsu dōmei*, which had supported Suetsugu's position during 1938, became openly critical of Hiranuma's proclivity to maintain the "status quo."[36] Some journalists described the new premier as an "old tiger," whose reformist zeal had dissipated with old age.[37]

The division of opinion on the right over Hiranuma's policies shattered what hopes remained for the coalescence of a unified right-wing political force. Instead, the right wing polarized into two camps during 1939. Their disagreement centered largely on conflicting priorities in foreign policy, but also on different attitudes towards radical political change. In December 1939, those who had supported Hiranuma earlier prepared to form the *Kōa mekkyō kurabu* (Develop Asia-Destroy Communism Club), which wished a minimum of domestic political change and advocated that Japan's foreign policy be based on opposing the Soviet Union. In opposition to this group, the "reformists" an-

[35] Naimushō keiho-kyoku, *Shōwa 14–nen–chū ni okeru shakai undō no jōkyō* (Secret), December 20, 1940, pp. 211, 215.

[36] *Ibid.*, p. 211.

[37] See, for instance, Yamaura Kan'ichi's article on Hiranuma in January 1939, "Hiranuma Kiichirō ron," in Yamaura, *Konoe jidai no jinbutsu,* p. 50. Tsukui Tatsuo—a "reformist" right-wing journalist and political activist—described Hiranuma in a postwar interview as having been a bureaucratic ally of the "Diet liberals." *Tsukui Tatsuo-shi danwa sokkiroku* (Nihon kindai shiryō sōsho B–6), (Tokyo: Nihon kindai shiryō kenkyūkai, 1974), pp. 150–51.

nounced they would form the *Tōa kensetsu kokumin renmei* (Popular Federation for the Construction of East Asia). This latter group included Suetsugu's supporters, Nakano Seigō, Hashimoto Kingorō, Tatekawa Yoshitsugu, General Matsui Iwane, Shiratori Toshio, and others who advocated radical attacks on the parties at home and the speedy conclusion of a military alliance with Germany and Italy abroad. As opposed to the former group's fixation on the USSR as Japan's chief enemy, the *renmei's* activities were mainly directed against Great Britain and her support of Chiang Kai-shek.[38]

During his short eight-month tenure as premier, Hiranuma remained impervious to the demands of the "reformist" right wing for sweeping political change. In April, his Cabinet did decide to restructure the Movement for Mobilizing Popular Morale, but the decision was designed to heighten spiritual mobilization, rather than to create a new basis for exercising political influence. Under the slogan "Material and Spiritual are One and the Same!" a limited degree of economic mobilization under the movement's auspices was sanctioned, through public campaigns against excessive domestic consumption, inefficient uses of resources, and inflation. The slogan, however, proved less a mandate for converting the movement into an organ promoting economic reform than a justification for limiting it, as before, to the promotion of vague principles of the national spirit. The main activities of the movement between April 1939 and April 1940 were confined to campaigns to stimulate savings, commemorate the anniversary of the China Incident, promote the observation of "Service to the Ideal of Asian Development Day," encourage frugality in the use of electricity and gas, prevent tuberculosis, revere the gods, serve the state during wartime by using less rice,

[38] Naimushō keiho-kyoku, *Shōwa 14–nen–chū ni okeru shakai undō no jōkyō* (Secret), pp. 2, 214–15, 320. Naimushō keiho-kyoku, *Shōwa 15–nen–chū ni okeru shakai undō no jōkyō* (Secret), December 20, 1941, p. 580.

serve the state by planting trees, and so on. Steps were taken to maintain the movement's overall disengagement from partisan politics by making the organization suprapartisan, with members from all parties and factions serving on committees running its activities.[39]

Hiranuma's conservative approach to domestic politics, and Konoe's semiwithdrawal from the forefront of national politics (he participated occasionally in Cabinet meetings as a minister without portfolio, and replaced Hiranuma as president of the Privy Council), brought a halt to the various movements to form a new political mobilization organ. Kido, appointed home minister by Hiranuma, indicated that the government was uninterested in reviving any of these movements. Speaking to the press en route to the shrines at Ise, the home minister observed, "The 'national reorganization' and 'new party' questions can only be understood in connection with former Premier Konoe personally. . . . To me, the words 'national reorganization' seem insulting to the people. I question the wisdom of having the government try to impose this thing from above."[40] In short, there would be no governmental effort to take up the issues posed during the ministerial conferences of late 1938. The creation of a new popular political organization was contingent on Konoe's leadership, and the prince was clearly unwilling to become involved in such an endeavor at that time. Indeed, for the duration of the Hiranuma government's reign, political interest at the Cabinet level, and among right-wing groups as well, shifted from domestic reform issues to the weighty question of whether Japan should enter a military alliance with Germany and Italy, and against whom such an alliance should be directed.

THE PARTIES AND "PUBLIC" MOBILIZATION

During the latter half of the Konoe government and the entire period of Hiranuma's tenure in office, Cabinet poli-

[39] See YKUS, pp. 30–34.   [40] Ibid., p. 25.

cies were oriented toward using existing political and economic structures with minimum disruption, rather than subjecting them to fundamental reform. The parties capitalized on this lull in the series of challenges to their institutionally derived powers to reassert their importance as intermediary agencies between the government and the people. Their supporters in business, whether in the "old" or "new" *zaibatsu*, likewise enjoyed a respite after sustained challenges to the capitalist ethic of profit making. The government invoked the Mobilization Law in several areas, but in all cases obtained the approval of the National General Mobilization Council packed with Diet representatives. Most of the imperial decrees issued during this period under the Mobilization Law were designed to increase the productivity of workers, and thus benefited businessmen as much as the state.[41] The battle over invoking Article xi of the law resulted in controls over profits, but at a sufficiently high level of profits to maintain private incentives to expand production. Official intervention in key industries such as electric power continued, but the private sector of the economy found that it could live quite well with government controls at the existing levels. During this period, therefore, party representatives of big business' interests found it relatively easy to support the status quo, and even advanced new proposals for increasing defense production that would enhance profits further.[42] Similarly, the failure

[41] For a list of cases where the National General Mobilization Law was actually invoked, see Board of Planning, "Invocation of the National General Mobilization Law," *Tokyo Gazette*, ii.21 (March 1939), 20–21.

[42] See, for example, the Seiyūkai's new industrial policy of 1939, which called for the consolidation of vital industries, matching government investments in private enterprise, and the preservation of private controls over management. Kuhara conceded that this plan would greatly increase profits, but his party proposed that half of the profits be turned over to the government to improve social welfare, in lieu of increased taxes on business. See Kuhara Fusanosuke, *Zenshin no kōryō* (Tokyo: Taichisha, 1939), pp. 87–140, especially pp. 128–

209

of the bureaucracy to implement plans for a "reorganization of the people" (*kokumin sai-soshiki*) left the *meibōka* in a relatively secure position at the head of their communities, and again facilitated party identification with the government.

As succeeding wartime governments appealed for "unity throughout the nation" (*kyokoku itchi*) and popular solidarity with government (*kanmin ittai*), many party politicians began shifting the emphasis of their definitions of the party as an intermediary between the people and the state. The role of the party as articulator of the people's interests was slowly cast aside, while politicians proclaimed the parties' essence in terms of transmitting and articulating the state's interests to the people. In its clearest form, this view posited the party as a vital and permanent organ of state, with the specific function of mobilizing popular support for governments in which it would naturally hold a preeminent position. While in form this proposal resembled the organs discussed at the ministerial conferences of the Konoe government, in fact and in intent it differed from those plans significantly. Rather than checking the influence of the parties nationally and locally, it sought to expand the national power of the party men and protect their local bases of support. By presenting themselves as mobilizers of public support for governments in a period of heavy state demands on the people, party men hoped to regain recognition by the other political elites that they were essential figures in the preservation of unchallenged elite control in wartime as well as peace. Such recognition, they hoped, would be accompanied by new offers to share in power in the Cabinet.

This rationale for wartime party power, of course, underlay the bipartisan *Tōa saiken kokumin renmei* "public"

31. Nakajima also called for more state financing and credit guarantees to expand essential businesses, and more extensive government controls over labor. See Moro Masanori, *Ijin Nakajima Chikuhei hiroku* (Nitta-chō, Nitta-gun, Gunma-ken: Jōmō ijin denki kankōkai, 1960), pp. 198–204.

mobilization campaign of late 1938. After an auspicious beginning, however, the campaign encountered the same apathy in the countryside that bedeviled leaders of the official Movement for Mobilizing Popular Morale. The parties worked through the leaders of their local *jiban*, and confined their approach to the masses to exhortation, rather than organization. Nevertheless, the concept of a mobilization party continued to enjoy favor in party circles, particularly among Seiyūkai leaders who hoped it might restore the organizational integrity of the party as well as the influence of its members. Discipline within the Seiyūkai had been deteriorating badly since early 1937, and by the end of that year, a number of politicians in the party had begun agitating for the creation of a new party under Konoe's leadership. In view of the debilitating factional struggles over the party presidency waged between the Nakajima-Maeda factions and Hatoyama's supporters, this desire for a new president and a new party was perhaps not surprising. By fall 1938, however, Konoe had made clear his lack of interest in leading a new party, and Seiyūkai partisans were obliged once again to turn inward in an attempt to resolve the bitter differences dividing the party.

Nakajima and Hatoyama suspended their battles long enough for the party to remain intact during the 74th Diet session, but immediately after the Diet closed in late March 1939, the presidency issue was again joined. Kuhara Fusanosuke now emerged from a two-year period of relative inactivity occasioned by his suspected complicity in the February 26th Incident, and plunged into the struggle for power in the Seiyūkai. It had become clear, however, that if a full meeting of party members were held, Nakajima would be elected president. Hatoyama's position had so deteriorated that his principal efforts were directed towards preventing the convening of a general party conference to decide the presidency. Kuhara also aligned himself with Hatoyama, by proposing that instead of a general meeting to select a new president, a small presidential succession committee be

211

established with the authority to choose a successor to Suzuki. As part of the attempt to frustrate Nakajima's election, Suzuki, who had surrendered his presidential powers to the four proxies, suddenly dismissed the proxies and arbitrarily appointed three of Nakajima's opponents, including Kuhara, as replacements. Nakajima's backers responded by declaring that these new proxies and Hatoyama had been expelled from the Seiyūkai.

Nakajima then scheduled a general party convention for April 30, which the party's existing leadership declared invalid. It is not clear whether his opponents deliberately boycotted the meeting, or were prevented from attending, but whichever the case, Nakajima was unanimously elected as the new party president. On May 11, Kuhara declared himself to be the "legitimate" successor to Suzuki, and on May 20, his self-annointment was confirmed at a convention attended by those who had been absent from the April 30 meeting. In essence, the Seiyūkai had now divided into two parties, the "Nakajima Seiyūkai" and the smaller "Kuhara Seiyūkai" (called the "legitimate Seiyūkai" in the press). The remnants of Hatoyama's following joined forces with Kuhara as a consequence of their bitterness towards Nakajima's high-handed solution of the impasse over the presidency.[43]

By the summer of 1939, the leaders of both Seiyūkai organizations had formulated plans that emphasized "public" mobilization in wartime as the key to the resuscitation of party power. Nakajima's views on the policies his party should follow to gain strength were contained in an "Outline of a Reform Policy" he drafted in June 1939. To accomplish Japan's international mission, Nakajima wrote, the unique Japanese world view must be understood by the people at home. The government thus needed to win its

[43] For a general account of the Seiyūkai wrangle, see Shiraki, *Nihon seitō shi*, pp. 281–82. For Nakajima's perspective, see Watanabe, *Kyojin Nakajima Chikuhei*, pp. 348–49. One small segment of the party refused to align with either of the two competing groups.

own people's support through an extensive ideological campaign, explaining the relevance of Japan's plans for a New
East Asia to the lives of the Japanese people. Nakajima
emphasized that an important role in this mobilization of
public support should be played by a strong party. "Japan's
unique world view must be spread among the people as
political thought, so that the people are aware of the nation's objectives and their own duties, and cooperate with
controls to produce great national power. For this, a strong
political organization—that is, a strong political party—is
necessary. The Cabinet should stand on the strength of such
a party."[44]

Nakajima's plan indicated his interest in using the party
to enhance a nationalistic consciousness among the masses.
Significantly, however, he proposed to accomplish this end
through an ideological campaign, rather than through any
proposal to extend the organization of the party (even as a
semiofficial organ of state) into the countryside beyond the
nexus of *meibōka*-Diet member ties that characterized the
existing level of community integration into national politics. In short, Nakajima did not appear interested in any new
mass organizational effort that would undermine local social
and political traditions or the authority of the *meibōka* who
organized the *jiban* of his party's membership. While he
sought to enhance party power at the national level, the
local activities of his new party were to be "public" rather
than "political" in nature, for they were not to constitute
any direct challenge to the customary prerogatives of existing elite groups in the village or their ties to the state
through the Diet. Kuhara, like Nakajima, was relatively satisfied with the existing political and economic systems, apart
from the fact that party influence beyond the Lower House
had waned. His own program for a new mobilization party
was characterized by an elaborate organization designed
to enhance party power nationally and integrate the citizen-

[44] "Kakushin seisaku no taikō," June 1, 1939, in Moro, *Ijin Nakajima
Chikuhei hiroku*, pp. 198–206.

ry into the state. However, like Nakajima's more modest proposal, Kuhara's concept was oriented toward "public" mobilization of citizen support for state policies rather than "political" mobilization of new groups in an attack on the legal or traditional prerogatives of existing elite groups. Indeed, Kuhara's advocacy of a one-party system earlier in the decade had been predicated on the continuing recognition of the political primacy of the *meibōka* locally, and the conversion of the election system from a mechanism for articulating conflicting interests into a ritual for mobilizing popular support for the policies of the government and the permanent government party. This concept of a "public" mobilization party continued to dominate Kuhara's thinking in 1938, as his idea expanded from a simple one-party system in the Lower House to a proposal for the creation of a hierarchical series of popular councils (*kokumin kyōgikai*).[45] Their primary membership was to be drawn from the Lower House and local assemblies, but they were also to encompass all political forces and mass groups from the national to the village and town levels. The network of councils was to be the nucleus of a new monolithic party, a "great popular organization" financed by government funds.

According to Kuhara's plan, the premier was to serve as chairman of the national party-council, and appoint members from representatives of the Upper House, civil and military officials, and other groups, in addition to the preeminent Lower House contingent. He was also to have the power to select members of local party-councils from vocational groups in addition to the preeminent force of local assemblymen.

As Kuhara noted, his plan for local councils resembled

[45] The following discussion is based on: "Dai-Nippon teikoku kokumin kyōgikai soshiki taikō (an)," in Imai and Itō, eds., *Kokka sōdōin,* pp. 80–82; "Dai-Nippon teikoku kokumin kyōgikai sōan," and "Kokumin-teki seiji kessei yōryō," in *Kido monjo,* pp. 377–85; Kinoshita Hanji, *Shintaisei jiten* (Tokyo: Asahi shinbunsha, 1941), pp. 66–67; and Kuhara, *Zenshin no kōryō,* pp. 1–85.

the proposals of the Home Ministry Local Affairs Bureau to create a network for organizing and integrating the entire citizenry into national affairs. Kuhara, however, sought to integrate the citizenry through a new party controlled by Lower House representatives; the Local Affairs Bureau wished to integrate the citizenry through official and semi-official organizations under its own control. Kuhara wished to preserve and expand the powers of popularly elected representatives at the national and local levels by making them the central force of the councils; the Home Ministry wanted to work through the bureaucracy at the expense of Diet influence nationally, and through the mayors at the expense of local assemblies in the towns and villages.

In essence, Kuhara's party-councils would provide the framework for the management of political conflict nationally and locally. At the national level, this plan constituted a bold effort to reassert the functions of the political party as an arena for the harmonization of elite conflict. It differed from the parties of the 1920s primarily in the rejection of two-party competition in the Diet. Under a single-party system in which the Cabinet and Diet were under party control, party decisions could be implemented through the other organs of state without conflict, manifesting the harmony of the imperial system. At the local level, the party-councils would still be dominated by the traditional political leadership, which controlled the assemblies and would consolidate its control over other local groups through the party-councils, dominated by assembly-men. *Meibōka* and local "elder statesmen" were also to serve as advisors to the local councils. At election time, they would continue to mobilize their communities' participation in politics, as previously. The integration of the citizenry into Kuhara's new official hierarchy was thus designed to minimize challenges to the established position of local elites in politics. At the same time, elections under the new party system would no longer be competitive, and would function primarily to articulate popular identification with and support of the party-controlled government and its policies. Strong authoritarian leadership at the apex of the party-council hierarchy would insure that party programs and mobilization campaigns reflect the policies of the ruling elites rather than challenge the legitimacy of their control of the state. The links running from the Cabinet and Diet through the party-councils to the *meibōka* and local communities would thus become the major official channel of popular control and "public" mobilization.

This new emphasis by Seiyūkai leaders on the party as an agency of "public" mobilization implied a new type of party, a new type of election, and a broader range of party activity. The new party would provide channels for popular expressions of support for governments, but not opposition. It also promised to increase political participation in party-sponsored local activities, and to integrate more people (in theory, all the people) directly through its mobilization efforts on the national and local levels. At the same time, the new party would be closely identified with the government, holding a central position in it. As a semiofficial organ of the state, its status would differ from that of other political groups or parties that remained outside of its organization. The new party would enjoy a permanent control of the Diet and the premiership. Diet elections would therefore become again a method of expressing public support for elite government. The party would hence provide a popular affirmation of the legitimacy of the government and policies with which it was associated. On the other hand, elections would no longer serve to articulate popular interests through the selection of one party or another to represent the people in the Diet; rather, their sole function would be to mobilize public support for official policies by the government party. To put it briefly, Kuhara and Nakajima de-emphasized the utility of the old two-party and multi-party models as the means for providing popular ratification of governments and their policies, minimized the party's potential to generate political conflict and divergent popu-

216

lar interests, and increasingly stressed the importance of mass national integration, local party activity, and "public" mobilization.

The proposals of the Seiyūkai leaders never went beyond the planning stage in 1939. Moreover, they were not representative of the complete spectrum of "mainstream" party thought. In the Minseitō, Machida Chūji remained wedded to a more balanced definition of party functions, and committed to the preservation of the party organization on which his personal political influence rested. He reaffirmed the conservative viewpoint at the general Minseitō congress of January 1940:

> In only one year, we have seen the unfortunate spectacle of three changes in the wartime Cabinets. My own experience in previous governments has taught me that Cabinets with weak bases, those which lack a motive force absolutely essential in times of war, cannot surmount the difficulties of the times. To be capable of truly bearing the strain of the situation, a wartime Cabinet must reflect a firm concert between the military and parties based on the people. Cabinets which are not rooted in the general will of the people will of course be unable to produce political results.[46]

In short, Machida continued to justify the parties' claim to a share of Cabinet power on the grounds that the parties represented the will of the people. While he agreed with Kuhara and Nakajima that parties must mobilize popular support for governments, the president of the Minseitō also emphasized the representative function of the parties. He saw no reason why politicians should depart from traditional party organizations, or why the parties should claim to function any differently from in the past. This conservative ("liberal") viewpoint continued to hold an important

[46] Matsumura Kenzō, *Machida Chūji-ō den* (Tokyo: Machida Chūji-ō denki kankōkai, 1950), p. 363.

217

place in party thinking, not only among Machida's followers but in Hatoyama's retinue and the minority *Shamin* faction of the Shadaitō. However, like the views of Kuhara and Nakajima, it was subjected to a severe challenge by the appearance of a new campaign for a "reformist" party.

The Campaign for a New "Reformist" Party

During the first eight months of 1939, political interest was briefly deflected from the China Incident as Japanese forces in the field adopted a strategic policy of holding and consolidating previous gains.[47] The major political controversy of the Hiranuma government centered on the proposal that Japan enter into a military alliance with Germany and Italy. Since the Cabinet could only agree to such an alliance as a means of neutralizing the threat of the Soviet Union in the Far East, supporters of the proposed pact were dealt a severe blow when Germany and the Soviet Union concluded a Non-Aggression Pact in August. In response to this sudden and dramatic development in the international climate, Hiranuma promptly resigned and was replaced by General Abe Nobuyuki.

General Abe was a pleasant and easy-going man from Kanazawa prefecture, who had risen to the top ranks of the Army without having ever commanded troops in the field. Although he had friends and relatives throughout the various civilian elite groups, he himself had never been an active figure in interelite politics. The new premier entrusted the duties of organizing the Cabinet to his son-in-law, Colonel Arisue Seizō, who was then serving as chief of the Military Affairs Section of the Army Ministry. According to the memoirs of Yatsugi Kazuo, then a civilian advisor of the Army, Arisue had great hopes for capitalizing on Abe's appointment to execute far-reaching domestic and political reforms in consonance with the Army's pro-

[47] DR, I, 571–75.

gram of establishing a national defense state. Believing that their reform program would meet with strong resistance from the bureaucracy and Diet, as in the past, Arisue and Yatsugi planned to have Abe dissolve the Diet and hold elections in which a new "Nationalist Masses Party" would marshal public support for the reform plans. They anticipated that if the government could produce a strong show of public confidence in this fashion, conservative resistance to reform could be overcome. The one party leader they looked to in organizing this new political reform force was Nagai Ryūtarō, the anti-mainstream "reformist" politician from Kanazawa.[48]

Nagai was highly receptive to these plans, and took an active role in the formation of the Abe government. Indeed, for many years he had been a consistent advocate of establishing a new mass-based political party.[49] Nagai's interest in mass organization, which long antedated the China Incident, made him an anomaly among *kisei seitō* leaders in the 1920s and early 1930s. He had consistently criticized the Diet parties for representing the interests only of capitalists and landlords, and urged the Minseitō to adopt policies based on broad popular interests rather than on the desires of these bourgeois groups. In 1935, he had recommended that the parties be recognized as public organs of the state, and that election costs be borne by the state instead of the parties and their capitalist supporters. In 1936, he reiterated his belief that the major purpose of Diet politicians was to bring the government into touch with mass opinion and to educate public opinion. Again in early 1937, he had urged the Minseitō to become a party of mass-oriented politicians.[50]

[48] Yatsugi, *Shōwa dōran shishi*, II, 86–104.

[49] For a recent English-language study, see Peter Duus, "Nagai Ryūtarō: The Tactical Dilemmas of Reform," in Albert M. Craig and Donald H. Shively, eds., *Personality in Japanese History* (Berkeley and Los Angeles: University of California Press, 1970), pp. 399–424.

[50] "Nagai Ryūtarō" hensankai, ed., *Nagai Ryūtarō*, pp. 302–307 and 334–49.

In other words, prior to the China Incident, Nagai conceived of the political party as an essential organ of state, through which mass interests could be articulated and expressed in national policy making. Parties that shared power in government could also obtain popular support for Cabinets through their political actions and political education of the masses. While he increasingly emphasized the role of the parties as mobilizers of public support after 1937, Nagai never abandoned his earlier view that the parties should articulate popular interests as well. His view of party functions thus did not differ greatly in theory from Machida's. However, Nagai's complaint with the Minseitō under Machida's leadership was that it was oriented, not towards mass interests, but only towards the interests of select groups of people.[51] By the fall of 1939, he was anxious to enlist Army backing for the conversion of the Minseitō into a mass-oriented political force, and fell in with the plans of Arisue and Yatsugi.

Machida, however, greatly resented Nagai's covert association with the Army, and refused to sanction Arisue's request that Nagai be appointed to Abe's Cabinet. Only after the Army applied great pressure on the Minseitō leadership was Nagai given party permission to become a member of the government. Several other party men known to favor the creation of a pro-Army "reformist" party were also given

[51] Nagai's populism was accompanied by his energetic efforts to mobilize mass support for the war in China. He often lent his considerable oratorical skills to the defense of Japan's Asian policies, in his own speeches and, occasionally, by helping Konoe draft public statements. In his view, the war increased the need to mobilize the public, since it imposed greater burdens on the citizenry. Unless the people cooperated in programs restricting consumption, particularly of imported goods, and conserving domestic resources, Nagai warned, "they themselves would be responsible for the destruction of Japanese civilization." See his widely circulated speech commemorating the first anniversary of the Marco Polo Bridge Incident, in Nagai Ryūtarō, *Watakushi no shinnen to taiken* (Tokyo: Okakura shobō, 1938), p. 344.

appointments in the government as parliamentary vice ministers and councilors.[52] However, the Minseitō refused to become the nucleus of Nagai's plan for a new reformist mass party, or to offer positive cooperation with Abe unless Nagai were expelled from the Cabinet. Hence, when Abe asked that Machida, too, join the government to strengthen its ties with the parties, the Minseitō president curtly refused to do so. He was willing to cooperate with Abe, but not with the scheme of Nagai and the middle-echelon Army officers for radical reform.[53]

While Abe was unwilling to fire Nagai, the reform plans were quickly shunted aside under his direction. The premier continued to show the same degree of goodwill towards party leaders that Hiranuma had professed. In December, he established a program of semimonthly meetings with the presidents of both Seiyūkai factions, the Minseitō, Kokumin dōmei, and Shadaitō. Through this gesture, he was able to retain the good will of the leadership of the parties, but he deeply disappointed Nagai and other proponents of a new party in the government.

Nagai's association with the Abe government thus had little impact on the nation's politics or economy, but the problems he and his Army friends encountered with the

[52] It was widely noted at the time that Machida was not disposed to approve of Nagai's appointment. Nagai's biography indicates that he and the chief Cabinet secretary were obliged to see Machida two or three times during the negotiations over Nagai's status. "Nagai Ryūtarō" hensankai, ed., *Nagai Ryūtarō*, p. 429. The press also indicated Machida's opposition to Nagai's appointment. See Yamaura Kan'ichi, "Gotō-shu kaidan to seiji yōsō," *Chūō kōron*, #629 (January 1940), p. 62. One wonders about Abe's motives for telling Baron Harada that he was displeased about Nagai's selection himself, but that it was the result of leaving the matter in Machida's hands. See SKS, viii, 63. Additional information regarding the formation of the Abe government was obtained in interviews with Yatsugi Kazuo by the author, November 6 and 25 and December 16, 1968, in Tokyo.

[53] Machida was offered a Cabinet position by Abe in the hope that mainstream Minseitō support could be gained for the forthcoming Diet session. Machida refused the offer on November 24, 1939.

Minseitō illustrated two important developments. First, pressures were again emanating from the Army for the creation of a new party to mobilize political support for its program of reform. Second, Nagai and other lesser party figures were prepared to create a new mass political organization on behalf of the Army, in the belief that the military's reform proposals were vital from the viewpoint of national defense and essential to the welfare of the citizenry. Collaboration with the Army in forming a new "reformist" party, in their view, was also the one viable approach left to the restoration of party power in the Cabinet. This perception of the dilemmas and opportunities for parliamentary politicians was also shared among many junior members of the *kisei seitō* and members of the smaller parties and Diet factions. Moreover, when the Abe government found itself beleaguered by domestic problems at the end of the year, this viewpoint became a critical factor in the parliamentary movement to overthrow the government.

The central foreign policy concerns of the Abe regime focused on the creation of a new Chinese government led by Wang Ching-wei, and on the maintenance of Japan's noninvolvement in the European war that broke out in September. While the government was able to pursue these policies without difficulty, its performance on domestic issues provoked widespread antipathy. In view of conservative and bureaucratic opposition, the premier was obliged to shelve the Army's proposals for a new Trade Ministry and a revision of the civil service system that would permit greater military participation in the administration of national affairs. The most serious problems confronting the Cabinet, however, were economic. The combined influence of the China Incident's drain on national resources and a severe drought created serious national shortages of food and power. The drought produced a shortage of water, while coal was being diverted to the Army in China; the result was an insufficient supply of electric power in the

222

homes and enterprises of all Japanese. The government could do little to assuage popular discontent on this matter, and also demonstrated an inability to deal with the food shortage. The drought reduced the rice yield in western Japan, Korea, and Taiwan below expectations, and black market transactions above the fixed rice price (38 yen/ *koku*) became commonplace. A thriving black market business was also done in goods that could no longer be imported legally because of the need to retain Japan's gold and foreign currency for the purchase of military supplies abroad. The government sought to prevent inflation during this difficult period by announcing a price freeze on all commodities, but this action only stimulated illicit selling and buying. Finally, the government raised the fixed price of rice to 43 yen/*koku* in November, and prohibited the use of white rice in a futile effort to destroy the black market.[54]

As a consequence of these problems, popular resentment grew against the government, the bureaucracy that administered the various economic restrictions, and even the war in China, which was in part responsible for the discomfort in daily life. Diet members touring their home districts prior to the 75th Diet session took note of this discontent, and returned to Tokyo with the desire to use the economic issue to propel their parties back into power. They were discouraged, however, by the attitude of party leaders, whose relationship with Abe ranged from benevolent neutrality to strong support. Abe's government included three party politicians—Nagai, Akita Kiyoshi, and Kanemitsu Tsuneo (a former Seiyūkai member who had refused to align himself with either Nakajima or Kuhara). All three were political mavericks, who shared an interest in the formation of a new political party. None was popular with the *kisei seitō* leader-

[54] Hayashi Shigeru, *Taiheiyō sensō* (Nihon no rekishi, XXV) (Tokyo: Chūō kōronsha, 1967), p. 131; Fujiwara, Imai, and Tōyama, *Shōwa shi*, pp. 174–75.

ship, and their presence in Abe's government was more irritating than gratifying to party leaders.[55] At the same time, however, both Kuhara and Machida had an interest in keeping Abe at the helm of government. Abe's chief Cabinet secretary, Endō Ryūsaku, enjoyed considerable influence in the government and was Kuhara's protégé. Machida had been able to blunt the sharpest thrusts of the Army's reform program through his skillful manipulation of Abe's desire for greater party support.

Finding their leaders unreceptive to a campaign against Abe, many junior members of the major parties turned instead to work with the *Jikyoku dōshikai*, a coalition of Diet members sympathetic to national socialism, who belonged to the Tōhōkai, Kokumin dōmei, and Nippon kakushintō (led by Etō Genkurō and Akamatsu Katsumaro). The *dōshikai* had been formed on November 20, as a preliminary step towards fusing the participating groups into a new reformist party, and sought support by leading the attack on the government's failure to manage the economy properly. The *dōshikai* won the backing of large numbers of Diet members for its attack on the government, and became the nucleus of the campaign to bring about Abe's downfall. A group of Diet supporters of this campaign, spanning all of the parties, was soon formed. Calling itself a "Conference of Concerned Diet Members" (*Yūshi daigishi-kai*), it secretly began to collect signatures on a resolution calling for the government's resignation. When the Diet session convened on December 26, the resolution was dramatically made public with the signatures of 240 Diet members, and on January 7, 1940, a formal Diet petition favoring Abe's resignation was signed by 276 Diet members. The Abe government was thus forced to consider either dissolving the Diet and calling new elections, or stepping down from office in face

[55] Kanemitsu worked closely with Kiya Ikusaburō, a journalist, during most of 1939 to promote the new party movement. See Kiya Ikusaburō, *Konoe-kō hibun*, p. 35, and Kiya, *Seikai gojū-nen no butai-ura*, p. 218.

224

of this barrage of criticism. Kuhara advised Abe to remain in office and make him (Kuhara) a minister in order to undermine the Diet's attack. Nagai, Kanemitsu, and Akita urged the premier to dissolve the Diet and form a new "reform" party to win the ensuing election. However, when the Army leadership informed Abe it would not sanction new elections at a time when popular morale was at its nadir, the premier reluctantly agreed to resign on January 16.[56]

CONCLUSION

The vicissitudes of the reform movement from 1937 to 1940 provided an accurate index of the power position of the political parties. Despite the decline of party influence in the Cabinet, the parties, *zaibatsu*, and *meibōka* remained strong enough to weather the storm of "political reform" sentiment directed against them in the name of national mobilization and the need to prosecute the war in China. The invitations to Nagai and Nakajima to attend the Eight-Minister Conference meetings in the final months of the Konoe government indicated that mobilization and reform could not be carried out by excluding the political parties and their supporters from the formulation and execution of domestic policies. The parties had managed to preserve, and tried to expand, their roles as mediating agencies between the people and government despite the desire of the right wing to undermine their position, and despite the efforts of bureaucrats to create a new mobilization structure free of party and *meibōka* influence. Party men in the Diet still

[56] See Shiraki, *Nihon seitō shi*, pp. 284–86; Sugihara, *Atarashii Shōwa shi*, pp. 173–76; and Sugihara, *Kokumin soshiki no seiji-ryoku*, pp. 23–24. A list of the signatories on the January 7 petition was published in the *Asahi shinbun*, January 8, 1940. The list included eighty-one Minseitō members, seventy-nine members of the Nakajima Seiyūkai, forty-six from the Kuhara Seiyūkai, thirty-two Shadaitō members, twenty-nine members of *Jikyoku dōshikai* and nine independents.

225

retained sufficient influence to veto governmental budgetary and legislative proposals, if they wished. This ability was great enough to dissuade men such as Kido from pressing the demand for political reform too far. Fearing that conservative opposition to the government would prove detrimental to the execution of important wartime policies, Konoe opted to avoid domestic turmoil by minimizing the disruptive effect of political reform on the positions of the political parties. Moreover, the government chose not to challenge business and the men of local influence, in hopes of gaining their cooperation in the execution of wartime economic policies. Hence, the Cabinet in the end responded to the call for reform by simply acquiescing to Konoe's reaffirmation of "public" spiritual mobilization.

The official commitment to spiritual mobilization was symbolized and reconfirmed by the appointment of Hiranuma as Konoe's successor. Contrary to the expectations and fears of many politicians, Hiranuma proved to be more effective as an ally of the parties than he had been as an adversary in the previous years. Moreover, the moderation of his approach to the parties was not idiosyncratic, but a reflection of changing sentiments among "Japanist" groups in the right wing. As the dimensions of reform required by the "national defense state" became known, many "Japanist" groups who had opposed the prevailing political and economic systems in the 1920s, and urged "purifying" reform in the early 1930s, also came to oppose drastic domestic reform as "socialistic" and inconsistent with Japan's national essence. This tendency was accelerated by the war in China, which "Japanists" insisted could be prosecuted successfully by spiritual mobilization and spiritual unity rather than institutional reform. Hence, their position shifted from alignment with the "reformist" camp in the early 1930s to growing sympathy with the conservative opposition to the "reformists." Justice Minister Shiono's participation in the new party talks with Suetsugu in October 1938 symbolized both the final, futile moment of collaboration between the two major segments of the right wing, and the growing rapprochement between the "Japanists" and conservative forces. While Shiono agreed to the formation of a new party, his principal party collaborators were not even the anti-mainstream elements of the two major parties, as might have been expected, but the faltering Seiyūkai mainstream faction led by Hiranuma's old colleague, Suzuki Kisaburō, and self-proclaimed "liberal," Hatoyama Ichirō.

Emerging from the battles of the Konoe government, party leaders thus found new allies in their struggle against the "reformist" camp. Indeed, despite enactment of the National General Mobilization Law, they and the Lower House they dominated continued to be a force to be reckoned with in the formulation of national policies and the struggle for power among the national political elite groups. From 1939 to the fall of 1940, they concentrated on orienting their activities in directions that might earn them a larger role in the political process, and restore their credibility as national leaders. Machida, Nakajima, and Kuhara all collaborated closely with the government, and were prepared to use their party organizations as agencies of "public" mobilization on behalf of any Cabinet that abjured radical reform. The leaders of the two Seiyūkai parties made proposals to revise the fundamentally competitive nature of the party system, and to create one new party that would enjoy permanent hegemony or monopoly over the Diet while serving as the agency of popular mobilization for the state. At the same time, they shared the interest of the Home Ministry and other bureaucratic agencies in integrating the citizenry more fully into national affairs. Integration, however, did not imply sharing political power with the masses, or even basing national policy on popular viewpoints. Rather it meant arousing in them a sense of identification with imperial government and a willingness to make personal sacrifices for the sake of Japan's mission in East Asia. By redefining the role of the political party as the crucial

227

linkage between the state and the citizenry, and by establishing permanent control over the Diet, advocates of a monolithic or hegemonic party system hoped to increase their leverage in negotiating with the nonparty elite groups, and in Kuhara's case, create a new extra-Cabinet forum for the reconciliation of competing elite ambitions and policy proposals.[57] They hoped, thereby to regain control of the premiership and the Cabinet. Meanwhile, the Minseitō under Machida adhered to more conventional definitions of party function, insisting on the importance of popular representation as well as popular controls and mobilization.

None of the mainstream leaders, however, took any concrete steps in 1939 to go beyond supporting the Hiranuma and Abe governments and opposing further reform (or disruption) of the political and economic systems. Their subordinates continued to despair of regaining influence beyond the Lower House, and looked toward coalitions with small national socialist and reformist parties to overthrow the mainstream leadership of their parties. They hoped to create a new "reformist" party in the Diet, and work with the Army and other reform groups for the transformation of the political and economic systems. Nagai Ryūtarō proved to be the party leader who sympathized most strongly with this position, and by the beginning of 1940, his own withdrawal from the Minseitō appeared to be only a matter of time.

The denouement of the Diet's campaign against the Abe Cabinet reflected the magnitude of the challenge to party leaders' power positions from within their own organiza-

[57] The term "hegemonic" is borrowed from Giovanni Sartori, "The Typology of Party Systems—Proposals for Improvement," in Erik Allardt and Stein Rokkan, eds., *Mass Politics: Studies in Political Sociology* (New York: Free Press, 1970), pp. 322–52. "One-party" systems outlaw the existence of any other party. "Hegemonic" party systems permit subordinate parties to exist, so long as the hegemony of the party in power cannot be challenged. Other parties are permitted to exist only as satellite parties, for they may not compete with the "hegemonic" party in antagonistic terms or on an equal basis.

tions. The parties' membership had demonstrated that party leaders could no longer exert firm discipline over their forces. Even the Minseitō, which prided itself on its unity and internal discipline, split squarely down the middle when the petition against Abe was signed. Inasmuch as a party without discipline was virtually powerless as a force in national affairs, the spectacle of massive *kisei seitō* defections to the anti-Abe campaign provided a further stimulant for the movement to dissolve the old parties and create a new party. For party leaders, the lesson of the anti-Abe campaign was clear. If they wished to retain control over the groups they led, it would be necessary to reconcile the "reformist" sentiments of the junior membership with their own support of the "status quo." Failure to do so would permit the growing "reformist" coalition of small factions and parties to strip large numbers of *kisei seitō* parliamentarians away from their parties, and into a new party movement in which men like Adachi, Nakano, Akamatsu, Kanemitsu, Nagai, and Akita would have the leading roles. Handling this vexing problem became the chief task of party leaders in the first half of 1940.

Ironically, the chaotic conditions within the major parties, and the strong new party initiative taken by the smaller parties in early 1940, coincided with a brief period in which it seemed the parties were on the verge of attaining renewed political eminence. The simple fact that a Diet-centered campaign had again resulted in the resignation of an Army-supported government led to speculation in the press that Machida would soon become premier.[58] The rise of popular discontent with governments in which they had no voice fostered the hope among many party politicians that the senior advisors to the throne (*jūshin*) would now see fit to choose a party man to lead the new government.

[58] See, for example, Tsukui Tatsuo, who viewed the possible appointment of a party Cabinet with grave misgivings. "Seikyoku no tenki to gunbu no sekimu," *Chūō kōron*, #629 (January 1940), pp. 55–61; and Fujiwara, Imai, and Tōyama, *Shōwa shi*, p. 175.

Such hopes, however, were not to be realized. Given the renewed pressures for domestic reform in the Army, Machida was totally unacceptable to the military, and no longer had complete control over the 169-man Minseitō contingent in the Diet. Working in close concert, Privy Seal Yuasa Kurahei and Harada Kumao were able to install Admiral Yonai Mitsumasa as Abe's successor. Yonai's appointment provided anti-leadership politicians with new evidence that they would never regain power under their present leaders. As Yonai's government took office in the middle of January, a large number of Diet members in the *kisei seitō* and the smaller groups were only waiting for an opportunity to demonstrate their willingness to dissolve their parties and establish a new mass party in collaboration with the Army.

CHAPTER VI

The Birth of Konoe's New Political Order

INTRODUCTION

THE first six months of 1940 were a period of tumultuous change for the world and Japan. Europe was at war, and Germany was getting much the best of it. In April, the Nazis occupied Norway and Denmark. In May, the war opened on the Western Front, and Hitler's troops marched through France, Holland, Belgium, and Luxembourg. Paris fell in mid-June, and Britain's defeat seemed only a matter of days or weeks. The United States sought to bolster Britain's flagging fortunes with material and financial support, and also reacted strongly to Japanese restrictions on American commercial interests in China. In January, President Franklin Roosevelt escalated the "moral embargo" on airplanes, parts, and credits to Japan into the abrogation of the American-Japanese Treaty of Commerce and Navigation. The possibility of a total American embargo on war materials to Japan thereafter became a vital factor in American-Japanese relations, and in determining Japan's response to changing world conditions.

Within Japan, there was also a great deal of tumult, impelled by these international events and by the ongoing competition for power among various elite groups. The political parties began the year with a demonstration of their residual strength against the Abe government, and then rushed forward to extend their influence in the "new political order" (*shin seiji taisei*) proposed by Konoe Fumimaro. Party men hoped Konoe's leadership would make a new party the focal point of managing elite conflict outside the Cabinet, since the prince was well connected with all elite groups and was an experienced political mediator.

231

They believed Konoe would create a new hegemonic or monolithic party and thought such a party would establish permanent control over the premiership. In an effort to regain their extraparliamentary influence, nearly all existing political groups were willing to dissolve their organizations by the middle of the summer, and did so in response to Konoe's encouragement. When it later became clear that Konoe's new order was not a new party, but a challenge to their influence and the Diet institution, party leaders joined the attack on the new order at the end of the year, and emerged from this final challenge to their institutional prerogatives with their original organizations formally dissolved but their parliamentary power actually intact.

The new political order idea developed in the context of a rapidly changing international environment. Japan's leaders perceived the involvement of the Western colonial powers in a European war as a "golden opportunity" for expanding into Southeast Asia, and extending the "New Order in East Asia" into a "Greater East Asian Co-Prosperity Sphere." The "South" held the promise of valuable resources and strategic advantage in fighting the Chinese and establishing Japan as an autonomous power capable of defending her growing empire against the Soviet Union or the Anglo-American powers. These perceptions were heightened by a sense of urgency on the part of the Japanese. There was a possibility that unless Japan moved south quickly, Germany might claim the colonies of the conquered European powers as her own. Moreover, Japan desired rapid access to Southeast Asia's resources in order to replenish and guarantee her stocks of vital materials before the United States imposed a total embargo on Japan. Finally, with Chiang Kai-shek's foreign supporters diverted to the conflict in Europe, a number of influential Japanese leaders believed that the moment was ripe to bring about China's capitulation to Japan, on the battlefield or at the conference table.

To meet all of these contingencies, Prince Konoe and

232

other political leaders agreed that the entire citizenry must be integrated more fully into the life of the state. They worked tirelessly to strengthen mass identification with the state through the manipulation of nationalistic symbols (particularly the throne), propaganda relating Japan's international policies to the lives of the citizenry, and plans for new "national unity" organizations. They intensified earlier efforts to enhance mass support for the government and mass participation in the implementation of national policies.

Although Japan moved with relative smoothness from a semicentralized administrative system of *bakufu* and *han* in the Edo period to a centralized nation-state after 1868, the process of political integration was not considered complete by Japanese leaders even in 1940. Before 1853, most Japanese had strong parochial loyalties, and tended to identify themselves as members of specific functional classes or inhabitants of particular domains. In the 1860s and Meiji era, the samurai class became politically integrated into "the nation," although parochial loyalties persisted and were evidenced most prominently in national politics through the *hanbatsu*. By the end of the Meiji era, all of the growing number of national elite groups owed their primary political loyalty to the nation-state. However, directing the ordinary citizen's loyalties and sense of identification beyond the village or town to the nation remained an ongoing task on the agenda of the nation's leadership. War—first with China in 1894–1895 and then with Russia in 1904–1905—did much to strengthen peasant identification with the state. The national system of education, and particularly its courses on Japanese history and ethics, fostered nationalism among the young.

On the other hand, the system of local administration did not fully penetrate into the villages and towns. Parochialism remained strong in many areas, and villagers' primary concern with local, rather than national, issues remained a distinguishing characteristic of mass political behavior. At election time, candidates for public office did little to offend the parochial sensibilities of their constituents, and more often than not, campaign promises centered on the satisfaction of local interests rather than on the enactment of broad national policies. By the early part of the twentieth century the political parties had made a small but important contribution to the process of national political integration by serving as a vital link between the community and the state. However, the parties as institutions did not really penetrate the village. Their links to the countryside were fragile and indirect, being embodied in the relationship of the community to *meibōka*, the *meibōka* ties to party candidates, and the candidates' ties to the national party. The pressures for national integration grew rapidly after 1930, as Japanese leaders felt a growing need to gain popular support and mobilize mass energies toward the fulfillment of national policy objectives. Increasingly, the integrating function of the parties was regarded as inadequate, and they were attacked as disintegrative influences. The competition of the two major parties added another divisive element to other conflicting ideological and interest positions in national and local politics, and was decried and disparaged as a simple manifestation of the parties' lust for power. Even many party leaders recognized by late 1938 and 1939 that the existing party organizations and activities did not contribute to the wartime quest for greater national integration. They sought to adapt themselves to this new task by participating in the Movement for Mobilizing Popular Morale, and creating their own movement with similar goals. Nakajima proposed still another spiritual mobilization drive in 1939, which would center exclusively on his new party. However, only Kuhara's plan for the popular-council party sought to create a national organization that penetrated all the way into the village.

The new political order and "high-degree national defense state" concepts were, above all, expressions of the desire of Japan's wartime leaders to intensify the process of national integration, to elevate citizen attitudes toward the state from passive compliance with orders from above to active support for the state. The ultimate goal of national integration as conceived by the leadership was the complete negation by the citizen of the self, and self-affirmation solely in the context of "fulfilling the duties of the loyal subject to the throne." The excessive passion with which individualism, liberalism, socialism, private interests, and class identity were attacked in the "Shōwa teens" (1938–1944) was explicit evidence of the importance attached to having individuals identify themselves primarily as members of the nation. The political struggle over the creation of the new political order in 1940–1941 became the anvil on which the institutional framework for systematic efforts at national integration was hammered out.

In scope and in purpose, therefore, the movement for a new political order dwarfed the movement for a new "reformist" party in 1938. Nevertheless, the two campaigns had much in common. The Army and its civilian supporters launched a new attack against the domestic "advocates of the status quo," and proclaimed the need to restructure the nation to meet the military requirements of Japan's foreign policies. The new order movement thus began as a direct political attack on the institutional prerogatives of those who were opposed to policies deemed "vital" for Japan's international mission; and, in this sense, it closely paralleled the campaign against the opponents of those reforms deemed "vital" to the five-year plans in 1938.

The pattern of Prince Konoe's response to the "reformist" campaign of 1940 also bore a strong resemblance to his behavior in 1938. He sympathized with the advocates of reform, but as a noble, remained reluctant to assume the leadership of a new political party. Nevertheless, as in 1938, he appeared on the verge of overcoming his aversion to party movements, provided that intensive "political" mobilization did not impede the nation's ability to prosecute and end the war in China. Konoe's proposed new order was

235

indeed "political," and highly divisive, for it challenged the institutional prerogatives of every major elite group with political influence: the parties, the bureaucracy, business, and even the military. In planning to bring all elite groups and the citizenry under his control, Konoe implicitly challenged the diffusion of political power legitimized by the Constitution and Cabinet system. The unique style of national integration he sought thus bore within it the danger of shattering the national cohesiveness provided by adherence to commonly accepted laws and norms of political behavior, before the higher level of "national unity" he sought could be attained. Konoe's actions demonstrated that he was willing to risk this danger and issue a direct challenge to the defenders of the "status quo," provided there was an opportunity to end the war in China before creating the new order.

Throughout the first half of the year, Konoe and certain elements in the Army held great, if ill-founded, hope that a truce could be negotiated with Chiang Kai-shek. This optimism coincided with the prince's announcement of the campaign for the new political order. In the second half of the year, however, it became increasingly and then conclusively evident that Chiang would refuse to surrender at the negotiating table what the Japanese were unable to procure on the battlefield, and Konoe's enthusiasm for "political" mobilization waned. Unwilling to risk dividing the nation while troops fought in the field, Konoe thereafter confined his efforts to more conventional approaches to national integration and mobilization of popular spiritual and economic energies on behalf of the state. He soon denounced the "highly political" nature of the new order. As in late 1938, Konoe agreed finally to confine policy making and control over mobilization within existing (and diffuse) patterns of elite political and economic power holding.

Konoe's decisions during the year had a profound bearing on the fate of the political parties, and the responses of party men to his new order campaign were a decisive fac-

236

tor in determining the scope and degree of their influence during the last years of imperial Japan. The outcome of Konoe's challenge and the response by the parties and other elites demonstrated, as in 1938, the persistence of the "limited pluralism" of power holding in imperial Japan, and the strength of the constitutional, legal, and traditional systems of legitimizing power that underlay that pluralism. Konoe was unable to monopolize control of access to the institutions of legitimized political power, and the Army, despite its immense influence over foreign and domestic policy, also found itself frustrated in its efforts to establish a dictatorship after 1941. Party politicians and other nonmilitary elite groups continued to enjoy the prerogatives of power bestowed upon them by their occupancy of legitimized institutions of imperial government; and indeed, under General Tōjō Hideki's wartime regime, party influence beyond the Lower House began to grow once more.

Army Perspectives on Politics and Diplomacy

By January 1940, the nation had been fighting in China for thirty months, and the Army was anxious to terminate hostilities as quickly as possible. Prior to the outbreak of the China Incident, the Army's central concern had been to develop Japan's military and economic capacity to fight the Soviet Union. The war with China deflected the nation from this task, and skirmishes with the Soviet Army at Nomonhan in mid-1939 suggested that the "Northern Defense" problem could not be ignored much longer without dire consequences. However, there was no agreement within the Army on how to end the China Incident. Some officers still believed that the Chungking government could be brought to its knees through the determined application of military force. After thirty months without success, however, this view no longer enjoyed the support it had received in the earlier stages of the war. A second approach to the Incident gained wide currency during 1939. Most actively

237

pursued by Major General Kagesa Sadaaki, it called for the establishment of a new central Chinese government and Kuomintang leadership under Wang Ching-wei, to attract the support of the Chinese people away from Chiang Kai-shek. A third approach emerged in late 1939. Essentially, while recognizing the need to continue planning for the Wang government, a number of Army officials were convinced that the creation of a new regime would not in itself suffice to induce Chiang's surrender. Hence, they believed renewed efforts must be made to reach a diplomatic settlement of the Incident through direct negotiations with Chiang Kai-shek. What further distinguished the second and third approaches from one another was the willingness of those subscribing to the latter to postpone or even undermine the establishment of Wang's government in the event Chiang could be induced to end the war.

These three approaches formed the dominant currents of thought in military circles during early 1940. As the year began, Army officials had already decided on a policy regarding the China Incident that took account of these approaches:

> We shall take advantage of the new international situation by pushing forward with the plans for Wang while simultaneously concentrating our efforts at home and abroad on quickly resolving the China Incident at the time his new central Chinese government is established. If this does not succeed, we must move firmly to assume a long-term war footing. . . .

> The key to resolving the China Incident lies in establishing a strong central government. Towards this end, while moving ahead wtih the Wang plans, we must also develop plans for Chungking. By providing points on which Wang and Chiang agree, we shall bring about a truce with Chungking and a union of Wang and Chiang. . . .[1]

[1] DR, ii, 7.

The cardinal principles of the Army's China policy were thus threefold: continuation of the plans to establish a new Wang government; intensification of the attempt to effect a truce with Chiang and a unification of the Chungking regime with Wang's government; and, in the event these plans failed to materialize, determination to prepare the Army and the nation for a prolonged period of warfare in China.[2]

The Army's approach to negotiations with Chiang took place under the rubric of the "Paulownia Plan" (*kiri kōsaku*). The plan had its origins in a secret meeting of a few Army Ministry and General Staff officers late in the summer of 1939. Also attending was the emperor's brother, Prince Chichibu, then attached to the General Staff. These men agreed that the China Incident could not be terminated without recourse to negotiations with Chiang Kai-shek, and dispatched one of their number, Lieutenant Colonel Suzuki Takuji, to Hong Kong to establish contacts with Chungking representatives as a prelude to a possible peace conference. By December, Suzuki had made contact with a man introduced as Soong Tzu-liang, a brother of Madame Chiang and noted Kuomintang financier T. V. Soong. In February 1940, other officers from the General Staff and China Expeditionary Forces (CEF) joined the talks; and by late February, the CEF command had become so sanguine about the prospects of the discussions that it forecast the declaration of a truce by mid-March.[3]

The principal obstacles to agreement in Hong Kong were

[2] The Abe government took a major step forward in committing Japan to support of Wang on January 8, 1940, when the terms of collaboration between Wang and Japan worked out by Kagesa and the *Ume kikan* (Plum Blossom Organ) were ratified by the Cabinet. See KF, II, 34–38.

[3] *Nishiura Susumu-shi danwa sokkiroku*, II, 227–33; Usui Katsumi, "Nit-Chū sensō no seiji-teki tenkai," in NKSG, IV, 229–30. The Paulownia Plan is discussed in some detail in Boyle, *China and Japan at War*, pp. 289–93. In Japanese, see Imai Takeo, *Shina jihen no kaisō* (Tokyo: Misuzu shobō, 1964), pp. 112–50; 326–75.

the Japanese demands for Chinese recognition of the independent status of Manchukuo and the right of Japanese troops to be stationed in North China. On these points, neither side would yield, and the talks were suspended in mid-March. Chiang finally sent word to Hong Kong, requesting that the establishment of Wang Ching-wei's new central Chinese government be delayed from late March to April 15, to give him more time to consider the peace terms. Although the Paulownia Plan participants were prepared to accept this request, Wang's associates in Nanking and his backers in the Japanese Army and government were less receptive, and regarded Chiang's request as a tactic designed solely to delay the creation of a rival Nationalist regime. On March 30, after a four-day delay, Wang's government was established. The Japanese realized, however, that once formal Japanese recognition of Wang as the legitimate central government had been extended, Chiang was unlikely to resume the negotiations begun in Hong Kong. Consequently, Japanese recognition of the new regime was deferred pending the negotiation of a treaty between Nanking and Tokyo. In April, ex-premier General Abe was dispatched to Nanking to begin lengthy talks on the treaty and Japanese recognition.

The CEF was undaunted by these developments, and continued to seek an opportunity to resume negotiations with Chungking. During April and May, it sought to establish jurisdiction over Abe's diplomatic mission, in order to direct the talks with Wang toward the successful implementation of a truce with Chungking. "The primary duty of the new central government," read one CEF directive, "is related to the plans for Chungking."[4] At the same time, CEF Chief of Staff General Itagaki went to Tokyo to request more troops to apply military pressure on Chungking to accede to a negotiated truce. After a considerable debate over the wisdom of allocating more troops and materiel to

[4] Usui, "Nit-Chū sensō no seiji-teki tenkai," p. 238.

China, Itagaki's request was granted on April 22, and plans were made for his forces to attack the strategically located city of Ichang. The Army Ministry and CEF agreed, however, that the additional troops could be employed in China no later than the end of the year, and that if they failed to bring about Chiang's agreement to end the war, they would be withdrawn and the Army would shift to a long-term war footing and occupation in China, in conjunction with recognition of the Wang government. The new troops were quickly employed in the CEF's campaign to seize Ichang in mid-June, and aerial bombardments from the newly occupied city were launched on Chungking to soften Chiang's resistance to surrender. In addition to these military pressures, the Army expected that the imminent collapse of Britain, long regarded as Chiang's principal source of outside aid, would further induce the generalissimo to come to the conference table. They counted also on the disintegration taking place in the alliance between the Nationalist and Communist forces in China to encourage Chungking to reach accord with the Japanese.[5]

On May 18, preliminary discussions between Soong and Japanese Army representatives were held on resuming the talks, and on June 4, the formal talks began again in Macao. The negotiators soon agreed that General Itagaki, Chiang Kai-shek and Wang Ching-wei should meet in the immediate future to eliminate the obstacles to a general accord for peace. News of this agreement quickly reached Tokyo. On June 24, the emperor was informed that the vice chief of the General Staff had flown to China to set up Itagaki's meeting with the two Chinese leaders in Changsha in early July. The emperor was so excited that he proposed to defer his annual summer excursion to Hayama in order to be available if any important news came out of the Changsha

[5] *Ibid.*, pp. 234–35; DR, ii, 36–39. This agreement was embodied in an Army Ministry policy decision on May 18, entitled "Shōwa 15, 16–nen o mokuhyō to suru tai-Shi shori hōsaku." See Hata Ikuhiko, "Nit-Chū sensō no gunjiteki tenkai," in NKSG, iv, 65.

talks. Clearly, hopes for a settlement of the China Incident were now at their highest point since late in 1937.[6]

In the meantime, the Army also began studying the domestic policies and programs that would be needed regardless of whether a satisfactory truce agreement could be negotiated.[7] Additional impetus to this study was provided from late spring by the dream of southern expansion. Domestic policy would center on the establishment of Japan as a "high-degree national defense state," where all of the nation's energies were integrated and focused on increasing the military capabilities of the state. The establishment of the national defense state would allow Japan to fight in China for a prolonged period of time, while enabling the military services to attend simultaneously to the neglected problems of strengthening defenses in the north against the Soviet Union, and expanding southward.

The Army's desire to establish a high-degree national defense state in 1940 was the principal motive behind its renewed interest in political affairs and political reform. The Army wished to institute stricter government control over the economic resources and activities of the nation than had been obtained by the compromises of the two previous years, streamline the administrative structure to reduce "sectional" friction in policy making, and open the bureaucracy to fuller participation and control by military officers. The Army was well aware of the political opposition that would arise against the implementation of these

[6] Imai, *Shina jihen no kaisō*; Imai Takeo, *Shōwa no bōryaku* (Tokyo: Hara shobō, 1967), pp. 158–61; Usui, "Nit-Chū sensō no seiji-teki tenkai," p. 236; Kido, *Kido Kōichi nikki*, II, 796. This optimism is also attested to in DR, II, 40; and Hata, "Nit-Chū sensō no gunjiteki tenkai," p. 70.

[7] The Army's study was done in collaboration with Yatsugi Kazuo, the general secretary of the *Kokusaku kenkyūkai*. The research results were embodied in a lengthy outline ("Sōgō kokusaku kihon yōkō") of the overall proposals that formed the basis for subsequent Army policy positions during much of 1940. For a text of the outline, see YKUS, pp. 43–48.

reforms. Planners of the national defense state in the Army Ministry and Cabinet Planning Board were therefore determined to overcome this opposition by organizing a strong political support group in the Diet, and establishing a Cabinet sympathetic to the Army's domestic and foreign policy goals. From this viewpoint, 1940 began quite inauspiciously. Despite years of Army inveighing against the pernicious political influence of the parties, Diet forces had risen dramatically to drive General Abe from the premiership. The major parties, especially Machida's Minseitō, were regarded as close political allies of the business interests who would most strongly oppose the establishment of strong government controls over the economy. For the moment, at least, the parties seemed strong, and the possibility of a party-led government was even mooted seriously in the press and among politicians.

Abe's failure, like that of General Hayashi three years earlier, served as a pointed reminder that Army control of the premiership was an ineffective means of exerting Army political influence for any prolonged period. It was evident that the Army was ill-equipped to serve as an agency for the harmonization of elite views and ambitions, and that this defect would preclude Army control of the elites under the existing system of political institutions. Moreover, the alternative of a coup d'état seemed less viable than ever, particularly in view of the Navy's commitment to the existing system of constitutional government and the emperor's known revulsion for the rebels of 1936. Army Ministry officials directly charged with managing the Army's political activities (the Army minister, vice minister, and chief of the Military Affairs Bureau) were quick to recognize their dilemma, and in the wake of Abe's resignation, they immediately decided to spare the Army the further embarrassment of another short-lived Cabinet led by a general. Their choice as a successor to Abe was Prince Konoe.[8]

[8] For examples of this Army viewpoint, see the comments made to Harada by Major General Mutō Akira, chief of the Military Affairs

This decision forestalled the plans of several middle-echelon officers and pro-Army party men to install General Sugiyama Hajime as premier while retaining him on active duty.[9] The Army leaders remained committed to Konoe, who in turn refused to assume the responsibility of resolving the economic problems that had accumulated and intensified during the latter half of 1939. As a result, perhaps, of the political inexperience of the newly appointed chief of the Military Affairs Bureau, Major General Mutō Akira, who insisted on backing Konoe, the Army now found itself without any candidate or strategy to follow. Thus, despite the fact that the Army was the most powerful individual elite group by 1940, it was obliged to surrender its voice in the selection of the new premier.

Seizing this opportunity, Privy Seal Yuasa, Baron Harada, and Admiral Okada Keisuke secured the premiership for Admiral Yonai Mitsumasa. As navy minister, Yonai had objected strenuously to the Army's unrestrained advocacy of a military alliance with Germany and Italy during the Konoe and Hiranuma governments. His new foreign minister, Arita Hachirō, was also recognized as a stubborn

---

Bureau, and by Sugiyama himself. SKS, viii, 155–56. Also note Mutō's recollection that the prospect of an Army general as Abe's successor was disturbing in view of the failures of the Hayashi and Abe governments. Mutō Akira, *Hitō kara Sugamo e* (Tokyo: Jitsugyō no Nihonsha, 1952), pp. 50–51.

[9] The idea of a Sugiyama Cabinet and a new party led by Sugiyama was forwarded at the time by a number of people, including Sakurauchi Yukio and Sakurai Hyōgorō (both of the Minseitō), Yuzawa Michio of the Home Ministry, Yamazaki, Taki Masao, and Yatsugi. Yatsugi later recalled that it was from this time that he and the *Kokusaku kenkyūkai* became seriously interested in the formation of a new political party. The idea was quashed, however, by the opposition of senior Army officials, most prominently, Major General Mutō. See Yatsugi, *Shōwa dōran shishi*, ii, 130–50; Yatsugi Kazuo, "Rikugun gunmu-kyoku no shihaisha," *Bungei shunjū* (October 5, 1954), pp. 99–101. Yatsugi confirmed these points in an interview with the author in Tokyo on November 25, 1968.

opponent of Army influence in formulating Japan's foreign policy. Army supporters of an Axis Pact—as a lever to be used in extracting a settlement of the China Incident—had been badly shaken by the Russo-German Non-Aggression Pact in August 1939. The appointment of Yonai now seemed to strike another blow at their hopes to conclude a military alliance with Hitler and Mussolini. The Yonai government also seemed a poor vehicle for realizing the establishment of a controlled economy. Of particular concern to the Army was the fact that no fewer than four ministerial portfolios were held by mainstream figures from the major political parties. The combination of Yonai, Arita, and four party men in the Cabinet so disturbed Army officers that the emperor found it prudent to elicit a promise of Army co-operation with the Cabinet as soon as it was formed. On January 14, he was able to secure Army Minister Hata Shunroku's pledge that the Army would at least "go along" with Yonai.[10]

Hata's assurances notwithstanding, the Army was deeply perturbed by the change of government in January. Many officers believed that Yonai's appointment had simply been the product of a political intrigue by the "liberal" advisors surrounding the throne. Realizing that their political adversaries had temporarily gained the upper hand, a number of Army officials soon began searching for a new political strategy to insure a fuller and more receptive hearing for Army views than might be expected with Yonai and the parties dominating the Cabinet.

The chaotic internal condition of the political parties afforded an opportunity for the Army to reduce the influence of its opponents and enhance its own political position within two weeks of Yonai's appointment. On February 2, Saitō Takao mounted the rostrum of the Lower House, against the wishes of the Minseitō leadership, and

[10] SKS, VIII, 174. The four party men given Cabinet posts were Matsuno Tsuruhei, Shimada Toshio, Katsu Masanori, and Sakurauchi Yukio.

245

proceeded to deliver a stinging critique of previous governments' policies related to the China Incident. Saitō was particularly critical of the moralistic overtones of the government's position, arguing that war was a struggle of power between the strong and the weak, and not a conflict between right and wrong. Wars were fought for survival, he asserted, not for moral principles. He went on to contend that the Wang government would be of little use to Japan, and that Chiang would never join forces with Wang.[11]

In view of the fact that the Army was pursuing a policy of establishing Wang's regime, seeking a truce with Chiang and working towards a fusion of the Chungking and Wang governments, a number of Army officials were deeply offended by Saitō's tirade. Many also felt that his criticism of the "holy war" ideals embodied in the "New East Asian Order" demeaned the sacred cause for which thousands of their comrades-in-arms had died. Reaction in the Army to Saitō's speech thus bordered on outrage. As soon as the Diet had adjourned for the day, the Army's observer stormed into the office of the speaker of the House (Koyama Shōju) and demanded that the offensive passages of the Saitō speech be stricken from the Diet's minutes, "to avoid the possibility that Chungking might see the speech as a split in continued Japanese support for the battle." Meanwhile, in the Cabinet chambers of the Diet building, Overseas Development Minister General Koiso Kuniaki and Education Minister Matsuura Shingorō were voicing their displeasure with the way Saitō had blasphemed Japan's high moral purposes. The two ministers insisted that some form of disciplinary action be taken against Saitō. Koyama finally complied with these demands, instructing the House

[11] Saitō Takao, *Saitō Takao seiji ronshū* (Izushi-machi, Izushi-gun, Hyōgo-ken: Saitō Takao sensei kenshōkai, 1961), pp. 2–3. Since the latter part of Saitō's speech was eventually stricken from the Diet minutes, historians have encountered great difficulty in locating a full text of his comments. The only published version of the complete text known to the author may be found *ibid.*, pp. 19–41.

secretaries to delete the entire second half of Saitō's speech from the record.[12]

Koyama's concession did not mollify the Army, however, for there was a strong feeling among Army officers that the Saitō speech provided an excellent opportunity for a real political showdown against their detractors in the Diet.[13] Under further Army prodding, Koyama was obliged to establish a special Diet commission to investigate the advisability of punishing Saitō by expelling him from the Diet. While there was little legal basis for drumming Saitō out, the Seiyūkai and Minseitō had brought about the expulsion of Shadaitō member Nishio Suehiro under similar circumstances in 1938. The special commission met for over a month, while each party and faction debated the wisdom of expelling Saitō from the Diet. The debate provided the Army with an opportunity to discover who in the Diet were its strongest allies, and the Diet's response proved remarkably gratifying. Despite the opposition of Saitō's supporters in the Minseitō, in the Hatoyama faction of Kuhara's Seiyūkai, and in the *Shamin* faction of the Shadaitō, the overwhelming majority of the Lower House acceded to the Army's demands and finally voted to expel Saitō from the Diet in early March.

Major General Mutō was now preparing to retrieve some of the ground he had surrendered at the beginning of the year. After reviewing the consequences of the Army's inept approach to selecting Abe's successor, Mutō came to the conclusion that despite the liabilities of having the Cabinet led by a general, Konoe's refusal to assume the premiership

[12] Maki Tatsuo, "Gun no seiji kan'yō to kokunai jōsei," unpublished memoir in the archives of the Japan Self-Defense Agency War History Room. For a detailed treatment of the Saitō incident from the Army's perspective, see Bōeichō bōei kenshūsho senshi-shitsu (Hara Shirō), *Daihonei rikugunbu Dai Tōa sensō kaisen keii*, I (Tokyo: Asagumo shinbunsha, 1973), 270–76 (hereafter cited as *Sensō kaisen keii*). See also Koiso Kuniaki jijōden kankōkai, ed., *Katsuzan kōsō* (Tokyo: Koiso Kuniaki jiden kankōkai, 1963), p. 692.

[13] Maki, "Gun no seiji kan'yō to kokunai jōsei."

left the Army with no alternative to preparing for an Army Cabinet and driving the coalition under Yonai out of power. As a crucial step in the preparations for this eventuality, Mutō now sought to create a new Diet party that would be responsive to the wishes of the Army, and forestall the problems Hayashi and Abe had encountered during their tenures in office. The new party would be used to outweigh conservative opposition to the programs of radical economic and administrative reform envisioned as part of the establishment of a national defense state. Mutō had reason to assume that his new stratagem would prove successful, for several parties had been bitterly divided internally over the Saitō issue, and the desire to form a new political party had become pervasive among Diet politicians. In the wake of Saitō's resignation, the *Shamin* faction led by Abe Isoo and Katayama Tetsu finally withdrew from the Shadaitō and its domineering leader, Asō Hisashi.[14] Kuhara's Seiyūkai remained intact, but was now permanently riven between the Hatoyama faction and the rest of the party. With the strength of these two parties weakened by dissension and attrition, their leaders became more interested than ever in creating a new political organization.

The Army thus found a growing number of parliamentary allies with whom to work in creating its new party. For example, Seiyūkai politician Hida Takushi believed that

in light of the China Incident, the contents of Saitō's speech could not be regarded as favorable for the nation. I felt strongly that Diet members should band together and be more conciliatory towards the military, uniting to lead the haughty Army and serving as the base rock of the nation, rather than creating friction with the Army as Saitō had. Feeling this way, I began serious negotiations with young men in the Army. In these political talks,

[14] The *Shamin* faction subsequently attempted to form a new party, the Kinrō kokumintō, under the leadership of Abe Isoo. The party was banned by the Home Ministry on the day it was formally organized.

three or four men attended from the Army Ministry, the General Staff, Air Headquarters, and the Office of Military Education. Much of the work was done by Lieutenant Colonels Kinoshita [Hideaki] and Suzuki [Kyō]. This was one manifestation of my fervent hope that Japan would remain steadfast in her preeminent position in the Orient.[15]

Other Diet members shared Hida's interest in Japan's international position, and in creating a new political alliance. On March 9, the Diet sought to mitigate any impact Saitō's speech might have in Chungking by unanimously passing a Lower House resolution supporting the prosecution of the "holy war" (*Seisen kantetsu ketsugi-an*). Meanwhile, on March 5, anti-Machida forces in the Diet began meeting to discuss ways of using the Saitō incident to weaken the strongest party—the Minseitō—and undermine its opposition to a new party aligned with the Army. These forces, composed of junior members of both Seiyūkai organizations, the Shadaitō, the *Jikyoku dōshikai*, and the First Lobby Club became the nucleus of the "League of Diet Members Supporting the Prosecution of the Holy War" (*Seisen kantetsu giin renmei*).[16]

The central figure in the League was Yamazaki Tatsunosuke. Like Hida, Nagai Ryūtarō, and a number of other Diet members, Yamazaki had close ties with certain elements in the Army. Once the Diet session had ended, and a number of junior Minseitō members had joined the League, Yamazaki and the Army Military Affairs Bureau began active planning to convert the 100-man League into a new pro-Army political party. In the Army Ministry, the key figures involved in these plans were Major General Mutō and Major Maki Tatsuo, head of the Political Affairs

[15] Hida Takushi, *Seitō kōbō gojū-nen* (Tokyo: Kokkai tsūshinsha, 1955), p. 397.

[16] This organization should not be confused with *Seisen kantetsu dōmei*, formed in July 1939 by Kataoka Shun and others connected with the *Shinpeitai* incident.

Division under Mutō. During late March and April, Mutō's staff worked closely with League members, while Mutō himself was in contact with Maeda Yonezō of Nakajima's Seiyūkai.[17] Mutō was eager to create a new party that would dominate the Diet, and prevent party leaders from obstructing the Army's program of economic and administrative reforms. Those working with Mutō in the League were seeking to take the first step back to power by using Army support to supplant the Minseitō as the largest group in the Lower House. Once a strong party had been formed by League members, they might become an integral part of the coalition committed to the Army's reform program, and enjoy again a place in the Cabinet chambers.

The strategy of Mutō and Yamazaki was to gain the approval of Kuhara and Nakajima (who were seen as more "reformist" than the "liberal" Machida), and weaken Machida's ability to resist the new party. The Army's patronage of junior members in both major parties, as well as of Nagai in the Minseitō, made it increasingly dangerous for party leaders to ignore Mutō's plans. Nakajima and Kuhara were indeed willing to form a new mobilization party in collaboration with the Cabinet, even an Army-led Cabinet, but only within the limits of the Army's commitment to the economic and political "status quo." Their "reformism" was far more limited than that of the Army and many young party members. Torn between the potential disintegration of their parties as younger members defected to the Army's support group, and the danger of being manipulated by the Army into sanctioning political and economic reforms that ran counter to their interests and the interests of their supporters, Kuhara and Nakajima found themselves in a profound dilemma.

While Machida consistently indicated his opposition to the formation of a new party, Kuhara and Nakajima sought to escape their quandary by turning to Prince Konoe—the

[17] *Sensō kaisen keii*, I, 276–77.

one man whom the Army would find acceptable as a new
party leader and who might, in his own words, "check as
much as possible the group in the military which easily
became reckless and impatient, while also accepting those
of their demands which were rational."[18] From mid-March,
therefore, Konoe again became the focal point of the Army
and parliamentary efforts to create a new political party.
During March and April, leaders of all parties became
anxious to learn the position Konoe would take towards the
formation of a new party. Machida's emissary visited the
prince in late March to sound him out on the subject, and
Konoe, Machida, and Maeda Yonezō conferred on the proposed new party shortly thereafter. Meanwhile, Kuhara
and Nakajima indicated to Konoe that they would dissolve
their parties and join any new political organ Konoe agreed
to lead.

KONOE'S RETURN TO THE POLITICAL SPOTLIGHT

While Prince Konoe was not anxious to assume the personal leadership of a new political party, he, too, was disenchanted with the direction of politics during the first half
of 1940. Although he had refused to be considered as Abe's
successor at the beginning of the year, he alone among the
ex-premiers (*jūshin*) had opposed Yonai's appointment as
premier, and he was mightily displeased by the admiral's
appointment. For the first time since the February 26th
Incident, a premier had been selected contrary to Konoe's
wishes. Konoe seems to have been anxious to see Yonai
replaced, but he himself was uninterested in the premiership until the end of May. Until that point, his real political
goal was to become the leading official at Court, taking over
the duties of the failing Prince Saionji. Chief among these
duties, of course, was the responsibility for selecting premiers, the most important single task in the process of

[18] KF, II, 72; Kido, *Kido Kōichi nikki*, II, 670.

managing elite conflict under the Meiji constitutional system. Late in 1939, while serving as president of the Privy Council, Konoe had proposed with Kido that the duties of organizing and directing the selection process for premiers be transferred from the privy seal's responsibilities to the Privy Council.[19] He again proposed such a plan to Harada for Saionji's consideration at the beginning of May 1940. Had his plan been accepted, it is doubtful that Konoe would have ever resigned from the Privy Council presidency. Saionji reacted coolly to the plan, however, and when Privy Seal Yuasa suddenly fell ill and indicated his intention of resigning, Konoe abruptly shifted his tactics and pleaded with Harada to be appointed as Yuasa's successor.[20]

While Kido supported Konoe's bid for preeminence at Court, Harada and Saionji resolutely opposed permitting Konoe and his right-wing sympathies to penetrate the inner sanctum of the palace. The emperor concurred, noting that "Konoe might be good as privy seal but he has too many types of people around him. . . ."[21] Excluded from the post, Konoe agreed to the appointment of Kido, his closest political associate, as Yuasa's successor on June 1. Although the two men were subsequently to have their political differences, neither ever again took up the question of restricting the privy seal's powers, and Kido played an important role in the selection of premiers until the end of the war. However, it had become abundantly clear to Konoe that he would not be permitted to assume the position of the emperor's principal advisor—either in his capacity as president of the Privy Council or by appointment as privy seal. If he wished to regain a preeminent position in politics, Konoe now had little alternative to becoming premier once more. As he lamented on June 1, "I really didn't want to get

[19] Kido, *Kido Kōichi nikki*, ii, 755–56 (diary entry for November 10, 1939).

[20] SKS, viii, 231–32 and 242.

[21] *Ibid.*, p. 252.

involved in political movements again, but now it looks unavoidable."[22] Judging from the support for his candidacy shown by the Army, parties, and even Yuasa in January, Konoe could scarcely doubt that becoming premier would be easy. The central question was, rather, when he would seek the post and what he would try to accomplish with it.

In his memoirs, Konoe relates the frustration of having been unable to control the Army during his first Cabinet. This frustration was the product first of his struggle with Ishiwara and the General Staff to have Japan's military might thrown against China in late 1937 and early 1938, and second from the premier's subsequent inability to harmonize operational plans in China with his changing diplomatic and political strategy on the China question. Now, as he faced the prospects of organizing a new government, Konoe "finally concluded that the military could be checked and the China Incident resolved only if a popular organization were formed which differed from the parties, which was rooted in all the people, and had political strength to be employed in checking the military."[23]

It is important to note that Konoe disagreed less with the overall thrust of Army policy, both in 1937–1938 and in 1940, than with the political system that allowed the services independence from the premier in determining their strategy and tactics in military operations. He was certainly in basic sympathy with the Army's approach to the China question in late 1939 and early 1940. In December 1939, as the Paulownia Plan was getting underway, he observed that while there appeared to be no alternative to setting up the Wang regime, Japan "would naturally get through to Chungking covertly." As the plan developed in early March, he told Harada that "we must speak directly with Chiang," and spoke approvingly of the Army's shift from a policy

[22] Ashizawa Tsutomu, "Ningen Konoe Fumimaro: Yabe Teiji nikki no naka kara," *Bungei shunjū*, LI.13 (September 1973), 168.

[23] *Ibid.*, and Konoe, *Konoe Fumimaro-kō no shuki: ushinawareshi seiji*, pp. 24–25.

of full support for Wang to a more direct search for a means of ending the war. When the talks stalled between mid-March and May, Konoe became extremely pessimistic, but on May 17, he confided to Harada again that contact with Chungking might be established after all, and pressure applied on Chiang to end the war. He alluded frequently to the possibility of having Akiyama, his chief link to Chiang, act as an intermediary between Tokyo and Chungking, with the blessings of both the Japanese Army and Konoe himself. By mid-May and early June, as the Macao talks got underway, he was more sanguine than ever about the possibilities of reaching some agreement with Chungking.[24]

Konoe's sympathies with the Army's policy positions went still further. In March, he clashed with the Yonai government by supporting the Army's proposal to conclude a military alliance with Germany and Italy, feeling with the Army that such a pact would serve as a useful diplomatic lever in prodding Chiang to the conference table. Later in March, he proposed that he undertake a six-month journey abroad; and his secretary indicated that Konoe's itinerary would be limited to Germany, Italy, and the USSR. Konoe's plan was quashed by Foreign Minister Arita, who feared the prince would seize the diplomatic initiative from the Foreign Ministry, and seek a tripartite or quadripartite alliance with the countries he was scheduled to visit. Konoe's views on expanding to the south were also close to those of the Army, for he was convinced that "the ultimate development of the Greater East Asian Co-Prosperity Sphere was the path to Japan's destiny."[25]

Konoe's foreign policy views were, however, clearly at odds with those prevailing in the Yonai government, particularly when the issue was Konoe's central concern, the resolution of the China Incident. The prince favored a strengthening of Japan's diplomatic position through alli-

[24] SKS, VIII, 129, 179, 191, 193, 247.
[25] Ibid., pp. 211–19 and KF, I, 223.

ance with the Axis and the Soviet Union, and negotiating with Chiang while preparing for long-term warfare in China. The government, especially Foreign Minister Arita, was less than enthusiastic about this approach. While preliminary work on an Axis Pact went on in the Foreign Ministry during the spring of 1940, Arita and Yonai were known to oppose the conditions Germany insisted upon: namely, that the pact apply to relations with the United States and Britain as well as any other third power. As for the China issue itself, Arita held that direct talks with Chungking would prove fruitless, and only obstruct the conclusion of a treaty with Wang and the extension of diplomatic recognition to his regime. Japan, affirmed the foreign minister, must bolster the Wang government, rather than negotiate with Chiang.[26] There was thus a subtle contrast between the Cabinet's focus on Wang, and the Japanese Army's new "Policy for Dealing with China" (*Tai-Shi shori hōsaku*), which sanctioned the Wang plan but also approved of efforts to negotiate with Chiang until the end of the year. In this policy, approved on May 18, the Army conceded that if the peace effort failed, Japan would have no alternative to focusing its China policy on Wang, and girding the domestic economy and administration for a prolonged and expensive period of occupation in a long-term war strategy.[27] Recognizing the costs of long-term war, however, the Army remained willing to seek peace through direct talks with Chiang. As of May 1940, Konoe's sympathies lay with the Army's two-pronged approach, rather than with the singular program of support for Wang endorsed by the Yonai Cabinet.

Konoe's principal strategy from mid-May was thus to bring Japan into a closer diplomatic and military relationship with the Axis, negotiate with Chiang while preparing for long-term warfare, and take whatever domestic steps would be required to gird the nation against the conse-

[26] SKS, viii, 247 (entry of May 17, 1940).
[27] DR, ii, 36–38.

quences of these policies. In other words, he wished to overturn the Yonai government's policy of hesitation in dealing
with Chiang, Hitler, and Mussolini, and restructure the
nation's economy to deal with an anticipated period of iso-
lation from the resources and finances of the United States.

Konoe's attitude towards the new party movement in the
Diet and the Army reflected his foreign and domestic policy
goals. Until mid-May, when he told Harada of the impending reopening of the negotiations in Macao, Konoe remained
uninterested in leading a new political force. During April,
he, Arima, and Kido discussed the new party issue on several occasions, but Konoe showed little evidence of interest
and Kido noted that the prospects of a new party were slim.
Konoe confirmed Kido's judgment on May 5, when he told
Harada that he doubted the feasibility of a new party. Once
he had been denied a position at the Court, however, and
the talks with Chiang's representatives were rescheduled,
Konoe's attitude changed markedly. In response to inquiries
from Kuhara and Kazami Akira (a key figure in the Diet's
campaign for a new party), Konoe urged Kazami on May
18 to become fully involved in the campaign for the new
party, and promote the dissolution of the parties. A week
later, Konoe met with Kido and Arima to discuss the tactical approach to be used vis-à-vis the Diet, in light of the
likelihood that Konoe would soon be asked to replace
Yonai. The three men agreed to take no positive steps towards establishing a new party prior to Konoe's appointment as premier, but to reconsider their course of inaction
in the event the new party movement in the Diet developed
spontaneously.[28]

Within a week, events had forced a reconsideration.
Kazami and his colleagues quickly drew up plans for a new
party committed to the establishment of a national defense
state, an adjustment and invigoration of diplomacy, and

[28] Kido, *Kido Kōichi nikki*, II, 781 (entry of April 19, 1940) and
786–87; SKS, VIII, 287; Kazami, *Konoe naikaku*, pp. 197–200; and
Arima, *Seikai dōchūki*, pp. 190–91.

the establishment of a new political order. As Kazami later recalled, the term "new political order" was adopted in place of "new party" because he knew Konoe believed reference to the latter would connote a selfish desire to obtain political power through the new organization. To the Diet members in the new party movement, the rhetoric of a "new political order" was simply verbal shorthand for the creation of a new political party under Konoe. During the course of discussions among Kazami, Maeda, Yamazaki, and Nagai, it was decided that the new party should exclude the main body of the Minseitō under Machida, and Hatoyama's faction of the Kuhara Seiyūkai, from their plans. It was also secretly agreed that the participating parties would dissolve themselves as soon as the preparations for the new political order (new party) had been made. All of the small Diet parties agreed to dissolve and merge into the new party, and Kuhara had already endorsed the plan. Nakajima finally overcame his reluctance to appear to follow Kuhara's lead, and also lent his public support to the call for a new party. On June 3, with the backing of every major Diet figure and faction (except Machida and Hatoyama), the new party movement in the Diet (i.e., the League) adopted a formal resolution to create a new political party. The organization would reject liberal notions of political competition in the Diet, and class-oriented concepts of class competition, and would instead work closely with a government sharing its viewpoints. The party would have a nationwide organization, integrating all citizens into the life of the state, and its primary function would be to lead the people.[29]

The following day, as the Macao talks got underway, Konoe responded to the events of the moment with a public volte-face on the new party question. Speaking to the press, he revealed that "for a long time I have believed in the necessity of a new political order. In order to deal with the

[29] Kazami, *Konoe naikaku*, pp. 202–203; Kido, *Kido Kōichi nikki*, II, 787; *Tōkyō asahi*, June 3, 1940 and June 4, 1940; YKUS, p. 8.

critical situation, a strong new political party must be created through this new order." While waiting to assess the outcome of the Macao talks, however, Konoe hedged his own position of leadership in the new political organization.

> I am now unable to discuss publicly the question of my own participation in the new party. To leave my present post requires the prior approval of the emperor, and also involves the Cabinet. I will say, however, that the absolute prerequisite for establishing a new party is the dissolution of the old parties. I may previously have said that the time was not ripe for a new party, but the thinking of party men now has changed considerably. . . . It will be a difficult undertaking, but as a Japanese citizen I pray for its success.[30]

Shortly after making this statement, Konoe told Harada that he planned to remain in his post as president of the Privy Council for the present, implying that he would not yet resign to lead the new party movement. He also noted that Akiyama had informed him of the resumption of the talks with Chiang's emissaries, and indicated that he would not seek the premiership until such time as negotiations with Chungking had gotten underway.[31]

During the first three weeks in June, both the Macao talks and Hitler's campaigns seemed to go very well. While Japanese bombardiers used Ichang as a base to force Chiang to the negotiating table, careful preparations were being made in Macao for a mid-July Changsha conference among Itagaki, Chiang, and Wang. Paris fell, and a German invasion of Britain seemed imminent. Konoe now decided that the moment had arrived to assume direct command of the government and the movement to create a new political organization. So great was his sense of urgency that he insisted on resigning immediately, despite the impending

---

[30] For an account of Konoe's press conference, see *Tōkyō asahi*, June 5, 1940.

[31] SKS, viii, 259 and 268.

visit of the Manchurian emperor to Japan. Yonai reluctantly accepted the prince's resignation on June 24, uncertain what hopes Konoe nursed for "the establishment of a strong national-unity order to deal with unprecedented changes at home and abroad."[32]

Konoe's sanguine outlook on the China Incident was not shared by the Yonai government. Foreign Minister Arita correctly assumed that unless Japan revised the terms offered and rejected by the Chinese on several occasions, the prospects for a negotiated end to the war were slim. It is difficult to explain why Konoe and the Army officers connected with the Paulownia Plan felt otherwise. Certainly, they placed a great deal of faith in the impact on China of a German victory over England and a military alliance between Japan and Hitler. Perhaps they were also encouraged by the responsiveness of Soong and other Chinese with whom they were talking in Hong Kong. The real question, however, was how much Japan would compromise to obtain a truce or peace settlement. At no time did Konoe intimate the concessions, if any, he would sanction to end the war. Aside from a willingness to negotiate with Chungking, and a belief that such negotiations would result in Chiang's capitulation, he and the Paulownia Plan Army representatives differed little in substance from the government's adherence to the policy of annihilating Chiang's regime. Nonetheless, he and his Army colleagues were optimistic about ending the war in June and July of 1940, and that optimism was eventually carried to the emperor himself. With the war behind them, Japan could move south, free herself of dependence on American resources, and strengthen her northern defenses. However misplaced

[32] Ordinarily, the president of the Privy Council would have had an important role to play in the formalities of welcoming the Manchurian emperor and entertaining him. In the view of many officials, Konoe's resignation would have been better deferred until the visit had been concluded, if only for the sake of protocol. See Kido, *Kido Kōichi nikki*, II, 793. See also, *Tōkyō asahi*, June 25, 1940 and KF, II, 92.

Konoe's optimism may have been, it propelled him into the new order movement and launched his quest for the premiership.

Once Konoe had indicated his interest in assuming command of the movement for a new political organization, Major General Mutō happily abandoned his plans for a Cabinet to be led by an Army general and supported in the Diet by a coalition of small parties and anti-mainstream figures from the *kisei seitō*. Mutō now shifted his support away from the League's campaign and directed it towards Konoe. On June 10, Mutō met secretly with Kanemitsu Tsuneo to convey the Army's interest in Konoe. He confided that the Army wished to see the formation of a new party and new government, both to be led by the prince. He and his Army colleagues hoped Konoe's popular political force (*kokumin-teki no seiji suishintai*) would be linked closely with the government but exclude the leadership of the major political parties.[33]

During the next month, as Konoe more openly declared his readiness to lead the new order movement and serve as premier, the Army prepared the way for his return to power. Army officers became increasingly fearful that the Yonai government would not move swiftly enough to capitalize on events in Europe and conclude a pact with the Axis. They fretted that Germany might claim control of the Southeast Asian colonies that belonged to the powers it conquered, and worried that temporizing on the Axis Pact might also cost Japan vital diplomatic leverage in dealing with Chungking. The government's lukewarm attitude towards the talks with Chiang and the Axis Pact was well known. Moreover, even if the China Incident were not resolved, the Army was now committed to southern expansion, an end to economic dependence on the United States and Britain, and the creation of a high-degree national

[33] "Kanemitsu, Mutō gunmu-kyoku-chō kaidan naiyō" (June 10, at Hoshigaoka Tea Room), in Imai and Itō, eds., *Kokka sōdōin*, pp. 157–58; Maki, "Gun no seiji kan'yō to kokunai jōsei."

defense state. Army representatives indicated that Japan must henceforth be allied politically with the Axis, and associated economically with a sphere of autonomy embracing Southeast Asia. The economic and political abandonment of the sinking Anglo-American ship would, in the Army's view, require a fundamental revision of domestic political views, and a "strengthening" of the domestic political and economic order.[34]

While Army Minister Hata sought to abide by his commitment to the emperor regarding Army support for Yonai, a number of officers had already decided that their policy views would never be enacted until Konoe had replaced the admiral as premier. Vice Minister Anami Korechika subscribed to this view, as did many of his subordinates. The General Staff was, if anything, more adamant than Anami in seeking Yonai's ouster, at least partially because of the government's negative attitude towards the efforts to negotiate with Chungking. On July 4, Vice Chief of Staff Sawada Shigeru visited Hata to say that the General Staff felt Yonai's resignation to be essential. Sawada sought to overcome Hata's inhibitions about bringing down the government by presenting him with a memorandum from Prince Kan'in, the chief of staff and a member of the imperial family. Kan'in's message to Hata read as follows:

Japan must resolve the China Incident as quickly as possible. In order to accomplish this, however, it is first necessary not only to strengthen the domestic order, but also to take urgent and decisive action in dealing with the endlessly changing international situation. But in observing the policies of the present government, we find them unassertive and unresponsive. We cannot but assume that this government will be unable to extricate us from the present situation. Meanwhile, such weakness will have a damaging influence on the spirit and co-

[34] See explanation of this policy to Navy officials by Colonel Usui Shigeki on July 4, 1940, in DR, II, 51.

hesiveness of our armed forces. It is now essential to organize a strong national-unity government which will unhesitatingly carry out firm policies. We earnestly hope that the Army Ministry will take appropriate action with regard to the above.[35]

The Army minister was not averse to seeing the Yonai government resign, but he wished to avoid the onus of violating his pledge to the throne and spare the Army from the opprobrium which would follow unilateral action on his part. Between July 6 and July 8, Hata discussed his difficult position with the senior officers of the Army, Prince Kan'in, General Sugiyama, and Marshal Terauchi. Finally, he was persuaded to bring the government down, and Vice Minister Anami reported to Kido on the 8th that

> in the last four to five days, we have reached the point where a change in government may be at hand. The Army wishes to put to good use the dramatic changes in the international situation. However, the Yonai government's nature makes it an extremely unsuitable government for carrying out talks with Germany and Italy, and it may act too late in any case. We are now decided that a change in government is unavoidable if this moment is not to be missed. The Army is united in backing Prince Konoe as the next premier. When he returns from Karuizawa on the 10th, he should see the Army minister. An important message will then be sent to Yonai.[36]

Konoe did not wish to be publicly associated with the Army's overthrow of Yonai, so he remained secluded in Karuizawa beyond the 10th, and continued discussing plans for the new order with a few close advisors. Hata was thus left to bear the full brunt of responsibility for ending the life of the Cabinet. On July 14, the Army minister formally

[35] *Sensō kaisen keii*, I, 312 contains the text of this message, as excerpted from the unpublished diary of Hata Shunroku.

[36] Kido, *Kido Kōichi nikki*, II, 801.

urged Yonai to dissolve the government. When the stubborn admiral refused to yield to this advice, Hata himself resigned on the 16th, citing "the need to reform the domestic political order to cope with world conditions."[37] The Army announced that it would have difficulty finding a replacement for Hata, and Yonai was obliged to submit his government's resignation to the emperor that evening. The following afternoon, Kido summoned the *jūshin* to recommend a new premier, and within thirty minutes they had unanimously agreed that Konoe should be asked to form a new government.

KONOE'S VISION OF A NEW POLITICAL ORDER

Between the time when Konoe became interested in returning to the premiership in mid-May, and the installation of his government in late July, he and his advisors held frequent meetings concerning the nature of the new political order he was proposing, and the prince himself made several public statements on the subject. As the emperor had aptly phrased it, Konoe had "many types of men around him," and each had his own prescription for a new political structure. Konoe limited his own public remarks to general observations about the ills of the existing political system, and on several occasions appeared to contradict previous positions he had taken on the type of political reforms he would like to have implemented. Nevertheless, a perusal of the prince's statements in public and private during this period suggest the general approach he hoped to take in reforming Japanese politics.[38] They also reveal three

[37] KF, II, 110.

[38] This discussion is based upon the following sources: Konoe's meeting with Arima and Kido on May 26, in Kido, *Kido Kōichi nikki*, II, 786–87; Konoe's statements, public and unreleased, regarding his resignation as president of the Privy Council, in KF, II, 90–92; Konoe's comments to Harada, in SKS, VIII, 275–76; Konoe's remarks to Yabe, in KF, II, 81–82; Konoe's July 8 press conference, in Oda Toshiyo,

fundamental points of interest. First, Konoe did not equate the term "new political order" with "new party," as many Diet politicians did. Second, in order to realize his policy objectives, the prince was prepared to transform the political system constructed by the Meiji oligarchs into a highly organized and monolithic political structure, in which the Cabinet, and the premier in particular, would exercise dictatorial powers over the occupants of other military and civilian institutions of state. Finally, Konoe was bent on fully integrating the entire citizenry into the life of the state to cope with the massive burdens of expansion and preparation for war.

From the outset, Konoe made it clear that he hoped to resolve the perpetual problem of harmonizing Cabinet-Diet relations by creating a one-party system, in which all of the previously existing parties would dissolve themselves and reorganize under Konoe as new party president and premier. He had, however, no intention of permitting the leaders of the old parties to dominate the new party and Diet, for he doubted their willingness to sanction the domestic policy proposals he hoped to enact as premier. Instead, he privately calculated that when the old party members joined the new party, they would constitute only forty percent of the membership, while "new" and "reform-minded" members made up the remaining sixty percent.

Konoe wished to enhance the premier's access to information about military operations, and to strengthen the premier's ability to control military activities in the field and in domestic policy making. He thus proposed the creation of a Supreme Defense Council (*Saikō kokubō kaigi*) consisting of the premier, both service ministers, and the two

---

Yokusan undō to Konoe-kō (Tokyo: Shunpei shobō, 1940), pp. 8–10; and Konoe's meetings with the designated Army, Navy, and foreign ministers of his new Cabinet, July 18–19, in KF, ɪɪ, 118–19. For Kido's views on the proposed Supreme Defense Council, see KF, ɪɪ, 78. For Yabe's plans, see KF, ɪɪ, 104, and Ashizawa, "Ningen Konoe Fumimaro."

chiefs of staff. The sources of leverage that would enable the premier to exert control over the military through this council were never made clear, perhaps because to do so would have immediately provoked military opposition to the council as a clear violation of the institutional prerogatives of the armed forces. Konoe also sought to limit the military's political influence by engulfing the armed forces in his proposed "popular organization." At the time, and again in his memoirs, Konoe asserted that a strong political force rooted in the people was required to "check the military." On some occasions, he proposed that the popular organization be constituted in such a way as to permit military participation in it, to "fuse the military and the people" in principle, but in fact to provide institutional leverage for the organization's leadership (under Konoe) to control military activities in the political and economic fields.

While Konoe mused publicly about the new popular organization, he was never definitive about its composition. His chief advisors, including Professor Yabe Teiji of Tokyo Imperial University, nevertheless proposed that the popular organization be composed of hierarchically arranged guild organizations that would link politics to the economic life of the people, and similar groupings of cultural groups (i.e., youth groups, educational organizations, and so on) to integrate and control the people in still another network. Yabe's approach was finally sanctioned by Konoe and became the skeleton of the "popular" element of the new political order. What is important to note about this approach to popular organization is that it provided a new channel for popular political participation and for linking the people to the state, and would supercede the Diet's importance, and the importance of Diet groups, in this vital function. The new popular organization thus promised to provide an important challenge to the institutional prerogatives of Diet members and their local supporters, the *meibōka*. Moreover, it sought to establish an institutional framework for integrating the lives of the entire citizenry into national affairs.

265

The new popular organization, if implemented as Konoe and his closest advisors proposed, would also have had the effect of supplanting the government ministries and the semiofficial and official organs under their jurisdiction as a principle linkage between the people and the state. This attack on bureaucratic influence was extended through a number of other proposals made by Konoe in the context of creating a new political order. For example, he proposed a new policy-making organ, to be responsible directly and solely to the premier, which would absorb many of the policy-making and coordinating duties of the established ministries. The new organ was to be staffed by officials and nonofficials alike. Konoe sought to make further inroads into the bureaucracy's power over administration and policy making by proposing to reform the system guaranteeing the status of officials so that the premier could appoint men from outside the bureaucracy—be they talented civilians, new party members, or military men—to important civil service positions.

The vagueness that characterized Konoe's public statements on these proposed innovations in the political system was calculated to conceal the extent to which the institutional prerogatives of every major elite group would be challenged by the prince's vision of a new political order. By the time Konoe had accepted the premiership, however, all of the elites were sensitive to the fact that the new order proposal represented both a grave threat to their power bases in the imperial system, and an opportunity to expand their political influence beyond the institutions in which they were based to new areas of political control. It was the feeling of imminent opportunity which, combined with Konoe's great popularity, led other elite groups to rush forward in support of him and his new order plans; and it was the sense of danger which he sought to mitigate by abstract discussions in the press of the new order.

The new political order forwarded by Konoe in the middle of 1940 emanated from the belief that the structural

diffusion of political power that was institutionalized by the
Meiji political system could no longer serve Japan well in
a period of national crisis. Konoe had long ceased to believe
that the Diet and election system were adequate instruments of popular integration, and he regarded bureaucratic
struggles for administrative prerogatives as signs of "sectionalism" that prevented the high degree of administrative
integration required by a national defense state. He was
likewise troubled by the growth of military influence
throughout the government, not because he disagreed with
the Army's views, but because the autonomy of the services
made it impossible for premiers to coordinate government
and military approaches to problems unless the civilian
branch of the government agreed simply to defer to and
follow the wishes of the military. Moreover, the military
was internally divided on many important policy issues,
such as how to solve the China Incident, whether to ally
with Germany and Italy, and whether Japan should concen-
trate on northern defense or southern expansion in the face
of certain Anglo-American opposition. Intraservice rivalries
and policy disputes within the Army and Navy made it
doubly difficult for the premier to harmonize the affairs of
state with those of the supreme command.

Konoe and many other Japanese leaders in 1940 were
critical of the concept of "separation of powers," holding
that it was a legacy of decadent Anglo-American liberalism.
At the same time, they were profoundly impressed by the
obvious effectiveness of the Nazi and Fascist systems in
mobilizing and integrating the energies of the state toward
specific goals. Of course, Konoe's new order construct was
no more a mere imitation of the German and Italian systems than party government in the 1920s had been a wholesale adoption of Anglo-American political institutions.
Nevertheless, Konoe and his advisors were anxious to integrate the political and economic power of the state, and
were inspired, if not reduced to slavish aping, by the success of the German and Italian experiments. By the same

267

KONOE'S NEW POLITICAL ORDER

token, the chauvinistic *kokutai* ideology of the 1930s, which accompanied and rationalized Japan's quest for regional and world preeminence, led her leaders to emphasize the native origins of "national unity"—the natural communal spirit of the village, the sacrosanct and indestructible bonds linking a paternalistic emperor to his children-subjects, and so on—rather than the advantages of adopting foreign models of totalitarian organization. But while this insistence on the divinity and inviolabilty of the throne rationalized strict popular controls, it ultimately complicated the task of challenging or reforming the institutions of government that had previously been sanctioned by the imperially bestowed Constitution.

Konoe was not insensitive to the legal and constitutional problems raised by his radical program. Publicly, he promised that

> while organizing the new order, we will faithfully respect our Constitution. The Constitution is a great and ever-lasting canon; changing it is absolutely unthinkable. However, according to the Constitution, Japanese politics are to be stabilized through a balance of power. The new order, on the other hand, will be completely organized and concentrated on the lines of national policy. There would appear to be some legal problems involved here, but the new order will respect the Constitution, always proceeding in accord with its workings.[39]

Privately, however, Konoe was willing to reinterpret the spirit and letter of the Constitution to conform to the new order. As he told Yabe on July 14,

> Whenever a new Cabinet is formed these days, the emperor always warns the new premier on three points: respecting the provisions of the Constitution, avoiding any upheavals in the business world, and cooperating with the Anglo-American powers. When I become premier, he'll probably issue the same warnings again. But

[39] Oda, *Yokusan undō to Konoe-kō*, p. 10.

268

the emperor's view of the Constitution is based largely on the old liberal interpretations of men like Saionji and Yuasa. His concern for stability in the economy even leads him to worry about the fluctuation of stock prices, and his foreign policy views are based on a sentiment favoring the Anglo-American powers.

But politics in Japan today cannot be run in accordance with these imperial wishes. . . . If he gives me the same instructions, I cannot simply agree to form a new government and walk away. Instead, I would like to tell him that interpretations of the Constitution must change with the times. I would add that in these semiwartime conditions, we must have economic controls and planning, and cannot worry about the ups and downs of each stock quotation. And I would ask him frankly to recognize that in the present international situation, the Anglo-American attitude requires us to strengthen our relationship with Germany and Italy, even if only for the sake of negotiating later with the British and Americans.[40]

In the days following his designation as premier, Konoe took the first steps toward insuring that his government would be amenable to the policies and institutional reforms he endorsed. Before formally accepting the premiership, he held a private round of policy discussions at his *Tekigaisō* residence with Matsuoka Yōsuke, his choice as foreign minister, Lieutenant General Tōjō Hideki, and Vice Admiral Yoshida Zengo, the Army and Navy selections for the service portfolios. The timing of these discussions was of great importance, for Konoe was implicitly threatening to renounce the premiership unless the four ministers could agree on the policies to be followed henceforth. The Army's policy proposals were adopted as the basis of discussion and informal agreement during the talks.[41] There is no evidence to suggest that Konoe was coerced into supporting

[40] KF, ii, 106–107.
[41] SKS, viii, 292; Maki, "Gun no seiji kan'yō to kokunai jōsei"; Yatsugi, "Rikugun gunmukyoku no shihaisha," p. 106.

269

the Army's foreign and military policies, or that he was unwittingly made a "robot" of military interests, as he and historians have often lamented after the fact. On the contrary, the prince was in a strong position to see that the discussants conformed to his own views on foreign and domestic policy (see Figure 5).

Satisfied with the accord reached among his key ministers, Konoe proceeded to organize his Cabinet. Realizing that the foreign policies adopted by his government would inevitably divorce Japan economically from Britain and the United States, Konoe invited men into his Cabinet who were prepared to restructure the economy into a highly planned and controlled system. Hoshino Naoki, who had been the top Japanese official in Manchuria, was appointed Chief of the Planning Board, with the rank of minister. Kishi Nobusuke, another influential economic planner in Manchuria, was invited to serve as minister of commerce and industry. He preferred to serve as vice minister, however, and the portfolio went to Kansai industrialist Kobayashi Ichizō instead. As finance minister, Konoe appointed Kawada Retsu, an experienced budgetary expert from the ministry's bureaucracy. Aside from these appointments, Konoe's selections were oriented towards the question of the new political order. Yasui Eiji, who had been advising Konoe on the new order during the previous month, was given the Home Ministry portfolio. Kazami Akira, a leader of the new party movement in the Diet, was given the position of justice minister. Three other posts were left vacant, presumably to be filled by representatives of Konoe's new party or new order when it was established. Finally, Konoe appointed Tomita Kenji as the chief Cabinet secretary. Tomita was a vigorous opponent of party influence, and had served for six months as Suetsugu's top police officer in the Home Ministry during the first Konoe government. He was later appointed governor of Nagano prefecture in December 1938, and had frequent opportunities to see the vacationing Konoe in Karuizawa. In the weeks immediately

FIGURE 5. On July 19, 1940, the leading members of the second Konoe cabinet gathered at Konoe's Tekigaisō residence to discuss the contours of Japan's national policies. From left to right, Konoe Fumimaro (prime minister), Matsuoka Yōsuke (foreign minister), Yoshida Zengo (navy minister), and Tōjō Hideki (army minister).

preceding Konoe's appointment as premier in 1940, Tomita was invited to consult with the prince on the plans for the new political order. When the Konoe Cabinet was formed, he was asked to continue this work in an official capacity. He and Home Minister Yasui were regarded as close associates and political allies.

The new government addressed itself immediately to a number of important issues which had been discussed at *Tekigaisō*. With regard to the foreign and military policies to be adopted, a Liaison Conference was convened on July 27, marking the first occasion such a conference had been held since Konoe had severed relations with Chiang in January 1938. At this conference of Cabinet and military command officials, the foreign and defense policy agreements reached at *Tekigaisō* were adopted officially as the new government's policies. For the first time, the use of force in southern expansion was given official sanction, although it was subject to a number of conditions enumerated in the new policy. This decision had far-reaching significance in the months ahead, and many historians have regarded it as the first serious step toward Pearl Harbor.[42] While the new policy continued to regard the China Incident as holding high priority in the nation's policies abroad, the "southern question" had now been elevated by both the Army and the Cabinet to a position of commensurate importance.

Appended to the decision on foreign and defense policies was a section dealing with the domestic policies to be adopted in conjunction with the ambitious program abroad. The services had already agreed that domestic policies should be geared towards the sole objective of strengthen-

[42] For a full text of the Liaison Conference policy, entitled "Sekai jōsei no suii ni tomonau jikyoku shori yōkō," see Gaimushō, ed., *Nihon gaikō nenpyō narabi ni shuyō bunsho*, ii (Tokyo: Hara shobō, 1966), 437–38. For a commentary in English on the significance of this policy decision, see Butow, *Tojo and the Coming of the War*, pp. 150–53.

ing Japan's ability to fight total war. While they still differed on some points regarding the implementation of this program, they concurred on the need to streamline and centralize decision-making and administrative procedures, as well as on the development of mechanisms for the total mobilization of men, materiel, and morale throughout the nation. The enhancement of Japan's capacity to wage war was to be defined as the goal of the nation, and all other goals were to be subsumed beneath this sacrosanct objective. As Maki Tatsuo later remarked succinctly, "To the Army, the words 'new order' meant reorganizing the political and economic system under the unified will of the state leading to a high-degree national defense state establishment."[43]

The Liaison Conference of July 27 agreed that the domestic order should "be transformed into a national defense state on the basis of the new international situation." There would be a strengthening of political controls, a broader invocation of the National General Mobilization Law, the establishment of a wartime economy, a stockpiling of war materials and an increase in shiphold capacities for the transport of necessary goods, increased production and replenishment of military supplies, a raising of public morale, and a unification of public opinion. While the entire Cabinet, including Konoe, and both services could readily agree on these general guidelines for domestic policy, it was unlikely that specific policies could actually be implemented without encountering strong opposition from a variety of political and economic groups.

A similar observation can be made for the July 26 Cabinet agreement on "An Outline of Basic National Policies" (*Kihon kokusaku yōkō*). The "Outline," which had been drafted in the Planning Board under Hoshino's supervision, restated in general terms the defense and foreign policies that the Liaison Conference would approve a day later. It

[43] Maki, "Gun no seiji kan'yō to kokunai jōsei."

called for an emphasis on resolving the China Incident by capitalizing on the current international situation, and for a replenishment of the nation's armaments on the basis of establishing a national defense state. Finally, it noted Japan's interest in the construction of a new order for *Greater* East Asia, reflecting a new departure towards the south. Essentially, however, the "Outline" was intended to be a blueprint for the establishment of a domestic political and economic order through which the above objectives might be attained. This blueprint called for the creation of a new political order to integrate all national affairs. Within the new political order, a new popular organization was to be established on the basis of vocations, and the Diet system would be reformed to adjust to new but undeclared functions. The bureaucratic system was also to be somehow restyled to conform with the new emphasis on streamlining administration and focusing on specific national goals. There were also provisions for a planned economy, with stringent controls over finance, production, and consumption. Finally, the "Outline" stressed the importance of cultivating a national morality that put loyal service to the state before private interests and personal material welfare.[44]

Within a week of the formation of the Cabinet, therefore, a general framework had been established within which a wide variety of differing "new order" proposals would be debated. However, Konoe himself dealt with the new order issue gingerly during his first few weeks as premier. According to one of his associates, he seemed uninterested in pushing ahead with the monumental task of creating the new order, and sought to avoid any consideration of what a new order might require.[45] Konoe's lethargy was probably due to his knowledge that the reforms he desired would create a political furor, and he wished to defer debate on them until

[44] A text of "Kihon kokusaku yōkō" may be found in Gaimushō, ed., *Nihon gaikō nenpyō narabi ni shuyō bunsho*, ii, 436–37.

[45] *Gotō Ryūnosuke-shi danwa sokkiroku* (Naiseishi kenkyū shiryō dai–66, 67, 68, 69–shū) (Tokyo: Naiseishi kenkyūkai, 1968), p. 160.

the negotiations with Chungking had effected a cessation of
hostilities on the continent. However, instead of flying to
Changsha in mid-July for scheduled talks with Itagaki and
Wang, Chiang Kai-shek requested a postponement of the
meeting to mid-August.[46] Konoe obviously wished to delay
any concrete new order decisions until after that meeting.
Unfortunately for him, however, each political elite group
was now clamoring for the premier to take steps to bring
(their version of) the new order into existence. Furthermore, popular interest in the new order had been stimulated earlier by Konoe's own resignation and comments to
the press, and the entire nation was anxious to see what
proposals Konoe would forward. Having ridden back to
power on the wave of public support for his commitment
to the new order, Konoe was now unable to drop his public
posture of enthusiasm for the project without exposing himself to charges that he had promoted the new order movement simply in order to become premier. The prince had
maneuvered himself into a position from which he was
obliged to produce *some* new order proposal, whether the
Changsha talks succeeded or even took place.

ELITE RESPONSES TO KONOE'S NEW POLITICAL ORDER

Konoe's new order plans aimed at consolidating the
policy-making structure of the central government, and redefining the context in which elite competition for power
took place. Moreover, they sought to establish an entirely
new structure integrating the citizenry into the state, providing new channels of popular participation in national
affairs and new implements of popular control. Many of
Konoe's advisors wished him to create a "new popular organization" before he assumed the premiership, in order to
wage a partisan campaign against opponents of fundamental domestic reform both in and out of government. Konoe,

[46] Horiba, *Shina jihen sensō shidō shi*, p. 419.

however, seems never to have considered mobilizing a mass movement against the government, and even when he resigned from the Privy Council in June, he indicated privately that he would be willing to create the new political order as chairman of an official government commission, rather than as a private citizen.[47]

On the other hand, even after becoming premier, Konoe remained reluctant to clarify the nature of his approach to popular mobilization. The critical question was whether his new popular organization would be a partisan body, galvanizing popular support against domestic opponents of the new political and economic systems he had in mind, or whether it somehow would contrive to embrace political figures of all persuasions and seek a "public" mobilization of support in terms of the nation's mission in Asia. The stakes in this issue were high, for they involved the right to mobilize, organize, and control the population of Japan. To phrase it in other words, the matter of deciding the nature of the new popular organization was intimately related to determining who would assume control over the political and economic energies of the Japanese people. During the month of August 1940, the political elites made known their respective positions on these weighty questions, and thereby suggested the lines of political conflict that would characterize the effort to establish a new political order in Japan.

The "new party" advocates in the Diet saw in Konoe's new order an opportunity to enhance their position in national politics while confirming their position as a principal link between Tokyo and the local community. In order to accomplish this dual objective, they were willing and even eager to dissolve their old party organizations. The inclusion of "new party" planner Kazami in Konoe's government and the three vacancies in the Cabinet seemed to confirm expectations that a political party would soon be estab-

[47] SKS, VIII, 275–76.

lished under Konoe's leadership. In anticipation of this event, the Shadaitō formally dissolved itself on July 6, and Kuhara disbanded his party organization on July 16. Others, however, proved slightly more cautious. Nakajima indicated that he would dissolve his party only after Konoe had given concrete evidence of a willingness to form a new party. The Minseitō, meanwhile, continued trying under Machida's leadership to forestall the disintegration of its forces.

However, unlike Kazami's group and the League, Konoe's political strategy vis-à-vis the Diet had been to embrace *all* party forces in his projected mobilization movement, and he was unwilling to tolerate the continuation of any organized Diet group. On the eve of his investiture as premier, therefore, the prince discussed the problem of the parties with the nation in a radio address designed to speed the dissolution of the parties still in existence. In his address, he bitterly attacked the parties as selfish power-seeking manifestations of liberalism, democracy, and socialism, and condemned their tendency to oppose governments in the Diet as inconsistent with the *kokutai*.[48]

Faced with this withering appraisal of political parties, Nakajima was no longer able to resist the importunities of his party colleagues, who begged him to dissolve the party and rally to Konoe's standard before they were left out of the new order or new party. Within a week of Konoe's radio address, Nakajima's Seiyūkai had formally announced its dissolution. President Machida of the Minseitō managed to hold out a bit longer, but the anxieties of the new party advocates within the Minseitō eventually forced him to surrender as well. On July 26, thirty-seven Minseitō members, led by Nagai Ryūtarō, withdrew from the party, reducing the Minseitō delegation to only 132 members. Machida's subordinates, like those of Nakajima's Seiyūkai a few weeks earlier, became increasingly apprehensive

[48] For an English text of Konoe's radio address, see *Tokyo Gazette*, IV.2 (August 1940), 45–47.

about being left out of Konoe's new political order and on August 15, Machida reluctantly announced the dissolution of the last of Japan's major parties.

The new order envisioned by the members of the defunct political parties was revealed three days later in a statement by their spokesman organization, the Association for Promoting a New Order (*Shintaisei sokushin dōshikai*).[49] The association, which excluded the Machida and Hatoyama factions, denounced individualism, democracy, parliament-centered government, majority rule, liberalism, and socialism. Instead, it called for the establishment of a political ethic of service to the state and adherence to the "leadership principle" (*shidō genri*, a Japanese adaptation of the German *Führer prinzip*). Apart from this expression of political philosophy, the association made a vigorous effort to defend the institutional and customary prerogatives of party members, and sought to expand their powers vis-à-vis the other elite groups through the new order. It rejected any intensification of bureaucratic controls over the people, claiming that official intervention in mobilization would "cool the political ardor of the people." The Diet group clearly sought to maintain the prerogatives of the old parties as the principal organs of popular political mobilization and participation through this argument. It further attacked the implementation of any system of vocational representation in national affairs as a manifestation of the "impure" desire to articulate private economic interests at the expense of the national interest. Needless to say, the association wished to prevent the creation of a hierarchy of guilds as the principal form of popular control because of the effect it would have on the Diet's position as representative of the popular will, and on the position of the parties' local supporters in the community and financial backers in the business world. In addition to defending the prerogatives of the party men, however, the association also called for a new party that

[49] YKUS, pp. 56–58.

would serve as the bridge uniting civilian government with the military command, and facilitate the implementation locally of economic and administrative tasks essential to the prosecution of the nation's foreign and defense policies.

The association plan gave close attention to the mobilizing functions of the proposed new party. The party would consist only of "reformists" endowed with a high degree of political consciousness, and a conviction of faith in the *kokutai*. In less elegant phraseology, this statement amounted to a pledge to exclude Diet conservatives such as Machida and Hatoyama from the new organization. Joined in a commonly shared spirit of reform, members of the new party would play a vital role in mobilizing the masses by "leading and enlightening" the people. In other words, the duty of the party was to provide political leadership for the masses. It was to advise the government in policy making, educate the people about established policies, and assist in the implementation of domestic policies. In short, the association's new order proposal called for the creation of an organization independent of, but closely linked to government; little was said about articulating popular wishes and interests as the nation embarked on the perilous and demanding path to the fulfillment of her historic mission abroad. In essence, members of the disbanded parties hoped to enhance their position as the preeminent representatives of the state in the local communities from which they were elected. They sought to prevent the expansion of bureaucratic control over the countryside, and attempted to block the creation of any new organs of popular representation based on vocational groups.

While Arima and Kazami were close to the association, it is not certain how strongly they endorsed this new order proposal. In 1938, they had sought to create a new political organization based on the nationwide network of agrarian guilds. Had this plan succeeded, the new party or organization would have been in direct competition with Diet politicians for political influence in rural Japan. By 1940, Arima

279

and Kazami had softened their position towards the parties somewhat, as evidenced by their active participation in the new party drive during the spring.

In July, Arima proposed the "establishment of a new political party composed of ex-party members and others, and a federation of vocational groups (primarily the guilds) which would become the moving force of the new party." Federation leaders would be members of the new party from the beginning, in much the same way that proletarian parties rested on the political strength of unions and had union representatives serve among the party leadership.[50] Arima's plan promised to have a profound impact on the local political structure, for the new party's members would acquire new *jiban*, the guild memberships. Equally important, the guilds would become the focal point of economic and political life in the village or city. They would thus tend to displace the local agrarian, commercial, and industrial elites that had previously aligned with the parties. Understandably, these elites were hostile to Arima's plan, which they believed was aimed at collectivizing all economic activity in the name of establishing the national defense state and the new order. Within a short period of time, Arima was barraged with criticism for being a "Red."

Whatever their differences, Arima, Kazami, and the association were all proposing that the new political order consist mainly of a new national political organization independent of existing government institutions. It was hardly likely that their plans would escape severe attack from the bureaucracy, for they were seeking to create a nationwide network for the economic and political control of the citizenry divorced from both the Home Ministry and the Ministry of Agriculture and Forestry. Home Minister Yasui, his subordinates, and Chief Cabinet Secretary Tomita (a former Home Ministry official) were particularly anxious to

[50] Arima Yoriyasu and Miki Kiyoshi, "Taidan: Shin seiji taisei," *Kaizō*, xxii.15 (Jikyoku-han 9, August 2, 1940), pp. 65–66.

assure that the Home Ministry's position in local administration was not undermined by the movement for a new
political order. Indeed, the Home Ministry not only sought
to prevent other groups from establishing a preeminent
position in local affairs, but attempted to use the movement
for a new order and national defense state to enhance and
consolidate its jurisdiction over the cities, towns, and
villages.

As noted earlier, officials of the Home Ministry Local
Affairs Bureau had been seeking for several years to integrate local administration more fully under the centralized
control of the ministry. Although these plans were unsuccessful in 1938, they were not jettisoned. In September
1939, Hazama Shigeru, the chief of the Local Affairs
Bureau, ordered the nation's governors to establish *burakukai* and *chōnaikai* throughout the country where they did
not already exist, to "carry out the thrust of important national policies—the National General Mobilization Law,
behind-the-lines support, increasing productive power, encouraging savings, collecting funds, adjusting materiel with
prices—and to become a structure that gets all the people
to cooperate and work together."[51]

The *burakukai* and *chōnaikai* still lacked legal status,
however. In early 1940, further efforts were made to integrate local economic administration into the network of
Home Ministry controls. Citing the unequal ability of various local areas to meet national demands (because of
uneven industrial development and variations in land productivity), the Home Ministry implemented a wartime tax
reform in which the central administration assumed the
major burden for collecting local tax revenues. This measure in effect undermined the final vestiges of local autonomy, while relieving the towns and villages of wartime eco-

[51] "Shi-chō-son ni okeru burakukai mata wa chōnaikai nado jissen-
kō no seibi jūjitsu ni kansuru ken," cited in Ari, "Chihō seido," n. 2,
pp. 203–204. For earlier comments on this aspect of Home Ministry
thinking, see Chapter v, *supra*.

nomic burdens that were too great to handle on a local basis. Hazama later insisted that the new tax system revolutionized the political and economic structure of the nation on a scale commensurate with the Taika Reform thirteen centuries earlier.[52] While this assessment overstates the case, the administrative directive that enacted the reform curtailed many of the remaining vestiges of autonomy in the cities, villages, and towns, and brought them and their leaders increasingly under the jurisdiction of the Home Ministry. Despite these administrative measures, however, little progress was made in confirming the integration and centralization of local administration legally. The Yonai government would not sanction any legislation to alter the structure of local government during its tenure in office.

When Yasui became the new home minister in July, Hazama became vice minister, and he pressed ahead with the Home Ministry's program of centralizing control over local administration. By the end of July, Hazama had drafted a new set of instructions to all governors, urging them to accelerate the creation of *burakukai* and *chōnaikai* as the basic units of Home Ministry administration.[53] These instructions were designed to assure the preeminence of the Home Ministry in administering local affairs, establish the *burakukai* and *chōnaikai* as the basic units of popular life and local administration, strengthen the powers of town and village mayors in governing local areas, and integrate the mayors into the Home Ministry administrative network. The *burakukai* in the villages and *chōnaikai* in the cities were to embrace all residents. They were to become the

---

[52] Hazama also explained after the war that the 1940 tax reform became the basis of Japan's current system of local taxation. *Hazama Shigeru-shi danwa sokkiroku* (Naiseishi kenkyū shiryō dai–31, 32, 33–shū) (Tokyo: Naiseishi kenkyūkai, 1965–1966), p. 114.

[53] Author's interview with Hazama Shigeru, Tokyo, March 2, 1968. The instructions were formally issued by the new home minister, Yasui Eiji, on September 11. For a text of the instructions, see YKUS, pp. 93–97.

coordinating agencies for all local organizations (in particular, the guilds hitherto independent or under the supervision of the Ministry of Agriculture and Forestry), and, "as regional units of the people's economic life, start up the functions necessary for the implementation of a controlled economy and the provisions of the necessities of life." They were to serve as the distributing agencies in the rationing system, and be responsible for the collection of funds and materiel to be directed toward the war effort. They were also to be the basic organizations for moral indoctrination and the cultivation of a sense of spiritual community locally. Furthermore, they were to function as the principal channel through which the people could "assist the imperial rule" (*banmin yokusan*); in other words, they were to serve as the vehicles of political participation in the village and city.

Under the auspices of local mayors, leaders of the *burakukai* and *chōnaikai* were to hold regular meetings (*jōkai*) at which they would be informed of administrative directives from Tokyo to be implemented locally. The *burakukai* were to be organized along the lines of existing hamlet organizations (which were informal, having been carryovers from the Tokugawa system of rural towns and villages), while the somewhat more artificially constructed *chōnaikai* were, in principle, to organize in correspondence with the *machi* or *chō* in the cities. Chairmen of the *kai* were to be selected in accord with local methods for choosing community leadership, but all appointments were to be confirmed by the mayors. Just as the *burakukai* and *chōnaikai* were to become a formal part of the local administration substructure, community organizations (*rinpo-han* or *tonari-gumi*) were to be established within them as official subunits. These subunits were to comprise approximately ten households each, and where possible were to follow the *gonin-gumi* (five-family groups) and *jūnin-gumi* (ten-family groups) that already existed informally in some areas.

283

Coupled with Hazama's detailed administrative directive was a plan by Yasui to make the *burakukai* and *chōnaikai* the basic units of popular political activity. He tried to institute a new system of candidacy, to replace the designation of candidates by the various parties. Under his plan, candidates would be nominated at the lowest level by the *buraku*, at the next level by the village or town and city-district (*shi, gun*) leaders, and finally by the *ken* (prefecture) and *fu* (metropolis) leadership.[54] Since all officials of these bodies were ultimately to be responsible to the Home Ministry, its control over the selection process was virtually assured by Yasui's scheme (although independent candidacies were still to be legally recognized in principle). Yasui's election reform proposal was designed to realize in fact the concept announced by Hazama in his instructions to the governors: the *burakukai* and *chōnaikai* would become the basic units of popular "assistance of the imperial rule."

If successfully executed, the Yasui-Hazama plans promised to guarantee not only that the Home Ministry's local administrative and political powers would be greatly enhanced, but also that the ministry would be unchallenged as the major conduit between the central government and individual Japanese citizens. While Hazama had already stolen a march on the parties and the Ministry of Agriculture and Forestry, his instructions to the governors lacked the force of law and were still subject to negotiation or revision in the months ahead. Party members, for instance, realized that the Home Ministry program would shatter their local *jiban*, which rested on the local political preeminence of the *meibōka*. They were also bitterly opposed to the proposed restrictions on free candidacies. The Agriculture Ministry similarly recognized that the new *burakukai-chōnaikai* structure, under the supervision of the

[54] *Yasui Eiji-shi danwa dai–5–kai sokkiroku* (Naiseishi kenkyū shiryō dai–19) (Tokyo: Naiseishi kenkyūkai, 1964), p. 39.

284

city, town, and village mayors, would undermine its supervisory position over the local economic guilds.

It was the Army, however, that provided the strongest opposition to the Home Ministry. Seeking to overcome opposition to the establishment of a national defense state, the Army preferred creating a radical partisan mass movement and party to employing administrative guidance. While welcoming the establishment of a local substructure to implement national economic policies, Army officials opposed the Home Ministry's monopoly of local controls. No popular enthusiasm was to be expected if the movement were led and controlled by the bureaucracy, and there was little chance that the Home Ministry would be as responsive to Army views and pressures as local groups that the Army hoped to mobilize in support of its programs.

The Army's vision of the new political order was elaborated secretly in mid-July.[55] In order to obtain a total national commitment of economic energies to military requirements, the Army proposed a series of administrative reforms, coupled with the creation of a new mass mobilization organization. In interpreting the call for "strong politics," the Army indicated that political leadership should be strengthened in four ways through administrative reform. First, the premier should enjoy what amounted to dictatorial authority. He was to be empowered to decide any issue over which contending groups were unable to agree. He was also to be vested with full authority to plan and carry out national mobilization. Second, political leadership would be strengthened if interministerial competition were

---

[55] " 'Sekai jōsei no suii ni tomonau jikyoku shori yōkō' chū dai–4–jō kokunai shidō ni kansuru gutaiteki yōmoku." This statement was submitted to the Navy, which amended it somewhat. This document is part of a collection of Navy Ministry materials (hereafter referred to as Navy Ministry archives) microfilmed and kept at the Institute of Asian Economic Affairs (Ajia keizai kenkyūjo) in Tokyo. I am grateful to the late Kishi Kōichi of the institute staff for providing me with access to this valuable documentary source.

curtailed. Hence, the Army proposed to consolidate and reduce the number of ministries. Moreover, as Ishiwara Kanji had proposed in 1937, the post of cabinet minister (*kokumu daijin*) was to be divorced from the position as chief administrative official of a ministry (*gyōsei chōkan*). Cabinet officers would thereby no longer be responsible for or responsive to specific (or "sectional") bureaucratic constituencies, and might provide more authoritative leadership when concerned only with the "national" interest. As a further curb on ministerial "sectionalism," a Central Personnel Bureau was to be established, taking appointments out of the hands of the individual ministries and placing it under the control of the premier, through the bureau. Finally, to integrate the planning of war-related economic policies then under study in individual ministries, the Planning Board was to be expanded and given greater supervisory authority. As the office primarily responsible for wartime economic controls, it would become a Control Ministry (*Tōseishō*). Ministerial authority would be greatly reduced by these plans, and "supraministry" agencies such as the Planning Board would become more influential. Moreover, through new personnel regulations, military officers could be assigned to key positions in the civilian bureaucracy.

To overcome the political opposition of various groups whose economic interests would suffer most from a total focus on a wartime economy, the Army formulated a three-part program. The first plan was to launch a "spiritual" or "public" mobilization drive, which affirmed the morality of service to the state (*kokka hōkō*) and, conversely, the immorality of putting private or personal interests before those of the nation. Where persuasion and education failed, the authority of the state was to be used to control the freedom of the press and suppress all criticism of the nation's wartime policies. The "spiritual" approach to mobilizing support for national defense state policies was directed at cultivating an individual sense of duty to and identification with the state and throne.

A second approach focused on mobilizing support and minimizing opposition to the Army's plans by establishing political control over all areas of organized group activity. This was the thrust of the Army's proposal for the creation of a new popular organization (*kokumin soshiki*). The organization was to embrace all political parties, cultural, social, and economic groups, thereby assuring that it reached the entire citizenry and, in its political activities, "brought politics to all the people" (*"seiji no shintō"*). The new organization would not only involve all citizens in national politics, but would also provide the vehicle through which national policies were enacted by the people. In other words, the *kokumin soshiki* was to be an active political force locally, the focal point of popular activities related to wartime economic and political life. This proposal approximated Konoe's idea of a new popular organization of national integration.

Further details of Army thinking on the new political order and new popular organization were made public on August 21 as the proposal of Yatsugi Kazuo's *Kokusaku kenkyūkai*. This proposal was drawn up through the combined efforts of the Military Affairs Bureau, Colonel Akinaga Tsukizō of the Planning Board, and Yatsugi.[56] After reiterating briefly the importance of a planned economy, the need for a heightened public awareness of the primacy of national (public) interests over private interests, and the desirability of administrative reforms, the Yatsugi plan focused on the formation and operating procedures of the new popular organization. It was to be a new, mass political party, although quite different from both the "infantile" plan for a Diet-centered new party proposed by the association and the government-sponsored organization proposed by a number of bureaucrats. The party was to consist not only of members from the defunct parties but also of power-

[56] For a slightly abridged text of the *Kokusaku kenkyūkai* proposal, see YKUS, pp. 64–71; a complete version is available in Imai and Itō, eds., *Kokka sōdōin*, pp. 316–26.

ful leaders from all sectors of Japan's political power structure: government, both Diet Houses, the financial world, and so on. Ex-party members would be allotted a role in the new party, but not an exclusive or dominant position of leadership, as the association wished. While the party was to be set up by a commission staffed by civilians, officials, and military officers, and chaired by Konoe, it would be independent of the existing bureaucratic structure. The plan also called for reform of the election law and for a new political organization law to sanction the existence of this quasi-official political party, but opposed any introduction of vocational representation in the Diet for fear of intensifying the Diet's proclivity to represent private economic interests. In sum, the Army's new party plan provided for the creation of a new leadership organ, formally independent of official or military leadership, but guided in some way by a commission composed of civilian, military, and official representatives. The leadership organ itself was to include members of the old parties, as well as representatives of nonparty groups.

Through the Army's proposed party, a new force would be created in local political and economic affairs. The party was to absorb existing mass movements such as the labor unions, agrarian guilds, and the national spiritual mobilization drive, and convert them from individual government-run movements lacking the ability to inspire popular participation and support into a unified system of national integration capped by a party. Through these links to local communities, the party was to communicate and execute national policies (*jōi katatsu*) rather than encourage the articulation of local interests and views (*kai jōtatsu*). In other words, the party's function was defined in terms of popular leadership and its relationship to the government rather than in terms of popular representation. Its chief mobilization functions, therefore, were to be determined by government policies, rather than by popular political demands. Among the local activities of the party were to be

288

the establishment of owner-worker production committees in factories and mines to increase production, creation of similar committees in the villages to stimulate food production, the fostering of a new popular life movement in the *tonari-gumi*, *chōkai*, and *burakukai*, emphasizing frugality and limited consumption, and propaganda agitation on behalf of the production-increase and "new life" campaigns through literature, the arts, movies, and radio broadcasts.

The Army expressed a general interest in directing and capitalizing on the energies and reformist zeal of young men locally who were willing to challenge the influence of the old local elites in village and town affairs. However, it had no organized local support group on which to rely. Soldiers on active military duty were prohibited by imperial edict from membership in political organizations, while local *Zaigō gunjinkai* leaders were not fully trusted to carry out the wishes of the Army's central headquarters.[57] Throughout the 1930s, the Army's influence in the *seinendan* and *sōnendan* organizations had grown, but these groups were even less firmly under Army control than the reserve associations. The central question, therefore, was whether the Army could provide a formal organizational apparatus and leadership positions in the new party for the challengers of the established local power structure.

Officials of the Home Ministry and Ministry of Agriculture and Forestry saw the creation of an Army-inspired mass party in terms of the establishment of a new nationwide network outside the jurisdiction of either ministry. Since the Army had posited the new party as the central organ of mass mobilization and the key body in the local execution of national policies, civilian officials could only conclude that their authority would be severely under-

---

[57] The *Zaigō gunjinkai* local leadership had previously demonstrated its willingness to act independently of the Army Ministry's wishes. See Richard J. Smethurst, "The Military Reserve Association and the Minobe Crisis of 1935," in Wilson, *Crisis Politics in Prewar Japan*, pp. 1–23.

mined by the Army's plans. Particularly in the Home Ministry, the reaction to Yatsugi's proposals was swift and bitterly hostile.

Political relations among the elites were thus unusually strained during August 1940, as Konoe prepared to fulfill his public promise of a new political order. By mid-August the Changsha talks had still not taken place, while elite pressures on the premier to structure the new order in accordance with one political viewpoint or another grew steadily. It was impossible for Konoe to postpone the new order indefinitely, and further delay would only add to the apprehensions and speculation over its nature. The final prod that moved Konoe to action did not come from a truce in China, as the prince had hoped, but rather from the domestic tensions that had arisen in the wake of his announcement of support for the new order. This fact was of vital importance in the weeks and months ahead, for it meant that, barring a breakthrough at Changsha, the nation would be moving ahead with strengthening its northern defenses and expanding southward, while still involved in a full-scale long-term war in China. In these circumstances, Konoe might well be expected to abandon his plans to mobilize a political movement against the institutional prerogatives of those who opposed his policies, as he had in 1938. If Japan kept fighting in China, Konoe seemed likely to use the new political order simply to assure that so long as the conflict continued, the existing degree of national unity in Japan did not disintegrate.

Throughout the second and third weeks of August, the press carried daily reports of the imminent establishment of a "Preparatory Commission for Establishing the New Political Order." On August 22, Konoe finally submitted to the Cabinet his roster of nominees for this commission, and the Cabinet indicated its approval of Konoe's selections.[58]

[58] For biographical data on commission members, see *Tōkyō asahi*, August 23, 1940 and Oda Toshiyo, *Konoe shintaisei no zenbō* (Tokyo: Kōkoku Nippon shinbunsha, 1940), pp. 234–41.

As the press quickly observed, Konoe's list was marked by an effort to strike a "balance of power" among various political forces. Six members of the Lower House were chosen, representing all shades of opinion on the new party and new order issue. Several ex-Home Ministry bureaucrats with expertise in questions of local politics and administration were also selected. Other commission members were appointed as unofficial representatives of business, the agrarian guild movement, the "reformist" and "Japanist" right-wing groups, and the press. In addition, all eleven Cabinet members were appointed to serve on the commission. To facilitate commission discussions, an eight-man secretariat was established to draft agendas, policies, and organizational plans. Included as members of this important organ were Chief Cabinet Secretary Tomita, Murase Naokai (chief of the Cabinet Legislative Affairs Bureau), the chiefs of the Army and Navy Military Affairs Bureaus (Major General Mutō and Rear Admiral Abe Katsuo), and Vice Minister Hazama of the Home Ministry.

By the end of August, the nation was waiting anxiously to see what plan would result from the efforts of these men, who, as Japanese observers phrased it, might now be sleeping in the same bed but were likely to have different dreams. Throughout the month, Konoe and his staff had been working on the guidelines to be followed in the deliberations of the commission. Government and Army officials suggested amendments and deletions to Yabe's drafts to bring the text of these guidelines more closely into line with their own plans. Mutō, for instance, sought vainly to tone down all negative references to the concept of a new totalitarian party.[59] Hazama and the Home Ministry succeeded in eliminating from the text many suggestions that the new order would establish a system of local administration to rival the Home Ministry network.[60] Finally on

[59] SKS, viii, 320; KF, ii, 139; Tomita Kenji, *Haisen Nihon no naisoku: Konoe-kō no omoide* (Tokyo: Kokin shoin, 1962), p. 81.

[60] *Hazama Shigeru-shi danwa sokkiroku*, p. 133.

August 26, the commission's secretariat reached agreement on the wording of the guidelines, and the following day, the Cabinet expressed its approval as well. On August 28, Prince Konoe delivered the text of the guidelines as his personal instructions to the first meeting of the commission. The construction of a new domestic order for Japan had begun.

CHAPTER VII

The Political Parties and Japan's Wartime Political Order

INTRODUCTION

THE formal dissolution of the major political parties took place in the month preceding the establishment of Japan's new political order. Dissolution took place at a time when the parties were internally divided, and under severe attack from Konoe, the bureaucracy, and the Army. Nevertheless, the circumstances that brought an end to the party organizations in imperial Japan did not signify their powerlessness or capitulation in the competition for power. Instead, the events of mid-1940 indicated the parties' desire to enhance their influence beyond the Diet as well as the desire of other elite groups to undermine the significant influence parties had retained by virtue of their institutional prerogatives in the Diet and their links to the countryside. Although the parties dissolved, the influence of party men in the Diet and the countryside survived.

For nonparty elites, the survival of party power in wartime posed two fundamental problems. The first related to harmonizing the always troublesome relationship between the Cabinet and Lower House. Many party members retained their personal connections with the bureaucratic, military, and business groups. After 1932, however, these nonparty elites dealt directly with each other in the Cabinet. Under Konoe's aegis from 1937 to 1941, they struck important, if not always consistent, compromises without seeking party mediation. In the latter half of the 1930s, connections between party members and nonparty elites were really significant only in the context of gaining Diet approval for the Cabinet's compromise policies, and from June 1941 to April 1943, the Cabinet did not include a single minister from the old parties. When a proposal reached the Diet, each nonparty elite group sought to use its connections with Diet members to defend those aspects it supported in the compromise, and undermine those features of the policy in question that its adversaries in the Cabinet had insisted upon as the price of Cabinet unity. The Diet retained the right to veto legislation not covered by the National General Mobilization Law, and also enjoyed majority representation on the National General Mobilization Council. Diet members' prerogatives in these bodies, combined with the competition among the Cabinet elites, thus permitted parliamentary forces to retain a voice in wartime policy making.

After 1940, the desire to manifest at least external national unity grew stronger among Japan's leaders. On the one hand, this desire led to the expulsion of the iconoclastic Saitō Takao from the Lower House and the disappearance of public debate over Cabinet policies on the floor of the Diet. On the other hand, the Cabinet paid a growing price for the Diet's display of "national unity." It was often obliged to negotiate with party leaders before the Diet opened publicly, and pigeonhole or modify controversial legislation to preserve the unanimous support of the Diet. The mediation efforts of parliamentary leaders grew in importance during wartime, although they were still confined to managing the Lower House, and not the Cabinet. The parliamentary leaders' role resulted in restoring some of their lost prestige and tightening their once-tenuous grip over the rank and file. Later, their price for unanimous Diet consent increased, as wartime pressures obliged the government to submit bills that might previously have been deferred or toned down. By April 1943, party leaders had reappeared in the Cabinet, and the number of party men in the Cabinet increased slowly thereafter.

294

The second problem occasioned by the persistence of party power concerned the question of how to integrate popular political energies and channel them towards the attainment of established national objectives. Phrased differently, the issue was one of insuring that the imposition of heavy wartime burdens on the populace would not create passive or active resistance to national policies, and would, in fact, be met with active support and participation in the implementation of these policies. For the elites who opposed party power, this question required a decision on whether to challenge or accept the traditional nexus of relationships running from the community through the *meibōka* and individual party member into the Diet.

During the war, bureaucratic controls over citizens' lives greatly increased, as the tasks of economic mobilization and maintenance of public morale became more important. Assuring popular recognition of the wartime regime's legitimacy remained an important concern of the ruling elites, and they promoted many campaigns to justify the extensive scope of state controls in the name of imperial rule. Even the most ardent advocates of state controls, however, agreed that controlled popular political participation in national affairs remained a vital instrument for the legitimization of elite rule. The legitimacy of the traditional political conduit of citizen participation in politics as the exclusive channel of popular political participation was challenged in 1940 by the creation of a new hierarchy of popular councils in the new political order. It was also challenged in 1940–1941, and again in the 1942 general elections, when the Army endeavored to replace the old party men with "new faces" in the Lower House, and the traditional political elites of the countryside with a new reformist coalition. In all cases, the strength of the parties and their local allies, and the widespread desire to avert a public display of discord in the body politic, resulted in the failure of the challenges. This concluding chapter in the history of Japan's prewar parties thus demonstrates again the degree to which party men retained a share of national power and contributed to the maintenance of "limited pluralism" and the constitutional system of diffused political responsibility.

DETERMINANTS OF POPULAR MOBILIZATION IN 1940

As Prince Konoe approached the meetings of the Preparatory Commission for Establishing a New Political Order in August 1940, he was faced with a vexing cluster of immediate problems. The rapidly changing international situation and the need for domestic adjustments to international developments had a profound impact on the way he would use the new political order as a vehicle for national integration and popular mobilization. In mid-August, the Chungking government sought through Lieutenant Colonel Suzuki to obtain from Konoe a public announcement of his willingness to negotiate with Chiang and abandon the Japanese government's commitment to Wang Ching-wei's regime. Both Suzuki and Konoe vetoed this request as premature, but on August 22, the premier sent a personal letter to Chiang emphasizing the importance and value of the recent Sino-Japanese talks in Hong Kong and implying by his remarks a desire to pursue them further. Army Minister Tōjō and Suzuki went to Konoe's office to obtain the premier's written statement, and it was presented to Soong in Hong Kong with the approval of CEF Chief of Staff General Itagaki. Soong assured the Japanese that Konoe's letter would prove satisfying to Chungking, and the CEF again began preparations for the proposed Changsha conference.[1]

While Konoe, Itagaki, and Foreign Minister Matsuoka remained sanguine about the possibilities of quickly negotiating an end to the Incident, others were less certain that such an approach would succeed. Within the Army, it had

[1] SKS, VIII, 322; Kido, *Kido Kōichi nikki*, II, 816; Horiba, *Shina jihen sensō shidō shi*, pp. 419-22.

already been decided on May 18 that negotiations could be pursued only until year's end. If the Paulownia Plan initiative and the intensified military pressure provided by the new troops placed under Itagaki's command in the spring did not succeed in bringing peace by the end of 1940, Japan was to prepare for a long-term occupation of conquered Chinese territory. Efforts would be continued to cut off support for Chiang from the United States and Great Britain by occupying strategic areas in Southeast Asia, while the Wang government received official recognition and support from Japan. It was hoped that Chiang would in time surrender, as his outside sources of aid were closed off and as Japan, supported by a military alliance with Germany and Italy and enriched by the resources of Southeast Asia, applied additional diplomatic and military pressures on Chungking. At any rate, the Paulownia Plan could not be sanctioned indefinitely.

Konoe still believed that if a settlement with Chiang materialized, the nation could afford a "highly political" challenge to the constitutionally sanctioned independence of those elite groups who insisted on supporting the Wang regime or opposed the establishment of a high-degree national defense state. In Konoe's view, certain groups of Army officers remained committed to the establishment of the Wang government, and would be difficult to control unless the premier gained additional political leverage from the new political order. Moreover, influential courtiers and financiers, such as Harada and Ikeda Seihin, had expressed their disapproval of negotiating with Chiang throughout the early months of 1940, and would have to be neutralized politically if the Changsha talks were successful.[2] Even more importantly, however, the sweeping state controls over the nation's economy and polity, and the rationalization of all economic activity from the viewpoint of wartime requirements would obviously be opposed with vigor by the

[2] For example, see SKS, viii, 193 and 209.

zaibatsu, many Diet representatives, and local elites. For all of these reasons, Konoe continued in mid-August to think of the new political order in terms of a new "political" mobilization effort to undermine the institutional bases of support for opponents of his foreign and domestic policies.

At the same time, however, the prince was obliged to consider the possibility that the negotiations with Chiang's representatives would not bear fruit. Continuing the war in China would add greater burdens to the citizenry, on top of the duties imposed by the anticipated rupture of economic relations with the United States and the need to replenish Japan's northern defenses against the Soviet Union. In other words, Konoe had to consider the effects of establishing a high-degree national defense state on the citizenry's willingness to tolerate and support policies that imposed growing official constraints on their livelihood. Although the Japanese people bore up magnificently under the burdens placed on them by Japan's expansionist policies, leaders such as Konoe became increasingly fearful of popular resistance to elite government. Perhaps, as Fujiwara Akira has argued, this excessive anxiety about revolution from below was occasioned by the psychological and political distance between courtiers like Konoe and the common people.[3] The fear was shared by nonnobles as well, however, and was probably a consequence of their having witnessed the Russian Revolution and a variety of other manifestations of mass politics in other countries. At any rate, Konoe on several occasions indicated his concern that popular war weariness might someday erupt into revolution, and legislation was being prepared to strengthen still further the power of the police to suppress expressions of popular discontent against the war and official national policies.[4]

[3] Fujiwara Akira, "Kyūchū gurūpu no seijiteki taido," in Hashikawa Bunzō and Matsumoto Sannosuke, eds., *Kindai Nihon seiji shisō shi II* (Kindai Nihon shisō shi taikei, IV) (Tokyo: Yūhikaku, 1970), pp. 379–80.
[4] Kazami, *Konoe naikaku*, p. 258.

Apart from repression, however, Konoe believed with most Japanese leaders that the populace must evince positive support for national policies if the nation was to survive its international crises. The people must be brought to identify more closely with the legitimacy of the imperial government and its goals, and be integrated more fully into the processes of policy implementation. The prince no longer believed that the existing linkage between the citizen and the state through Diet elections was sufficient for the necessary evocation of popular identification with the government, and he wished to have all people integrated and "participating" in national affairs through new economic and cultural organizations. That is, he wished to raise the popular level of tolerance and participation by mobilizing the consciousness of the people as members of the nation. He sought to persuade the people that all subjects were intimately involved in the work of the throne, and that each had important duties to fulfill. Konoe's spiritual mobilization would thus on the one hand be pre-emptive—to prevent the possibility of popular resistance as had occurred in other countries, and in a more positive vein, it would seek to promote the public's willingness to sacrifice for the state as the citizenry had done during the first Sino-Japanese and Russo-Japanese wars.

If the war with China continued, Konoe was prepared to abandon the new order as a vehicle for divisive "political" mobilization against his opponents, and use it primarily as an integrating ("national unity") institution for the "public" mobilization of citizens, in support of Japan's international mission and whatever domestic measures elite groups could approve through the existing means of conflict management in the Cabinet and Diet. As of August 1940, Konoe was still considering the new political order as a vehicle for both kinds of popular mobilization, "political" and "public." As his hopes for a settlement with Chiang faded in September, and vanished by late November, the prince would ultimately concede the futility and imprudence of "political" mobilization, and the new order would become a set of

299

institutions for mobilizing the morale and sense of identification of the citizenry with the government and the national policies that elite groups with power sanctioned by
the imperial system might approve.

PREPARATIONS FOR THE NEW POLITICAL ORDER

The commission began its deliberations at the premier's
official residence on August 28, 1940. The first order of business on the agenda was a speech by the premier, outlining
the task of the commission. Prince Konoe began his address
by indicating that the new political order was intimately
related to the prosecution of Japan's policies abroad.[5]

> If [Japan] is to bring the China Affair to a successful
> conclusion while adjusting herself to the international
> situation, and take a leading part in the establishment
> of a new world order, she must concentrate upon the
> accomplishment of this task the moral and material re-
> sources of the nation to the utmost degree so as to be
> in a position to take independently, swiftly, and resolute-
> ly appropriate measures to meet whatever situations may
> arise. To this end Japan must perfect a highly organized
> national defense structure. Consequently, there has arisen
> the pressing demand for the setting up of a new struc-
> ture in politics, economy, education, culture and in all
> phases of the life of the State and of the people.
>
> . . . Whether or not Japan can firmly set up such a strong
> national structure will decide the fate of the nation.

In other words, Japan required a strong domestic structure
in order to respond with flexibility and resolution to "whatever situations may arise" in bringing the China Incident
to a close, adjusting to new relationships among the major

[5] The English text of Konoe's speech may be found in the *Tokyo
Gazette*, iv.4 (October 1940), 133–36. For the original Japanese version, see YKUS, pp. 83–86.

world powers as Germany marched victoriously through Europe to the English Channel, and building a new international order among all nations of the world.

During the course of his address, Konoe further intimated that the new order would embody a new system of political participation to supplant elections, and a political structure that would eliminate any "tendency toward conflict between those who govern and those who are governed." The new structure would consist of a nationwide network of economic and cultural organizations, integrating all people into the process of formulating national economic and cultural policies. Only under such a system, the prince declared, could "the entire strength of the nation . . . be concentrated on carrying out the national policies." The elimination of political opposition required "not merely a spiritual movement in the narrow sense but one aiming at uplifting the political ideals and enhancing the political consciousness of the nation. . . . The movement is highly political in nature."

These remarks of the premier could only be interpreted as a pledge to challenge the prerogatives of existing elite groups with a "highly political" movement, centered on a "nuclear body" of able men from all social and economic strata who had not been active participants in the established institutions of government hitherto. Consequently, in the discussion between commission members and Konoe that followed the premier's speech, the "political nature" of the new order became a focal point of inquiry. Once again, Konoe affirmed that "the range of activities of the new order extends to the economic and cultural spheres, as well as to all aspects of the people's lives. The main points distinguishing the new order from a second spiritual mobilization movement are that it will have political power to take action. That is why a nuclear organization is essential."[6] The premier did not elaborate on the "political nature" of this nuclear body, but instead asked the

[6] YKUS, p. 100.

301

chief of the Cabinet Legislative Bureau, Murase Naokai, to clarify for the commission the legal status of the new order.

As the chief legislative expert of the government, Murase attempted to describe the new order's character in terms of Japanese laws regarding political associations (*seiji kessha*). Murase declared that since the new order movement did not aim at any private goals, or at organizing a new opposition force against the government, but was rather committed to public and "national-unity" tasks, it was not to be regarded legally as a *seiji kessha*.[7] His analysis amounted to a declaration that even if the new order were to be political, it was not to be regarded as a political organization. If Murase's tortured definition proved acceptable, women, youth, and military men would be permitted to join the new order movement.

This definition was unlikely to survive unchallenged. The commission convened again on September 3, and Konoe was again present to answer questions. "Japanist" representatives Kuzuu Yoshihisa and Ida Bannan anxiously inquired about the guiding spirit of the new order, the composition of the nuclear body of the new order movement, and the degree to which the nuclear body would be independent of the government. They further solicited Konoe's views on the relationship the movement would have with other political groups.[8] As their questions belied, Ida and Kuzuu suspected that Konoe was planning a radical coalition, which would become the only legal political organization or party in Japan, monopolize access to the Diet and Cabinet, and prevent the existence of other political organizations. Konoe attempted to assuage their doubts by assuring the commission that the new order movement would be guided by the spirit of the *kokutai*, and would not seek to establish any legal prohibitions on the right of other political organizations to exist. Nevertheless, the prince noted pointedly, he

[7] *Ibid.*, p. 101.   [8] *Ibid.*, p. 105.

hoped that all political groups still in existence would dissolve of their own accord.[9] As for the remaining questions raised by Ida and Kuzuu, Konoe referred them to the actual new order proposal, which had been drawn up by the commission's secretariat, and was on the agenda as the main order of business for the second meeting.

Chief Cabinet Secretary Tomita was then called upon to explain the new order proposal (see the chart, p. 304).[10] He indicated that the heart of the new political order would be contained in two major institutional innovations, which threatened the prerogatives of the Diet and, perhaps, the bureaucracy. First, all Japanese were to be organized through vocational and cultural groups into two new national popular organizations. The organization of vocational groups was to include guilds of agrarian workers and industrial workers. In the case of the latter, all employees of a given enterprise or factory would be organized into a unit guild, and each unit guild would be fused into a larger guild embracing all enterprises of the same industry. The resulting federation of industrial and agrarian guilds would compose the Supreme Economic Council (*Saikō keizai kaigi*). The second popular organization—comprising cultural groups—would embrace educational and technical groups, neighborhood physical fitness groups, newspaper publishing associations, and groups connected with the arts, youth work, women's activities, social work, and religious activity. When joined together, they would stand as the Supreme Cultural Council (*Saikō bunka kaigi*). These two organizations were to be linked (it was as yet unclear whether or not they would also be subordinate) to the government's ministries. The establishment of these two organizations through which the people could fulfill their duties as subjects and be integrated into the life of the state was posited as one objective of the new order.

[9] *Ibid.*, pp. 105–106.

[10] For the details of the secretariat's proposal, see *ibid.*, pp. 101–109.

303

The proposed organization of the New Political Order

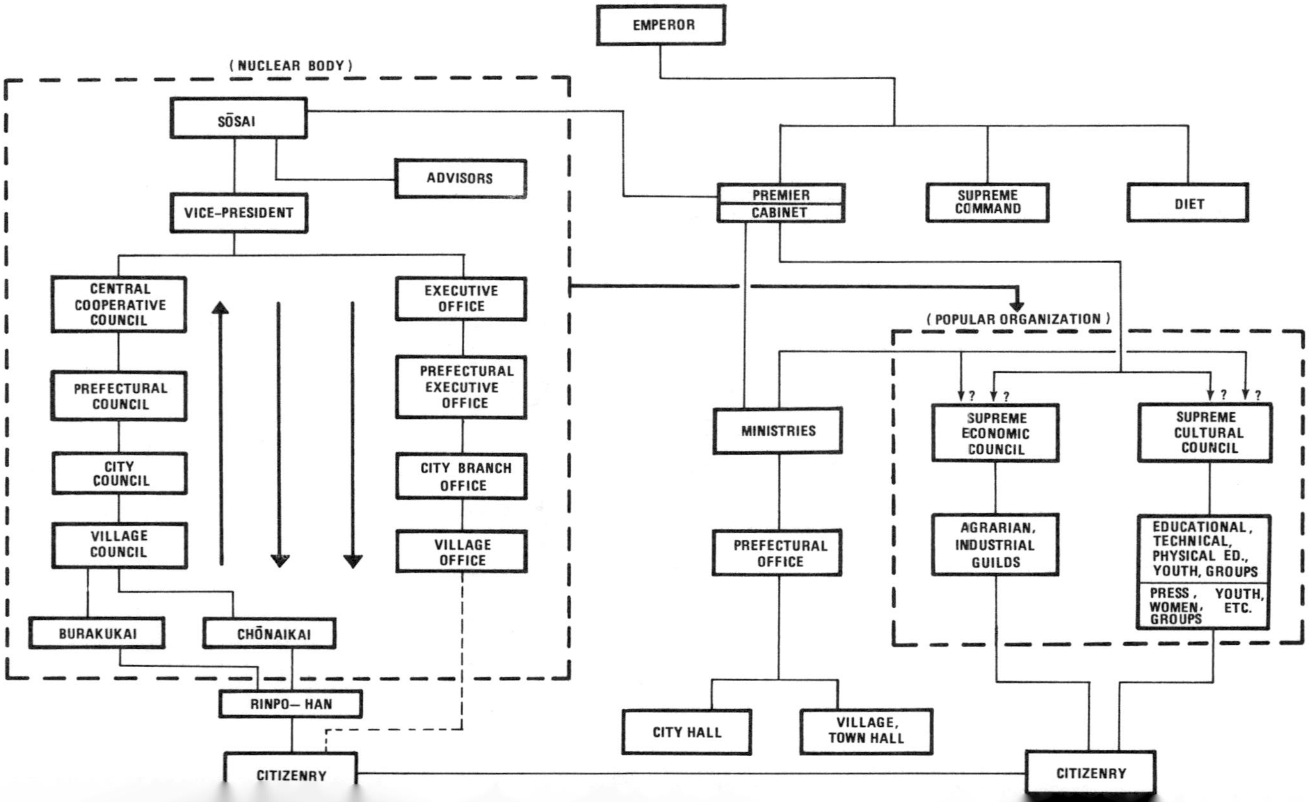

The second feature of the new order plan was the establishment of a nuclear body, which would be an advisory unit for the premier and would propel the movement for the creation of the aforementioned vocational and cultural organizations. While emphasizing that this nuclear body was not a political party, Tomita indicated that it would have four important political duties. First, it was to work with the government in formulating national policies and in executing them. Second, it was to organize popular groups into the Supreme Economic and Cultural Councils. Third, its members were to assume a leading position in the Diet. Finally, it was to establish close liaison with the government and the military. To perform these duties, the nuclear body was to be constructed in two parts, an executive office and a series of cooperative councils. The main duties of the executive office would be to participate in the formulation and execution of national policies in Tokyo, and to convey to the people through local branches the policies that had been decided. It was also to "harmonize government and military" by embracing civilian and military leaders in a new political institution, a measure that implicitly undermined the centrality of the Cabinet and threatened the independence of the military and civilian arms of government.

The cooperative councils were likewise to be organized at the national and local levels, supplanting the Diet and local assemblies. In Tokyo, a central cooperative council of roughly three hundred members was to meet. Smaller councils were to be established at the prefectural (*dō-fu-ken*) and old county (*gun*) levels. In the cities, towns, and villages, councils were also to meet, but it was recognized that already existing councils at this local level might serve in the capacity of cooperative councils. The function of cooperative councils in the *buraku* and within urban wards was to be exercised by the *burakukai* and *chōnaikai*, and in neighborhoods by the neighborhood associations (*rinpo-han, tonari-gumi*). The primary purpose of this hierarchy of councils would be to replace existing independent legislatures as the forum for articulating the views of the people to the government, and gaining additional popular sanctions for government policies.

The entire nuclear body was to be presided over by a president (*sōsai*) and vice president (*fuku-sōsai*). All decisions and personnel appointments were to be made formally by the *sōsai* (naturally, Konoe) and he was to work closely with the premier. No decision had yet been made, however, on the vital question of whether the premier himself would automatically become the *sōsai* or whether a *sōsai* could remain in office while premiers and their governments changed. At the core of this question was the issue of whether the new political order was to be a vehicle for the dictatorship of Konoe as an individual, or of Konoe and his possible successors as premier. What seemed clear either way was that the nuclear body apparatus provided Konoe with a potentially powerful organization through which to mobilize political support for domestic reforms, or generate a heightened degree of public tolerance to forthcoming economic restrictions in daily life. Both "political" and "public" mobilization would be possible through the nuclear body itself and the economic and cultural organizations that were to be led by the nuclear body.

The commission was asked to discuss this proposal, although all final decisions regarding it were formally left for Konoe to make. A number of commission members promptly raised questions concerning the structure and operation of the new order as proposed by the secretariat. The fear was expressed that the new order would make the *sōsai* too strong, and would enable him to establish a government "outside the government" similar to a *bakufu*. Horikiri Zenjirō, a career Home Ministry bureaucrat, contended that the Supreme Economic and Cultural Councils should be based on the *burakukai* and *chōnaikai* regional organizations rather than on new vocational organizations. He also urged a closer integration of the local cooperative councils into the activities of local government officials. In

306

other words, Horikiri wished to see the local organization of the new order brought more firmly under Home Ministry supervision. Diet members sitting on the commission voiced different views. Ogawa Gōtarō of the Minseitō mainstream feared that the nuclear body, with its cooperative councils, would usurp the responsibilities of the Lower House, while Nagai Ryūtarō and Kanemitsu Tsuneo from the anti-mainstream and splinter groups saw in the nuclear body an opportunity to create a new political party. Nagai urged that the executive office be explicitly designated as a permanent organ, and that the nuclear body itself become a party with the task of mediating between popular political views and government policy making. He further urged that the nuclear body have the power to decide national policy, and that the Cabinet's role in the new order be confined to the execution of these policy decisions. He added that the Supreme Economic and Cultural Councils should be subordinated to the nuclear body, so that their functions, too, would become a part of the execution of the policies it decided. Nagai's views on strengthening the functions of the executive office and nuclear body were seconded by "reformist" right-wing leaders Hashimoto Kingorō and Nakano Seigō, who likewise sought to convert the nuclear body into a totalitarian party that would replace the Cabinet as the central policy-making organ of state.[11]

On this note, the second meeting of the commission adjourned. On the basis of the first two meetings, two points had become clear. First, Konoe seemed determined to create a new "political" movement and had taken an active part in the early discussions of the commission. Second, a sharp debate was developing among commission members over the nature of the new order. Party men seemed divided between those who favored transforming the new order into a totalitarian party and those who feared the new order would restrict their activities in the Diet. Right-wing commission members were also at odds over the new order. The

[11] *Ibid.*, pp. 109–11.

greatest fear of "Japanist" right-wing members was that the new order would create a powerful political organization beyond the scope of the constitution and the law. Their efforts were therefore directed towards assuring that the new order was limited to spiritual mobilization, and did not infringe on the rights and duties of constitutionally sanctioned institutions. The "reformist" right wing, on the other hand, shared the hopes for a totalitarian party expressed by Nagai and other "reformist" advocates in the Diet. They regarded the Constitution as an obstacle to be overcome in establishing a strong force, rather than as sacred canon to be revered and preserved. In the midst of this controversy, the Home Ministry seemed anxious to prevent the new order from becoming a new network of national administration free of bureaucratic supervision or control. All Home Ministry efforts, therefore, were to be directed toward absorbing the apparatus and leadership of the new order under Home Ministry supervision.

During the next two weeks, the commission met four more times. Konoe attended some of these meetings, and missed others. Not once during those two weeks did he again comment on the nature of the new order, or on his hopes for the creation of a "highly political" movement. His biographer notes that even before the new order was formally launched, "Konoe's ardor towards it had cooled notably."[12] This apparent change of heart was attributed to a variety of factors by historians and by those who placed great hope in the new order as a new force in Japanese politics. It was charged that Konoe was dissuaded from his original intention to create a new party by the threats of "Japanist" terrorists, that he was influenced by accusations that the new order would be an illegitimate replica of the *bakufu*, that he was "used" by fascist forces he sought to control, and that his weak courtier character prevented

[12] KF, ii, 200.

him from carrying out his original plans.[13] No doubt the difficulty of overcoming opposition to the new order was considerable, but not surprising to a man with Konoe's political experience. His hesitation at this point emanated not from a sudden recognition that he would encounter opposition, but rather to changes (or the absence of change) in the international environment that raised the risks of "political" mobilization and made the alternative of "public" mobilization more attractive.

The optimistic hopes for a negotiated settlement with Chungking suddenly evaporated in early mid-September, 1940. On September 5, Chiang Kai-shek denounced the Konoe letter of August 22 as a forgery, and Konoe confessed to Harada that he had been badly misled when he was induced to write the letter.[14] A week later, the Army's chief aide-de-camp at Court noted that the Paulownia Plan had reached an impasse, and the CEF representative in Hong Kong sent a recommendation to his superiors urging that the meeting at Changsha be postponed. On September 19, the CEF formally announced the suspension of the Paulownia Plan.[15] Thenceforth, the Army turned toward developing its strategy for a long-term occupation in China, coupled with the extension of diplomatic recognition and support for the Nanking regime. From the Army's perspective, the possibility of a negotiated settlement with Chiang had, for the time being, disappeared.

The collapse of the Paulownia Plan initiative was a seri-

---

[13] Maki, "Gun no seiji kan'yō to kokunai jōsei"; Hara Shirō, quoted in Nakamura Kikuo, *Shōwa rikugun hishi* (Tokyo: Banchō shobō, 1968), p. 277; KF, ii, 197 and 200; Nakamura, *Shōwa seiji shi*, p. 152; Maeda Yonezō denki kankōkai, ed., *Maeda Yonezō den*, p. 426; Okada Takeo, *Konoe Fumimaro: Tennō to gunbu to kokumin* (Tokyo: Shunjūsha, 1959), p. 252; Tanaka Sōgorō, "Taisei yokusankai: Nihonteki fuashizumu no shōchō to shite," *Rekishigaku kenkyū*, #212 (October 1957), p. 4; Aritake, *Shōwa keizai sokumen shi*, p. 428; Hasegawa, *Shōwa kenpō shi*, p. 143.

[14] SKS, viii, 336; DR, ii, 125.

[15] Kido, *Kido Kōichi nikki*, ii, 821; DR, ii, 126.

ous blow to Konoe's hopes for a quick settlement of the China Incident. However, no sooner had the Army dropped the plan than Foreign Minister Matsuoka announced his intention to bring about a diplomatic settlement of the war. In Matsuoka's opinion, the Incident had to be ended quickly so that Japan would be free to deal with the hostile Anglo-American reaction expected when the Axis Pact was signed. He was soon bragging that he expected confirmation that negotiations could begin with Chungking within two weeks. During October, Tajiri Aigi, a diplomatic official serving with Abe in Nanking, was dispatched to Hong Kong to explore the possibility of negotiations with Chien Yung-ming and Chou Tsou-min. He was accompanied by Matsumoto Shigeharu, as Konoe's personal emissary. At the same time, Konoe informed Harada that Matsuoka had taken charge of the plans to negotiate with Chungking. Despite these efforts, however, and despite Army Minister Tōjō's willingness to defer the extension of diplomatic recognition to Wang if Chungking gave positive evidence of a willingness to negotiate, Matsuoka's plan ended in failure. On November 28, a liaison conference between the government and supreme command decided to extend diplomatic recognition to Wang immediately, and Matsuoka himself angrily denounced Chiang's apparent interest in negotiations as being nothing more than a political plot.[16]

By the end of November, Konoe's hopes for ending the China Incident quickly had been completely shattered. Indeed, there had been only a glimmer of hope for success after the collapse of the Paulownia Plan in September. Con-

[16] Indeed it was, for Chungking's posture of interest in Matsuoka's plans was calculated to arouse American apprehensions that Chiang would come to terms with Japan. Washington responded on November 30 with a massive loan and aid program for Chiang. See Boyle, *China and Japan at War*, pp. 299–304. Also, Kido, *Kido Kōichi nikki*, II, 825, 827, and 831; SKS, VIII, 376; Tanemura Suketaka, *Daihon'ei kimitsu nisshi* (Tokyo: Daiyamondosha, 1952), p. 36.

sequently, the premier's focus in domestic affairs shifted away from "political" mobilization. Between mid-September and the end of November, he temporized while watching the progress of Matsuoka's last-ditch efforts, and thereafter he moved to eliminate completely the "political-ness" of the new political order. After late November, Konoe's sole interest in the new order would be to develop it as a vehicle to integrate the public into a system of wartime economic controls, strengthen the public's spiritual identification with the imperial throne and the state, and implement whatever measures the established elite groups might agree on as essential to wartime mobilization. Any affinity he may have felt earlier for the advocates of a new political force vanished, and instead he found common cause with the "Japanists" and the Home Ministry. The actual development of the new order under Konoe's leadership closely paralleled the shifts in the prince's attitude toward domestic affairs. Between early September and late November, there was a steady withdrawal from the original plan to create a new political force. During this period, Konoe remained largely silent, being careful in his few public pronouncements to avoid any mention of the plan for a "highly political" movement. From late November, when all hope had been lost for Sino-Japanese negotiations, the new order developed primarily as a second movement to mobilize popular morale, exactly as Konoe had come to desire.

The evisceration of the "political" quality of the new order began during the last four commission meetings. Between the second and third meetings, the secretariat of the commission had drawn up an outline that would have converted the nuclear body of the new order movement into a "*kai*," or association. This terminology was adopted to avoid any uncomplimentary comparisons of the new order to the old political parties (*tō*). The third commission meeting, on September 6, was marked by hot debate over the wisdom of creating a new party. Unable to reach any consensus on this question, the commission designated eleven

311

of its members as a subcommittee to examine the issue further and to report back at the next commission meeting. The subcommittee report was submitted at the fourth session on September 10. Again, however, there was considerable discussion over the question of whether the new order nuclear group should be a *kai* or not. Nagai, Kanemitsu, and Hashimoto were particularly adamant in contending that the nuclear group should be a political party. Ultimately, the commission agreed that the new order should consist of both a *kai* of leaders to guide the new order movement, and a nationwide movement embracing all of the people. This agreement was the result of an uneasy compromise between those who sought to develop the new order as a new party organization and those who wished to prevent the launching of any partisan movement by opposing the exclusion of anyone from the new order.[17]

By September 10 a further refinement of the original proposal by the secretariat had also been made, probably by Konoe as the final arbiter of the plan. The Supreme Economic and Cultural Councils, whose establishment had recently been declared to be a primary goal of the new order movement, were quietly dropped from the new order plans. With them went the plans for a new organization of the people based on vocational and cultural groups, and one of the key challenges to the bureaucracy. The new order, whether political or not, whether partisan or not, would be geographically based as the Home Ministry wished. Of the two original institutional innovations contained in the new order proposal, one had now been eliminated. The new order would henceforth be focused exclusively on the "nuclear body," which, in turn, had been subdivided into a *kai* and a national movement. Since one of the original objectives of the popular movement (the creation of two new popular organizations) had been deleted from the

[17] YKUS, pp. 120 and 122.

plans, it became more important to develop a clear statement of goals to determine whether the new order would engage in "political" or "public" mobilization. At this juncture, however, Konoe was unwilling to commit himself to any specific program. Until his views became known, it would not be possible to agree on a "proclamation" (*sengen*) announcing the launching of the new order or a "platform of action" (*jissen kōryō*).

Once a discussion of the goals and objectives of the new order had been deferred, the commission was left with little to do. Clearly, no decision could be made as to whether the *kai* should be partisan until Konoe indicated the functions it was to fulfill. The fifth commission meeting accomplished little, while the sixth, on September 17, met only to ratify names for the *kai* and movement. Arima, as the acting commission chairman, revealed that the nuclear body would be named the Imperial Rule Assistance Association ([IRAA] *Taisei yokusankai*), while the popular movement it would lead would be called the Imperial Rule Assistance Movement (*Taisei yokusan undō*). He added that Konoe had decided that the premier would automatically serve as president of the IRAA, linking the new structure to the government rather than to Konoe personally. As the sixth meeting drew to a close, Konoe asked its members to continue their support for the new order, and promised to make his decisions regarding it consistent with the *kokutai* and the Constitution. The commission was then formally dissolved.[18]

The plans for the IRAA that emerged from the commission's discussions called for a two-part structure under the president (premier). There was to be an executive office, with local branches, and a series of cooperative councils from the national to the local level. During the ensuing weeks, the main questions regarding the IRAA concerned the personnel to be selected to run the office, and the "plat-

[18] *Ibid.*, pp. 130 and 132.

form of action" to be promulgated. Eleven men were selected as permanent directors to supervise the work of the office; together, they represented all of the conflicting viewpoints expressed during the commission's sessions, and each of the permanent directors had, in fact, been a commission member.[19] All other commission members were selected as either regular directors or advisors to the IRAA. Personnel were also appointed for important staff positions in the central office, and chiefs were selected for several of its bureaus and sections. Arima Yoriyasu was designated as overall chief of the office (*jimu-sōchō*), and concurrently as one of the office's five bureau chiefs, heading the General Affairs Bureau. Other bureau chiefs chosen were Maeda Yonezō (Diet Bureau), Gotō Ryūnosuke (Organization Bureau) and Obata Tadayoshi (Planning Bureau).[20]

These appointments gave little indication of Konoe's plans for the IRAA. With the press on October 4, he limited himself to stressing the spiritual features of the new order movement: "This movement is in one sense ideological— to clarify the *kokutai*. I myself feel that the true sense of *kokutai* and the way of the subject (*shindō*) are not yet fully comprehended. This is true everywhere: in business, government, and elsewhere. The ideological goal of this movement is to clarify the *kokutai* concept." He coyly deflected other questions by protesting that he had been totally immersed in the question of foreign policy (the Axis Pact had been formally signed a week earlier), and would have no more to say on the new order until he had spoken with Arima and Gotō.[21]

[19] *Ibid.*, p. 136. Selected were Arima Yoriyasu, Ida Bannan, Nagai Ryūtarō, Nakano Seigō, Hashimoto Kingorō, Furuno Inosuke, Gotō Fumio, Maeda Yonezō, Hatta Yoshiaki, Ōguchi Kiroku, and Ōkubo Ritsu.

[20] *Ibid.*, p. 136. Gotō was the director of the *Shōwa kenkyūkai* and a long-time associate and political errand boy of Prince Konoe. Obata was a prominent executive in the Sumitomo group of businesses. Ōta Masataka, a member of the defunct Seiyūkai, was subsequently appointed chief of the Policy Bureau.

[21] *Tokyo asahi*, October 5, 1940.

Establishment of the Imperial Rule
Assistance Association

The IRAA's program of action was scheduled to be revealed on October 12, Konoe's birthday and the day selected for the launching of the new organization. As the *Tokyo asahi* noted, the permanent directors were to discuss the texts of an IRAA "proclamation" and "platform of action" on October 9. It was anticipated that these texts would differentiate more clearly between the Imperial Rule Assistance Movement and the old Movement for Mobilizing Popular Morale; and the nation would then have some idea of the "political nature" and specific policies of the IRAA.[22] On October 9, the assistant secretaries of the old commission met and drafted texts for Konoe to issue. As the Army's Maki Tatsuo later recalled, the texts of the "proclamation" and "platform of action" described a highly political movement with the nucleus of a new political party.[23] These texts were discussed by the permanent directors of the IRAA on the same day, and Arima brought them to Konoe's residence on the evening of October 11 for final approval. Konoe began amending them to the point where the texts were no longer legible, and after wrangling over their contents with Arima until 2 A.M., he suggested that Arima go home. Seven hours later, Arima called on Cabinet Secretary Tomita to learn what Konoe would say at the inaugural meeting scheduled to begin in an hour. Tomita had no news for Arima until 10 A.M., when Konoe appeared at his office, recounted the details of the previous evening's debate with Arima, and directed Tomita to prepare a statement of greeting for the IRAA meeting. Tomita quickly complied, and within thirty minutes, Konoe had an innocuous pronouncement to deliver.[24]

[22] *Ibid.*

[23] Maki, "Gun no seiji kan'yō to kokunai jōsei," and personal interview of Maki by the author in Tokyo, October 5, 1968.

[24] Arima Yoriyasu, *Yūjin Konoe* (Tokyo: Kōbundō, 1949), p. 33; Arima, *Seikai dōchūki*, p. 203; Tomita, *Haisen Nihon no naisoku*, pp. 86–87.

315

Shortly after the meeting was opened, Konoe was called upon to deliver his inaugural speech (see Figure 6). The crux of it was that

> our Imperial Rule Assistance Movement must cast off the old-fashioned laissez faire style, and create a new order of service to the state. . . . As regards the platform of the Imperial Rule Assistance Movement, I understand that it was debated seriously on several occasions in the commission's meetings. But I believe, and I pray, that the movement's platform may be summed up in saying that we shall fulfill the way of the subject in assisting the imperial rule (*taisei yokusan no shindō jissen*). Indeed, it may be stated that other than this, there is no platform or proclamation (*sengen*). If I were to express the platform and proclamation of the movement at this time, it would be "carrying out the way of the subject in assisting the imperial rule." In other words, "We should serve the throne night and day, faithfully in our own particular situations." This I believe, and it was I who decided that no platform or proclamation would be issued today.[25]

As Konoe concluded his remarks, his audience reacted in amazement. Depending on their own individual political viewpoints, they had come to the IRAA meeting either hoping or fearing that they would witness the birth of a dynamic new force in Japanese politics. Instead, the premier had presented them with a new structure aimed only at the vaguely defined spiritual objective of "fulfilling the way of the subject in assisting the imperial rule." There was no platform of action, no ringing proclamation of a new political order to distinguish the IRAA from the old spiritual mobilization movement. The *Asahi* wondered critically how anyone could regard the IRAA as a strong new political structure, while others simply shook their heads in confusion over Konoe's purposes. It appeared that at the

[25] YKUS, pp. 137–38.

very moment when Konoe had raised high the standard of political reform, he had chosen to sound the death knell of the "highly political" IRAA and its popular movement.[26]

FIGURE 6. Konoe Fumimaro inaugurated the Imperial Rule Assistance Association on October 12, 1940, with a vaguely worded speech that obscured the plans he had for the "new political order."

This view, however, endows Konoe's actions with a greater sense of purpose than, in fact, they had at the time. During this period, Konoe was still uncommitted about the program of the IRAA, waiting to see whether Matsuoka could bring about an agreement with Chungking to negotiate an end to the China Incident. Since the prospects for peace in China were far from bright, he had obviously shifted away from his early commitment to "political" mobilization, but until the results of the Tajiri-Chien talks were ascertained, he withheld any decisive effort to steer the

[26] *Ibid.*, p. 138 and KF, II, 201.

IRAA towards an exclusive preoccupation with spiritual mobilization. As the casual way in which his inaugural address was prepared clearly demonstrated, Konoe was not yet ready to do anything about the IRAA.

Following the inaugural ceremonies of October 12, Konoe divorced himself almost completely from the new order movement until the end of November. He attended none of the IRAA functions, and did not participate in the frequent meetings and discussions of IRAA leaders during this period.[27] While the premier withdrew to the sidelines, however, political controversy continued to attend the establishment of the IRAA's organizational apparatus and the definition of the IRAA's position in national politics. Only after late November did Konoe begin to deal with these problems, and between December and the IRAA's reform in April 1941, his approach to the controversy over the IRAA determined the final nature and importance of the new political order.

The argument over the organizational apparatus of the IRAA was intimately related to the dispute over the political nature of the new body. Essentially, the question was whether the IRAA was to become a new party, an administrative organ under the Home Ministry, or a nonpartisan "public" body with the simple purpose of mobilizing popular morale. Political leaders' attitudes towards the local organization of the IRAA were primarily determined by their positions on this key issue. The strongest proponents of converting the IRAA into a new political party were Army Ministry officials involved in the new order movement, "reformist" right-wing group leaders such as Nakano and Hashimoto, members of small Diet parties and splinter groups such as Kamei Kan'ichirō, Akamatsu Katsumaro, Nagai Ryūtarō, and Kazami Akira, and IRAA leaders Arima and Gotō. In discussing the personnel to be appointed to positions in the IRAA branches, these men urged the selec-

[27] Sekiguchi Tai, "Naikaku kaizō to Yokusankai kaisō," *Kaizō*, XXIII.9 (May 1941), 119.

tion of "new" men: individuals unconnected with the bureaucracy, the old parties, and the local elites, which together constituted the main existing linkage between the community and national policies. In short, they called for the emergence of new local leadership in politics. The most vigorous opposition to this view came, naturally, from Home Ministry bureaucrats and *meibōka* who had no wish to be displaced from their preeminent positions in local affairs.

The opening salvo in the political struggle over control of the IRAA locally was fired on September 11, when Home Minister Yasui issued the directive to governors that had been drafted in July by Vice Minister Hazama. As noted earlier, the directive called for the establishment of *buraku-kai* and *chōnaikai* as the basic units of Home Ministry administration.[28] Two days later, the Army gave some indication of its plans for converting the local organization of the new order into a powerful political force working to overcome domestic opposition to a national defense state. At the fifth session of the commission, Army Minister Tōjō delineated the degree to which military men would be involved in the new order movement. Envisioning the creation of a "strongly political" nuclear body, Tōjō declared that the Imperial Rescript to Soldiers and Sailors, issued in 1882, prohibited the participation of active-duty military men in political affairs. Despite Murase's convoluted interpretations of the new order's nonpolitical nature, therefore, soldiers and sailors would be unable to take an active part in creating a new political order. Tōjō noted further that the reservists were also enjoined by imperial proscription from entering political associations en bloc. In other words, the service ministers were unprepared to permit the political penetration of the armed forces and the reserves by placing them under the control of a new political organization. On the other hand, the Army Minister declared, both services were in complete sympathy with the concept of a new political order, and there were two important ways in

28 See *supra*, pp. 282–83.

which they might make a positive contribution to its realization. First, the minister, vice minister, and chief of the Military Affairs Bureau in both services might belong to the nuclear body and serve as advisors. Second, and of greater significance, members of local reserve association units could, and would be urged to, join the new order movement on an individual basis.[29]

The Army evidently placed a great deal of hope in the ability of the association's membership to dominate the local activities of the IRAA. According to naval intelligence, the directors of the Army Reservists' Association sought from mid-September to place reserve officers in positions of leadership in the *burakukai, chōnaikai,* and *rinpo-han* units of the new order organization. On October 2, Lieutenant General Koizumi Rokuichi, the general director of the Army Reservists' Association, issued a top secret directive to all leaders of local reservist units, giving them detailed instructions on how to participate as individuals in the local branches and cooperative councils of the IRAA. Koizumi directed that local reservist leaders send "as many of their members as possible" into the IRAA, and asked that preliminary lists of reservists who would participate be forwarded to him.[30]

Other groups also sought to gain a leading position in the local branches of the IRAA. Hashimoto Kingorō issued orders to the members of his small political party, the *Dai-Nippon seinentō,* calling on them to become the central

[29] YKUS, pp. 129–30. For an English-language translation of the "Imperial Rescript to Soldiers and Sailors," see William Theodore de Bary, Tsunoda Ryusaku, and Donald Keene, comps., *Sources of Japanese Tradition* (New York: Columbia University Press, 1958), pp. 705–707.

[30] Kaigunshō hōmu-kyoku, "Jōhō: Rikugun no Yokusankai ni taisuru taido," October 25, 1940, Top Secret, and Koizumi Rokuichi (Teikoku zaigō gunjinkai sōmu), "Taisei yokusankai ni yakuin-kyū sanka-hō no ken tsūchō," Directive #511, Top Secret, October 2, 1940, in Navy Ministry archives.

figures in the Imperial Rule Assistance Movement. Hashimoto urged his colleagues to use the platform of the movement to attack liberalism, socialistic elements, and the spiritual mobilization organization, all of which had, in his view,
lost favor in the public eye.[31] Nakano Seigō had similar
hopes for his party, the *Tōhōkai*, while Arima Yoriyasu had
not yet abandoned his hope that the young members of the
agrarian guild movement might become the moving force
of the IRAA locally. Gotō Ryūnosuke, who for years had
been involved in the activities of youth associations (*seinendan*) and young adults' associations (*sōnendan*), sought to
place these groups at the heart of the local political activities of the IRAA.

The various plans of these leaders to convert the IRAA
into a political party through the organization locally of
"new" political forces became a major issue during the first
ten days of October. During this period, there were staff
meetings almost daily on the vital question of who would
lead the local branches of the IRAA. The proponents of a
new political force advocated that nonofficials be selected
as branch chiefs, while representatives of the Home Ministry, supported by "Japanist" leaders, sought to place local
leadership in the hands of the governors and local officials.
At times, the discussions became quite heated. In preliminary meetings, Lieutenant Colonel Maki was the chief
spokesman for the advocates of nonofficial local leadership,
while Tomeoka Kiyoo and Okamoto Shigeru of the Home
Ministry hoped to place officials in command of local IRAA
units. On two occasions, the debate became so stormy that
Maki stalked out of the meetings. The IRAA permanent
directors, meeting on the same question on October 4, saw
a similar display of temper. Hashimoto and Nakano insisted
that nonofficials be selected as branch chiefs, and when

[31] Kenpeitai, "Jōhō: Dai-Nippon seinentō no tai-shintaisei undō
hōshin shishi sono ta ni kansuru ken," #221, October 2, 1940, in Navy
Ministry archives.

Kuzuu Yoshihisa, the bearded leader of the "Japanist" *Kokuryūkai*, objected, Nakano threw his walking stick at Kuzuu and strode angrily out of the room.[32]

At last, however, a temporary compromise was reached. After the Home Ministry had rejected an Army proposal to appoint the governors as honorary branch chiefs, while nonofficials ran the branches in actual fact, Lieutenant General Mutō consulted with the Army's division commanders stationed throughout the country. The commander of the Hirosaki division urged that local officials, rather than non-officials, be placed in charge of the IRAA branches, and the other commanders supported this view. Perhaps they shared the apprehensions of the chief of the Naval Bureau of Military Affairs, who believed that placing reservist officers in leading IRAA positions locally would be dangerous because the reservists were not firmly enough controlled by the Army Ministry. Whatever the reasons for their position, Mutō became resigned to some official control over the local branches. At the next meeting of IRAA officials, he sided with the Home Ministry on the question of local branch chiefs, saying that unless they were placed in charge, the branches might become centers of anti-government activity. After a telephone call to his party head-quarters, Hashimoto agreed to go along with Mutō's new position, but Nakano again stomped out of the meeting in protest. On October 7–8, the nation's governors met for their annual conference in Tokyo, and reaffirmed their desire for official control over the IRAA branches. A final face-saving decision was reached by the permanent directors on October 9. Rather than appointing a branch chief, each prefectural (*fu* and *ken*) branch was to be led by a committee of ten men, nominated and chaired by the governor. His nominees would be forwarded to the permanent directors

[32] Maki, "Gun no seiji kan'yō to kokunai jōsei"; *Sensō kaisen keii*, I, 446–47; also, interview of Matsumae Shigeyoshi by the author, in Tokyo, June 20, 1969.

for screening, and then passed along to Konoe for final approval.[33]

The Home Ministry wasted little time in self-congratulation over its success in assuring its governors a prominent role in the formation of the prefectural branches of the IRAA. Its long-range objective was to extend official control into the towns and villages, and to assume the responsibility for guiding the *burakukai* and *chōnaikai* that would be sanctioned when the IRAA apparatus was established.

During the next month, the governors selected their committees. Although the composition of branch committees differed from prefecture to prefecture, typical ten-man units contained the prefectural assembly speaker and perhaps one or two additional assembly men, a prominent local business leader, a newspaper publisher, a few village and town mayors, a local reservist association leader, and perhaps the head of the prefectural agrarian guild.[34] Similar committees were formed to run the IRAA branches of the six metropoli (*fu*). In response to criticism in the press that the governors had only selected local leaders of the "old order," Home Ministry spokesmen replied weakly that thirty percent of the committeemen chosen were either reformists of a new stripe or political unknowns. The permanent directors met for six hours on November 18 to consider the governors' selections. In the absence of any pressure from Konoe to weed out leaders of the "old order," the directors finally felt obliged to pass the lists along to the premier intact.[35]

[33] Maki, "Gun no seiji kan'yō to kokunai jōsei"; *Hazama Shigeru-shi danwa sokkiroku*, p. 134; Kaigunshō gunmu-kyoku-chō [kara] chinshufu sanbō-chō ni, "Taisei yokusankai chihō shibu ni taishi kaigun jinji-bu-chō mata wa chihō kaigun jinji-bu-chō no kyōryoku ni kansuru ken shinshin," November 1940, in Navy Ministry archives; author's interview wtih Matsumae Shigeyoshi; *Japan Chronicle*, October 9, 1940; *Sensō kaisen keii*, I, 446–47.

[34] For complete lists of committees formed, see *Tokyo asahi*, November 19–21, 1940.

[35] *Ibid.*, November 20, 1940.

On November 23, Konoe formally approved of the governors' choices without comment, and the branches were established without disrupting long-standing political and social relationships in the countryside.

Under Gotō's leadership in the IRAA Organization Bureau, a renewed effort was made to organize "new" forces locally through the establishment of IRAA branches at the city, town, and village levels. The branch committees formed at these levels, however, were similar in composition to those formed at the prefectural and metropolitan levels, and on December 15, Gotō angrily protested that few young or new faces had appeared on the rosters of the local committees. However, he and other advocates of a new political force were able to appoint "new" men to the posts of General Affairs Section chief and Organization Section chief in the local branches. These section chiefs proved to be the strongest local advocates of a new political order in the countryside, and they repeatedly petitioned Konoe and the government to carry out the original plans to infuse the Imperial Rule Assistance Movement with a political character. Under Gotō's direction, a training program was established for local IRAA organizers, in which they were presumably to be instructed in the arts of political organizing. These training sessions, which began in mid-December, drew the fire of such "Japanist" IRAA leaders as Permanent Director Ida Bannan and Regular Director Kobayashi Jun'ichirō, who criticized the ideology being implanted in the local leaders' minds by "Reds" selected by Gotō and Arima.[36]

While Gotō, Arima, and their supporters in the IRAA central headquarters continued their efforts to select and indoctrinate local men as the nucleus of a new political force, Army leaders working with the IRAA had already acknowledged the victory of the Home Ministry on the

[36] YKUS, p. 159; Ida Bannan and Kobayashi Jun'ichirō, "Taisei yokusankai-nai kaimu no tōsei ni tsuite," [January] 1941, in Imai and Itō, eds., Kokka sōdōin, pp. 449–52.

question of local branch leadership. However, being unwilling to surrender the new order to government officials,
Mutō and Maki became active from December in seeking
to recruit a new political force under the auspices of the
IRAA East Asia Section. Working with East Asia Section
Chief Kamei Kan'ichirō and his assistants (including Sugihara Masami), Mutō, Maki, and Colonel Satō Kenryō attempted to form a new coalition of forces from radical
agrarian youth groups, small- and medium-size business
guilds, Army reservists, and "reformist" right-wing groups
led by Hashimoto, Nakano, and others. Participation was
also solicited from a limited number of Diet members who
shared the goal of founding a new reform party.[37]

The new coalition was to be known as the "Federation
for a Popular Movement to Construct the Greater East
Asian Co-Prosperity Sphere" (*Dai-Tōa kyōeiken kensetsu
kokumin undō renmei*). Although the expressed goal of the
proposed federation was simply to unify ideological movements in Japan regarding the development of a new Asia,
its actual purpose was to circumvent the Home Ministry's
growing control over the existing IRAA apparatus and create a new political party.[38] The Home Ministry objected
strongly to the formation of a new partisan group within
the IRAA, and insisted that if a federation were formed,
it be expanded to include *all* right-wing groups, not simply
those interested in forming a new party. The Home Ministry's purpose, according to Maki, was to convert the federation into a control organization, to facilitate the policing
and supervision of right-wing groups constantly agitating

[37] Information on the federation is based primarily on a reading
of the unpublished papers of Kamei Kan'ichirō. Supplementary data
was provided in an interview by the author with Kamei in Tokyo,
October 14–15, 1969. See also, Satō Kenryō, *Dai-Tōa sensō kaikoroku*
(Tokyo: Tokuma shoten, 1966), p. 286; and interview by the author
with Maki Tatsuo, Tokyo, October 5, 1968.

[38] Interviews with Maki Tatsuo and Kamei Kan'ichirō; Maki Tatsuo,
"Watakushi to shintaisei undō: gun no kitai to genmetsu," *Rekishi
to jinbutsu*, #32 (April 1974), p. 46.

325

THE WARTIME POLITICAL ORDER

for an "overthrow of the status quo," and to dilute the reformist character of the federation through the addition of
"impure" ("Japanist") groups.[39] The Army and Home Ministry thus clashed over the establishment of a new political
force in early 1941, as they had the previous fall in the context of determining leadership of local IRAA branches.

The fate of the proposed federation was ultimately decided within the larger context of a number of important
actions taken by Prince Konoe in February and March 1941.
Before discussing these, however, it is necessary to review
the attitudes of the members of the defunct parties towards
the IRAA; for in the final analysis, the Diet proved as strong
an obstacle to the plans for a new political force as did the
Home Ministry.

THE PARTIES AND THE IRAA

Once the IRAA was formed, parliamentary leaders sought
to work through it to strengthen their control over the Diet
rank and file, and to extend their power beyond the Lower
House. Most Diet leaders were given posts as permanent
directors, directors, or advisors in the IRAA, and they also
established control over the IRAA Diet Bureau. So long as
the IRAA held out the possibility of serving as the vehicle
for a restoration of party influence in the Cabinet, the rank
and file seemed willing to accept this distribution of posts.
Their central concern, like that of the defunct parties' leaders, was, after all, to regain a share of Cabinet power for
the parliamentary forces. Only twenty-five Lower House
members from the Hatoyama faction and the Shadaitō's
Shamin faction refused to join the IRAA Diet Bureau. The
small parties and splinter groups similarly saw the IRAA
as a vehicle for the expansion of their influence. They
tended to take a more aggressive part in IRAA activities
than did the members of the old Minseitō and Seiyūkai,

[39] Interview with Maki Tatsuo.

326

and generally were the only Diet members to hold staff posts in the IRAA outside the Diet Bureau.[40]

During the early months of the IRAA's existence, it served as the focal point of political competition among parliamentary groups and between the Lower House forces and the other elites. Cleavages became apparent when Diet leaders began to consider the possibility that the IRAA would not be a new political party and that some new organization might be required in the Lower House to govern committee assignments, allocate responsibilities for questioning government officials, and negotiate agreements among members for joint actions in voting on government-proposed legislation. The urgency of creating a new organ was intensified in leaders' minds by the realization that unless such a body were established, they would have no organized control over the actions of the Lower House membership, and would lose their bargaining power in dealing with the government and other elites.

On September 30, the senior leaders of the Lower House decided to organize the Diet Members' Club (*Giin kurabu*) to preserve their control over these important Lower House activities. Five "founders" of the club were designated to begin discussions on its formation: Yamazaki Tatsunosuke, Sakurai Hyōgorō, Okada Tadahiko, Kiyose Ichirō, and Kawakami Jōtarō. However, as the representatives of the small parties and groups in the Diet, Kiyose and Kawakami sought to delay the formation of the club. The forces they represented soon met at the Sannō Hotel to plan a strategy

[40] Baba Motoharu and Nakahara Kinji, for example, were vice section chiefs in the General Affairs Bureau; Miwa Jūsō was chief of the Liaison Section in the Organization Bureau; Ōta Masataka became chief of the Policy Bureau with Funada Naka and Kamei Kan'ichirō serving as section chiefs under him; and Akamatsu Katsumaro was a section chief in the Planning Bureau. Of these, only Ōta came from a major party, the Seiyūkai, but, in fact, he was a member of a small splinter group that remained unaffiliated with either Kuhara or Nakajima. YKUS, pp. 148–50.

for obstructing the club's creation.[41] Despite their opposition, talks among Diet leaders continued, and by the time the IRAA was formally launched, the five "founders" were joined in preliminary discussions by Maeda Yonezō, the chief of the IRAA Diet Bureau, Akita Kiyoshi, Ōasa Tadao, and Sakurauchi Yukio.[42]

Konoe's refusal to build a new party gradually undercut the position of those who sought to work through the IRAA to create a political force independent of the senior party leadership. By November 1, party leaders had decided to establish the club independent of the IRAA. The club was to be in existence only during the forthcoming (76th) Diet session, and was to include as members all current and former Diet representatives wishing to join.[43] By insuring their control of the Lower House through the club, parliamentary leaders hoped to increase their political leverage within the IRAA, and guarantee that the IRAA would not develop as a threat to their hegemony in the Lower House.

Had Konoe still desired to undermine the position of the party politicians, he might well have sought to prevent the reinforcement of control over the Lower House by its old leadership. By the end of November, however, the premier's political strategy had changed. His government now began to encourage the formation of the club and the prince began preparations to eliminate the IRAA's capability for "political" mobilization. In a conversation with Kido on November 27, Konoe indicated that he was planning to obtain the resignations of Justice Minister Kazami and Home Minister Yasui, and would bring Hiranuma into the Cabinet either as Yasui's replacement or as a minister without portfolio.[44]

[41] The central figures of the Sannō Hotel group were Hida Takushi, Akamatsu Katsumaro, Minami Teizō, Nishikata Toshima, and Kamei Kan'ichirō. See Kenpeitai, "Jōhō: Giin kurabu kessei ni taisuru bōshi undō," #224, October 4, 1940, in Navy Ministry archives.

[42] Kiya, *Seikai gojū-nen no butai-ura*, pp. 283–84.

[43] Yokogoshi Eiichi, "Mu-seitō jidai no seiji-ryoku gaku," Part I, *Nagoya daigaku hōsei ronshū*, #32 (1965), p. 20.

[44] *Ibid.*; Kido, *Kido Kōichi nikki*, II, 838.

Kazami had been Konoe's main channel of communication with the small parties and younger members of the major parties who advocated a "reformist" party, and his removal portended a clear shift by Konoe away from the establishment of a new political party. The reasons for Yasui's ouster were less clear. He claimed Tōjō wanted him out of the Cabinet, but he also alluded to his controversial election reform proposal as a factor in his downfall.[45] Both the Army and the old political parties resented the Home Ministry's attempt to monopolize control over local politics. At the end of November, the clash between the Home Ministry and the Diet forces over reforming the election law reached its maximum intensity, and Konoe's removal of Yasui seemed calculated to mollify the Lower House as much as the Army. Taken together, Konoe's encouragement of the Diet Members' Club and removal of Kazami and Yasui appeared to be part of a general strategy to placate the established leadership of the Lower House on the eve of the Diet session, rather than proceeding with his original plan to undermine their position through the IRAA. Hiranuma's appointment to the Cabinet seemed to confirm this appraisal of Konoe's new strategy. As a leader of the "Japanist" right wing, Hiranuma had from the start opposed the IRAA as an illegitimate, *bakufu*-like political force. Bringing him into the government was thus another omen of the premier's decision to shift the focus of the IRAA away from "political" mobilization and towards the stimulation of "public" spiritual identification with the throne.

THE NEW ECONOMIC ORDER

Konoe's actions in late November and early December took place against the additional backdrop of a serious new domestic controversy. From September 1940, Colonel Akinaga Tsukizō, Minobe Yōji, and a number of other

[45] *Yasui Eiji-shi danwa dai–5–kai sokkiroku*, pp. 51–53. For the Yasui election plan, see *supra*, p. 284.

"revisionist" bureaucrats in the Planning Board had begun formulating a set of new economic policies as part of the overall plan to establish a national defense state.[46] By mid-November, these plans had been drafted and submitted to the Cabinet for consideration by the ministers concerned with economic affairs. The ministers immediately objected to the Planning Board's suggestion that management of the nation's major industries be removed from owners' hands and placed under state control, and that all other private economic activity be subjected to governmental supervision. The attack on the board's "new economic order" plan was spearheaded by Commerce and Industry Minister Kobayashi Ichizō, and was strongly supported by Railways Minister Ogawa Gōtarō and other parliamentary representatives in the Cabinet, spokesmen for the business and finance communities, and the "Japanist" right wing. These groups claimed that nationalizing the management of industry was tantamount to establishing communism in Japan, and represented a denial of the legal right to hold private property.

The strongest defenders of the "new economic order" were the Army and IRAA officials outside the Diet Bureau. The new economic program, according to the Army, was consistent with the requirements of national defense. This viewpoint was echoed by the anti-capitalist elements in the "reformist" right wing, socialists and national socialists in the IRAA such as Miwa, Akamatsu, and Kamei, as well as by Arima, whose primary concern had been righting the imbalances of wealth and political influence enjoyed by the industrialized cities vis-à-vis the agrarian countryside. The lines of battle over the government's economic policy were clearly drawn between the Planning Board, Army, and IRAA staff on one side, and the business community, major party leaders, and "Japanist" right wing on the other. Be-

[46] For a recent detailed study of these policies, see Nakamura Takafusa and Hara Akira, " 'Keizai shintaisei,' " in Nihon seiji gakkai, ed., "Konoe shintaisei" no kenkyū, pp. 71–133.

tween the two contending coalitions stood the premier—
whose Cabinet's tenure in office was now at stake—and an
uneasy populace, for whom the "new economic order" portended greater constraints on daily living and a further
denial of the necessities of life.

Faced with this political standoff, Konoe acted swiftly
to create a Cabinet consensus on economic policy. Between
November 23, when the crisis became full blown, and
December 7, the Cabinet moved to mitigate the most controversial aspects of the Planning Board's economic proposals while gearing the nation's economy to support the services' defense policies. On November 27, an economic
conference was officially established, comprising the nation's leading businessmen and financiers.[47] The creation of
this organ over the Planning Board's objections assured the
nation's entrepreneurs that they would have a voice in the
setting of economic policy. On December 1, the economic
ministers of the Cabinet prepared a revised formula for
economic planning that afforded private enterprise an independent role in the nation's economic activities. This revised
plan drew the immediate fire of the Army and IRAA, who
considered it too mild. Nevertheless, on December 7, the
Cabinet approved the new economic policy as revised by
the economic ministers. The new policy contained no mention of state management or formal control over private
business.

Much to Konoe's chagrin, the leadership of the IRAA staff
did not accept this compromise settlement with good grace.
Instead, many IRAA leaders stepped up their call for radical economic reforms, and criticized the government for its
lackluster performance in the realm of economic policy
making. From the premier's viewpoint, the IRAA was now
not only unnecessary for "political" mobilization, but also
a genuine nuisance and threat to the successful implementation of the government's economic policy. It appeared
that if IRAA leaders were permitted to engage in "political"

[47] *Tokyo asahi*, November 28, 1940.

331

mobilization activities, they would support economic reforms too radical to win consensual support among the
elites. Rather than mobilizing public support and tolerance
of the government's economic policy, the IRAA's energies
would be directed toward mobilizing opposition to the government's economic policy decision. The hostile attitude of
the IRAA staff on this issue all but sealed the fate of its
leadership in Konoe's eyes. Within six weeks, he was in-
forming a delegation of local IRAA leaders that he had
come to recognize in November the need to shake up both
the personnel and organization of the IRAA.[48]

The new economic order controversy not only provided
Konoe with an additional motive for permanently abandoning his plan to use the IRAA as an organ of "political" mobilization, but also gave him specific inducement to eviscerate
the IRAA's ability to engage in political activities. On
December 6, Hiranuma was brought into the government as
a minister without portfolio, and when Yasui and Kazami
were relieved of their posts on December 21, they were replaced by Hiranuma and Lieutenant General Yanagawa
Heisuke (of the old Imperial Way faction). Neither of the
two new Cabinet appointees was inclined to disrupt the
economic system in order to steel the nation for its imminent ordeal of economic autonomy. Both shared Konoe's
desire to convert the IRAA from a potentially dangerous
political organization into an organization specifically engaged in mobilizing spiritual identification with the emperor and public tolerance of government policies.

The Parties' Attack on the IRAA

By the time the 76th Diet session convened at the end
of December, Konoe's disenchantment with the IRAA had
become readily apparent. The response of parliamentary
groups to the IRAA during the Diet session reflected their

[48] YKUS, p. 208.

awareness of the shift in the prince's attitude and their own particular political ambitions. Members of the former small parties and factions continued to regard the IRAA as a useful vehicle for advancing their political fortunes and "reformist" programs, and stood among its foremost defenders. During late December and early January, small party and faction members bore the brunt of the IRAA's efforts to defend itself against charges from the business community, House of Peers, and "Japanist" right wing that the organization was run by socialists and camouflaged communists.[49] Simultaneously, Kamei, Akamatsu, and Nagai became involved with the Army in planning a new political force under the aegis of the East Asia Section of the IRAA.

Meanwhile, the Diet Members' Club was formally established on the eve of the Diet session. While the club embraced virtually all members of the Lower House, there was a great deal of parliamentary disagreement over the approach to be taken toward the IRAA.[50] The old-line Diet leadership recognized that Konoe's attitude had turned negative toward the IRAA, but still hoped to expand its influence in IRAA circles, and to use its dominant position in the Diet Bureau to reassert its control over the parliamentary rank and file. In response to the position of the parties' leadership, two divergent lines of argument developed within the club. The Hatoyama and *Shamin* factions contended that the Lower House should take a strong position against both the IRAA and the Konoe government. Others, however, continued to hope that Konoe could be induced to lead a new political force which would restore their influence in the Cabinet. While they, too, agreed that the IRAA should be attacked in the Diet, they were resolved to endorse the Konoe government's policies and encourage

[49] *Ibid.*, pp. 170, 185–86, and 188.
[50] When the club was established on December 20, 1940, Ozaki Yukio and five other Diet members refused to join. Iwanami shoten henshū-bu, ed., *Kindai Nihon sōgō nenpyō* (Tokyo: Iwanami shoten, 1968), p. 324.

the premier to rely on them for political support in the execution of his legislative program.[51] In short, while they had abandoned hope that the IRAA would provide them with a channel for returning power in the Cabinet, they continued to cling to the illusory hope that Konoe was still willing to form a new political party with them.

The various positions of these parliamentary groups became manifest in the Diet debate over the IRAA budget in January and February, 1941. Originally, when the IRAA was being considered as a political organization, the possibility of funding it through private contributions and dues had been raised. After its creation in October 1940, the IRAA had been financed by private funds from the major *zaibatsu*, procured by Arima, Gotō Ryūnosuke, and their staff. In the wake of the "new economic order" issue, however, business turned hostile toward the IRAA, and funds were cut off. By January, therefore, it was obvious to the IRAA staff that its principal source of funds would have to be the government. A budget request for thirty-seven million yen for the fiscal year 1941 was submitted during the 76th Diet session, and became the focal point for the Diet's attack on the IRAA.

Alignments in the Lower House on the IRAA question were readily discernible by the third week in January. While senior party leaders negotiated with the government over the legislative calendar, 350 younger and middle-echelon Diet members organized a support group for the Konoe government. Meeting at the Imperial Hotel, they were quickly labeled the "Imperial Hotel faction" by the press. Their dual objectives were to oppose the development of the IRAA—which had failed to become the new party they desired—and to encourage Konoe to form a new party centered on them. Not surprisingly, the Hatoyama faction and *Shamin* opponents of both the government and the IRAA did not participate in the Imperial Hotel discus-

[51] Yokogoshi, "Mu-seitō jidai no seiji-ryoku gaku," pp. 21–23.

sions. Also absent was a group of former Minseitō politicians who, led by Kawasaki Katsu, had been Machida Chūji's staunchest supporters before the dissolution of their party. Throughout 1940 and 1941, this group remained consistently negative toward the formation of a new party through the IRAA or by any other method. The most significant feature of the Imperial Hotel faction was that it also excluded representatives of the small parties and splinter groups, who continued to support the IRAA and attempted to convert it into a "reformist" organization.[52] The division between the Imperial Hotel faction and the men from the small parties and factions represented the first split in the ranks of the old League of Diet Members Supporting the Prosecution of the Holy War, and a step toward the reintegration of junior members of the old parties into groups controlled by the established parliamentary leadership.

Within the IRAA, officials from the small parties and splinter groups joined with other national and local IRAA officials to reiterate the importance of maintaining the original reformist nature of the organization. Konoe, of course, was now unwilling to consider this position, and instead he entered a series of negotiations with Lower House leaders to prevent the outbreak of another major political crisis. On January 21, he and Machida worked out a compromise to avert a direct confrontation between the government and Diet on the political and economic reform proposals advocated by the Army, Planning Board, and IRAA. In exchange for Machida's agreement that the Diet would not challenge the government's legislative program, Konoe, Tōjō, and Admiral Oikawa Koshirō (the new Navy minister) agreed not to submit about one-third of the bills prepared for the Diet's consideration. Measures to be withheld included the election reform bill, bills related to government control over industrial and agricultural associations, and a measure de-

[52] *Ibid.*, p. 23.

THE WARTIME POLITICAL ORDER

signed to establish government control over the distribution of electric power.[53] The Konoe-Machida compromise assured that the only issue on which the Diet would challenge the government would be related to the IRAA itself.

The premier was, of course, now amenable to compromising on the IRAA question as well. On January 22, he indicated to local IRAA officials that he favored a reform of the IRAA, and he simultaneously gave Hiranuma wide latitude in criticizing the "political" nature of the IRAA. On January 24, the new home minister obligingly told the Diet that the purpose of the IRAA was to effectuate a policy of *banmin yokusan* rather than *taisei yokusan*. The distinction was more than just a semantic one. *Taisei yokusan* connoted a specific role in policy making and government; *banmin yokusan* referred more generally to the relationship of the people (and IRAA) to society and the emperor. In other words, the home minister said, the principal goal of the IRAA was merely to inform the people of government policy, so that they could as loyal subjects carry out the emperor's wishes.[54] Four days later, Hiranuma stated clearly in the Diet that the IRAA was not to be regarded as a "political" organization (*seiji kessha*), but rather as a "public" organization (*kōji kessha*).[55] The inference to be drawn from Hiranuma's comments was that the IRAA would be denied any role whatsoever in policy making and articulating popular interests. It was to serve only as a public agency of spiritual and economic mobilization.

Hiranuma's position proved to be the formula Konoe followed in extricating himself from his previous commitment to a new political order and in converting the IRAA into a spiritual movement. On February 2, the Imperial Hotel fac-

[53] Furusawa Isojiro, "The Wartime Non-Party Diet," *Contemporary Japan*, x.4 (April 1941), 462–64.

[54] Edogawa Ranpo, ed., *Kawasaki Katsu den* (Tokyo: Kawasaki Katsu den kankōkai, 1956), p. 276.

[55] KF, ii, 201.

tion of the Diet informed Konoe that he had two choices if he wished to avoid a showdown in the Lower House over the IRAA budget. If he converted the IRAA into a new political party dominated by Diet forces, the large IRAA budget would be quickly approved by the Lower House. The premier's alternative was to cut the IRAA budget back, and convert the organization into a "public" institution. Senior party leaders endorsed this proposition on February 10, but added that the premier would have to fire IRAA officials from the small parties and factions as well as those who had supported the "communistic new economic order."[56] The premier was opposed to the first alternative, since he had no desire to preside over the creation of a new political party. By the same token, he faced heavy pressure from the Army and Navy to preserve the IRAA in its original form. On February 6, Army Minister Tōjō publicly expressed the Army's support for a political IRAA, and the chiefs of the Military Affairs Bureaus of both services reaffirmed this position on February 12.[57] Meanwhile, a coalition of eighty-four Diet members led by Kawasaki Katsu organized at the *Chūō-tei* restaurant in order to propose a complete evisceration of the IRAA. Kawasaki used the forum of the Lower House budget committee to attack the IRAA as a political entity, and echoed Hiranuma's views about the difference between *taisei yokusan* and *banmin yokusan*. The Minseitō politician contended that the Diet alone was accorded the constitutional prerogative of serving as the channel for the people's *taisei yokusan*. The only legal form of mass participation in the political system therefore lay in electing members to the Lower House. Hence, the IRAA's claim to act as an additional agency of popular participation in policy making and political mobilization was unconstitutional. Thus, Kawasaki concluded, the IRAA's character should be clearly defined as distinct

[56] Yokogoshi, "Mu-seitō jidai no seiji-ryoku gaku," p. 28.
[57] *Ibid.*, p. 31.

from the functions of the Diet and separate from the political process.[58]

Konoe's response to these conflicting pressures was to placate a majority of the Diet. To mollify the services he sought to undermine the more strident anti-IRAA position of the *Chūō-tei* group, but his primary interest lay in reaching agreement with the Lower House on a modified budget for the IRAA. To accomplish this end, he formulated a twofold tactical approach. First, he repeated the same tactic he had employed in 1938 to gain Diet approval for the National General Mobilization and Electric Power Laws. In other words, he permitted rumors to circulate that he might again be interested in forming a new political party outside of the IRAA framework. If the Diet Members' Club were expanded to include the House of Peers, Konoe would be eligible to join it and convert it into a new party.[59] Such a proposal alarmed the senior party leaders, who dominated the club and used it to control the rank and file. If the Upper House were brought into the club and it was converted into a new political organization, many members would be outside their control, and their grip on club leadership might be fatally undermined. However, rumors of a new Konoe party were music to the ears of young and middle-echelon new party advocates in the Imperial Hotel faction. By holding out the prospect of a new party, Konoe was able to generate a more cordial atmosphere in the Lower House and induce the ex-party men to be receptive to his solution of the IRAA question.

The second feature of Konoe's approach to the Diet consisted of a compromise he reached between February 7 and 14 with the senior leaders of the Lower House. They agreed to approve the government's scaled-down budget request of eight million yen for the IRAA in return for Konoe's

[58] *Ibid.*, p. 28; for the text of Kawasaki's remarks, see Edogawa, ed., *Kawasaki Katsu den*, pp. 254 ff.

[59] Yokogoshi, "Mu-seitō jidai no seiji-ryoku gaku," p. 36.

promise to reorganize the IRAA as a "public" organization and dismiss IRAA officials who advocated using the IRAA in policy making and mass "political" mobilization. To Konoe, this was a cheap price to pay for quelling the Diet's hostility, for the concessions demanded of him were entirely consistent with his own plans for the IRAA. On February 8, Konoe agreed in the Lower House budget committee that the IRAA should operate as a "public" organization, working in cooperation with the government. It was not to be permitted to formulate policies independent of government control.[60]

With that, the issue was virtually settled. The bargain between the government and Lower House was sealed formally on February 23, in a budget committee exchange between the committee chairman and Hiranuma, standing in for Konoe. The chairman asked the home minister to clarify once and for all the government's position on the IRAA. Hiranuma replied on cue that the government regarded the IRAA as a "public" body, and would take severe steps against any effort to involve the organization in political activities as defined in the Public Security Police Law. He added that the government intended to reform the structure of the IRAA and change its personnel.[61] With this reassurance, the IRAA budget was sent to the Diet floor for approval. Kawasaki made one final effort to reduce the IRAA budget for 1941 to three million yen, but his motion was voted down by an overwhelming margin. The Diet then immediately approved the eight-million-yen budget proposal. Konoe was now able to convert the IRAA into an agency for mobilizing popular morale (the original movement for this purpose having been absorbed into the IRAA in October of the previous year). On March 11, the Cabi-

[60] *Ibid.*, pp. 17, 25, and 31; KF, ii, 202.
[61] For an account of this exchange, see *Kanpō gogai—Shōwa 16-nen 2-gatsu 23-nichi, Dai 76-kai teikoku gikai shūgiin giji sokkiroku dai 17-go*, pp. 261–62.

net directed its secretariat to draft a proposal for IRAA reform.[62]

EFFORTS TO ENHANCE PARTY AND HOME MINISTRY POWERS

As the Diet prepared to adjourn, the schism between the leaders and rank and file of the old parties began to open once more. Again, the issues of managing the IRAA and forming a new political party proved to be the touchstone of disagreement. The basic issue involved a decision by the Diet forces over how their influence could best be extended beyond the Lower House. The old leadership, spearheaded by Machida and Nakajima, pressed the government to reform the IRAA in such a fashion as to allow its control by them. They insisted that the government carry out its part of the February compromises by converting the IRAA into an administrative unit. The cooperative councils, which threatened the positions of Diet men and their local allies, were to be dissolved, and a study commission established to investigate important administrative problems. The bureaus of the central office of the IRAA would be supplanted by committees led by permanent directors drawn largely from the Lower House, while the Diet Bureau itself was to be dismantled. In brief, these demands were designed to reorganize the affairs of the IRAA under the leadership of the old party leaders.[63] They would distribute committee posts to other Diet members, who would thereby gain widespread access to official administrative posts for the first time since 1932. At the same time that party influence was extended into the administrative realm, therefore, the Diet leaders' ability to reward their political followers and reinforce the rank and file's feelings of obligation and loyalty to their leaders would be enhanced.

[62] Yokogoshi, "Mu-seitō jidai no seiji-ryoku gaku," p. 33.
[63] *Ibid.*, p. 34.

340

While the rank-and-file Diet members in the Imperial Hotel faction were not averse to this plan for gaining access to administrative positions, many of them were more interested in pursuing the possibility of a new party headed by Konoe. Led by Kazami Akira, the faction attempted to take a preliminary step toward this objective by bringing the House of Peers into the Diet Members' Club; subsequent efforts were planned to convert the club into a new party led by Konoe. As previously mentioned, the parties' leadership was opposed to this plan because it feared a loss of control over the affairs of the Lower House. By April, therefore, the competition for influence within the Diet had again emerged along with efforts to extend Diet members' influence into other areas of the government.[64]

Konoe himself took little notice of the new party campaign after the IRAA's budget had been approved. From the premier's viewpoint, the central political task was to reform the IRAA without overly antagonizing the military services. He did this by announcing a structural reform of the IRAA, accompanied by the resignations of all national IRAA officials. While this approach disappointed the advocates of a "political" IRAA in the services and on the IRAA staff, they could at least derive consolation from the premier's refusal to turn the IRAA over to the control of the old parties. The plans for the new IRAA called for the appointment of a vice president to run the organization in the premier's name. This post, which had hitherto been unfilled, was now occupied by Lieutenant General Yanagawa. Three of the five bureaus in the IRAA central headquarters—the Planning, Policy, and Diet Bureaus—were dissolved to eradicate any connection between the IRAA and policy making or parliamentary scrutiny of government legislation. The men selected as the new chiefs of the remaining General Affairs and Organization Bureaus had had

[64] *Ibid.*, pp. 37–38; also, letter from Ikezaki Tadataka to Kido Kōichi, June 28, 1941, in *Kido monjo*, p. 583.

341

long careers in the Home Ministry. Nagai Ryūtarō was placed in charge of the newly created East Asia Bureau, but the new party he had earlier planned with Kamei and Mutō was converted into an ideological movement promoting the ideals of Japan's mission of leadership in Asia. In addition, a Central Training Office was established in the IRAA headquarters, not for political indoctrination but to train local IRAA officials in the art of mobilizing popular consciousness of the subject's duties toward the throne.

The cooperative councils were maintained to promote a spirit of popular participation in affairs relating to the livelihood of the citizens. Locally, the governors were formally installed as IRAA branch chiefs, and at lower levels Home Ministry influence was strengthened through the *burakukai* and *chōnaikai*. The hopes of Lower House leaders to dominate the IRAA were thus rudely shattered. A new group of research committees was established for Diet members to participate in the organization's affiairs; but these committees were merely placed in an advisory relationship with the vice president, not in control of IRAA headquarters, as the Diet leaders had wished.

In essence, Konoe had turned the leadership of the IRAA over to the Home Ministry and the advocates of spiritual mobilization. The revised structure of the organization's central headquarters reflected this change well. It was neatly divided between local administration (through the General Affairs and Organization Bureaus) and spiritual mobilization (through the Central Training Office and the East Asia Bureau, with its ideological emphasis on Japan's international mission). The only area of IRAA activity not thoroughly "de-politicized" was the group of research committees. In the months ahead, the committees were the scene of a renewed call for a "political" IRAA, but since they were simply advisory organs, their position carried little weight. So far as Konoe was concerned, the reformed version of the IRAA represented the final solution to the new political

342

order issue. Until his resignation from the premiership, immediately preceding Japan's attack on Pearl Harbor, neither the political system nor the balance of power among the elites underwent further significant change.

EFFECTS OF THE NEW POLITICAL ORDER

Perhaps the most striking feature of the IRAA was the minimal impact it had on political institutions and relations among the elites. The relationship of the Cabinet, Diet, and military services was ultimately left unchanged by the IRAA. In itself, the IRAA did not enable either the Cabinet or the military to impose new constraints on the independence of one another, nor did it permit either of them to deprive the Diet of its constitutional prerogative to approve budgets and represent the people. Some historians have argued that the new order marked the culmination of a decade-long trend in which parliamentary influence was reduced to nothing.[65] This contention, however, seems unwarranted. While the passage of the National General Mobilization Law in 1938 and its amendment in early 1941 meant a surrender of the Diet's privilege of approving or rejecting much important government legislation, this surrender was obtained only with the consent of the Diet itself, and was not unconditional. Members of both Houses maintained an important position on the National General Mobilization Council. Moreover, Lower House members retained their role and responsibility in confirming Cabinet policies through control of the purse strings. Indeed, it was this responsibility that ultimately provided them with the political leverage required to throw their weight effectively against the IRAA. Diet power was again exhibited in the government's agreement to drop one-third of its legislative

[65] Scalapino, *Democracy and the Party Movement*, pp. 387–89; Storry, *Double Patriots*, pp. 278–79; Hasegawa, *Shōwa kenpō shi*, p. 156.

343

program to get through the 76th Diet session. Finally, the Lower House had never served as the source of important legislation, leaving the task of preparing bills to the government's agencies. The fact that no important legislation emanated from the Lower House during the wartime period was thus a continuation of previous political practices, rather than an indication of any dramatic loss of power or initative in the Lower House.

The new order also had little effect on the operation of the Cabinet system and the continuing need for coalition among the elites. Governments were still formed and maintained by elite coalitions, as they had been since the Meiji era. The premier's authority over other ministers and other elites was not enhanced by the establishment of the IRAA. Thanks to his eminent social status, Konoe's freedom of action as premier was greater than most; it was not unlimited, however, and it was not increased by the establishment of the IRAA. Konoe himself keenly realized that premiers who did not control some extra-Cabinet agency to harmonize elite views and ambitions were particularly vulnerable to sudden overthrow when their Cabinets were unable to agree on important matters. Had the IRAA been constructed as a totalitarian organization, as the prince originally planned, the position of the president/premier might have become very strong indeed, and the balance of power between the premier and his ministers radically altered. However, Konoe's plans were revised, the IRAA did not become a party, and constitutional "limited pluralism" survived.

The political battle over the creation of the IRAA has often been seen as a struggle between the right wing and the "moderates," the fascists and the "constitutionalists," the "ultra-nationalists" and the "liberals."[66] These labels do more to obscure the nature of political conflict in the pre-

[66] For example, see Butow, *Tojo and the Coming of the War*, p. 159.

war period than to clarify it. For example, it was in opposition to the creation of a totalitarian, unconstitutional party
that ultra-nationalist "Japanist" right-wing groups attacked
the IRAA as a *bakufu*. The "Japanist" right wing was, moreover, joined in this attack by "moderates" in the Diet leadership and in the business world. Opposed to their coalition
were a number of participants in the struggle for political
power who, indeed, sought through the IRAA to create a
strong political force, distinct from the existing elites. These
men were extremely desirous of developing the IRAA as a
new party, based on an organizational effort directed toward masses of people who had never before participated
actively in politics. The "reformist" right wing, led by
Nakano, Hashimoto, and Suetsugu, the officials of the Army
Ministry's Military Affairs Bureau, and a large number of
new party advocates in the Diet, hoped Konoe would develop the IRAA as a new reform party based on mass organization. So, too, did many of the intellectuals and "revisionist" bureaucrats participating in the research of Gotō
Ryūnosuke's *Shōwa kenkyūkai*.

While all of them shared the common fate of losing the
battle to keep the IRAA "political," each group had its own
distinct design for a new and strong popular political force
to dominate the Cabinet, and a popular movement to re-
make the face of local politics. Many were anxious to
replace the nexus of local-national political ties existing
between men of local influence and the parties, or between
low-ranking officials and the Home Ministry in Tokyo.
Their motives and plans were radical and complex, and
many of them drew common inspiration from Western
totalitarian examples. But they differed greatly from one
another in their personal ambitions and policy goals, and
it is difficult to categorize them. Moreover, they failed, for
the civilian elites were for the most part unprepared to
accept their proposals.

The real winners in the new political order controversy
were the Home Ministry, the "Japanist" right wing, busi-

345

ness, and the Lower House leadership in the Diet. Of these, the victory of the Home Ministry was most readily apparent. Through the apparatus of the IRAA, particularly through IRAA direction of the *burakukai*, *chōnaikai*, and *tonari-gumi*, Home Ministry influence penetrated further into local affairs than at any previous time. The financial and administrative burdens of economic recovery from the depression and wartime mobilization had long since proved to be beyond the capabilities of the "local autonomy" system; and the growing role of the Home Ministry in local affairs represented a culmination of efforts begun early in the 1930s to integrate and centralize local administration to deal with these burdens. The Home Ministry legally exercised its enlarged role through control of key IRAA offices after April 1941, until its own authority to do so was confirmed by the Diet in 1943.[67]

At the same time, "Japanist" right-wing groups had succeeded in reaffirming the inviolability of the Meiji Constitution and the Cabinet system as they were created to preserve coalition elite rule in the late 1880s. The reform of the IRAA in 1941, and its subsequent role in wartime spiritual and economic mobilization, represented a vindication of their "Japanist" view that citizenry would respond forcefully and creatively to the challenges faced by the throne and state if properly informed of the crises at hand and the tasks required of the people.

The successes of the Lower House leadership in the IRAA issue were qualified, but nonetheless real. Machida failed to preserve the Minseitō, and Seiyūkai leaders Kuhara and Nakajima were frustrated in their earlier plans to create a new political party and regain control of the Cabinet. They were also unable to obtain control of the IRAA in April 1941. In this sense, they won little from Konoe's new order. By the same token, however, they re-

[67] For a full discussion of the penetration of Home Ministry influence into the system of "local autonomy," see Ari, "Chihō seido," pp. 163–208.

tained control of the Lower House, and preserved the Diet's prerogative to serve as the exclusive vehicle of popular political representation. As the chief brokers for the Lower House in debates with the government over legislation and budgetary proposals, they continued to wield sufficient political leverage to exact concessions from the Cabinet. Although the Diet was no longer a forum of public dissent by virtue of parliamentarians' patriotic self-restraint in the interests of external "national unity," compromises were privately extracted from the government as the price for Diet support of government policies.

The external manifestations of the competition for political power during the war were muted by the widely felt need to exhibit this unity in state affairs. Political competition, however, never ceased. Following its fruitless effort to displace established party leaders and conservative local elites in 1940–1941, the Army tried once more in 1942. The growth of Army influence among elites had, of course, been fostered greatly in the early 1930s by the elite consensus on a foreign policy of autonomy and expansion. It accelerated as the "crises" of the late 1930s led to reliance on the presumed expertise of Army officers in matters vitally related to the nation's survival. Following the early chain of dramatic victories in the Pacific in late 1941 and early 1942, the Army's prestige reached its zenith, and Premier General Tōjō attempted to capitalize on these gains to establish Army control over national and local politics. Early in 1942, the Army sought to remove the newly organized *Yokusan sōnendan* ([*Yokusō*], Imperial Rule Assistance Young Adults Association) from Home Ministry control in the IRAA, and make it a new political force, the "iron backbone of the wartime order."[68] Tōjō also instituted a new

[68] See "Dai-Nippon yokusan sōnendan shi," in YKUS, pp. 893–926. According to Maki Tatsuo, the effort to mobilize *Yokusō* as the nucleus of a new political force was the third and final effort by the Army in 1940–1941 to reshape local politics and convert the Lower House into a strongly promilitary body. Interview by the author with Maki Tatsuo, October 18, 1968.

commission to bestow official approval on certain candidates in the forthcoming election, and planned to use *Yokusō* campaigners to insure that only officially nominated candidates would gain seats in the Lower House.

The Army was unable to divorce *Yokusō* from Home Ministry influence, but together with the Home Ministry, Army leaders sought to make the "*Yokusan* Election" of 1942 the burial ground of residual party influence. From the start, however, this effort was doomed to failure, because the old party leaders had retained a considerable degree of political leverage, and *meibōka* still exercised firm control over *jiban*. Tōjō's Cabinet was obliged to select General Abe Nobuyuki as chairman of the nominating commission, and as premier, Abe had developed and exhibited a great deal of respect for the party leaders.[69] Under his chairmanship, the most active members of the new commission were again the leaders of the defunct political parties.[70] Through their influence, 234 incumbents from the Lower House received official nominations.

Despite the energetic efforts of the reformist campaigners from *Yokusō* and other groups, and the supervision of the election by anti-party officials in the Home Ministry, the "*Yokusan* Election" confirmed the strength of the old party forces. Of the 234 incumbents nominated by the commission, 200 emerged victorious. From the old anti-leadership groups of the Diet (including the Hatoyama and *Shamin* factions), 132 incumbents sought to retain their seats without official blessing. Forty-seven of them were reelected, as was Saitō Takao, who had been expelled from the Diet in March 1940. Indeed, only eighty-five incumbents failed to win either the commission's nomination or the voters' approval, and Tawara Magoichi was the only major figure from the defunct *kisei seitō* to lose his seat in the election.[71]

[69] See, for example, SKS, viii, 113.

[70] Maeda Yonezō denki kankōkai, ed., *Maeda Yonezō den*, p. 450; Hoshino Naoki, *Jidai to jibun* (Tokyo: Daiyamondosha, 1968), p. 212.

[71] Figures compiled from Asahi shinbunsha, ed., *Yokusan senkyo taikan* (Tokyo: Asahi shinbunsha, 1942).

The total number of new men elected to the Lower House
was 199, higher than in the elections of 1930 (127), 1932
(123) and 1936 (125), but not significantly different from
the 181 new men elected in 1928. Furthermore, the rather
high influx of new faces was at least partly attributable to
the unique five-year time span between the 1937 and 1942
elections. Satō Kenryō later acknowledged that the Army's
plan to infuse the Diet with "a new spirit" more sympathetic to military rule had been a failure. Similarly, those
who sought to challenge the parties' firm grip on their local
jiban pointedly criticized the nomination system for having
obstructed the election of more new men.[72]

The continuing viability of party leaders' influence after
the formal dissolution of the parties was a prominent feature of wartime politics. After party leaders had successfully parried the Army's attempt to control the 1942 election, party influence was apparent on many occasions
during the Pacific War. When the Army sought in late 1942
and 1943 to establish yet another new political force based
on *Yokusō*, the parties prevented the creation of an independent central *Yokusō* headquarters. Party leaders and
Home Ministry officials banded together to oppose the intrusion of a new force in local politics, and Premier Tōjō
was ultimately obliged to turn control of *Yokusō* over to
the Home Ministry, as Konoe had done with the IRAA in
1941.[73] Even the wartime challenges to the *meibōka*-party
member linkage from *Yokusō* and the Home Ministry did
not undermine Diet members' control over their local *jiban*,
and the *jiban* survived intact well into the postwar era.
Moreover, in view of the continued need for Konoe, and
later Tōjō, to compromise with the old Lower House leadership, the ability of party leaders to control the rank and file

[72] Tsukui Tatsuo, ed., *Nippon seiji nenpyō: Shōwa jūshichi-nen*, I
(Tokyo: Shōwa shobō, 1942), 235–36; Satō Kenryō, *Dai-Tōa sensō
kaikoroku*, p. 287. For a somewhat different perspective on the 1942
election, see Scalapino, "Elections and Political Modernization in
Prewar Japan," p. 283.

[73] See "Dai Nippon yokusan sōnendan shi," in YKUS, pp. 893–926.

was often fostered rather than threatened by the other elites. In turn, party leaders worked closely with the other elites in power and sought to mobilize support for the government. In April 1943, for instance, Yamazaki Tatsunosuke and Ōasa Tadao were made Cabinet ministers by Tōjō, while Uchida Nobuya was tapped for a Cabinet post in early 1944, and subsequently served as one of the governors-general in the decentralized administrative structure created in the closing months of the war. In the Koiso and Suzuki governments that followed Tōjō's fall from power, Shimada Toshio, Maeda Yonezō, Machida Chūji, Okada Tadahiko, and Sakurai Hyōgorō held ministerial portfolios. Little further evidence need be adduced to demonstrate that Japan's party leaders exercised influence outside the Lower House years after their party organizations had been formally dissolved, and that nonparty elites had been obliged to recognize the importance of the parties' role in the wartime system.

The success of party leaders in maintaining a share of political power during the war was understandably played down by party members during the immediate postwar period. As the victorious Occupation forces began their witch hunt for the culprits responsible for Japan's "conspiracy to commit aggression and crimes against mankind," it made little sense to boast about the ability of parliamentary groups to have enjoyed a share in the governance of the state. Nevertheless, senior party leaders survived the challenges of the nonparty elites, the right wing, and the anti-mainstream factions of their parties, and were ready at the end of the war to take part in the political affairs of state.

Wartime conditions permitted a continuation of important party functions, even though the formal party organizations had dissolved and the scope of party members' activity had been reduced. Party leaders continued to serve as mediators of elite conflict between the Cabinet and Diet, and as wartime conditions worsened, they were rewarded for their efforts with a small but growing share of prestige and power beyond the Lower House. They further contributed to the legitimization of elite rule by providing unanimous support by popularly elected representatives for those Cabinet proposals that reached the floor of the Lower House. Party men also continued to serve as a link in the chain of political participation in national affairs. And as leading members of the movements to intensify citizen self-identification with the fortunes of the state, they also contributed to the elites' efforts to promote national integration.

The overall influence of party men declined greatly between 1926 and 1942, and increased only slightly thereafter. Nevertheless, through the effective performance of critical functions during the war, they were able to preserve an important share of their earlier power, and when a new international and domestic climate was created after August 1945, they emerged as experienced performers of political tasks that remained vital to the survival of the Japanese state. The reward for their wartime performance was in many cases an Allied-imposed purge from public life for between three and seven years. However, those who inherited the parties' legacy and those who returned to parliamentary careers at the end of their purges carried on the work of the parties of imperial Japan, and capitalized on the new environment to acquire authority and great political power.

Epilogue

THE decline of Japan's political parties during the 1930s has been regarded by postwar historians as a development of great importance. On the one hand, the failure of the parties to retain control over the premiership and Cabinet has been regarded as a significant cause of the rise of militarism and Japan's "international outlawry." On the other hand, the parties' shortcomings and "failures" in the 1930s have been studied in terms of their impact on postwar political history and the future of Japanese democracy. While it may be inappropriate for the foreign observer to impose his own value judgments on the legitimacy of Japan's course of action abroad in the 1930s and 1940s, or to evaluate Japanese politics simply in terms of democratic theory, it nevertheless seems useful to conclude this study of the prewar parties with some brief observations about their impact on prewar policies and postwar politics.

A standard general view holds that the shift from party control of Cabinets to control by the miltary services and the bureaucracy produced a significant change in Japan's policies, setting Japan on a disaster course ending in World War II.[1] Others have argued that the end of party government in 1932 accelerated the trend towards fascism and militarism in Japan.[2] While there is considerable debate over the applicability of the "fascist model" to Japanese politics, it is generally agreed that the termination of party Cabinets had vast implications for increased military power and control, and resulted in the establishment of Japanese

[1] Fairbank, Reischauer, and Craig, *East Asia*, p. 580.

[2] Storry, *Double Patriots*, p. 124; Maruyama Masao, *Thought and Behaviour in Modern Japanese Politics* (London: Oxford University Press, 1963), p. 65.

militarism.[3] Since Japan was "peace-loving" under party rule in the 1920s, and warlike a decade later, it is often assumed that the central explanation of historical change in her international position lies in the replacement of party leaders by "militarists and fascists" at the helm of state. The seizure of power by forces inimicable to "cooperative diplomacy" is equated with the failure of the parties to maintain power, and evokes the need to explain the collapse of party government as an inevitable precondition to Japan's aggression. The Japanese invasion of Manchuria in 1931, under the auspices of a party-controlled government, is dismissed as an aberration stemming from independent action on the part of the militarists, implying that if the parties had retained control of national affairs, Japan might not have gone to war in China in 1937 or attacked Pearl Harbor in 1941.

This line of argument is suspect from a number of perspectives, and seriously distorts the nature of the parties' priorities and strategies during the 1930s. It also fails to take account of the dramatic changes in Japan's international climate around 1930, which fostered a reallocation of political power among the nation's elite groups. The focal point of national policy making shifted from the parties as managers of elite conflict to the military and bureaucratic specialists in mobilizing the nation to deal with the "period of emergency." The parties' fall from control of the premiership derived from a combination of their competitors' (and collaborators') perception of them as unequal to the tasks of national leadership, and a new international climate that made the claims to power and influence of other elite groups more credible and effective.

The advocacy of "cooperative diplomacy" by party Cabinets was only one cause of the attack against their leadership, and by 1931, the Seiyūkai had explicitly shed this

[3] Scalapino, *Democracy and the Party Movement*, p. 370; Shiraki, *Nihon seitō shi*, p. 115.

policy as a liability to the defense of Japan's interests and its own political position. By 1932, the Minseitō had followed the Seiyūkai lead in abandoning Shidehara Diplomacy, and thereafter, both parties repeatedly endorsed Japan's expansion into China and throughout Asia. Despite individual exceptions, party men as a group were never principled pacifists, and during much of the 1930s, they were among the most jingoistic elements of the ruling elite. One may argue that the parties compromised their principles by shifting from "international cooperation" to "autonomy" and sanctioning the use of force in the achievement of national objectives; but this position ignores the obvious fact that party leaders endorsed "international cooperation" in the 1920s because their supreme commitment was to the defense and enhancement of Japan's imperial interests. Their viewpoint was an accurate reflection of the imperialistic sentiments that pervaded the body politic in the 1920s, and it remained an accurate reflection of these sentiments during the more chauvinistic period of the 1930s. Had they been pacifists in principle, they would never have achieved power earlier, for they would have been poor managers of conflict among other elites who were fundamentally committed to the preservation of Japan's imperial position. Their approach to power was extremely pragmatic. It was rooted in principle primarily in the sense that party politicians, like politicians in other elite groups, consistently regarded the diminution of Japanese rights and interests in East Asia and the weakening of Japanese security in the Pacific as unacceptable policy alternatives.

It therefore required no abandonment of political principles for party politicians to endorse the policy of "autonomy" and the expansion of the nation's military establishment to underwrite this policy. However, the military and party elites faced a common dilemma in the 1930s. Implementing the military and economic policies regarded as vital to Japan's security required a concentration of the nation's resources in military and heavy industrial development, at the expense of the impoverished peasantry, whose interests the Army seemed so committed to defending, and local agrarian and business groups, whose interests were often represented by the parties. Ultimately, both national elite groups placed national security ahead of the popular standard of living in deciding official policies, a decision that was lamentable as much for the effects it had on the lives of the citizenry during the wartime years as for its unfortunate results in 1945. Nevertheless, the parties' endorsement of military expansion was consistent with their sense of mission as members of the ruling elite. Their policies proved fallible and unwise; but they required little compromise with the approach to power and the fundamental principles they had embraced in the 1920s.

The parties' endorsement of the fatal foreign and defense policies of the military was not the consequence of a lack of courage or political leverage, any more than it was the result of a compromise in principle. The parties lost control of the premiership after 1932, but maintained control of the Lower House and the principal channels of political participation by the citizenry. It is important to emphasize that even these limited institutional prerogatives would have been sufficient to deter the implementation of the policies that destroyed imperial Japan, had the parties been inclined to use them. Indeed, on several occasions, the parties fought vigorously and successfully against military attempts to limit their institutional prerogatives, and the prerogatives of their principal backers. Despite the undeniable threat of terrorism, and despite party members' desires to avoid frequent dissolutions of the Lower House and new election campaigns, the parties resisted much of the Army's domestic program on several occasions. Hence, they did much more than simply vie with one another in meaningless struggles for power; they retained an important voice in determining how Japan was to be governed as she dealt with the "period of emergency." As Japan's military commitments grew, the parties limited their public criticism of the gov-

355

ernment. Cessation of provocative interpellations in the Lower House was attributable, first to fundamental agreement with the foreign policies of the government, and second to a tacit agreement to work out policy compromises before debate began on the floor of the Diet. Party leaders shared the belief of nonparty elite groups that public debate over wartime policy was injurious to the strength of the nation, and impeded the effectiveness of Japan's diplomatic and military efforts in China and the Pacific. As leaders who supported Japan's international goals, they wished to mobilize the same spiritual support and national unity that had contributed to Japan's victories over China and Russia during the Meiji era. Voluntary restraint on the Diet floor limited the ability of the parties to embarrass the government, and perhaps weakened their leverage in the competition for power. They compensated for this loss by emphasizing their importance in the wartime system as popular mobilization agencies, and also used the government's desire for Diet unanimity to extract compromises on behalf of their supporters and themselves.

Having struggled against challenges to their institutional prerogatives for over a decade, the parties of imperial Japan left a variegated legacy to postwar political organizations. On the one hand, Japan was experienced in operating a system of parliamentary government, even if the parties had never been able to establish full control over the institutions of the imperial system. Moreover, despite the dissolution of the parties in 1940, informal political groupings persisted throughout the war, aligned under the same leaders who had presided over the party organizations. Many of these wartime groups proved to be the nuclei of the early postwar parties, prior to the purge. The very idea and desirability of forming political parties survived the dissolutions of 1940, and even during the war, Nakajima Chikuhei, Machida Chūji, Kishi Nobusuke, Prince Konoe, and other old or aspiring party figures laid plans for the formation of new political parties. After the war had ended, the new

356

parties sought to follow the strategy of their predecessors, becoming arenas for the management of elite conflict, and even adapting themselves to the existence of a powerful external military elite group (the Allied Occupation forces). Diet members' *jiban* remained surprisingly stable, and many Diet men returning from an enforced absence from politics in 1952 found that their old electoral organizations were still strong enough to return them to power. In addition to capitalizing on knowledge of the prewar parties' sources of strength, the postwar politicians sought to learn from their predecessors' failures. Postwar parties created much more powerful organs for the study and formulation of national policy than the prewar parties, and when the conservative parties found their control of the premiership challenged (by a Socialist coalition), they succeeded in implementing the plans entertained by party leaders in the 1938–1940 period for the creation of a new and well disciplined hegemonic conservative party.

On the other hand, it cannot be said that the parties of late imperial Japan provided postwar politicians with the inspiration to become democrats. Whether Japan today or at any time since 1945 has been a democracy is a question that falls beyond the scope of this study; but the prewar parties' contributions to postwar democracy were slight and perhaps inadvertent. Postwar parties have been responsive to the interests of specific constituencies, and the prewar parties also articulated the interests of their local and financial supporters. However, the *kisei seitō* linkage with rural elite groups proved, after the Meiji era, to be a negative factor in allowing the political system to absorb and articulate at a national level the interests and political views of the large masses of citizens subordinated to the political control of rural and urban *meibōka*. During the 1920s and 1930s the parties stood as defenders of traditional local authority against the encroachments of the central bureaucracy, but also worked to frustrate the politicization of the masses.

357

In retrospect, the parties were highly successful in warding off "reformist" challenges to their institutional prerogatives in the Diet and their role in linking the state to the people. However, the central dilemma of political reformists during the 1930s, whether their views approximated socialism or national socialism, and whether they looked to Konoe or the Army for support at the national level, was that the party-*meibōka* linkage and *meibōka* control over the political life of the community were too strong to overthrow without risking greater national divisions than the elites were willing to endorse in wartime. The parties' successes in this area were thus in part a consequence of the war itself, rather than of their satisfying the demands for greater political participation, better popular representation, and fundamental economic reform. The leveling effects of the war and radical Occupation reforms did much more to quiet the demand for reform and shatter the traditional monopoly of local political power by *meibōka* than any party program might have done. Conservative party politicians proved to be benefactors, rather than instigators, of this defusing of demands for new links from the people to the state.

Ultimately, the most important legacy of the parties of imperial Japan was the simple fact that whether they were democratic or not, they had once attained a remarkable degree of political influence under the Meiji Constitution, and had retained considerable power even under extremely adverse conditions in the late 1930s and wartime years. Many politicians recognized that in a more favorable domestic and international environment, parties could once again flourish if they functioned as they had earlier. When the war ended, virtually all members of the defunct parties were prepared to reorganize themselves into new political organizations that differed little from the groups they had dissolved five years previously. Even the Allied purge of many leading party figures did not prevent the reincarnation of the Seiyūkai and Minseitō with new names in the postwar era.

While the justice of purging Japan's political elites for their responsibility in the Pacific War is certainly questionable, Occupation authorities were not wrong to assert that most party men had shared the responsibilities of government. To claim a share of responsibility in imperial Japan's national affairs became a liability during the early postwar years; but most party men spent the better part of their political careers in quest of a share of this responsibility. They failed to hold the gains they had achieved by 1932, but as this study has demonstrated, they never stopped trying to retrieve what they had lost, and they were never obliged to surrender a good part of the power they had acquired.

Bibliography

Unpublished Sources, Japanese Language

"Arima Yoriyasu nikki."

Foreign Ministry Archives. Particularly *Honpō naisei kankei zassan*, Section III (Classification Number S1.5.0.0–1, continued).

Kamei Kan'ichirō papers.

Keishichō jōhō-ka. "Shintō juritsu undō gaikyō" (Top Secret). November 1, 1938.

Kido nikki kenkyūkai, ed. "Kido Kōichi kankei monjo sōmokuroku." 1967.

Konoe Fumimaro papers, Yōmei bunko, Kyoto.

Maki Tatsuo. "Gun no seiji kan'yo to kokunai jōsei," in Bōeichō senshi-shitsu.

"Mutō Akira nikki," in Bōeichō senshi-shitsu.

Naimushō keiho-kyoku. *Shōwa 12–nen–chū ni okeru shakai undō no jōkyō* (Secret). December 20, 1938.

———. *Shōwa 14–nen–chū ni okeru shakai undō no jōkyō* (Secret). December 20, 1940.

———. *Shōwa 15–nen–chū ni okeru shakai undō no jōkyō* (Secret). December 20, 1941.

———. *Shōwa 16–nen–chū ni okeru shakai undō no jōkyō* (Secret). December 20, 1942.

Navy Ministry Archives. Particularly *Kaigun shiryō* microfilms, in Institute of Asian Economic Affairs.

Unpublished Sources, English Language

Hugh Byas Collection, Sterling Memorial Library, Yale University, New Haven, Connecticut.

360

International Military Tribunal for the Far East. *Record of the Proceedings, Documents, Exhibits, Judgment, Dissenting Judgments, Preliminary Interrogations, Miscellaneous Documents* (Mimeographed). Tokyo, 1946–1949.

JOURNALS AND NEWSPAPERS

Bessatsu chimei. Particularly special issue: "Himerareta Shōwa shi." v.12 (December 1956).

Bungei shunjū. Particularly:
special issue: "Shintaisei-ka no bunka to chishikijin." xviii.13 (October 1940).
special supplement: "Shōwa memo." xxxii.11 (July 1954).
special supplement: "Dai-ni Shōwa memo—Tokuhon gendai shi." xxxii.16 (October 1954).
special supplement: "Shōwa no sanjūgo dai-jiken." xxxiii.16 (August 1955).
special issue: "Nippon riku-kaigun no sō-kessan." (December 1955.)
special issue: "San-dai Nihon no nazo." (February 1956.)
special issue: "Ima koso iu—shuyaku no memo." (April 1957.)
special issue: "Shōwa shi o ugokashita kaibutsu," xliii.2 (February 1965).

Chūō kōron. Particularly 1940–1941.

Contemporary Japan. 1932–1941.

Contemporary Opinions. Edited by Okamura Shigeyoshi. 1936–1941.

Japan Chronicle. June 1, 1940–January 31, 1941.

Kaizō. Particularly 1940–1941.

Kokka gakkai zasshi. Particularly:
special issue: "Kokunai kaikaku no sho-mondai, I." liii.9 (September 1939).
special issue: "Kokunai kaikaku no sho-mondai, II." liii.10 (October 1939).

Minsei.

Seiyū.
Shōwa dōjin. Particularly 1959–1964.
Sōnendan. 1935–1941.
Tokyo asahi. 1940–1941.
Tokyo Gazette. 1938–1941.
Toshi mondai. Particularly special issue: "Shi-sei fu-ken-sei kaisei-an hihan." xxx.1 (January 1, 1940).
Yokusan sōnendan undō. June 6, 1942–May 29, 1943.

INTERVIEWS

Gotō Ryūnosuke (4): February 29, 1968; March 14, 1968; March 25, 1968; April 5, 1968.
Hara Shirō (2): September 2, 1968; October 2, 1968.
Hata Ikuhiko: November 11, 1968.
Hazama Shigeru: March 2, 1968.
Imai Seiichi: August 21, 1968.
Kamei Kan'ichirō (3): October 14, 1969; October 15, 1969; October 28, 1973.
Katayama Tetsu: September 4, 1968.
Kido Kōichi: June 16, 1969.
Maki Tatsuo (2): October 5, 1968; October 18, 1968.
Matsumae Shigeyoshi: July 25, 1969.
Matsumoto Shigeharu: June 20, 1969.
Matsushita Yoshio: July 17, 1968.
Mutō Tomio: November 13, 1968.
Okumura Kiwao: October 31, 1968.
Ōta Kōzō: October 8, 1969.
Ōtsubo Yasuo: November 4, 1968.
Satō Kenryō: November 27, 1968.
Sawamura Katsundo (2): November 1, 1968; December 9, 1968.
Sugihara Masami (2): February 6, 1969; February 10, 1969.
Tōyama Shigeki: September 26, 1968.
Tsukui Tatsuo: September 30, 1969.
Ushiba Tomohiko: June 10, 1969.
Yamamoto Yūzō (2): September 6, 1972; October 12, 1972.

362

Yamazaki Tanshō (2): February 18, 1968; June 15, 1969.
Yatsugi Kazuo (3): November 6, 1968; November 25, 1968; December 16, 1968.

BOOKS, JAPANESE LANGUAGE
(All publishers in Tokyo unless otherwise cited)

Abe Genki-shi danwa sokkiroku. Naiseishi kenkyū shiryō dai–48, 49, 50, 51–shū. Naiseishi kenkyūkai, 1967.

Adachi Gan. *Kokumin undō no sai-shuppatsu.* Kasumigaseki shobō, 1940.

Adachi Kenzō. *Adachi Kenzō jijōden.* Edited by Izu Tomihito. Shinjusha, 1960.

Andō Yoshio, ed. *Shōwa keizai shi e no shōgen,* ii. Mainichi shinbunsha, 1966.

Aoki Tokuzō. *Taiheiyō sensō zenshi,* 6 v. Sekai heiwa kensetsu kyōkai, 1950–1952.

Aoki Yasuzō. *Nanajū-nen o kaerimite.* Edited by Asakura Yūji. Hachioji-shi: Aoki Hiroyuki, 1970.

Arima Yoriyasu. *Hitorigoto.* Koizumi insatsu kabushiki kaisha, 1957.

————. *Seikai dōchūki.* Nihon shuppan kyōdō kabushiki kaisha, 1951.

————. *Yūjin Konoe.* Kōbundō, 1949.

Aritake Shūji. *Shōwa keizai sokumen shi.* Kawade shobō, 1952.

Asahi shinbunsha, ed. *Shōwa jūgo-nen Asahi nenkan.* Asahi shinbunsha, 1939.

————, ed. *Shōwa jūhachi-nen Asahi nenkan.* Asahi shinbunsha, 1942.

————, ed. *Shōwa jūroku-nen Asahi nenkan.* Asahi shinbunsha, 1940.

————, ed. *Shōwa jūshichi-nen Asahi nenkan.* Asahi shinbunsha, 1941.

————. *Sōdōin-hō no zenbō.* Asahi shinbunsha, December 1938.

————, ed. *Yokusan senkyo taikan.* Asahi shinbunsha, 1942.

363

Asō Hisashi den kankō iinkai (Kawakami Jōtarō), ed. *Asō Hisashi den.* Asō Hisashi den kankō iinkai, 1958.

Baba Tsunego. *Konoe naikaku shi ron.* Takayama shoin, 1946.

———. *Kuni to jinbutsu.* Takayama shoin, 1941.

Bōeichō bōei kenshūsho senshi-shitsu. *Daihon'ei rikugunbu,* 2 v. Asagumo shinbunsha, 1967–1968.

——— (Hara Shirō). *Daihon'ei rikugunbu Dai-Tōa senso kaisen keii,* i, ii. Asagumo shinbunsha, 1973.

Chiba Saburō sensei kenshō kinen shuppan kankōkai (Hanami Tatsuji), ed. *Yonjūgo-nen no konjaku.* Chiba Saburō sensei kenshō kinen shuppan kankōkai, 1969.

Edogawa Ranpo, ed. *Kawasaki Katsu den.* Kawasaki Katsu den kankōkai, 1956.

Fujita Chikamasa, ed. *Shina mondai jiten.* Chūō kōronsha, 1942.

Fujiwara Akira. *Gunji shi.* Tōyō keizai shinpōsha, 1961.

———. *Nihon teikoku shugi. Taikei—Nihon rekishi,* vi. Nihon hyōronsha, 1968.

Fujiwara Akira, Imai Seiichi, and Tōyama Shigeki. *Shōwa shi.* Rev. ed. Iwanami shoten, 1959.

Fukai Eigo. *Sūmitsuin jūyō giji oboegaki.* Iwanami shoten, 1967.

Furui Yoshimi-shi danwa sokkiroku. Naiseishi kenkyū shiryō, unnumbered. Naiseishi kenkyūkai, no date.

Gaimushō, ed. *Nihon gaikō nenpyō narabi ni shuyō bunsho,* ii. Hara shobō, 1966.

Gotō Fumio-shi danwa dai-1-kai sokkiroku. Naiseishi kenkyū shiryō dai–4–shū. Naiseishi kenkyūkai, 1963.

Gotō Ryūnosuke-shi danwa sokkiroku. Naiseishi kenkyū shiryō dai–66, 67, 68, 69–shū. Naiseishi kenkyūkai, 1968.

Hamaguchi Fujiko, ed. *Hamaguchi Yūkō ikō: zuikanroku.* Sanseidō, 1931.

Hara Akira, Itō Takashi, and Nakamura Takafusa, eds. *Gendai shi o tsukuru hitobito,* 4 v. Mainichi shinbunsha, 1971–1972.

Harada Kumao. *Saionji-kō to seikyoku*, 9 v. Iwanami shoten, 1950–1956.

Hasegawa Masayasu. *Shōwa kenpō shi*. Iwanami shoten, 1962.

Hashikawa Bunzō and Matsumoto Sannosuke, eds. *Kindai Nihon seiji shisō shi II*. *Kindai Nihon shisō shi taikei*, IV. Yūhikaku, 1970.

Hashimoto Seinosuke-shi danwa sokkiroku. Naiseishi kenkyū shiryō dai–23–shū. Naiseishi kenkyūkai, 1964.

Hata Ikuhiko. *Gun fuashizumu undō shi*. Kawade shobō shinsha, 1962.

Hattori Takushirō. *Dai-Tōa sensō zenshi*, 8 v. Masu shobō, 1955.

Hayashi Shigeru. *Kindai Nihon no shisōka-tachi*. Iwanami shoten, 1958.

———, ed. *Sensō no jidai*. *Jinbutsu: Nihon no rekishi*, XIV. Yomiuri shinbunsha, 1966.

———. *Taiheiyō sensō*. *Nihon no rekishi*, XXV. Chūō kōronsha, 1967.

Hayashi Shigeru and Oka Yoshitake, eds. *Taishō demokurashii-ki no seiji: Matsumoto Gōkichi seiji nisshi*. Iwanami shoten, 1959.

Hayashida Kametarō. *Nihon seitō shi*, 2 v. Dai-Nippon yūbenkai kōdansha, 1927.

Hazama Shigeru-shi danwa sokkiroku. Naiseishi kenkyū shiryō dai–31, 32, 33–shū. Naiseishi kenkyūkai, 1965–1966.

Hida Takushi. *Seitō kōbō gojū-nen*. Kokkai tsūshinsha, 1955.

Hiranuma Kiichirō kaikoroku hensan iinkai, ed. *Hiranuma Kiichirō kaikoroku*. Hiranuma Kiichirō kaikoroku hensan iinkai, 1955.

Hirota Kōki denki kankōkai, ed. *Hirota Kōki*. Chūō kōron jigyō shuppan, 1966.

Hōchi shinbunsha seiji-bu, ed. *Shintaisei to wa donna koto ka?* Shintaisei kenkyūkai, 1940.

Hōmushō kōan chōsachō. *Senzen ni okeru uyoku dantai no jōkyō*, 4 v. Naikaku insatsu-kyoku, 1964–1967.

Horiba Kazuo. *Shina jihen sensō shidō shi.* Jiji tsūshinsha, 1962.

Horikiri Zenjirō-shi danwa sokkiroku, 3 v. Naiseishi kenkyū shiryō dai–7, 8, 10–shū. Naiseishi kenkyūkai, 1963–1964.

Hoshino Naoki. *Jidai to jibun.* Daiyamondosha, 1968.

Hoshino Naoki-shi danwa sokkiroku. Naiseishi kenkyū shiryō dai–24–shū. Naiseishi kenkyūkai, 1964.

Hosokawa Morisada. *Jōhō tennō ni tassezu,* 2 v. Isobe shobō, 1953.

Hosoya Chihirō, Saitō Makoto, Imai Seiichi, and Rōyama Michio, eds. *Nichi-Bei kankei shi: Kaisen ni itaru jū-nen (1931–1941 nen),* 4 v. Tokyo daigaku shuppankai, 1971.

Ikeda Chōya, ed. *Rikken Minseitō seisaku kōenshū.* Meiseisha, 1935.

Ikeda Seihin. *Kao: zaikai kaiko.* Sekai no Nihonsha, 1949.

———. *Kojin konjin.* Sekai no Nihonsha, 1949.

Ikeda Sumihisa. *Nihon no magarikado.* Senjō shuppan, 1968.

———. *Rikugun sōgi iinchō: Shina jihen kara Tokyo saiban made.* Nihon shuppan kyōkai kabushiki kaisha, 1953.

Imai Seiichi and Itō Takashi, eds. *Kokka sōdōin (2). Gendai shi shiryō,* XLIV. Misuzu shobō, 1974.

Imai Takeo. *Shina jihen no kaisō.* Misuzu shobō, 1964.

———. *Shōwa no bōryaku.* Hara shobō, 1967.

Imamura Takeo. *Ikeda Seihin den.* Keiō tsūshin kabushiki kaisha, 1962.

Inaba Masao, Usui Katsumi, Shimada Toshihiko, and Tsunoda Jun, eds. *Nit-Chū sensō (1). Gendai shi shiryō,* VIII. Misuzu shobō, 1964.

Inada Masazumi-shi danwa sokkiroku. Nihon kindai shiryō sōsho B–2. Nihon kindai shiryō kenkyūkai and Kido nikki kenkyūkai, 1969.

Inoki Masamichi, ed. *Nihon no nidai seitō.* Kyoto: Hōritsu bunkasha, 1958.

Inomata Keitarō. *Nakano Seigō no shōgai.* Nagoya: Reimei shobō, 1964.

Inoue Kiyoshi, ed. *Kindai (3). Nihon jinbutsu shi taikei.* VII. Asakura shoten, 1963.

366

Ishida Takeshi. *Gendai soshiki ron.* Iwanami shoten, 1967.
———. *Hakyoku to heiwa. Nihon kindai shi taikei,* VIII. Tokyo daigaku shuppankai, 1968.
———. *Kindai Nihon seiji kōzō no kenkyū.* Miraisha, 1956 and 1967.
Ishiwata Sōtarō denki hensankai (Irumano Takeo), ed. *Ishiwata Sōtarō.* Ishiwata Sōtarō denki hensankai, 1954.
Itō Kinjirō. *Kanryō washi ga kuni sa.* Hōunsha, 1940.
Itō Takashi. *Shōwa shoki seiji shi kenkyū.* Tokyo daigaku shuppankai, 1969.
Iwabuchi Tatsuo. *Yabururu hi made.* Nihon shūhōsha, 1946.
Iwanami shoten henshū-bu, ed. *Kindai Nihon sōgō nenpyō.* Iwanami shoten, 1968.
Izawa Takio denki hensan iinkai, ed. *Izawa Takio.* Haneda shoten, 1951.
Izu Tomihito. *Adachi-san no kokorogamae o kataru.* Chikura shobō, 1931.
Izumiyama Sanroku. *Tora daijin ni naru made.* Tōhō shoin, 1953.
Jikyoku kaibō chōsajo (Tokuda Kenji). *Seikai rimen shi nenkan* (gekan). Nihon bunka shuppankai, 1939.
Kaedei Kinnosuke, ed. *Shōwa jūroku-nen Kokumin nenkan.* Kokumin shinbunsha, October 1940.
Kamei Kan'ichirō. *Gojū-nen "gomu fūsen" o otte.* Edited by Sangyō keizai kenkyū kyōkai jimu-kyoku. N.p., 1968.
Kamei Kan'ichirō-shi danwa sokkiroku. Nihon kindai shiryō sōsho B–3. Nihon kindai shiryō kenkyūkai, 1970.
Kamishima Jirō, ed. *Kenryoku no shisō. Gendai Nihon shisō taikei,* x. Chikuma shobō, 1965.
Kanpō gogai (see *Teikoku shūgiin giji sokkiroku*).
Kase Toshikazu, Kawagoe Shigeru, Nishi Haruhiko, Oka Yoshitake, and Matsumoto Shigeharu, eds. *Kindai Nihon no gaikō.* Asahi shinbunsha, 1962.
Katayama Tetsu. *Kaiko to tenbō.* Fukumura shuppan, 1967.
Katō Kōmei-haku den hensan iinkai, ed. *Katō Kōmei,* 2 v. Hara shobō, 1971 (reprint).

Katō Yūsaburō-shi danwa sokkiroku. Naiseishi kenkyū shiryō dai–76, 77, 78–shū. Naiseishi kenkyūkai, 1969.

Kawanishi Toyotarō et al. *Tanabe Shichiroku.* Tanabe Shichiroku-ō shōtokuhi kensetsu iinkai, 1954.

Kawasaki Hideji. *Yūki aru seijika-tachi.* Sengoku shuppansha, 1971.

Kawasaki Katsu. *Kintei kenpō no shinzui to Taisei yokusankai.* Kohon seikokusha, March 18, 1941.

Kawasaki Takukichi denki hensankai, ed. *Kawasaki Takukichi.* Ishizaki shoten, 1961.

Kayaba Gunzō-shi danwa sokkiroku. Naiseishi kenkyū shiryō dai–46, 47–shū. Naiseishi kenkyūkai, 1966–1967.

Kazami Akira. *Konoe naikaku.* Nihon shuppan kyōdō kabushiki kaisha, 1951.

Kida Yasuo. *Minseitō sōran.* Minseitō sōran hensanjo, 1931.

Kido Kōichi. *Kido Kōichi nikki,* 2 v. Tokyo daigaku shuppankai, 1966.

Kido nikki kenkyūkai (Oka Yoshitake), ed. *Kido Kōichi kankei monjo.* Tokyo daigaku shuppankai, 1966.

Kikkawa Manabu. *Arashi to tatakau tesshō Araki. Rikugun rimen shi: Shōgun Araki no nanajū-nen,* II. Araki Sadao shōgun denki hensan kankōkai, 1955.

Kinbara Samon. *Taishō demokurashii no shakaiteki keisei.* Aoki shoten, 1967 and 1973.

Kindai Nihon shisō shi kōza, I: Rekishiteki gaikan. Chikuma shobō, 1959.

Kindai Nihon shisō shi kōza, V: Shidōsha to taishū. Chikuma shobō, 1960.

Kinoshita Hanji. *Gendai nashonarizumu jiten.* Kantōsha, 1951.

———. *Nihon kokka shugi undō shi,* 2 v. Iwanami shoten, 1952.

———. *Shintaisei jiten.* Asahi shinbunsha, 1941.

Kiya Ikusaburō. *Konoe-kō hibun.* Wakayama: Takanoyama shuppansha, 1950.

———. *Seikai gojū-nen no butai-ura.* Seikai ōraisha, 1965.

Ko-Baba Eiichi-shi kinenkai. *Baba Eiichi den.* Ko-Baba Eiichi-shi kinenkai, 1945.

Kobayashi Yūgo et al., eds. *Rikken Seiyūkai shi,* 7 v. Rikken Seiyūkai hensan-bu and Rikken Seiyūkai shuppan-kyoku, 1924–1943.

Koiso Kuniaki jijōden kankōkai, ed. *Katsuzan kōsō.* Koiso Kuniaki jiden kankōkai, 1963.

Kojima Kazuo. *Seikai gojū-nen: Kojima Kazuo kaikoroku.* Shin-Nihon keizaisha, 1952.

Kokumin seishin sōdōin chūō renmei, ed. *Shina jihen isshūnen kinen kōenshū.* Kokumin seishin sōdōin chūō renmei, 1938.

Kokusaku kenkyūkai. *Gyōsei shintaisei ni kansuru kenkyū hōkoku,* #27. Kokusaku kenkyūkai, March 1941.

Kokusei isshinkai (Uemura Kōyū), ed. *Kokusei isshin ronsō.* 20 v., 1935–1937.

Kōmei senkyo renmei, ed. *Shūgiin giin senkyo no jisseki.* Toppan insatsu kabushiki kaisha, 1967.

(Konoe Fumimaro). *Konoe Fumimaro-kō no shuki: ushinawareshi seiji.* Asahi shinbunsha, 1946.

(———). *Konoe Fumimaro shuki: heiwa e no dōryoku.* Nippon denpō tsūshinsha, 1946.

(———). *Konoe shushō enjutsu shū,* II. Edited by Atsuchi Narishige. N.p., February 11, 1939.

———. *Seidanroku.* Edited by Itō Takeshi. Chikura shobō, 1936.

(———). *Senji-ka no kokumin ni okuru Konoe shushō ensetsu shū.* Edited by Shinseiji kenkyūkai (Oka Tamao). Tōkōsha, December 1940.

"Konoe nikki" henshū iinkai, ed. *Konoe nikki.* Kyōdō tsūshinsha, 1968.

Kuhara Fusanosuke. *Kōdō keizai ron.* Chikura shobō, 1933.

———. *Zenshin no kōryō.* Taichisha, 1939.

Kuhara Fusanosuke-ō denki hensankai (Mima Yasuichi), ed. *Kuhara Fusanosuke.* Kuhara Fusanosuke-ō denki hensankai, 1970.

Kuribayashi Teiichi. *Chihō kankai no hensen.* Sekaisha, 1930.

Kyoto daigaku bungaku-bu kokushi kenkyū-shitsu, ed. *Nihon kindai shi jiten.* Tōyō keizai shinpōsha, 1958 and 1966.

Maeda Yonezō denki kankōkai (Aritake Shūji), ed. *Maeda Yonezō den.* Itō-setsu shobō, 1961.

Maejima Shōzō. *Nihon fuashizumu to gikai.* Kyoto: Hōritsu bunkasha, 1956.

Maruyama Masao. *Nihon no shisō.* Iwanami shoten, 1967.

Maruyama Tsurukichi. *Nanajū-nen tokoro dokoro.* Nanajū-nen tokoro dokoro kankōkai, 1955.

Masumi Junnosuke. *Gendai seiji to seijigaku.* Iwanami shoten, 1964.

――. *Nihon seitō shi ron,* 4 v. Tokyo daigaku shuppankai, 1965–1968.

Matsumura Kenzō. *Machida Chūji-ō den.* Machida Chūji-ō denki kankōkai, 1950.

Matsuoka Yōsuke. *Naze kisei seitō no kaishō o sakebu ka?* Seitō kaishō renmei shuppan-bu, 1935.

Minobe Tatsukichi. *Gendai kensei hyōron.* Iwanami shoten, 1930.

――. *Gikai seido ron.* Nippon hyōronsha, 1930 and 1946.

Mitani Taichirō. *Nihon seitō seiji no keisei.* Tokyo daigaku shuppankai, 1967.

Mitani Taichirō and Shinohara Hajime, eds. *Kindai Nihon no seiji shidō.* Tokyo daigaku shuppankai, 1965.

Miwa Jūsō denki kankōkai (Rōyama Masamichi), ed. *Miwa Jūsō no shōgai.* Miwa Jūsō denki kankōkai, 1966.

Miyazaki Masayoshi. *Tōa renmei ron.* Kaizōsha, 1938.

Miyazawa Toshiyoshi, ed. *Kenpō gikai.* Iwanami shoten, 1940.

Moro Masanori. *Ijin Nakajima Chikuhei hiroku.* Nitta-chō, Nitta-gun, Gunma-ken: Jōmō ijin denki kankōkai, 1960.

Muramatsu Shōfū. *Akiyama Teisuke wa kataru.* Dai-Nippon yūbenkai kōdansha, 1938.

Mutō Akira. *Hitō kara Sugamo e.* Jitsugyō no Nihonsha, 1952.

Myōga Fusakichi. *Nippon seitō no gensei.* Nippon hyōron-sha, 1929.

Nagai Ryūtarō. *Watakushi no shinnen to taiken.* Okakura shobō, 1938.

"Nagai Ryūtarō" hensankai (Matsumura Kenzō), ed. *Nagai Ryūtarō.* Seikōsha, 1959.

Nagata Tetsuzan. *Kokka sōdōin.* Osaka: Osaka mainichi shinbunsha, 1928.

Naikaku jōhō-kyoku, ed. *Yokusan gikai no sō-kessan.* Naikaku insatsu-kyoku, 1941.

Naimushō keiho-kyoku chōsa-shitsu (Hirotsu Kyōsuke). *Saikin wagakuni ni okeru gikai seido kaikaku ron* (Secret). March 1936.

Nakajima Kōsaburō. *Fūunji: Sogō Shinji den.* Kōtsū kyōdō shuppansha, 1955.

Nakamura Kikuo. *Shōwa kaigun hishi.* Banchō shobō, 1969.

———. *Shōwa rikungun hishi.* Banchō shobō, 1968.

———. *Shōwa seiji shi.* Keiō tsūshin, 1958.

———. *Tennōsei fuashizumu ron.* Hara shobō, 1967.

Nakamura Takafusa. *Senzen-ki Nihon keizai seichō no bunseki.* Iwanami shoten, 1971.

Nakano Masao. *Hashimoto taisa no shuki.* Misuzu shobō, 1963.

Nashimoto Sukehira. *Chūgoku no naka no Nihonjin.* Dōseisha, 1969.

Nashimoto Sukeyoshi. *Suzuki Kisaburō.* Jidaisha, 1932.

Nichi-Man zaisei keizai kenkyūkai shiryō, 3 v. Nihon kindai shiryō kenkyūkai, 1970.

Nihon gaikō gakkai (Ueda Toshio), ed. *Taiheiyō sensō gen'in ron.* Shinbun gekkansha, 1953.

Nihon hyōron shinsha, ed. *Yōyōko: Minobe Yōji tsuitōroku.* Nihon hyōron shinsha, 1954.

Nihon kindai shiryō kenkyūkai, ed. *Nihon riku-kaigun no seido, soshiki, jinji.* Tokyo daigaku shuppankai, 1971.

371

Nihon kokusai seiji gakkai, ed. *Nihon gaikō shi kenkyū: gaikō shidōsha ron.* Yūhikaku, 1966.

―――, ed. *Nihon gaikō shi kenkyū: Nit-Chū kankei no tenkai.* Yūhikaku, 1961.

―――, ed. *Nihon gaikō shi kenkyū: Shōwa jidai.* Yūhikaku, 1960.

――― (Taiheiyō sensō gen'in kenkyū-bu), ed. *Taiheiyō sensō e no michi,* 8 v. Asahi shinbunsha, 1963.

Nihon seiji gakkai, ed. *Nenpō seijigaku, 1972: "Konoe shintaisei" no kenkyū.* Iwanami shoten, 1973.

Nippon bunka chūō renmei, ed. *Nippon bunka dantai nenkan.* Nippon bunka chūō renmei, 1939.

Nippon kakushin nōson kyōgikai junbikai, ed. *Kessei daikai shiryō.* Nippon kakushin nōson kyōgikai junbikai, October 30, 1938.

Nippon kokumin undō kenkyūjo (Shimizu Shin), ed. *Nippon kokumin undō nenshi,* I. Kenbun shoin, 1943.

Nishiura Susumu-shi danwa sokkiroku, 2 v. Nihon kindai shiryō sōsho B–1. Nihon kindai shiryō kenkyūkai and Kido nikki kenkyūkai, 1968.

Oda Toshiyo. *Konoe shintaisei no zenbō.* Kōkoku Nippon shinbunsha, 1940.

―――. *Yokusan undō to Konoe-kō.* Shunpei shobō, 1940.

Ōdachi Shigeo denki kankōkai, ed. *Ōdachi Shigeo,* 2 v. Ōdachi Shigeo denki kankōkai, 1956.

Ogata Taketora. *Ningen Nakano Seigō.* Masu shobō, 1952.

Ogawa Heikichi monjo kenkyūkai, ed. *Ogawa Heikichi kankei monjo,* 2 v. Misuzu shobō, 1973.

Oka Yoshitake. *Konoe Fumimaro.* Iwanami shoten, 1972.

Okada Keisuke taishō kiroku hensankai, ed. *Okada Keisuke.* Okada Keisuke taishō kiroku hensankai, 1956.

Okada Takeo. *Konoe Fumimaro: Tennō to gunbu to kokumin.* Shinjūsha, 1959.

Ōkubo Toshiaki. *Taikei Nihon shi sōsho 3: seiji shi III.* Yamakawa shuppansha, 1967.

Ōkura Kinmochi nikki, 3 v. Nihon kindai shiryō sōsho A–3. Naiseishi kenkyūkai and Nihon kindai shiryō kenkyūkai, 1973–1974.

Ōtani Keijirō. *Shōwa kenpei shi.* Misuzu shobō, 1966.

Ōtsu Junichirō. *Dai-Nippon kensei shi,* 10 v. Hōbunkan, 1927.

Ōuchi Tsutomu. *Fuashizumu e no michi. Nihon no rekishi,* xxiv. Chūō kōronsha, 1967.

Rekishigaku kenkyūkai, ed. *Taiheiyō sensō shi,* 5 v. Tōyō keizai shinpōsha, 1953–1954.

Rikken Minseitō shi, 2 v. Rikken Minseitō shi hensan-kyoku, 1935.

Rikugunshō shinbun-han. *Kokubō no hongi to sono kyōka no teishō.* Rikugunshō shinbun-han, October 10, 1934.

Rōyama Masamichi. *Gikai, seitō, senkyo.* Nippon hyōronsha, 1935.

————. *Gyōsei soshiki ron.* Nippon hyōronsha, 1930.

————. *Nippon seiji dōkō ron.* 3rd ed. Kōyō shoin, 1936.

————. *Seiji shi.* Tōyō keizai shinpōsha, 1940.

————. *Tōa to sekai.* Kaizōsha, 1941.

Ryū Shintarō. *Nippon keizai no saihensei.* Chūō kōronsha, 1939.

Saitō Takao. *Saitō Takao seiji ronshū.* Izushi-machi, Izushi-gun, Hyōgo-ken: Saitō Takao sensei kenshōkai, 1961.

Sakurauchi Yukio. *Sakurauchi Yukio jiden: sōten isseki dan.* Sōtenkai, 1952.

Sassa Hiroo. *Jinbutsu shunjū.* Kaizōsha, 1933.

————. *Shōwa seiji hishi.* Nippon hōsō shuppan kyōkai, 1946.

Satō Kenryō. *Dai-Tōa sensō kaikoroku.* Tokuma shoten, 1966.

————. *Tōjō Hideki to Taiheiyō sensō.* Bungei shunjū, 1960.

Seiyūkai sanjūgo-nen shi. Seiyūkai sanjūgo-nen shi hensan-bu, 1936.

Sekiguchi Tai. *Jikyoku seiji gaku.* Chūō kōronsha, 1936.

Shigeta Asaji. *Kessen-ka no kokumin undō.* Shisō kokusaku kyōkai, 1944.

Shimizu Shigeo-shi danwa sokkiroku. Naiseishi kenkyū shiryō dai–74, 75–shū. Naiseishi kenkyūkai, 1968–1969.

Shimonaka Kunihiko, ed. *Dai-jinmei jiten,* 10 v. Fourth printing. Heibonsha, 1965.

Shimonaka Yasaburō den kankōkai. *Shimonaka Yasaburō jiten.* Heibonsha, 1965.

Shinobu Seizaburō. *Taishō seiji shi.* Keisō shobō, 1968.

Shiono Suehiko kaikoroku kankōkai (Matsuzaka Hiromasa), ed. *Shiono Suehiko kaikoroku.* Shiono Suehiko kaikoroku kankōkai, 1958.

Shiraki Masayuki. *Nihon seitō shi: Shōwa hen.* Chūō kōronsha, 1949.

Shirokita Toshi. *Konoe Fumimaro-kō no shisō to keirin.* Daimonji shoin, 1937.

Shisō no kagaku kenkyūkai, ed. *Kyōdō kenkyū: tenkō,* 3 v. Heibonsha, 1960.

Shōwa dōjinkai, ed. *Shōwa kenkyūkai.* Keizai ōraisha, 1968.

Shūgiin-Sangiin, ed. *Gikai seido nanajū-sen shi,* 12 v. Ōkurashō insatsu-kyoku, 1960–1963.

Suda Teiichi. *Kazami Akira to sono jidai.* Misuzu shobō, 1965.

Sugihara Masami. *Atarashii Shōwa shi.* Shin-kigensha, 1958.

————. *Kokumin soshiki no seiji-ryoku.* Modan Nipponsha, 1940.

————, ed. *Nis-Shi jiken kara Tōa kyōdōtai kensetsu e.* Kaibō jidaisha, 1938.

Suzuki Kisaburō sensei denki hensankai (Yamaoka Mannosuke), ed. *Suzuki Kisaburō.* Suzuki Kisaburō sensei denki hensankai, 1945 and 1955.

Suzuki Teiichi-shi danwa sokkiroku, ɪ. Nihon kindai shiryō sōsho B–4. Nihon kindai shiryō kenkyūkai and Kido nikki kenkyūkai, 1971.

Suzuki Yasuzō. *Seitō ron.* Nippon hyōronsha, 1943.

Taikakai (Gotō Fumio), ed. *Naimushō shi,* 4 v. Chihō zaimu kyōkai, 1970.

Takagi Sōkichi. *Shikan: Taiheiyō sensō.* Bungei shunjū, 1969.

———. *Taiheiyō sensō to riku-kaigun no tōsō.* Keizai ōraisha, 1967.

Takahashi Seigo. *Gendai no seitō.* Nippon hyōronsha, 1930.

Takeuchi Kakuji den kankōkai (Ōta Kōzō), ed. *Takeuchi Kakuji den.* Takeuchi Kakuji den kankōkai, 1960.

Takeyama Michio. *Shōwa no seishin shi.* Shinchōsha, 1956.

Tamura Shinsaku. *Myō Hin kōsaku.* San'ei shuppansha, 1953.

Tanabe Harumichi denki hensankai, ed. *Tanabe Harumichi.* Teishin kyōkai, 1953.

Tanaka Sōgorō. *Nihon fuashizumu shi.* Kawade shobō shinsha, 1960.

———. *Nihon no seitō.* Osaka: Sōgensha, 1953.

Tanemura Suketaka. *Daihon'ei kimitsu nisshi.* Daiyamondosha, 1952.

Teikoku gikai shūgiin giji sokkiroku. Particularly 1937–1941.

Togawa Isamu. *Shōwa gendai shi.* Kōbunsha, 1959.

Togawa Sadao. *Hashimoto Kingorō.* Rev. ed. Takunansha, 1942.

Tōgō Shigenori. *Jidai no ichimen: Tōgō Shigenori gaikō shuki.* Hara shobō, 1967.

Tokyo saiban kenkyūkai, ed. *Tōjō Hideki kyōjutsu-sho.* Yōyōsha, 1948.

Tomita Kenji. *Haisen Nihon no naisoku: Konoe-kō no omoide.* Kokin shoin, 1962.

Tōyama Shigeki, ed. *Kindai Nihon no seijika.* Kōdansha, 1964.

Tōyama Shigeki and Adachi Shizuko. *Kindai Nihon seiji shi hikkei.* Iwanami shoten, 1965.

Tsukui Tatsuo, ed. *Nippon seiji nenpyō: Shōwa jūshichinen,* I. Shōwa shobō, 1942.

Tsukui Tatsuo-shi danwa sokkiroku. Nihon kindai shiryō sōsho B–6. Nihon kindai shiryō kenkyūkai, 1974.

Tsunoda Jun, ed. *Ishiwara Kanji shiryō: kokubō ronsaku.* Hara shobō, 1967.

Ugaki Kazushige. *Ugaki Kazushige nikki*, 3 v. Misuzu shobō, 1968–1971.

Usui Katsumi. *Nit-Chū sensō*. Chūō kōronsha, 1967.

Wakatsuki Reijirō. *Kofūan kaikoroku*. Yomiuri shinbunsha, 1950.

Watanabe Kazuhide. *Kyojin Nakajima Chikuhei*. Hōbun shorin, 1955.

Watanabe Tsuneo. *Habatsu*. Kōbundō, 1958.

Yabe Teiji. *Konoe Fumimaro*, 2 v. Kōbundō, 1952.

———. *Konoe Fumimaro*. Jiji tsūshinsha, 1958 and 1967.

Yamaura Kan'ichi. *Konoe jidai to jinbutsu*. Takayama shoin, 1940.

———. *Mori Kaku*. Mori Kaku denki hensankai, 1940.

———. *Mori Kaku wa ikite iru*. Takayama shoin, 1941.

Yamazaki Tanshō. *Naikaku ron*. Takayama shoin, 1953.

———. *Naikaku seido no kenkyū*. Takayama shoin, 1942.

Yasui Eiji-shi danwa sokkiroku, 5 v. Naiseishi kenkyū shiryō dai–14, 15, 16, 18, 19–shū. Naiseishi kenkyūkai, 1964.

Yatsugi Kazuo. *Shōwa dōran shishi*, 3 v. Keizai ōraisha, 1971–1973.

———. *Shōwa jinbutsu hiroku*. Shin-kigensha, 1954.

Yokusan undō shi kankōkai (Shimonaka Yasaburō), ed. *Yokusan kokumin undō shi*. Yokusan undō shi kankōkai, 1954.

Yoshida Kei. *Denryoku kanri-an no sokumen shi*. Kōtsū keizaisha shuppanbu, 1938.

Yoshino Shinji. *Shōkō gyōsei no omoide: Nihon shihon shugi no ayumi*. Shōkō seisaku shi kankōkai, 1962.

BOOKS, ENGLISH LANGUAGE

Akita, George. *Foundations of Constitutional Government in Modern Japan, 1868–1890*. Cambridge: Harvard University Press, 1967.

Allardt, Erik, and Stein Rokkan, eds. *Mass Politics: Studies in Political Sociology*. New York: Free Press, 1970.

Allardt, Erik, and Yrjo Littunen, eds. *Cleavages, Ideologies and Party Systems*. Helsinki, Finland: Distributor, Academic Bookstore, 1964.

Beasley, William G. *The Modern History of Japan*. New York: Praeger, 1963.

Bergamini, David. *Japan's Imperial Conspiracy*. New York: William Morrow and Co., Inc., 1971.

Berger, Gordon M. "The Search for a New Political Order: Konoe Fumimaro, the Political Parties, and Japanese Politics in the Early Shōwa Era." Ph.D. dissertation, Yale University, 1972.

Borg, Dorothy, and Okamoto Shumpei, eds. *Pearl Harbor as History: Japanese-American Relations, 1931–1941*. New York and London: Columbia University Press, 1973.

Borton, Hugh. *Japan since 1931: Its Political and Social Developments*. I.P.R. Inquiry Series. New York: Institute of Pacific Relations, 1940.

—————. *Japan's Modern Century*. 2nd ed. New York: Ronald Press, 1970.

Boyle, John Hunter. *China and Japan at War 1937–1945: The Politics of Collaboration*. Stanford: Stanford University Press, 1972.

Butow, Robert J. C. *Japan's Decision to Surrender*. Stanford: Stanford University Press, 1954 and 1965.

—————. *Tojo and the Coming of the War*. Princeton: Princeton University Press, 1961.

Byas, Hugh. *Government by Assassination*. New York: Alfred Knopf, 1943.

Cohen, Jerome B. *Japan's Economy in War and Reconstruction*. Minneapolis: University of Minnesota Press, 1949.

Coox, Alvin D. *Year of the Tiger*. Tokyo and Philadelphia: Orient/West, Inc., 1964.

Craig, Albert M., and Donald H. Shively, eds. *Personality in Japanese History*. Berkeley and Los Angeles: University of California Press, 1970.

Craigie, Sir Robert. *Behind the Japanese Mask*. London: Hutchinson & Co., 1946.

377

Crowley, James B. *Japan's Quest for Autonomy: National Security and Foreign Policy 1930–1938.* Princeton: Princeton University Press, 1966.

―――, ed. *Modern East Asia: Essays in Interpretation.* New York: Harcourt, Brace and World, 1970.

de Bary, Wm. Theodore; Ryusaku Tsunoda; and Donald Keene, comps. *Sources of Japanese Tradition.* New York: Columbia University Press, 1958.

Dull, Paul S., and Michael Takaaki Umemura. *The Tokyo Trials: A Functional Index to the Proceedings of the International Military Tribunal for the Far East.* Center for Japanese Studies, Occasional Papers #6. Ann Arbor: Center for Japanese Studies, 1962.

Duus, Peter. *Party Rivalry and Political Change in Taishō Japan.* Cambridge: Harvard University Press, 1968.

Fahs, Charles B. *Government in Japan: Recent Trends in Its Scope and Operation.* I.P.R. Inquiry Series. New York: Institute of Pacific Relations, 1940.

Fairbank, John K.; Edwin O. Reischauer; and Albert N. Craig. *East Asia: The Modern Transformation: A History of East Asian Civilization,* II. Boston: Houghton Mifflin Co., 1965.

Feis, Herbert. *The Road to Pearl Harbor.* New York: Atheneum Press, 1965.

Fujii Shinichi. *The Essentials of Japanese Constitutional Law.* Tokyo: Yūhikaku, 1940.

Grew, Joseph. *Ten Years in Japan.* London: Hammond and Co., Ltd., 1944.

Gunther, John. *Inside Asia.* New York and London: Harper & Brothers, 1939.

Hackett, Roger F. *Yamagata Aritomo in the Rise of Modern Japan 1838–1922.* Cambridge: Harvard University Press, 1971.

Hall, John Whitney. *Japan from Prehistory to Modern Times.* New York: Delacorte Press, 1970.

Ike, Nobutaka. *The Beginnings of Political Democracy in Japan.* Baltimore: Johns Hopkins University Press, 1950.

————, ed. and tr. *Japan's Decision for War*. Stanford: Stanford University Press, 1967.

Ishida Takeshi. *Japanese Society*. New York: Random House, 1971.

Ishiguro Tadaatsu, ed. *Ninomiya Sontoku: His Life and "Evening Talks."* Tokyo: Kenkyūsha, 1955.

Jansen, Marius B., ed. *Changing Japanese Attitudes toward Modernization*. Princeton: Princeton University Press, 1965.

————. *The Japanese and Sun Yat-sen*. Cambridge: Harvard University Press, 1954.

Japan Times & Mail, ed. *Japan's Wartime Legislation–1939*. Tokyo: Jyapan taimuzu-sha, 1939.

Johnson, Chalmers. *An Instance of Treason*. Stanford: Stanford University Press, 1964.

Jones, F. C. *Japan's New Order in East Asia, 1937–1945*. London: Oxford University Press, 1954.

Kamesaka Tsunesaburo, ed. *The Who's Who in Japan, 1937*. Tokyo: Fuzufu in jyapansha, 1937.

Kornhauser, William. *The Politics of Mass Society*. Glencoe, Ill.: Free Press of Glencoe, 1959.

LaPalombara, Joseph, and Myron Weiner, eds. *Political Parties and Political Development*. Princeton: Princeton University Press, 1966.

Lu, David J. *From the Marco Polo Bridge to Pearl Harbor*. Washington, D.C.: Public Affairs Press, 1961.

Maruyama Masao. *Thought and Behaviour in Modern Japanese Politics*. London: Oxford University Press, 1963.

Maxon, Yale Candee. *Control of Japanese Foreign Policy: A Study of Civil-Military Rivalry, 1930–1945*. University of California Publications in Political Science, Number 5. Berkeley and Los Angeles: University of California Press, 1957.

Mayer-Oakes, Thomas Francis, ed. and tr. *Fragile Victory*. Detroit: Wayne State University Press, 1968.

Miller, Frank O. *Minobe Tatsukichi: Interpreter of Consti-*

tutionalism in Japan. Berkeley and Los Angeles: University of California Press, 1965.

Morley, James W., ed. *Dilemmas of Growth in Prewar Japan.* Princeton: Princeton University Press, 1971.

Morris, Ivan I. *Nationalism and the Right Wing in Japan.* London: Oxford University Press, 1960.

Najita, Tetsuo. *Hara Kei in the Politics of Compromise 1905–1915.* Cambridge: Harvard University Press, 1967.

Nettl, J. P. *Political Mobilization: A Sociological Analysis of Methods and Concepts.* New York: Basic Books, 1967.

Neumann, Sigmund, ed. *Modern Political Parties: Approaches to Comparative Politics.* Chicago: University of Chicago Press, 1956.

Ogata, Sadako N. *Defiance in Manchuria: The Making of Japanese Foreign Policy 1931–1932.* Berkeley and Los Angeles: University of California Press, 1964.

Peattie, Mark R. *Ishiwara Kanji and Japan's Confrontation with the West.* Princeton: Princeton University Press, 1975.

Quigley, Harold S. *Japanese Government and Politics: An Introductory Study.* New York and London: Century Co., 1932.

Reischauer, Edwin O. *Japan: Past and Present.* 3rd ed., rev. New York: Alfred A. Knopf, 1964.

Reischauer, Robert Karl. *Japan: Government—Politics.* New York: Thos. Nelson and Sons, 1939.

Rōyama Masamichi. *Foreign Policy of Japan, 1914–1939.* Westport, Conn.: Greenwood Press, 1973 (reprint).

Scalapino, Robert. *Democracy and the Party Movement in Prewar Japan.* Berkeley and Los Angeles: University of California Press, 1953.

Shigemitsu Mamoru. *Japan and Her Destiny.* London: Hutchinson & Co., 1958.

Shillony, Ben-Ami. *Revolt in Japan.* Princeton: Princeton University Press, 1973.

Smethurst, Richard J. *A Social Basis for Prewar Japanese*

380

Militarism: The Army and the Rural Community. Berkeley and Los Angeles: University of California Press, 1974.

Spaulding, Robert M., Jr. *Imperial Japan's Higher Civil Service Examinations.* Princeton: Princeton University Press, 1967.

Steiner, Kurt. *Local Government in Japan.* Stanford: Stanford University Press, 1965.

Storry, G. Richard. *The Double Patriots: A Study of Japanese Nationalism.* Boston: Houghton Mifflin Co., 1957.

Takagi Yasaka, ed. *Introductory Studies on the Sino-Japanese Conflict.* Tokyo: Japanese Council, Institute of Pacific Relations, 1941.

Takeuchi Tatsuji. *War and Diplomacy in the Japanese Empire.* Chicago: University of Chicago Press, 1935.

Tanin, O., and E. Yohan (pseuds.). *Militarism and Fascism in Japan.* London: Martin Lawrence, Ltd., 1934.

Tiedemann, Arthur E. "The Hamaguchi Cabinet: First Phase, July 1929–February 1930: A Study in Japanese Parliamentary Government." Ph.D. dissertation, Columbia University, 1959.

Titus, David A. *Palace and Politics in Prewar Japan.* New York: Columbia University Press, 1974.

Tōbata Seiichi, ed. *The Modernization of Japan,* i. Tokyo: Institute of Asian Economic Affairs, 1966.

Tōgo Shiba, ed. *Japan-Manchoukuo Year Book, 1938.* Tokyo: Jyapan-Manchukō nenkansha, 1938.

———, ed. *Japan-Manchoukuo Year Book, 1941.* Tokyo: Jyapan-Manchukō nenkansha, 1941.

Toland, John. *The Rising Sun: The Decline and Fall of the Japanese Empire 1936–1945.* New York: Random House, 1970.

Tolischus, Otto. *Tokyo Record.* New York: Reynal & Hitchcock, 1943.

Totten, George O., ed. *Democracy in Prewar Japan: Groundwork or Façade?* Lexington, Mass.: D. C. Heath and Co., 1965.

Totten, George O. *The Social Democratic Movement in Pre-war Japan.* New Haven: Yale University Press, 1966.

Tsurumi Yusuke. *Contemporary Japan.* Tokyo: Japan Times-sha, 1927.

Uyehara, Cecil H., comp. *Checklist of Archives in the Japanese Ministry of Foreign Affairs, Tokyo, Japan, 1868–1945, microfilmed for the Library of Congress, 1949–1951.* Washington, D.C.: Photoduplication Service, Library of Congress, 1954.

Ward, Robert E., ed. *Political Development in Modern Japan.* Princeton: Princeton University Press, 1968.

Ward, Robert E., and Dankwart A. Rustow, eds. *Political Modernization in Japan and Turkey.* Princeton: Princeton University Press, 1964.

Wheeler, Gerald. *Prelude to Pearl Harbor.* Columbia: University of Missouri Press, 1963.

Wilson, George M., ed. *Crisis Politics in Prewar Japan: Institutional and Ideological Problems of the 1930s.* Tokyo: Sophia University Press, 1970.

———. *Radical Nationalist in Japan: Kita Ikki, 1883–1937.* Cambridge: Harvard University Press, 1969.

Yanaga, Chitoshi. *Japan since Perry.* Hamden, Conn.: Archon Books, 1966 (reprint).

Yoshihashi Takehiko. *Conspiracy at Mukden: The Rise of the Japanese Military.* New Haven: Yale University Press, 1963.

Young, A. Morgan. *Imperial Japan 1926–1938.* New York: William Morrow & Co., 1938.

ARTICLES, JAPANESE LANGUAGE

Adachi Gan. "Kokumin saihensei undō no sōbyō." *Nippon hyōron,* XIII.13 (December 1938), 183–191.

Ari Bakuji. "Chihō seido (Hōtaisei hōkai-ki): burakukai chōnaikai seido," in Fukushima Masao, Kawashima Takeyoshi, Tsuji Kiyoaki, and Ukai Nobushige, eds. *Kōza:*

Nihon kindai-hō hattatsu shi—shihon shugi to hō no hatten, VI. Tokyo: Keisō shobō, 1959, 163–208.

Arima Yoriyasu and Miki Kiyoshi. "Taidan: Shin seiji taisei." *Kaizō,* XXII.15 (Jikyoku-han 9, August 2, 1940), 62–90.

Arima Yoriyasu and Murobuse Kōshin. "Nippon no saisoshiki: jihen no shori." *Nippon hyōron,* XIII.13 (December 1938), 322–338.

Arima Yoriyasu and Sasaki Sōichi. "Nippon seiji no konpongi: taidan." *Kaizō,* XXII.22 (December 1940), 66–91.

Ashizawa Tsutomu. "Ningen Konoe Fumimaro: Yabe Teiji nikki no naka kara." *Bungei shunjū,* LI.13 (September 1973), 166-190.

Baba Akira. "Kōain setchi mondai." *Gaimushō chōsa geppō,* VII.7–8 (July-August 1966), 46–83.

Baba Tsunego. "Konoe-kō to shintō." *Chūō kōron,* #615 (December 1938), pp. 228–235.

Fujita Shōzō. "Tennōsei to fuashizumu," in Iwanami Yūjirō. ed. *Iwanami kōza: Gendai shisō,* v. Tokyo: Iwanami shoten, 1957, pp. 153–187.

Fukuro Shunkichi. "Kansei seitō undō no zaseki." *Nippon hyōron,* XIII.13 (December 1938), 251–255.

Gotō Isamu. "Naikaku kaizō to Konoe-kō no seijika seishin." *Kaizō,* XXIII.2 (Jikyoku-han 14, January 2, 1941), 216–220.

———. "Shintaisei to Taisei yokusankai." *Kaizō,* XXII.20 (November 1940), 122–128.

Gotō Ryūnosuke. "Konoe Fumimaro o kataru." *Kōen,* #137 (December 15, 1968), pp. 1–34.

Gotō Ryūnosuke and Gotō Fumio. "Taisei yokusankai." *Keizai ōrai,* XIX.11 (November 1967), 166–179.

Gotō Ryūnosuke and Hosokawa Karoku. "Konoe-kō to watakushi." *Keizai ōrai,* XIX.12 (December 1967), 182–196.

Gotō Ryūnosuke and G. Richard Storry. "Konoe-kō ni tsuite kataru, I." *Shōwa dōjin,* v.2 (1959), 5–12.

———. "Konoe-kō ni tsuite kataru, II." *Shōwa dōjin,* v.4 (1959), 4–10.

Gotō Ryūnosuke, Wada Kōsaku, and Doi Akira. "Shōwa kenkyūkai to Shina mondai." *Keizai ōrai*, xx.11 (November 1968), 342–358.

Hata Ikuhiko. "Sanbō: Ishiwara Kanji." *Jiyū*, September 1963, pp. 140–149; October 1963, pp. 140–149; November 1963, pp. 144–151; December 1963, pp. 123–131.

Hayashi Shigeru. "Nihon fuashizumu no seiji katei." *Shisō*, #350 (August 1953), pp. 919–932; #351 (September 1953), pp. 1085–1102.

———. "Seitō wa doko e iku yo?" *Jiyū*, ii.2 (February 1938), 44–50.

Hosokawa Kamekichi. "Shintaisei to shi-chō-son jichisei." *Kaizō*, xxiii.2 (Jikyoku-han 14, January 2, 1941), 62–63.

Ichihara Ryōhei. "Seitō rengō undō no hasan: ' Teijin jiken' o shōten to shite." *Keizai ronsō*, lxxii.3 (March 1955), 161–182.

———. "Seitō rengō undō no kiban: 'zaibatsu no tenkō' o shōten to shite." *Keizai ronsō*, lxxii.2 (February 1955), 106–122.

Inumaru Giichi. "Gendai shi kenkyū kaisetsu," in *Iwanami kōza Nihon rekishi (Gendai 4)*, xxi. Tokyo: Iwanami shoten, 1963, 299–350.

Irie Taneomi. "Konpon rinen o ikketsu seyo." *Kaizō*, xxiii.3 (February 1941), 103–104.

Ishida Takeshi. "Fuashizumu-ki ni okeru kanryōteki shihai no tokushitsu." *Shisō*, #354 (December 1953), pp. 1446–1466.

Ishii Kin'ichirō. "Nihon fuashizumu no chihō seido: 1943-nen no hō-kaisei o chūshin ni." *Rekishigaku kenkyū*, #307 (1965), pp. 1–12.

Itagaki Takeo. "Hiranuma to Yanagawa." *Kaizō*, xxiii.2 (Jikyoku-han 14, January 2, 1941), 228–233.

Itō Takashi. " 'Kyokoku itchi' naikaku-ki no seikai saihensei mondai: Shōwa jūsan-nen Konoe shintō mondai kenkyū no tame ni." *Shakai kagaku kenkyū*, xxiv.1 (1972), 56–130.

———. "Rondon kaigun gunshuku mondai o meguru: sho-seiji shūdan no taikō to teikei." *Shakai kagaku kenkyū*, xvii.4 (February 1966), 1–162.

———. "Shintaisei undō to wa nani ka?" *Rekishi to jinbutsu*, #32 (April 1974), pp. 35–43.

———. "Shōwa jūsan-nen Konoe shintō mondai kenkyū oboegaki," in Nihon seiji gakkai, ed., *Nenpō seijigaku 1972: "Konoe shintaisei" no kenkyū*. Tokyo: Iwanami shoten, 1973, pp. 134–180.

Iwabuchi Tatsuo. "Konoe naikaku to gikai." *Kaizō*, xxiii.3 (February 1941), 146–151.

———, moderator. "Chihō no genjitsu." *Kaizō*, xxiii.2 (Jikyoku-han 14, January 2, 1941), 244–263.

Iwabuchi Tatsuo and Saitō Mitsugu. "Seikai yowa (4): 'Wakusei' Ugaki Kazushige o kataru." *Ronsō*, iv.5 (June 1962), 141–153.

———. "Seikai yowa (5): Konoe Fumimaro to Kido Kōichi." *Ronsō*, iv.6 (July 1962), 170–181.

"Kakushin ni hakusha suru hitobito." *Kaizō*, xxiii.2 (Jikyoku-han 14, January 2, 1941), 198–215.

Kano Masanao. "Sengo keiei to nōson kyōiku: Nichi-Ro sensō-go no seinendan undō ni tsuite." *Shisō*, #521 (November 1967), pp. 42–59.

Kawakami Jōtarō. "Konoe naikaku to shintō mondai." *Kaizō*, xx.5 (May 1938), 133–139.

Kinoshita Hanji. "Kokumin shugi undō no gen-dankai." *Chūō kōron*, #615 (December 1938), pp. 216–223.

Konoe Fumimaro. "Genrō, jūshin to yo." *Kaizō*, xxx.12 (December 1949), 32–36.

Kuhara Fusanosuke. "Nippon keizai kōryū no hōdo." *Kaizō*, xxiii.3 (February 1941), 196–215.

Maki Tatsuo. "Watakushi to shintaisei undō: gun no kitai to genmetsu." *Rekishi to jinbutsu*, #32 (April 1974), pp. 44–47.

Miki Kiyoshi, Yabe Teiji, Kazahaya Yasoji, Hayashi Kōkichi, Hozumi Shichirō, and Ishihama Tomoyuki. " 'Nippon seiji no saihensei' tōronkai." *Chūō kōron*, #634 (June 1940), pp. 98–119.

Minobe Tatsukichi. "Waga gikai seido no zento." *Chūō kōron*, #553 (January 1934), pp. 2–14.

Mitani Taichirō. "Kyūtei seijika no ronri to kōdō. *Sekai*, #251 (October 1966), pp. 190–195.

———. "Seijika no nikki." *Shakai kagaku dai-jiten geppō*, IV (October 1968), 3–5.

Miyazawa Toshiyoshi. "Gikai-kyoku no sekimu." *Kaizō*, XXII.23 (Jikyoku-han 13, December 2, 1940), 36–39.

———. "Gyōsei kikō." *Kokka gakkai zasshi*, LIII.9 (September 1939), 1195–1227.

———. "Taisei yokusan undō no hōriteki seikaku." *Kaizō*, XXIII.1 (January 1, 1941), 112–128.

Mori Tōhei. "Konoe naikaku no jinbutsu." *Kaizō*, XXII.15 (Jikyoku-han 9, August 2, 1940), 178–183.

"Mukashi no hoshutō, ima no hoshutō." *Asahi shinbun*, August 16–September 2, 1962.

Myōhōji Saburō (pseud.). "Gikai kakushin to gikai-kyoku." *Chūō kōron*, #640 (December 1940), pp. 114–119.

Nagai Michio. "Kazami Akira kaiken-ki." *Shisō no kagaku*, #4 (April 1959), pp. 4–7.

———. "Sogō Shinji kaiken-ki." *Shisō no kagaku*, #2 (February 1959), pp. 4–7.

Nakamura Takafusa. "Nihon sensō keizai no jōken: Nit-Chū sensō zengo" (Tokyo daigaku kyōyō gakubu). *Shakai kagaku kiyō*, XV (March 20, 1966), 57–92.

Nakamura Tetsu. "Kokubō kaigi ron." *Chūō kōron*, #637 (September 1940), pp. 18–29.

Nakano Tomio. "Nippon yokusan taisei." *Kaizō*, XXIII.2 (Jikyoku-han 14, January 2, 1941), 12–16.

"Nihon fuashizumu kankei hōgo shuyō bunken mokuroku." *Shisō*, #350 (August 1953), pp. 1004–1028; #351 (September 1953), pp. 1132–1156.

Nomura Shigetarō. "Shintō undō o hadaka ni suru." *Chūō kōron*, #615 (December 1938), pp. 236–243.

Okonogi Samata. "Yokusan gikai e no kitai." *Kaizō*, XXIII.3 (February 1941), 98–102.

Ōoka Jirō. "Kokumin saihensei ni odoru hitobito." *Nippon hyōron*, xiv.1 (January 1939), 172–179.

Ōta Masataka and Hoashi Kei. "Taidan: Kokumin seikatsu to sangyō saihensei." *Chūō kōron*, #640 (December 1940), pp. 100–113.

Ozaki Hotsumi. "Manshūkoku to Kyōwakai." *Chūō kōron*, #640 (December 1940), pp. 90–98.

Rōyama Masamichi. "Kokumin soshiki no kannen." *Nippon hyōron*, xiv.1 (January 1939), 66–74.

Sasaki Sōichi. "Senkyo shukusei no kokumin-teki jikaku." *Kaizō*, xvii.10 (October 1935), 2–39.

———. "Taisei yokusankai to kenpō-jō no ronten." *Kaizō*, xxiii.3 (February 1941), 8–48.

———. "Waga gikai seiji no sai-ginmi." *Kaizō*, xiv.1 (January 1932), 2–37.

Sassa Hiroo. "Kokumin soshiki mondai no kentō." *Chūō kōron*, #616 (January 1939), pp. 30–40.

———. "Shintō keikaku o meguru seikyoku no gen-dankai." *Kaizō*, xvii.10 (October 1935), 306–313.

Satō Kenryō. "Atarashii kokumin undō e no taibō." *Kakushin*, i.2 (November 1938), 44–52.

———. "Tōa kyōdōtai no kessei." *Nippon hyōron*, xiii.13 (December 1938), 97–103.

Satogami Ryōhei. "Taishō demokurashii to kizokuin," in Inoue Kiyoshi, ed., *Taishō-ki no seiji to shakai*. Tokyo: Iwanami shoten, 1971, pp. 251–279.

Sekiguchi Tai. "Naikaku kaizō to Yokusankai kaiso." *Kaizō*, xxiii.9 (May 1941), 114–121.

Shiraki Masayuki. "Naikaku kaizō no hyōri." *Kaizō*, xxiii.2 (Jikyoku-han 14, January 2, 1941), 164–169.

———. "Toyoda to Suzuki." *Kaizō*, xxiii.9 (May 1941), 138–143.

Shusetsu Sōshi (pseud.). "Yokusan undō no sai-shuppatsu." *Kaizō*, xxiii.5 (March 1941), 244–251.

Suzuki Yasuzō. "Yokusan gikai to wa nani ka?" *Kaizō*, xxiii.3 (February 1941), 72–82.

387

Tanaka Sōgorō. "Konoe Fumimaro." *Kaizō*, xxiii.2 (Jikyoku-han 14, January 2, 1941), 89–101.

———. "Taisei yokusankai: Nihonteki fuashizumu no shō-chō to shite." *Rekishigaku kenkyū*, #212 (October 1957), pp. 1–14.

Teraike Kiyoshi (pseud.). "Shin-seitō undō no tenbō." *Kaizō*, xix.3 (March 1937), 259–267.

Tsukui Tatsuo. "Seikyoku no tenki to gunbu no sekimu." *Chūō kōron*, #629 (January 1940), pp. 55–61.

Uchida Shigetaka. "Nippon seiji no shin-tenkai." *Kaizō*, xxiii.9 (May 1941), 34–43.

Yabe Teiji. "Atarashii seiji taisei to wa." *Shūkan asahi*, July 14, 1940.

———. "Konoe Fumimaro ikō kaisetsu." *Kaizō*, xxx.12 (December 1949), 37–38.

———. "Konoe Fumimaro to Kido Kōichi." *Bungei shunjū*, January 1966, pp. 220–228.

Yamaura Kan'ichi. "Gotō-shu kaidan to seiji yōsō." *Chūō kōron*, #629 (January 1940), pp. 62–68.

———. "Kaiso Yokusankai no hitobito." *Kaizō*, xxiii.9 (May 1941), 210–217.

Yatsugi Kazuo. "Rikugun gunmu-kyoku no shihaisha." *Bungei shunjū*, October 5, 1954, pp. 96–115.

———. "Tōjō no ketteiteki haiboku." *Bungei shunjū*, July 5, 1954, pp. 148–159.

Yokogoshi Eiichi. "Mutō jidai no seiji-ryoku gaku." *Nagoya daigaku hōsei ronshū*, #32 (1965), pp. 1–50; #33 (1965), pp. 35–93.

ARTICLES, ENGLISH LANGUAGE

Akinaga Tsukizo. "Coordination of Empire Efforts for High Power Defense State." *Contemporary Opinions*, #384 (June 5, 1941), pp. 1–3.

Arima Yoriyasu. "Japan's Agricultural Administration." *Contemporary Japan*, vi.2 (September 1937), 177–181.

Baba Tsunego. "Hirota's 'Renovation' Plans." *Contemporary Japan*, v.2 (September 1936), 166–177.

———. "Hostilities and Parliament." *Contemporary Japan*, vi.4 (March 1938), 590–600.

———. "An Opportunity for the Resuscitation of the Diet." *Contemporary Japan*, viii.3 (May 1939), 138–140.

———. "Reconstruction of Political Parties." *Contemporary Japan*, ix.5 (May 1940), 618–620.

Berger, Gordon M. "Japan's Young Prince: Konoe Fumimaro's Early Political Career, 1916–1931." *Monumenta Nipponica*, xxix.4 (Winter 1974), 451–475.

Board of Planning (Kikakuin). "On the National Mobilization Law." *Tokyo Gazette*, May 1938, pp. 1–9.

Chō Yukio. "From the Shōwa Economic Crisis to Military Economy." *Developing Economies*, v.4 (December 1967), 568–596.

Colegrove, Kenneth W. "The Japanese Cabinet." *American Political Science Review*, xxx (1936), 903–923.

———. "The Japanese Constitution." *American Political Science Review*, xxxi (1937), 1027–1049.

———. "Powers and Function of the Japanese Diet." *American Political Science Review*, xxvii (1933), 885–898; xxviii (1934), 23–29.

Colton, Kenneth E. "Pre-war Political Influences in Post-war Conservative Parties." *American Political Science Review*, xlii (1948), 940–957.

Crowley, James B. "Japanese Army Factionalism in the Early 1930s." *Journal of Asian Studies*, xxi.3 (May 1962), 309–326.

Deutsch, Karl W. "Social Mobilization and Political Development." *American Political Science Review*, lv.3 (September 1961), 493–514.

Duus, Peter. "Nagai Ryūtarō and the 'White Peril,' 1905–1944." *Journal of Asian Studies*, xxxi.1 (November 1971), 41–48.

Fahs, Charles B. "Political Groups in the House of Peers." *American Political Science Review*, XXXIV.5 (October 1940), pp. 896–919.

Fisher, Galen M. "The Cooperative Movement in Japan." *Pacific Affairs*, XI.4 (December 1938), 478–491.

Fridell, Wilbur F. "Family State (*Kazoku kokka*): An Imperial Ideology for Meiji Japan." *East Asian Occasional Papers*, II (Asian Studies at Hawaii #4). Harry J. Lamley, ed. Honolulu: Asian Studies Program, University of Hawaii, 1970, pp. 144–155.

Fujii Shinichi. "The Cabinet, the Diet, and the Taisei Yokusan Kai." *Contemporary Japan*, X.4 (April 1941), 487–497.

Funata Chu. "Outlines of the New Political Party." *Contemporary Japan*, IX.8 (August 1940), 994–1003.

Furusawa Isojiro. "The Wartime Non-Party Diet." *Contemporary Japan*, X.4 (April 1941), 461–476.

Furuta Tokujiro. "The Late Prince Saionji and the Genro System." *Contemporary Japan*, X.1 (January 1941), 64–70.

Hara Yuzo. "More is Expected of Konoye Cabinet than Preceding Regimes." *Contemporary Opinions*, #342 (August 8, 1940), pp. 1–3.

Hayashi Shiju. "New Structure Brain Trust Made Up of Arima, Yasui, Kazami." *Contemporary Opinions*, #354 (October 31, 1940), pp. 12–14.

Hoshi Yama (pseud.). "Konoye Pins Much Hope to Future of Throne Assisting Drive." *Contemporary Opinions*, #354 (October 31, 1940), pp. 7–8.

Hoshino Masao. "General Election Next Year and the New Political Order." *Contemporary Opinions*, #356 (November 14, 1940), pp. 12–14.

Iizawa Shoji. "Diet Members Unite." *Contemporary Japan*, X.10 (October 1941), 1261–1269.

Ikeda Isando [Hayato]. "Tax Revenues Increasing in Wartime Japan Since China Affair." *Contemporary Opinions*, #380 (May 8, 1941), pp. 6–8.

Ito Takashi. "Conflicts and Coalitions in Japan, 1930: Political Groups [and] the London Naval Disarmament Conference," in Sven Groennings, W. W. Kelley, and Michael Leiserson, eds., *The Study of Coalition Behavior.* New York: Holt, Rinehart and Winston, 1970, pp. 160–176.

Iwabuchi Tatsuo. "Prince Fumimaro Konoye." *Contemporary Japan,* v.3 (December 1936), 365–376.

Jansen, Marius B. "From Hatoyama to Hatoyama." *Far Eastern Quarterly,* xiv.1 (November 1954), 65–79.

Jen (pseud.). "The I.R.A.A." *Pictorial Orient,* ix.8 (August 1941), 276–281.

Kada Tetsuji. "The Theory of an East Asiatic Unity." *Contemporary Japan,* viii.5 (July 1939), 574–581.

Kashiwagi Saburo. "The Seventy-fifth Session of the Diet." *Contemporary Japan,* ix.5 (May 1940), 620–624.

Kihara Michio. "Baron Hiranuma: Resilient Force Behind Government." *Contemporary Opinions,* #380 (May 8, 1941), pp. 3–5.

Koellreutter, Otto. "National Socialism and Japan." *Contemporary Japan,* viii.2 (April 1939), 194–202.

Kuhara Fusanosuke. "The Basis for a New Party." *Contemporary Japan,* ix.7 (July 1940), 811–817.

Lasswell, Harold D. "The Garrison State." *American Journal of Sociology,* xlvi (1941), 455–468.

Maruyama Mikiji. "Neighborhood Unit Plays Vital Role in Fresh Political Setup." *Contemporary Opinions,* #349 (September 26, 1940), pp. 7–8.

Matsuo Takayoshi. "Sakuzō Yoshino." *Developing Economies,* v.2 (June 1967), 388–404.

Matsuoka Yosuke. "Dissolve the Political Parties." *Contemporary Japan,* ii.4 (March 1934), 661–667.

Minobe Yoji. "The Principles of the New Economic Structure." *Contemporary Japan,* x.2 (February 1941), 178–188.

Miyazawa Toshiyoshi. "Reform of Cabinet System and New Political Structure Drive." *Contemporary Opinions,* #344 (August 22, 1940), pp. 7–9.

391

Miwa Kimitada. "The Wang Ching-wei Regime and Japanese Efforts to Terminate the China Conflict," in Joseph Roggendorf, ed., *Studies in Japanese Culture*. Tokyo: Sophia University Press, 1963, pp. 123–142.

Morley, James W. "Check List of Seized Japanese Records in the National Archives." *Far Eastern Quarterly*, ix.3 (May 1950), 306–333.

Nagata Tetsuji. "New Political Party Still Object of Many Leaders." *Contemporary Opinions*, #165 (February 25, 1937), pp. 19–20.

Najita Tetsuo. "Inukai Tsuyoshi: Some Dilemmas in Party Development in Pre-World War II Japan." *American Historical Review*, lxxiv.2 (December 1968), 492–510.

Ogata Taketora. "Behind Japan's Greater Cabinet." *Contemporary Japan*, vi.3 (December 1937), 378–388.

———. "Whither the Political Parties?" *Contemporary Japan*, vi.1 (June 1937), 8–17.

Ozaki Hotsumi. "The New National Structure." *Contemporary Japan*, ix.10 (October 1940), 1284–1292.

Pyle, Kenneth B. "The Technology of Japanese Nationalism: The Local Improvement Movement 1900–1918," *Journal of Asian Studies*, xxxiii.1 (November 1973), 51–65.

Royama Masamichi. "Problems of Contemporary Japan." *University of Hawaii Occasional Papers*, #24 (January 1935).

Sartori, Giovanni. "The Typology of Party Systems: Proposals for Improvement," in Erik Allardt and Stein Rokkan, eds., *Studies in Political Sociology*. New York: Free Press, 1970, pp. 322–352.

Sato Kyonosuke. "A Survey of Those Believed Close to Prince Fumimaro Konoye." *Contemporary Opinions*, #341 (August 1, 1940), pp. 10–12.

Sauer, Wolfgang. "Nationalism: Totalitarianism or Fascism?" *American Historical Review*, lxxiii.2 (December 1967), 404–424.

Sekiguchi Yasushi [Tai]. "The Changing Status of the Japanese Cabinet." *Pacific Affairs*, xi.1 (1938), 5–20.

Shinobu Seizaburō. "From Party Politics to Military Dictatorship." *Developing Economies*, v.4 (December 1967), 666–684.

Shiratori Toshio. "Fascism versus Popular Front." *Contemporary Japan*, vi.4 (March 1938), 581–589.

———. "Preparing for the New World Order." *Contemporary Japan*, x.4 (April 1941), 435–442.

Silberman, Bernard S. "Bureaucratic Development and the Structure of Decision-Making in Japan, 1868–1925." *Journal of Asian Studies*, xxix.2 (February 1970), 347–362.

———. "The Political Theory and Program of Yoshino Sakuzo." *Journal of Modern History*, #31 (December 1959), pp. 310–324.

Smethurst, Richard J. "The Creation of the Imperial Military Reserve Association in Japan." *Journal of Asian Studies*, xxx.4 (August 1971), 815–828.

Spinks, Charles Nelson. "Japan's New Genro." *Contemporary Japan*, ix.7 (July 1940), 840–847.

Storry, G. Richard. "Konoye Fumimaro: 'The Last of the Fujiwara.'" *St. Antony's Papers*, vii. *Far Eastern Affairs*, #2. G. F. Hudson, ed. London: Chatto and Windus, 1960, pp. 9–23.

Suyekawa Ryugoro. "Factors Behind Establishment of New Political Structure." *Contemporary Opinions*, #346 (September 5, 1940), pp. 10–12.

Suzuki Kozo. "Cardinal Points in Establishment of National Defense State." *Contemporary Opinions*, #342 (August 8, 1940), pp. 7–9.

Taira Teizo. "New Political Setup Facilitates Sino-Japanese Peace Movement." *Contemporary Opinions*, #348 (September 19, 1940), pp. 1–3.

Takahashi Makoto. "The Development of War-time Economic Controls." *Developing Economies*, v.4 (December 1967), 648–665.

Takaishi Shingoro. "Prince Konoye: A Portrait." *Contemporary Japan*, ix.8 (August 1940), 984–993.

393

Takasugi Kojiro. "The Diet under the New Political Structure." *Contemporary Japan*, ix.11 (November 1940), 1398–1410.

Tetsuki Shinjin. "Important Personnel of Imperial Rule Assistance Association." *Contemporary Opinions*, #354 (October 31, 1940), pp. 4–6.

Turner, John E. "The Kenseikai: Party Leader vs. Party Liberal." *Far Eastern Quarterly*, xi.3 (May 1952), 317–324.

Wikawa Tadao. "Recent Strides in Our Cooperative Movement." *Contemporary Japan*, vi.1 (June 1937), 28–36.

Wilson, George Macklin. "A New Look at the Problem of 'Japanese Fascism.'" *Comparative Studies in Society and History*, x.4 (July 1968), 401–412.

Wray, William D. "Aso Hisashi and the Search for Renovation in the 1930s." *Papers on Japan*, v. Cambridge: East Asian Research Center, Harvard University, 1970, pp. 55–99.

Yabe Sadaji [Teiji]. "The Destiny of Europe." *Contemporary Japan*, ix.8 (August 1940), 955–963.

Yoshino Shinji. "Our Planned Economy." *Contemporary Japan*, vi.3 (December 1937), 369–377.

Index

395

345; attack reformist party plans (1938), 173, 206, 226; ideological principles, 28, 143, 163, 205–206, 346; and new political order (1940), 302, 308, 311, 329; and rapprochement with parties, 226–27; and spiritual ("public") mobilization, 183–84, 191, 308; and terrorism, 308; as victors in new political order issue, 345–46. *See also* right-wing groups.

jiban (electoral base), 15, 20–21, 105, 127, 174, 176–77, 211, 213, 280, 284, 348–49, 357

jichi-ken, see local autonomy

jichi seido, see local autonomy

Jikyoku dōshikai, 224, 225n, 249

jiriki kōsei, 69

jissen kōryō, see new political order, platform of action

jōkai, 283

jūnin-gumi, 283

Junsa mibun hoshō-rei, 64–65

jūshin (senior statesmen), 105–106, 182, 229, 251, 263

Kagesa Sadaaki, 238, 239n

kai (association), 311–13

Kakunōkyō, see Nippon kakushin nōson kyōgikai

Kamei Kan'ichirō: and Army plans for national mobilization (1934), 89; and IRAA, 318, 325, 327n, 328n, 342; and new economic order, 330, 333; and new party plans, 164, 166–74, 184, 191–93, 198

Kanemitsu Tsuneo, 223, 224n, 225, 229, 260; and new political order, 307, 312

Kan'in, Prince, 261–62

kanmin ittai (popular solidarity with government), 210

kannen uyoku ("idealist right wing"), *see* Japanists"

kanri mibun hoshō iinkai, see Commission on the Guarantee of Officials' Status

Karazawa Toshiki, 73–74

Katakura Tadashi, 96n, 98

Kataoka Shun, 249n

Katayama Tetsu, 248

Katō Kanji, 29, 36

Katō Kōmei (Takaaki), 181, 183

Katō Yūsaburō, 192, 198–99

Katsu Masanori, 245n

Katsura Tarō, 15, 165

Kawada Retsu, 270

Kawakami Jōtarō, 327

Kawasaki Katsu, 335, 337, 339

Kawasaki Takukichi, 57, 102–105, 113

Kaya Okinori, 116, 117n, 122–23, 140

Kazami Akira, 148, 155, 163, 196, 202, 204; and coalition Cabinet plan (1931), 41; as justice minister, 328–29, 332; and new party movement (1940), 256–57, 270, 276–77, 279–80, 318; and new party movement (1941), 341

ken (prefecture), 284, 322

kenpeitai, 166

Kenseikai, 15, 30, 181

Kido Kōichi, 51, 89, 146–47, 161, 191, 202, 208, 226, 252, 256, 262–63, 263n, 264n, 329

Kihon kokusaku yōkō, see "Outline of Basic National Policies"

Kikakuchō, see Cabinet Planning Office

Kikakuin, see Cabinet Planning Board

Kinoshita Hideaki, 249

kyokoku itchi (national unity), 210

Kyōwakai, 98–99, 174

League of Diet Members Supporting the Prosecution of the Holy War (*Seisen kantetsu giin renmei*), 249–50, 257, 260, 277, 335

local autonomy, 68, 200, 281–82

local elites, vii, x, 12, 14–16; as essential channels of mobilization, 216, 348; opposition to new party in IRAA, 319; political influence of, 20, 22–24, 26, 225; position challenged by government mobilization planning, 197, 199–200, 202, 210, 284; position challenged by new order movement, 265, 280; position challenged by rightists, 134, 167, 195; response to national integration campaigns, 24, 71, 202, 215; ties to parties, 26, 71, 73, 83–84, 167, 174, 177, 197, 213, 295, 345, 357–58

London Naval Treaty, 34–35, 39, 51, 60, 101–102

Lower House: budget control, 3; powers of, 4, 11; preserved, 347; threatened by new political order, 307;
elections for: *1890*, 12; *1924*, 18; *1928*, 51, 349; *1930*, 349; *1932*, 43, 349; *1936*, 56–58, 73–74, 74n, 349; *1937*, 119–20, 129; *1942*, x, 295, 347–49

Machida Chūji, 57, 100, 102–103, 128, 146, 154, 176–77, 217–18, 220–21, 224, 227–30,

243, 250–51, 257, 277–79, 335–36, 340, 350, 356

Maeda Yonezō, 57, 101–102, 104–105, 109, 114, 129–30, 146–47, 168, 204, 211, 250–51, 257, 314, 314n, 328, 350

Maki Tatsuo, 249, 315, 321, 325

Makino Nobuaki, 76

Makino Ryōzō, 149, 153

management of political conflict, 31, 252

"Manchurian Group," 96, 96n, 99, 116

Manchurian Incident, 38–40, 71

Maruyama Tsurukichi, 72

mass control, growing importance of, 72

Matsui Iwane, 207

Matsukata Masayoshi, 7

Matsumoto Shigeharu, 310

Matsuno Tsuruhei, 245n

Matsuoka Yōsuke, 269, 296, 310–11, 317

Matsuura Shingorō, 246

May 15 Incident, 44–45

Meetings and Political Associations Law (*Shūkai oyobi seisha hō*, 1900), 179

meibōka, see local elites

Miki Bukichi, 194

Minami Teizō, 328n

Minobe Tatsukichi, 60–63

Minobe Yōji, 329

Minseitō, 5, 15; and Abe Cabinet, 220–21, 225n, 229; as chief enemy of reformist party planners, 243, 257; conservatism of (1940), 217; control of Cabinet (1929–1931), 32–42; crushed in 1932 elections, 43; dissolves, 277–78; and first Konoe Cabinet, 146; internal conditions (1939),

404

National General Mobilization
Law, 145, 149–52, 154, 160,
227, 273, 281, 294, 338, 343;
Article XI controversy, 195,
209; Diet debate on, 152–57;
invoked, 175, 186, 189, 209;
significance of, 156–57
National Service Association
(NSA, *Hōkokukai*), 202–203
National Service Federation,
(NSF, *Hōkoku renmei*), 200–
203
"national unity" Cabinets, weakness of, 81, 130
new economic order, 329–332,
334, 337
new party movements: Akiyama-
Asō-Kamei party plans, 167ff,
192–93; anti-Machida forces
in Diet (1940), 278–79; anti-
mainstream parliamentary
coalition movements, 85;
Arima's rural party plans,
126, 163, 279–80; of Imperial
Hotel faction (1941), 341;
within IRAA, 325–26, 328;
"Kokken shakaitō," 98; Konoe-
centered party plans, 109–10,
114, 119, 129, 155, 168;
Kuhara-Tomita plans, 100,
106, 144, 148; Kuhara's plans
(1939–1940), 213–17; Mutō's
plan (spring 1940), 248–49;
Nakajima's plans (1939), 212–
13; Nationalist Masses Party
plan, 219; within new
political order campaign, 307–
308, 311–12; one-party movements, 75, 84–85; right-wing
coalition party plan, 142, 144,
147, 190–91, 206; Suetsugu-
Shiono plans (1938), 192ff;
Sugiyama party plan (1940),
244n; Ugaki party plan, 102,

154. *See also* Army, new party
plans; Association for Promoting a New Order; Federation for a Popular Movement
to Construct the Greater East
Asian Co-Prosperity Sphere;
Great Japan party; Greater
Imperial Japan Popular party;
Imperial Japan party; Im-
perial Rule Assistance Association; *kokumin kyōgikai*; new
political order; *Nippon kakushin nōson kyōgikai*; Ogikubo
talks (1936–1937)
new political order, viii, 231–32;
as challenge to political elites,
304; as dictatorship plan, 306;
eviscerated by Konoe, 311,
318, 335–43; and international
environment, 232, 309; Konoe
Cabinet's view of (1940),
274; Konoe's view of, 263–
69, 296–300; military participation in, 319–20; minimal
impact of, 343ff; and national
integration, 234–35; parties'
view of, 257, 278–79; platform of action (*jissen kōryō*),
313–14; proclamation (*sengen*), 313. *See also* Imperial
Rule Assistance Association
"new *zaibatsu*," 85, 100
Nippon kakushin nōson kyōgikai
(*Kakunōkyō*), 163, 164n, 195
Nippon kakushintō, 224
Nishikata Toshima, 328n
Nishio Suehiro, 156, 247
nōkai, 20, 24, 69–70
Nomohan, 237
*Nōson gyoson keizai kōsei
keikaku*, 69
Nōson jichi seido kaisei yōkō,
201–202

Privy Council, 4; and party
influence, 30, 252
proletarian parties, ix, 16;
Japan Communist party, 72.
See also Shakai taishūtō;
Shamin faction
"public" association (*kōji
kessha*), 180, 336, 339
"public" mobilization, 182–84,
186, 197–98, 203, 208–18,
276, 287, 306, 309, 313, 329
Public Security Police Law
(1900, *Chian keisatsu hō*), 179,
339
reformist right wing (*kakushin
uyoku*), 143; attacks Hiranuma
(1939), 206; attacks *kisei seitō*
influence, 137; and new political order, 307–308, 318, 345.
See also Hashimoto Kingorō;
Nakano Seigō; right-wing
groups; Suetsugu Nobumasa
Regulations for Meetings and
Associations (1880, *Shūkai
jōrei*), 179
repression: of anti-government
views, 298–99; of communists
(1932–1933), 72; of left wing
after 1925, 27–28, 181; of
liberals and socialists, 188, of
popular sovereignty advocates,
10, 183
reservists, 167, 289, 289n; as
integrating force, 23–24; and
new political order, 319–20,
322; ties to local elites, 20
"revisionist" bureaucrats, 86, 88,
88n; and electric power bill,
158; and new economic order,
330; support Army reform
plans, 95, 112
right of supreme command, 37
right-wing groups (*uyoku dan-*

tai), 134, 142; attack parties,
142, 144–45; seek new party,
142, 190–91, 206; split over
Hiranuma's policies, 205–207,
226–27; split over new political order, 307–308; unite on
war in China (1937), 144.
See also "Japanists"; reformist
right wing
Rikken minseitō, *see* Minseitō
Rikken seiyūkai, *see* Seiyūkai
rinpo-han, 283, 305, 320
rinpo kyōjo, 69
Rōyama Masamichi, 63

Saikō kokubō kaigi, *see* Supreme
Defense Council
Saionji Kinmochi, 4, 8, 43–45,
58, 88, 110, 251–52; antago-
nism toward Suzuki Kisaburō,
49–51; attacked by right and
young officers, 106; decision
to suspend party government,
52–53; decision to continue
national unity government
(1936), 76; and Konoe's appointment as premier (1937),
120–21, 123, 154; names
Inukai premier, 42; names
Konoe premier (1936), 77–
78; names Okada premier, 55;
as president of the Seiyūkai,
16; and Ugaki Kazushige, 103;
view of conflict management,
8; view of constitutional
monarchy, 8, 49. *See also
genrō*
Saitō Cabinet: economic recovery
policy, 68–70; foreign and
military policies, 60, 81. *See
also* Saitō Makoto
Saitō Makoto, 51–52; assassinated, 76

Saitō Takao: expelled from
Lower House (1940), 245–
48, 294; and national general
mobilization bill debate, 149,
152–53, 156; re-elected
(1942), 348
Sakomizu Hisatsune, 74
Sakurai Hyōgorō, 244n, 327, 350
Sakurauchi Yukio, 204, 244n,
245n, 328
sangyō kumiai, 20, 24, 69, 109,
193
*Sangyō kumiai seinen renmei
(Sanseiren)*, 163 167
Satō Kenryō, 325, 349
Sawada Shigeru, 261
seiji kessha, see political associations
Seimu chōsakai (Political Affairs
Research Councils), 62
seimu-jikan (parliamentary vice-
minister), 102
seinendan, 109, 167, 188, 193,
289, 321
Seisen kantetsu dōmei, 206, 249n
Seisen kantetsu giin renmei, see
League of Diet Members Supporting the Prosecution of the
Holy War
Seisen kantetsu ketsugi-an, 249
seitō rengō undō (movement for
two-party coalition), 99
Seiyū hontō, 18, 101
Seiyūkai, 3–4, 8–9, 15, 19, 30;
attacks London Naval Treaty,
36, 101–102; defeated in 1936
election, 56–57; demands
greater military role in defense
policy making, 37; divisions
within, 42, 46, 55–57, 99–102,
146; economic policies
(1939), 209n; fragments
(1939), 176–77, 193–94, 212;
new party movement sup-

porters in, 99–102, 168–70;
opposes "national unity" government, 55–57; and plan for
coalition Cabinet (1931),
40ff; presidential succession
dispute, 128, 211–12; presses
for amendment of active-
officer requirement for service
portfolios (1913), 91; strength
in 1937 assessed, 128–29. *See
also* Kuhara Seiyūkai; Nakajima
Seiyūkai; Seiyū hontō
sengen, see new political order,
proclamation
Shadaitō, *see* Shakai taishūtō
Shakai taishūtō, 147–48, 155,
164, 166, 168–69, 193, 249;
and Abe Cabinet, 221, 225n;
and covert government support
(1936); 73–74; dissolves, 277;
and Nagata Tetsuzan, 89; sup-
ports electric power legislation,
159–60. *See also Shamin*
faction
Shamin faction, 218, 247–48,
248n, 326, 333–34, 348.
See also Shakai taishūtō
Shidehara kijūrō, 35–41, 101,
354
shidō genri, 278
Shimada Toshio, 245n, 350
shindō (way of the subject), 314
Shinjō Kenkichi, 89n
Shinminkai, 171
Shinpeitai Incident, 249n
shinsei (direct imperial rule), 49,
76, 86
shin seiji taisei, see new political
order
Shintaisei sokushin dōshikai, see
Association for Promoting a
New Order
Shiono Suehiko, 119, 123, 191,
193–96, 226–27

410

Library of Congress Cataloging in Publication Data

Berger, Gordon Mark, 1942–
  Parties out of power in Japan, 1931–1941.

  Emanates from the author's thesis, Yale, 1972.
  Bibliography: p.
  Includes index.
  1. Political parties—Japan—History.   2. Japan—
Politics and government—1912–1945.   I. Title.
JQ1698.A1B46   1977   329.9′52   76–3243
ISBN 0-691-03106-1